THE PROCESS

Dictated by the Spirit
John Wilmont
Earl of Rochester

Psychography of
ARANDI GOMES TEXEIRA

English translation:
Rosario Huari Romero
Lima, Peru, July 2023

Original title in Portuguese:
"O Proceso"

© Arandi Gomes Teixeira 2002

Translated from the 3rd edition 2012

Reviewer:
Brian Morales Gonzales

World Spiritist Institute
Houston, Texas, USA
E-mail: contact@worldspiritistinstitute.org

About the Medium

Arandi Gomes Texeira is an incarnated spirit aware that he must evolve, physically and spiritually, in order to dignify her own existence.

In 1975 he looked for a spiritist house due to the need of one of her sons. To help him, she began to study intensely the works of Allan Kardec. In them she found rational answers to her old questions. After the spiritual treatment of her son, she stayed in the Spiritist house, with the purpose of assuming, intellectually and morally, the principles and postulates of the Spiritist Doctrine.

Her childhood and adolescence were permeated with phenomena; some physical, terrifying and even aggressive. She learned, then, to live with both planes of life. Once in the Spiritist Doctrine, she decided to study her mediumnity, educate it and exercise it in Spiritist practice.

In the late 1970s, a neighbor almost "forced" her to read a large book with silver covers. Initially she rejected it, due to a lack of time, but at his insistence, she glanced through it out of kindness. One afternoon, I decided to check it out. The work was "The Jew's Revenge." She narrates that right at the beginning of the reading she felt strange, emotional, and began to get angry, inexplicably, at this or that. She paused for a moment and asked herself, "Arandi, have you gone crazy?" How could she make demands like that, if she didn't know the work, had never heard of it, ignoring even the name of its author? So she looked into it and read: "J. W., Count Rochester." The impact was considerable - what a strange situation!

Arandi says that at this moment she comes to mind an idea: to challenge the author? She asked him, in a loud and clear voice: "Come to me! Appear to me...! I did not have to invoke him twice. He appeared in the middle of the room, smiling, dressed in the clothes of an English nobleman, showing great joy. So we were looking at each other. I was crying, a lot, and he was very happy. Since then, we never really separated from each other."

Other phenomena followed, and they began walking together every night during their corporal rest. "We wandered, many times, through different spaces and spheres; we talked a lot and he educated me about the works I should study. Eventually, he told me that we would write books. So it was and so it has been."

On her connection with Count J.W. Rochester she explains, "My connection with this spirit is very old. We walked right next to each other for a long time. We know quite well and respect each other deeply. Yes, there are many facts and countless revelations of other reincarnations, in the different periods he focuses on in his books."

As for Rochester's style and the use of several mediums, Arandi indicates that "in fact, Rochester's style is unmistakable. Highly regarded, he has a very eclectic audience. As for other mediums, depending on the reader to analyze, compare the works and draw their own conclusions.

The practice of psychography is almost always moving. After finishing the practice, many tears, gratitude to the author and the satisfaction of having succeeded, in spite of the obstacles, to carry it out. While I make the endless revisions and plans for the desirable editions, he is there, participating in everything, always."

The psychic novels do not prevent those interested in Spiritism from knowing Kardec's work, so much so, that those who do not study Spiritism lose a lot in the understanding of the spiritist novels. Rochester always bases his practices on the codification of

Allan Kardec (his only friend, since the time of ancient Egypt). We can, fairly, consider him one of the precursors of Spiritism, when he narrates stories of the ancient world and explains psychic phenomena, demonstrating an admirable knowledge of the spiritual plane.

Arandi does not see any inconvenience in psychic novels when they are based on Spiritist principles and postulates. When they are not, they may be novels, but they will never be spiritist. Their advantage lies in their objectives: to entertain, to make people dream, to move, to surprise, to educate, to clarify and to signal directions, teaching and transforming. Our dear author knows, like nobody else, how to create, weave plots and develop them, with mastery, in real stories or not; it doesn't matter, because, according to him, life is more fantastic than fiction.

Finally, she shares that when working on the novels of the dearest John Wilmot, Earl of Rochester, she is the first to benefit from the guiding light give it and the incomparable opportunity to practice and learn.[1]

---

[1] Excerpt from "Interview to Arandi Gomes Texeira" by Eliana Haddad, April 13rd, 2020. Published by Correio.new by Correio Fraterno URL: https://correio.news/leitura/entrevista-arandi-gomes

About the Spiritual Author

John Wilmot, Earl of Rochester was born on April 1 or 10, 1647 (there is no record of the exact date). The son of Henry Wilmot and Anne (widow of Sir. Francis Henry Lee), Rochester resembled his father in physique and temperament, domineering and proud. Henry Wilmot had received the title of Earl because of his efforts to raise money in Germany to help King Charles I regain the throne after he was forced to leave England.

When his father died, Rochester was 11 years old and inherited the title of Earl, little inheritance, and honors.

Young J.W. Rochester grew up in Ditchley among drunkenness, theatrical intrigues, artificial friendships with professional poets, lust, brothels in Whetstone Park and the friendship of the king, whom he despised.

He had a vast culture, for the time: he mastered Latin and Greek, knew the classics, French and Italian, was the author of satirical poetry, highly appreciated in his time.

In 1661, at the age of 14, he left Wadham College, Oxford, with the degree of Master of Arts. He then left for the continent (France and Italy) and became an interesting figure: tall, slim, attractive, intelligent, charming, brilliant, subtle, educated, and modest, ideal characteristics to conquer the frivolous society of his time.

When he was not yet 20 years old, in January 1667, he married Elizabeth Mallet. Ten months later, drinking began to affect his character. He had four sons with Elizabeth and a daughter, in 1677, with the actress Elizabeth Barry.

Living the most different experiences, from fighting the Dutch navy on the high seas to being involved in crimes of death, Rochester's life followed paths of madness, sexual abuse, alcoholics, and charlatanism, in a period in which he acted as a "physician."

When Rochester was 30 years old, he writes to a former fellow adventurer that he was nearly blind, lame, and with little chance of ever seeing London again.

Quickly recovering, Rochester returns to London. Shortly thereafter, in agony, he set out on his last adventure: he called the curate Gilbert Burnet and dictated his recollections to him. In his last reflections, Rochester acknowledged having lived a wicked life, the end of which came slowly and painfully to him because of the venereal diseases that dominated him.

Earl of Rochester died on July 26, 1680. In the state of spirit, Rochester received the mission to work for the propagation of Spiritualism. After 200 years, through the medium Vera Kryzhanovskaia, the automatism that characterized her made her hand trace words with dizzying speed and total unconsciousness of ideas. The narratives that were dictated to her denote a wide knowledge of ancestral life and customs and provide in their details such a local stamp and historical truth that the reader finds it hard not to recognize their authenticity. Rochester proves to dictate his historical-literary production, testifying that life unfolds to infinity in his indelible marks of spiritual memory, towards the light and the way of God. It seems impossible for a historian, however erudite, to study, simultaneously and in depth, times and environments as different as the Assyrian, Egyptian, Greek and

Roman civilizations; as well as customs as dissimilar as those of the France of Louis XI to those of the Renaissance.

The subject matter of Rochester's work begins in Pharaonic Egypt, passes through Greco-Roman antiquity and the Middle Ages, and continues into the 19th century. In his novels, reality navigates in a fantastic current, in which the imaginary surpasses the limits of verisimilitude, making natural phenomena that oral tradition has taken care to perpetuate as supernatural.

Rochester's referential is full of content about customs, laws, ancestral mysteries and unfathomable facts of History, under a novelistic layer, where social and psychological aspects pass through the sensitive filter of his great imagination. Rochester's genre classification is hampered by his expansion into several categories: gothic horror with romance, family sagas, adventure and forays into the fantastic.

The number of editions of Rochester's works, spread over countless countries, is so large that it is not possible to have an idea of their magnitude, especially considering that, according to researchers, many of these works are unknown to the general public.

Several lovers of Rochester's novels carried out (and perhaps do carry out) searches in libraries in various countries, especially in Russia, to locate still unknown works. This can be seen in the prefaces transcribed in several works. Many of these works are finally available in English thanks to the *World Spiritist Institute*.

"The rebirth of the flesh is the soul's conciliation with itself, offering a new opportunity to learn and live better."

Joanna de Ângelis, psychographed by Divaldo Franco
Nascente de bênçãos - LEAL Publishing House.

PROLOGUE

TAKING AS A POINT OF start the sordid and soulless judicial process that involved and destroyed Juan Gadelha, we can follow the "process" of soul's purification throughout their multiple existences. Here is where they weave their "faith", enlightening themselves from the inside out, gradually being redeemed before themselves and before God.

As silent spectators, will be analyzing the events and inner behavior that each person has, getting to know the secrets by using the power we were vested with.

By reviewing the many different cultures, our dearest Fata morgana, with all of its magic and lucidity, has revealed to us sometimes beautiful stories, but also with quite terrifying ones!

We were part of them and even now we find ourselves in this valley full of tears, suffering because of other's anger that ended revealing our imperfections, pointing out the debts we had acquired throughout the millennia.

Invigilant as we once were, proud and selfish, we attracted the pain we are suffering now, the one that made us to remember the true purpose of reincarnation!

Exhausted, sometimes deeply disappointed; exiled from this kind planet which by welcome us, has believed in our redeeming proposals. With our feet wounded and our hearts aching, we are in this incessant repetition of "to be born, to die, to born again, and make progress continuously, in accordance the Great law"!

In this context of separating the wheat from the chaff, it is crucial that we seek all the strength from our souls to reject the "Golden Calf" we are used to pray to, in order to finally turn our hearts and minds to the Holy lamb who has waited for us for a long time!

May we have the courage to do good and no longer to do evil that only generates pain and misfortune, which make our journey complicated and expose us to the risk of a new and shameful exile!

The Lord is with us and give us support in this new opportunity that has been granted to us out of mercy in response to our humble prayers and promises!

Time is short considering what we still have to do with determination and courage to do good, together with Jesus, exercising our condition as his brothers, children of the same father; in the urgent and deeply loving creation of a better world for everybody!

ROCHESTER

JUAN GADELHA

AS HE THINKS SERIOUSLY about his four decade of life and, even when he tried to remember harder, Juan couldn't think in anything that justified all the soul-wrenching pain that was tearing his heart.

Despite everything, he wasn't complaining; he was just shocked and intimidated.

Where did all that resignation come from? Not even he knew it.

The apparent calm when he received the accusations without anger, seen confusing even to his relatives who denied to help him in these terrible moments.

Juan analyzes his own situation:

The interrogatory had settled in suddenly and crudely, preventing him from defend himself fairly.

Anytime he tried to explain anything, they wouldn't listen to him.

In the authoritarian and pompous speech of the alleged "knights of justice", his weakened and stunned voice loses its power. The two lawyers who initially tried to defend him, suddenly changed their minds, replacing the initial enthusiasm of the first hours with a clear lack of commitment and openly switching to the side of the prosecutors.

What could be done when you are in such a situation?...!

Feeling insignificant, without any value. He seems to be witnessing events that has nothing to be with him. Overwhelmed, he starts to ignore everything that is happening around him. To those who look at him despicably, Juan looked like he has already accepted the disguise of cynicism and indifference in their faces. That's why, looking around, he found harsh expressions on faces that once smiled at him. Many were customers. Some owned him all kinds of favor, and even money.

The rude attitude of the prosecutors has a clear intention of tarnish his reputation as a decent man. The hasty and arbitrary accusations keep coming.

To avoid the terrific situation, he isolated himself, internalizing:

"-Oh, God! Why am I going through hell? You can search inside my soul! All these accusations are lies. It is all a sham!

Wake me from this nightmare, Lord! I wish that each one of the prosecutors could see, like you, into my soul and realized that I am not guilty! How can I accept what they say if my conscience is clear? I guess I am paying debts from past lives! I know in this life I have follow your commandments, but I also know you are upright and perfect, and is fair that I pay for past actions! Right now, my life is a mess.

Poor me!"

An uncontrollable and strong sweat wet the clothes already battered by the days he was in prison. He was marred and completely changed by gauntness and the lack of color on his face.

The "smart discussants" keep going with the slanderous speech, with more enthusiasm now. Everything that comes out of their mouths are just words of condemnation, materializing lies that people take as truth and are thus enthusiastically applauded by those who wants to silence the innocents.

Juan feels his body aching, his hands shaky and his feet tired. Automatically, he looked at his shoes and realized they are dirty. Usually, he always wears clean and polished shoes.

Proud of his appearance and physical beauty, he's even vain. His dark and luscious hair well-groomed by habit, is now tangled and hangs over a wide and noble forehead.

With the help of his thinning fingers, he tries to straighten them, something useless because his image has been already damaged.

The court is swarming with people. Most of them being there just for curiosity, waiting to see the morbid situations that are common in these trials. They enjoy the other's suffering; they are insensible animals who wants to see innocent blood running.

Overwhelmed by the pain, Juan already knows he is going to be sentenced. Due to technical problems, there is a recess in the trial, which gave him a moment of peace.

To his mind come the image of a strong six-year-old child, with rosy cheeks, dark hair and eyes the color of the sky.

"-Charles, dear! – he thought. – I miss you so much...!

I can hear his voice calling me! I would give everything to wake up from this nightmare, and see your innocent eyes; you in your pajamas, planning to jump on me to play with pillows and ending laughing and hugging...!

And right next to the bed head the photo of your mother, our beloved Cecile, would be looking at us tenderly...

We were so happy, until that damn fever had to took her away forever.

When she died, I thought I would die too, but I saw you so fragile and needed that I had to take care you. Now, my son, you're the greatest love of my life!

Will I go back home soon? Thinking in you gives me strength and at the same time weakens my soul!

My dear son, who will guide you, if I unfortunately, do not come back? I still don't know what the verdict will be from those, who are below God and above of regular men, that have decided about my fate.

I'd like to be more optimistic, but I don't have the strength I need to... I have heaviness in the chest and a clouded mind; I can't think straight in front of these people that only want to see me fall...

What will they tell you about me? Some people are imprudent and others are cruel! They won't hold back anything, not even because you are just an innocent child.

I have dedicated my life to the demanding and hard path of teaching, I wanted to contribute to the moral and intellectual education of my students.

They weren't my real children, but they had a special place in my heart.

Talking about children, I still remember how quickly, Cecile, the love of my life, and I wanted to start a family.

Until one lucky day, we discover Cecile was pregnant and you were coming to complete our lives. We were happier than ever!

Finally, we would be good kind of trees, the ones that bear fruit, perpetuating the species!

My heart was full and I happy. I tried to imagine how would be your features, your face. So, at last, God would give me the son I'd always dream of!

I would be your father, your friend, your guardian, my dear Charles!

And you were born! In that sacred time, you were like baby Jesus and your mother was the Virgin Mary, lighting up my world! You came with an aura of light, handsome and healthy!

Now, with six years old, you have fulfilled my intellectual and moral prospects. I have taught you everything you could understand.

And now, what will the days ahead be like?

It feels like I won't be able to get out from this procedure unhurt. Even less likely to escape from my executioners, I can't take so much more pain!

I will try to find some strength so I can write a post-mortem report that is going to be an inheritance for my soul, that will be suspended, safeguarded in your little hands, until you can give it back to me, with devotion and more importantly with the indisputable certainty of my innocence.

In these unspeakable moments of pain, like a premonitory vision, I can see you willing to answer me in this request that after my death will be a sacred duty for you. I know that in the future, you will redeem this present that by then will be the past...

My dear son, the one who asks for this is not your father, but a man on the edge of his grave making a full assessment of all that he has been, what he is now, and what he deserves. I'll make official the papers with my desires as soon as possible, then I'll leave them in trustful hands so that, at the right time, they be delivered to you.

The only inheritance I can leave you is my love and the moral lessons that I taught you. We never had money and luxuries in abundance, because the little we had I hard-earned honestly. It hurts me to leave you, however I trust in God, the one and only who created us and fulfills the needs of even the smallest creatures who live on earth. Remember that quote of the Book of Mateus, chapter 6, which we know so well:

"Look at the birds of the air; they do not sow or reap or store away in barns, and yet your heavenly Father feeds them. Are you not much more valuable than they? - Can any one of you by worrying add a single hour to your life?"

Your life will take the path that he wants for you and it has already been decided from your birth.

How did I end up in this situation? I don't even know, dear son; maybe you that stay in this world could search and discover the reasons. When it's time to leave this body that has provided me a dwelling place in this world, maybe I would be able to get answers. Please, have in mind this, doesn't matter where I go, I will keep loving and protecting you, my beloved son! I would love to hug you near to my heart once more! I leave this sorrow in God's hands! At such times I can only question the love of the creator for his children!

What keeps me going is my faith.

I feel bad for the ones that claim to be my executioners, because they are the ones that will suffer at the end! My son, I still don't believe I am part of this tragedy!

Despite all the limits, I'm still able to see the past, the present and future without barriers, like I'm looking from a far distance, on the top of a mountain.

What gives me such power? I don't know. It might be the coming of death...

I encourage you to become a lawyer, so that, from a chair, you can one day absolve me of all the nonsense that is now being throw to my face!

I already disassociated myself, slowly, maybe for physical exhaustion, from the reality, and hearing the call of the spiritual plane. I'll leave this world that one day welcomed me with open arms and from which men push me out without being able to understand them...

I feel like I'm on the threshold of infinity son, and there, one day we will meet again, happy and changed!

Noises bring him back from his stupor. It's time to continue with the trial…

Juan thinks in the fall of the "Divine lamb "and the time he had to carry that heavy notorious trunk towards the Cavalry.

After days and days of exhaustive reading records and evidence, despite the vein arguments of the alleged "knights of justice", the court sentenced Juan Gadelha to the maximum penalty.

He is taken to prison to wait for the execution of the judgment, where boldly, he writes a letter with his records and then give it to the Governor of his village, make him promise that will deliver the letter to Charles Gadelha when he reaches the legal age.

When Juan finished that matter, he asked the vicar that accompanied him for the consent to see and bid Charles farewell.

In the courtyard, he waits for his boy, who came holding the priest's hands.

With shining eyes, burning tears coming down on his disfigured face, he tries to smile while tenderly and desperately hugging his beloved son. Charles, very frightened, didn't recognize his father at first. He feels sorry for his father, he is still scared.

Talking with infinite tenderness, Juan identifies himself before his son.

The little boy starts sobbing because he cannot understand why his father is in jail or why he looks so sad…

Kissing his son's little face and head, sweetly caressing him through burning tears and trying to smile at him, Juan said to Charles:

- My beloved son! May God protect and watch over you! The holy angels will always be with you! Good bye, my son!

Eventually, he took his son back with the priest and, oddly, he stays quiet with a far-off almost shining look in his face.

The next morning, visiting him in an attempt to comfort him, the elderly and kind priest found him laid on the hard surface that he used as a bed.

During the time he was there, Juan has fearlessly shown his faith and submission for God. Words of anger or blasphemies were never told by him, thus reaffirming his commitment with the creator.

As he was giving the posthumous holy oils, preparing him for the burial, the priest was grateful to God for taking Juan to the kingdom of heaven, before the execution.

Looking inside that horrible cell, now with the door wide open, he understood that for him, it was never a prison, but some kind of release. Kneeling, on that rough and humid ground, he asked to the heaven for Juan's soul. From those hands, that were now inert, he always received innumerous offerings for the needy.

He feels sorry for Charles, who has lost his father. Now he will have to prepare him to cope with that pain. He had promised to Juan that he will take care of Charles. He will encourage Charles to honor devoutly his father's memory. The peace that filled Juan's soul since the acceptance of the things will be his lifelong reward.

The priest can already feel the paternal affection for the little boy. The first decision he will take after Juan's funeral will be to take the custody of the child.

He will be back for the burial.

Heading towards the exit, he turned around, looked at the dead body, grieving and big tears came down from his eyes.

Taking a handkerchief from his black coat's pocket, wiped his tears that continue falling. Deeply touched, he sighs painfully and shouted with a chocked voice:

"- *Consummatum est*! Beloved friend, Farewell! – and almost ran out, he left.

RECORDS

AT THE BEGINNING OF THE 18th CENTURY, in France, dealing with complicated financial transactions, in a privileged situation, we will meet a new admired and feared King Midas, who came (from an unknow place), saw and conquered lot of things.

The opportunist fawn over him trying to become his guest or just to get some benefit. But him, self-centered, arrogant and feeling superior to the rest, despises everyone.

His sophisticated and impeccable dress sense were a plus to his natural charming. With breathtaking blue eyes and his love conquests are the talk of the town. He is desired for women that craved for a profitable marriage, even if loveless. Aware of it, completely conceited, he uses it as a power to seduce others.

As he passed by, he left a trial of the most expensive parfums ever known...

He walks triumphantly, like a Cesar that gets in proud to the defeated and conquered cities that were crushed by his armies...

Smiley when he wants to be liked and, savage enemy when someone defies him, going to extremes in case he needs to silent the bold ones.

One day, he came to Rue de La Chappelle, Paris, bringing carriages full of merchandise, lots of money and valuable documents.

His good fortune and profits call into question his integrity.

Daily, conceited, he walks near Seine's River, admiring the beautiful city he had chosen to live.

Here and now, at night-time, lonely, he ponders; with a machiavellian expression. While he is shaving his well-groomed beard, laying on the back of the wooden chair, almost in an obsessive compulsion he is thinking in new ways to get money...

From distance, he is controlling "his new victims" while they are resting, ignoring the danger they are in, with that alleged kind man that, stepping down from his pedestal, paid attention to them or started a business with them.

He stands up, walks around that big and fancy living room that he uses as his private office, goes to the window, pushes the curtains and admire, amazed, Paris, the city of lights, that now looks very quiet.

Almost at dawn, he drew the curtains and walked toward his chambers, retiring. Even now his face showed an intriguing smile...

* * *

LET'S GO FURTHER BACK IN time and space.

Now we are in a catholic baptistery in England, the one, where thirty years ago served as location to give him the holy oils and where he was promised that with this sacrament, he was going to be free from original sin.

He grew up in a wealthy family, his parents were millionaires.

His life was full of whims, with even the smallest caprices satisfied, he became a tyrant since he was just a child. He found joy in making mischief and prank to his terrified servants.

Our little character wasn't loved by his family; he was barely noticed at home.

But…thanks to the twists of life, the wheel of fortune was on his side and every time his father did a commercial transaction, it went bad. His father completely disappointed and faithless, submitted himself to a careless life, leading him to a tragic and mysterious death.

His mother, used to a comfort and luxury life, lost all interest and ended up marrying to an unscrupulous man, who sucked her beauty and energy and took her with him, because she was never seen again.

The boy, nothing ready to the new oncoming situation, without having any clue, was sidelined by crooked men because of his innocence, which led him to become involved in an evil world.

With his petulant and aggressive temper, he pulled away everyone that tried to help him. Bad-tempered by nature, his attitude got worse when he got angry.

Reaching the twenties, already tired of that miserable life, he decided to change it and accept the heaven-sent offer a wealthy merchant had made him.

This kind merchant sympathizing with him and feeling sorry for his situation, gave him a job in one of his properties, believed in him when he said he wanted to change.

In company of the servants, he could feed better and take care of his appearance now.

He showed interest and strove to learn the new occupations, which gave his employer more hope and expectations about him.

Showing an exceptional intelligence, wisely dealing with the diverse accounting techniques, quickly became the most trusted employee of Sir. Jaime Sartorelli.

He felt pleasure in having any quantity of money. In those times, he could even feel a little smile that sometimes turned into a malevolent laugh. With remarkable diligence, he puts everything in order inside the drawers and cabinets, locking the lock carefully before struggling to give the set of keys to his employer.

During that time, the profits were vanishing as if by magic. Life was not something stays in one place, it was always changing, and just like that, the people that once were in a privileged position, were now living in poverty.

The social levels were nothing sure nowadays, and about that, Henry John Stanford was well aware. Because one day he had it all and the next one he had nothing.

IT WAS TIME OF splendor and grandeur...

During the age of absolutism, the King Louis XIV ruled under the theme of: *L'etat c'est moi* which meant that he was the absolute ruler of all France. He was capable of gather large multitudes, especially a great number of servants and libertine nobles. His entourage surrounding him was like how flies surround filth.

However, anyone who looked could see the contrast between "Louis the Great" and the pain of the people who were in need. You could see the evident social inequity...

Inside smelly basements, castles or gloomy fortresses, many miserable people are devoured by physical and moral sorrows. Mostly, ignoring the reasons and the responsible parties for sending them to these Dante's inferno.

The social conditions became quite chaotic. Any alleged offense against the king or the throne was punished by the confiscation of property, imprisonment or death.

Undoubtedly, there was already good and true virtue, because it has always existed in all times. In the midst of vices and corruption, the sacred souls wield their power through love and compassion, after all, those things were really important because they help to balance and align this stricken world lacking spiritual growth. May they be blessed in the name of God!

Every day, trusting his servant more and more, the employer of Henry put him in charge of almost all the financial activities and him, pleased, added enthusiasm into the job, producing unexpected and always welcome profits.

Distancing himself little by little, Sir. Jaime let Henry privileged mind take over most of the responsibilities, which would prevent him from problems and more fatigue that came over the years.

With servants, Henry became cruel; with the debtors, ruthless; defending with claws and teeth the fortune that was slowly remaining under his care.

Thanks to the circumstances, he became a friend and guest of Sir Jaime, allowing him to exercise his authority in the mansion and command in the domestic matters.

By that time, he had changed so much his appearance that he could easily pass for his employer's relative or son.

Once he had earned the trust of Sir Jaime, he started to look into his life. Anything was good for him, he showed himself friendly and helpful. With the time, he discovered that Sir Jaime had a teenage daughter who was interned in a monastery school.

Where even the family of the students have not influence in that place.

He had access to the family estate, the records, and even to the mail. Not wanting to waste the opportunity, he read the letters Sir Jaime's daughter wrote to her father in advance. Then he would proceed to carefully seal the letter again before handing it over.

When Sir. Jaime had lost his wife, he puts his daughter in a boarding school. He usually visits her weekly and, in their free time, they both travel around the world.

In return, she became in a dedicated student who was always among the best ones. However, while her intellect was impeccable, her temperament constantly gave problems for the school management.

The name of this new character is Eugene. On the outside, she had a peaceful beauty, but inside, she lacks something that make her truly shine. And, to avoid people notice this, she always wears exaggerated and glitzy ornaments that her father would buy for her. And this little tyrant, without realizing it, was carefully observed from the distance by her father's proficient servant.

After a while, Henry decides to meet her. To achieve this, he started to show so much

interest that Sir Jaime, like every father, proud and delighted, started having long conversations with him about his beloved child, then invites him to go with him on his next visit. Needless to say, Henry accepted the invitation with great joy and excitement! - Well, Henry - says the employer, - what a pleasure to have you coming with me to Eugene's school! In fact, I already think of you as my son, and that would make you the brother my dear daughter never had.

- It is an honor, Sir. I cannot wait to meet her.

- We will go together, soon. I promise I'll try to make time for it the next week.

- I appreciated. I already imagine her: kind and lovely like her father.

- Thanks for that, son.

Intrigued, Henry asks the other servants what they think about Eugene. Them, in a blunt way. answer:

- The girl is mean and stubborn – said the maid.

- Every time she comes home, she feels so bored that to amuse her a little, she gets a servant fired. We all end up suffering. Who does that kid take after? I don't think is like her parents, because her father is a nice person and her late mother was a saint! – said sincerely the butler.

The gardener, making a disapproving face at the servant, decided to remain silent, he prefers not to speak. He appreciates his employer very much and knows the great love he has for his daughter.

Pleased, Henry thought was best to finish the matter. He better show fraternally interested in the girl, at least in front of the servants.

* * *

MEANWHILE, AT THE SCHOOL, Eugene quietly thinks about her mother, who was always very sweet and kind. She also remembers her beautiful face, her bright eyes, her loving and calm voice, her luxurious dresses and jewelry...

Eugene has never overcome the loss of her mother. When she is at home, she searches avidly for the portraits and move them around the house. Very often, she finds her father admiring them, with a sad and nostalgic look...

He never loved another woman and even today he lives with the memories of that love... And so it will be, always (she counts on it)!

Burning tears flow and she sighs deeply, not realizing Sister Rosália is coming closer worried, because she saw her crying.

- Child, was it something wrong?

- No, sister. I was just thinking in my mother. Since she died, I cannot be happy!

- Really? That's not what it looks like, Eugene.

- I'm miserable. You're wrong if you think otherwise!

- Well, well, how can I believe it, when all I see is a pretty little girl who her father delivered every caprice because of his love?

- Do you blame him for that? - she asks, eyes blazing.

- No, Eugene. Your late mother, by God's side, must be thankful for the effort your father makes to make up for her absence.

- I will never forget my mother!

- And nor should you! Those who have passed away still deserve our attention and prayers.

- Do you know when will my father come? I have so many requests for him...

- That's why I am here, my child. This is a letter from him. Take it! With these words, sister Rosalia extends to her an envelope filled with loving pages, written with great affection by that extraordinary father.

- Eugene holds the letter in her hands, while keeps trying to hold back the previous thoughts so will not lose the thread of her memories.

- Aren't you going to open it, child? - asks the sister, surprised.

- What? Oh yes... I am still thinking about my mother... She was so beautiful! Why did she have to die? Why, sister Rosália? Why?! I miss her so much! I will never be able to get used to her absence!

I would like to tell her about my dreams and sorrows; hug her one more time, sit on her knees and listen again the beautiful stories she used to tell me...

- At that time, my child, you were so small!...Yet you still remember, must be because that period of childhood leaves a mark on our lives.

But today you are a grown up and a beautiful young woman. Despite the sadness. When we don't have the tools to change our destiny, we must be happy, despite everything. Do you understand?

- I can't and I don't want to understand, sister, she answers rudely, - I don't need your advice! Leave me alone with my memories. Perhaps you are talking because you don't have any. How can you understand me then? Excuse me, but I want to read my father's letter, okay?

- Sure, Eugene, take your time. Someday I will tell you my life, if you want to listen. Don't think that religious life is not entertaining. But now, doesn't matter. Be at peace. I hope the letter will bring you good news and comforts your needy little heart!

And the good sister leaves, bewailing the bad mood that seems to be part of Eugene's physical and spiritual life.

Her heart has become attached to this sad and arrogant little girl. She understands her more than she will ever know.

Deeply concerned, she goes to the school chapel to pray.

With a certain fury, Eugene opens the envelope and absorb in the multiple lines of love from his father. She reads over and over again. The handwriting is beautiful and clear.

"What does he mean by a pleasant visit?! – thinks upset. - Who will come, and what does he pretend? Will it be a servant? My father has a great number of them and has never

granted them this privilege! Why now? Whoever it is, I will show him who I am and what is his place!

He isn't worth the wait, must be one of those ordinary servants that life itself steps on…

Luckily, the holidays are coming.

My father is getting old, I need to be by his side…

These lessons are making crazy! They progress slowly! It is important that I take my rightful place soon, so I will be able to stop opportunist people like the one who is coming to see me. Surely, he is thinking of taking advantage of my father …I'll show him the reality!

Then she crushes the letter and, standing up suddenly from her seat, throws it into a nearby floral can. Returning from the chapel, sister Rosália saw her anger about the

missive. Noticing the redness in her cheeks and the theatrical attitude, came to the right conclusion, her father had somehow upset her.

Passing by, she left her alone to deal by herself the frustration.

Tapping her feet on the ground, Eugene goes to the yard, where she sat and continued ponder the same matter without joining the activities of her classmates.

The principal of the institute tolerates as much as she can her frequent misbehaviors, because Sir. Jaime contributes with great sums of money to the charity and has participated donating funds to the multiple school renovations in order to make it bigger, more modern, and functional.

Just like that, Eugene decided to give free rein to her darker thoughts. Thinking that someone could stopped her, she decided to hide her real intentions. The only who had listened about her real feelings was sister Rosália, because she was known for her extremely discretion and caring for the others, something she takes advantage of.

Her roommate, Marianne, who also admired Eugene, received from her crumbs of attention. Being always treated with contempt because of her kind and docile temper.

Eugene defends with claws and teeth everything she considers her property.

She studied harder, so maybe she could soon finish her education program. With only fourteen years, she asked the heavens to have enough patience to get to adulthood. The only pure feeling she has is the unconditional love for her dead mother.

She doesn't see herself a teenage no more, she already behaves like an adult, lecturing they classmates, the ones she considers fools and insignificant for her childish behavior. She is thinking in her future, if one day she will get married, she would like to do it with someone who has social status, a powerful man!

Well, well, dear readers, things are started to become interesting. Our little character doesn't have idea that, gently, with an enigmatic smile on its lips, Nemesis is coming for her.

* * *

SO MANY CHARACTERS FROM THIS STORY, will cross path in the course of their life, to interfere somehow in the events of other people's life.

Leaving for a while the ones we already know, let's move through the story to meet new ones.

Let me introduce you *Mademoiselle* Madelaine D'Or Alvarado, blessed with physical and spiritual attributes that everybody adores, especially men. Who are more vulnerable to physical beauty, and that why beautiful women must be very careful in this world.

Madeline has a dark and smooth skin that match with a dark black hair as ebony. Big kind eyes of the same color of her hair that shine as stars, reflecting the pureness of her soul. With a perfect nose and small mouth made to smile.

She's slim and shapely, she seems to be taller than she is. She likes to wear dresses made of dak fabric with little fun and light details that help her to elongate her figure.

Her long hair is usually tied on top of her head, what make her look like a queen, beauty, worthy and noble. Those small feet, that look like they have the wings of Mercury because of how fast they walk help her in her daily chores, on which the harmony of the village and its inhabitants hang…

She is the eldest of her siblings. Everyone who could see her would say she is just fifteen years old, but she actually is twenty years old.

Her parents had tried to set her up with the best prospects, but she refuses by saying she will wait for her prince charming that will come in a white horse. She is pretty sure that he will be a good man and will be willing to help the poor and defend the oppressed…

She is naive by nature, always ready to do good and simple things. She is a pleasant person, like a song of praise to the Creator.

Smart, always determinate to learn more. Her father, fascinated because of the physical, intellectual and moral gifts of her daughter, encourages her.

Without underestimate his other children who loves them equally, Madeleine is the apple of the Count Santiago Luiz de Alvarado's eyes. Every day she wins her father's heart, because of her multiple qualities and dedication. He wouldn't know how to live without his daughter, even if he's happy with his marriage. The Countess Bettine D'Or Alvarado makes him blissful, because he feels she is the woman of his life.

But the Count, smart and intuitive, doesn't feel good with all that happiness, he's afraid that what he is living now, can be sort of an early compensation for the problems that could come in the future.

Madeleine, alongside with her parents direct the education of her two younger siblings, and she also helps her mother with the household duties.

Her sister Soraya is twelve and her brother Fabian is just six.

They all live in an old castle, where the order and aesthetic can be appreciated in every angle. Most of the furniture are upholstered in crimson velvet with details in gold. Abundant flowers, artistically distributed, and together with ornamental plants that perfume and decorate all the spaces.

At the music room, on the piano, was placed a basket full of nice, a *corbeille*, tasty things that came from one of a Madelaine's persistent admirers.

The white marble, covert in a wide red carpet, stairs. The various rooms are decorated with very good taste and practicality.

In Madelaine's chambers, we can see: books, brushes and paints, canvases and painting easels, sewing boxes, embroidery and, in a corner, near a large window, a loom still filled with thick and colorful threads.

The chambers of Soraya were a replica of Madelaine's.

At Fabian's we can see several toys from all over the world that his father brings him when he returns from his travels. Currently, an all-white wooden horse with a seat and natural hair is still rocking, while the little boy is running towards the very tidy kitchen, where we see the servants dressed in white, happily attending to their chores.

In front of a huge copper pan, dear Ignácia mixes the sweets that the family is going to eat. It is because of this pleasant smell that Fabian approaches and kindly asks for "a little bit" to taste. Laughing, sweaty from the steam, she stops and places in an earthenware bowl a small portion of jam in syrup, stirring it to cool it. She affectionately kisses the child, who sits patiently waiting.

The pantry, carefully organized, was next to the large kitchen.

Into the enormous courtyard, we can see a large laundry room, where the men and women boiled the clothes in big cauldrons. The steam that comes out pervade the place. The pieces of garments are carefully scrambled for their cleaning. There are different vessels where the servants put the clothes after being selected and separated per sectors, going from garments of the family and servants.

In a different part of the house, in huge deposits, other servants are already washing the pieces that will be boiled and dried in an open and sunny area. Going downstairs to inspect this duty, Madelaine runs into Fabian enjoying the sweets. She advises Ignácia to give him less sweets so as not to ruin the boy's appetite before lunch. Ignácia takes some of the candy and Fabian makes a mumble of displeasure. Caressing his head, Madelaine kisses him with a smile as she goes to the music room, where Soraya is practicing ardently on her violin.

She, immersed in playing her favorite tunes, does not notice her sister's arrival.

Madelaine comments:

"How beautiful you are, my sister! Fabian and you have inherited the blonde beauty of the French through our mother! I resemble dad and his compatriots from Andalusia, golden land of sun and passion! We only have physical differences, because spiritually we are the same. Thank God! May he keep us united".

Madelaine is an excellent pianist. Whenever she plays, an emotive silence falls between heaven and earth. On these occasions, the castle is also reverently silent. When she sings, especially beautiful arias and gentle madrigals, she seems to reach phases of the soul inaccessible to mortals, and at such moments, inexplicable burning tears run down her beautiful face. Giving her the appearance of the weeping of an angel who, having to live in this world, misses the one to whom her beautiful spirit should belong.

The countess also plays and sings a duet with her husband, who is an excellent tenor. Together they perform the popular operas.

Arriving at her chambers, Madelaine calls herout:

- Corine, come here! Don't run away! I need to talk to you.

Pretending to be in a hurry, the maid tries to slip away, but knowing Madelaine, she desists.

She is sixteen years old, beautiful and attractive. Her eyes are big and mischievous. With copied gestures she answers:

- Yes, *Mademoiselle*, what do you need from me? I am here organizing your artistic material...

- Since early this morning you have been running away from me, and you should know by now that it will be useless. You are only postponing a necessary conversation for both of us.

- Really, *Mademoiselle*, I've been very busy!

- Well, listen once more: I don't want you to receive flowers, or anything from strangers!

Much less to put them in the salon hall, creating illusions in the heads of others, and worse than that, compromising myself in a very dangerous way! Don't you realize that?!

- Pardon me, *Mademoiselle*," she replies, rolling her eyes, while with her hands she nervously tucks in her white, starched apron. - It's just that the Baron André of Villefort was so insistent!

He really begged me! Poor man, he is always hanging around the house, peeking in the windows in order to catch a glimpse of you! He is so obstinate in his devotion to you! I pitied him. Imagine he said that the corbeille was a token of gratitude for heard you sing!

From a distance; sneaking dangerously behind the walls. He also told me, very wisely, that her voice is as mellow as a nightingale's!

Madelaine, who, while listening, is rummaging through paints and brushes, turns to her and concludes:

- Corine, be wise, pay no attention to strangers! If advice is not enough, then take it as an order!

That man really annoys me, he constantly harasses me!

If I find out that you keep on facilitating his access to me, taking in count that this is a dangerous invasion of my privacy, I will be forced to dismiss you without hesitation.

I see no other way, since you continue to turn a deaf ear to my constant and exhaustive admonitions!

Think about that and decide if you want to keep working for us!

- Please, *Mademoiselle*! I really like working in here and for your family! I'll obey everything you say!

- All that matter to me is that you comply with your duties. Now, let's go to work!

Making a well-studied and sincere reverence, Corine quickly goes away through the corridors, while Madeleine keeps with a sense of worry that reflects on her face.

And Corine, while walking started thinking in the money she gets from the errands she does for the Baron.

Clearly, always keeping in mind the happiness of Madelaine!

The Baron is a full-grown man, elegant and powerful; good-looking, wealthy, and a widower.

One night, at a music concert, he saw Madelaine and fell madly in love with her. He never gave her a break again, constantly pursuing her, using a lot of resources and Corine's ambition.

Madelaine feels threatened. She thought of speaking to her father, but fears retaliation from this man she doesn't know.

He, in the other hand, counts on her power to make what he considers his dearest dream come true: to marry her. The more Madelaine eludes him, the more he desires her. He knows no limits and has no restraints. His life is mysterious and very private.

When he comes across Corine, he asks anxiously:

- How is my goddess doing?

And Corine tells him something interesting, which he listens to in astonishment, and then rewards her by promising her more and more.

Grateful and cheerful, she concludes that Madelaine may be very beautiful and intelligent, but there is nothing practical about her...

Ah, if only that handsome, rich, fragrant man would look at her! - Corine takes a deep breath as she shakes her well-constructed body. Elegant, she dresses in the latest fashions, to make people think, that she is a noble. She is charming, full of life, and has miraculous plans. She knows the sensual force she carries, but will carefully choose the one who has the 'privilege' to give her the life she desires.

She is theatrical in her manners and claims to be the defender of everything and everyone...as long as it interests her. She is aware of Madelaine's supervision; however, she thinks she is too smart to be caught doing something wrong.

The castle breathes love and work. Its residents are averse to the decadent and corrupted life of court salons. For this reason, they are politically guarded. Its heraldry speaks of a glorious past. The present is the fruit of much effort in building a more just and peaceful world.

On previously scheduled dates, they promote events with games, sports and artistic entertainment. For these activities, the best of the best people gathers who, like them, harbor in their hearts the same ideal of life.

On these occasions we can see, scattered along the various alleys, on the banks of the singing streams, in kiosks, under balconies, on the lush lawn or on spacious rooftops, the most diverse art being worked on right there, by amateur artists or specialists.

Music is mixed here and there, where the instrumentalists surpass themselves in talent.

The prizes are different, according to a series of criteria.

There, new and poor artists are promoted, giving them the funds to invest in their work.

Small works of art emerge as if by enchantment, dazzling those who come to appreciate the art or collaborate. The competitions don't create conflict, they only invite to greater effort.

It is a beautiful picture, in its colors and sounds, in the joyful bustle and in the good results.

In the distance, in the old hunting lodge, athletes of all kinds settle and organize themselves in preparation for the competitions.

In a large open-air amphitheater, actors show off, either in epic verses, the presentation of monologues or plays by renowned authors of the time.

The Creator, surely, looking at all that is done there, must feel more confident in the future of human kind.

Finally, forgetting the jagged towers and the size of the castle, we can glimpse there a normal residence, in which this family progresses showing love.

Madelaine moves between two opposite worlds: hers, noble by birth, luxurious and comfortable, and the world of misery, to which she courageously throws herself to rescue the unfortunate, wiping away their tears, relieving their hunger, clothing them, or medicating them according to their needs, or, still, admitting them to appropriate institutions several treatments.

She is part of a selfless group that helps the many needy people of Paris, a consequence of the prevailing situation, of the alarming contempt for the human being and the extreme attachment to riches.

These philanthropic works are centralized in a church called Our Lady of Mont'Serrat.

Father Estanislau, the parish priest, found in the good heart of Madelaine and the financial resources she represents, what was needed to pull out of the misery and ignorance countless unfortunates.

Whoever sees her in the infirmaries of the Parish House, with her messy hair, sweaty face, hands stained with medicines, running around in a filthy apron, will hardly recognize the beautiful and elegant Madelaine D'Or Alvarado!

At their entrance, toothless mouths smile, pain eases and hope for better days reaches hopeless hearts of the world. When she sees the benefits, asks for silence.

Trusting in God, she is the mistress of herself and of her feelings. Her strength is the example.

Along with the necessary stuffs, she brings for the little ones treats and candys made with extreme care by Ignácia, who, when sees the various baskets, comments, touched:

- They are for the poor people you are helping, my little girl!

With love, Madelaine guides and teaches the women to leave the wrong path and to go back to the correct paths of love, while supporting them to survive with dignity.

She explains to the mothers, indicating to them adequate behaviors for the loving and responsible exercise of the divine gift of motherhood along their little children.

She listens to the old people's narratives, the common " back in my days" while they, with shining eyes, relive things from the past and never forgotten...

She fixes their sheets and pillows; she reads them beautiful novels...

When it's time to leave at the end of the working period, she leaves her protected people comforted, less disillusioned and more confident in life.

On Sundays, at the time of the mass, whoever sees her entering the church, luxuriously dressed, will hardly recognize her as the friend of the unfortunate people.

Father Estanislau, in comparing the "two Madelaines", cannot say which of them is the more beautiful.

When she arrives, she goes to the sacristy and there, reverent, while kissing his hand, she says, smiling friendly:

- I kiss not only the hand of the priest, but the hand of the selfless man whom I admire and respect!

The good priest embraces her tenderly, fixes his gaze on the image of Jesus and thinks, "Thank you, Lord, for this virtuous soul. Protect her!"

And with cloudy eyes he tells her:

- Thank you, my child. Now go! Your family is waiting for you!

She returns to her seat and, in fervent prayer, accompanies the mass. Sometimes, those who look at her will feel that her radiant spirit glides through regions inaccessible to others. From time to time, people catch a glimpse of a silent tear running down her cheek, as happens when she plays and sings, detaching herself from the world around her. At the end of the liturgy, the various groups disperse toward the exits. Softly, with Soraya and Fabian, Madelaine watches, with great emotion her parents hugging each other, lovingly, when her gaze crosses with the baron at the back of the church, he seems to be waiting for her.

Polite, he bows, greeting her with a fiery look and a thin smile on his lips.

Annoyed, she ignores him and continues her way, feeling closely watched by him.

Noticing her tense, Soraya asks her:

- What's the matter, Madelaine? You look nervous!

- Don't worry, everything is fine, my sister! - she answers, hurrying her pace. They reach the central courtyard, where the carriages await their respective owners.

The caged horses and coats of arms indicate the social status of each family.

Richly dressed, most of them display their latest costumes. Makeup in pink tones, crimson on the lips, men and women show a lot of vanity.

The children, proud, hunched by their heavy clothes, copies of the adults, are a reflection of the times.

But... In stark contrast, the ragged ones dare to stretch out their hands to beg for alms to buy a loaf of bread or a hot drink.

Some give them alms to escape persecution or to be charitable. After all, a few moments ago they heard the preaching of the Gospel...

Others, more credulous and frivolous, approach in front of everybody, and, opening their silk, leather or velvet purses, take out a few Louis D'Or, jingling them, before placing them in the hands of the unfortunate.

A few minutes later, the gibberish ceases and the place become silent and deserted.

Next Sunday, everything will be repeated as in a common social act.

Loudly, the carriages leave one after the other.

In one of them, discreet and comfortable, are the Alvarado's family. They laugh and exchange impressions about the beautiful Sunday. Fabian relates, smiling, how he saw a dusty lady, dressed in lace, full of jewels, sleep to the point of snoring during the priest's sermon.

Count Louis and Countess Bettine snuggle, tenderly. She sighs, introspectively, still expanding the spiritual resources that she received during the time she was in the mass directed by her dear friend, Father Estanislau. In her ears still sound the words of the Sermon of the Mount, so well explained by him. Sometimes she was moved to tears.

While the children excitedly disputed the sun's rays through the curtains of the vehicle, Madelaine watched with great attention the scenes of daily life that enchant her so much.

She is easily moved by the simplest things in life: a mother with her child on her lap, servants moving from one place to another in search of the various errands of their employers, children tugging at the hands of adults when they want to stay longer watching this or that...

The sun overwhelms her, cheers her up, and the intense blue sky fills her with peace. Intrigued, she asks herself: How long will we be happy? There is so much misery and pain around us! When will it be our turn to suffer? And her chest becomes tight.

Observing her, affectionately, the Count was able to guess her thoughts. He knows her deeply. He respects her and looking outside he admires the beautiful Sunday. Everyone will have a lot to do when they get to the castle.

Shouting a loud "Whoo!" and tightening the reins, the coachman stops the carriage. At a run, Fabian jumps out and enters the wide doorway, followed closely by Soraya.

The servants, well oriented, are already in the midst of the great assembly of the special Sunday. Each one assumes their own responsibility, so the successes achieved correspond to the expectations of the Alvarado family.

The decoration of the castle transports us to the Greek temples or the Champs Elysées, without their sumptuousness and paganism.

Wandering around, we stumble upon a hexagonal stand made of fabric, half a meter off the ground. There, on a large piece strategically arranged on the floor, there were several musical instruments.

Among them, we highlight a rich jade-colored lute, inlaid with precious stones that form a delicate floral motif. From the neck of this instrument hang narrow golden ribbon that seems to tell about its owner, an important character in this story.

The extroverted uncle Richard has brought him to introduce him to the family.

At this point, he takes him through the halls in search of Madelaine, whom he adores. He meets his brother and sister-in-law, and introduces them to the guest. The hosts hasten to sympathize with the boy.

Pursuing his intention, uncle Richard went in search of his niece, and found her busy with the servants, completing the decoration of the colonnades of the gardens with garlands of mosses and tiny flowers.

Quickly and gracefully, she arranges the small bouquets. Then, she comes down from the small stall, when she finds her uncle smiling at her. Happy to see him, she asks him affectionately:

- My dear uncle, how are you?

- Me, my goddess? I am very well, and you?

- I am fine.

- Madelaine, may I present my friend, the Marquess Charles D'Alençon. I know his family is noble and nice. I have invited him to come and play the lute, to liven up the party, but without competing for the prize since he doesn't need it. I have been telling him about these events for some time now, and it was not until today that I managed to convince him to attend.

Madelaine stares the Marquess in the face. Their eyes meet and he smiles in fascination. For the first time, she feels intimidated by a man. What strange feelings invade her, in front of those beautiful translucent green eyes? Where does she know him from?...

Trembling, she holds out her hand to him, which he delicately kisses, making her blush, for no apparent reason. Finally, she comments:

- Very nice to meet you, Monsieur Marquess!

- Likewise, kind *Mademoiselle*.

Surprised by his niece's unusual shyness, uncle Richard continues:

- Dear Madelaine, my young friend is virtuoso on the lute.

He composes musical pieces that delight all who hear them.

Today he has brought us a new one to listen!

- We thank you, sir, and remain at your disposal for anything you may need. We want you to feel at home.

Bowing, elegantly, face to face with Madelaine, he responds, in a friendly manner:

- Rest assured, I feel better than ever!

I confess that I cannot find the appropriate words to express how happy I am to meet you. I would like to recite exquisite verses to you instead of telling you conventional phrases. But in the most important moments of our life, we are almost always at a loss for words because the heart internalizes everything, clear and wise by nature!

Pleasantly surprised, trying to hide her emotion, she replies:

- Well, everything I have just heard seemed to me pure poetry! But I must conclude that you should be accustomed to say it to all the beautiful women who attend the salons of the court!

- You are wrong, let me tell you. I rarely go to the salons you mention. I'm almost a misanthrope, devoted to letters and music, which consume my time. Sometimes, however, I attend a few meetings with my dear parents, but I assure you that no one else has ever heard from me what I have just told you.

Richard, laughing, bursts out:

- By Jupiter's beard, anyone can tell you two are attracted to each other! You didn't even wait for me to leave! My God, the youth of today!

Deeply confused, Madelaine defends herself:

- Dear Marquess, please excuse my uncle's diatribes. As your friend, I must tell you that you are very witty.

As for you, I understand you are trying to tease me, but I am too busy at the moment. Excuse me, I'll be right back!

Saying this, she hurried away, causing Charles to smile slightly, and his uncle exclaimed:

- You're angry! Well, why? Excuse us, Marquess! Madelaine doesn't usually behave like that!

Following the silhouette of the girl, who walks away at a slow pace, he calmly responds:

- You can put your heart at ease and forget the apologies, my friend. I have never been so well impressed in all my life! - it seemed to him that Madelaine, for some reason, had escaped.

In the company of Richard, he decided to go for a walk, enjoying the cheerful hustle of this Sunday...

At every corner of the road, he hopes to see the girl again.

Beside him, chatting and gesticulating a lot, his friend continues:

- Charles, do you know why my brother, the Count Santiago Luiz and his family are offering this expensive and stressful meeting?

- No, you haven't informed me yet!

- Well, it is always time to correct our mistakes! Here, several meetings are held in the name of culture and the arts in general. On Sundays some benefactors come, discover new talents, and help them.

- And how do they do this?

- With financial resources.

- I figured as much! I think that, along with real talent, one comes across characters who are not very noble. I wonder if they're not, sometimes encouraging idleness or, who knows, funding vices?

- No, Charles. They are careful to make a meticulous analysis, to then give them an opportunity and sponsoring them. After their victories, the artists leave here some references, so there is a proper follow-up.

- Will those who are dishonest lose their money?

- That's right!

- Have there been any similar cases?

- Of course, there have been. A lot of people think they can move up in life without any

effort.

- What about an author with only one work?

- Yes, it seems to us that, in executing it, they have made use of strange resources, because in their attempt to repeat the feat, the longed-for inspiration escaped them as if by magic! But others do provide joy, grow and strive more and more.

- Artists are, in general, unique people, don't you think, dear Richard?

- And sometimes they are eccentric, Charles! There are the arrogant ones, like gods who had descended from Olympus, for whom "ordinary" men are worthless, even if they possess great abilities like them, but they didn't care and keep in negation!

- And for those, what is the procedure of the sponsors?

- The sponsors are equally proud to put up with them for a long time, so they leave them alone.

- Ah, the humans! When will it learn that it is part of a whole and must harmonize with everything?

- Well, my young friend? The only reasonable people in this world are you and me! - replied Richard, with a loud laugh.

Madelaine, who was approaching, heard him and hurried away unseen. She feared her uncle would go on in the same way, ... and compromise her.

But, despite the huge effort she makes to concentrate on the event, she could not. She feels detached from the projects and the meeting. Recently, she saw the Marquess and her heart skipped a beat.

Her cheeks flushed.

Her father had questioned her several times, without success, and had given up on knowing the reason for her remarkable distraction.

Her mother noticed a slight discomforting in her. Moving closer, she hugged her shoulders and kissed her. There is so much to do and no time for personal problems.

In the kitchen, the movement is amazing. Meats roasting in breads of all shapes, cakes and sweets exquisitely prepared.

Fruits, in large wicker baskets, are scattered around the various delicious refreshments.

In the large hall, handmade tablecloths cover long tables decorated with floral arrangements decorated with floral arrangements that stretch the length of it, forming a large semicircle. In the center, glittering trophies and medallions are fastened with black velvet ribbons. Small, delicately carved hardwood boxes hold rich jewels. These are the prizes. The cash offerings will be made on the spot, in honor of the various guests.

The house and the garden already show many people who, arriving in groups, spread out little by little through the rooms and specific sectors. Each one looking after their own interests or simply observing those preparing for the various contests, in a pleasant bustle that announces great joys.

Charles and Richard continue talking:

- My friend, what do you think about my niece Madelaine?

- Well, Richard, from everything I see, I'm sure the world still has a way to go. When a family gets together with friends, for the sake of legitimate progress, we breathe easier, much more confident! I'm sorry it took me so long to accept your invitation. I realize now how much I've missed out!

- That's not exactly what I asked you, dear friend!

- I know, Richard. As for her, let me get to know her better and then I'll judge her. For now, I can tell you that I am very, very impressed. I feel that today is not the right day to win her friendship. I have been able to observe the many tasks involved in this great confraternity.

- You can come back as often as you wish.

- It will be a great pleasure for me. Now, Richard, excuse me. I'm going to practice on the lute strings. I must prepare myself so as not to make a fool of myself in front of so many competitors. Ah, by the way! As for the prize, in fact, I wish to compete for it! It makes the competition more exciting. In case I win it, I will use it right here, in the fairest way.

- Of course, Charles. You should take note. Rules are made to be to be followed. I will find my brother and inform him your decision. As always, I am right! It seems that out of the two of us, it is you who has more spiritual maturity. I admire your common sense, my young friend. See you later! Make yourself at home and come back to sign your participation.

- I'll be right there, thank you.

In fact, Charles intended to look for Madelaine and headed inside without stopping. He walks through several halls, but does not see her. He goes through the gardens, and she is not there either. He enters the castle, pretending to admire the heraldry of the various banners and coats of arms scattered throughout the corridors. He heard one maid inform the other that Madelaine was upstairs, finishing washing her siblings. Strategically positioned, he waits for her to come down and surprise her.

After about fifteen minutes, he hears the sound of footsteps and sees the children coming downstairs very well dressed. A few minutes that seem like centuries, a rustle of silks makes his heart skip a beat.

When he looks up, he sees Madelaine, elegantly dressed, adorned with jewels, her hair up, her face fresh and flushed. She is dazzling. With light steps she descends majestically, when she crosses his path. He flinches slightly, unable to conceal his surprise.

Gently stepping forward, Charles offers her his hand, while, with an ardent gaze, he declares:

- It was worth the wait, *Mademoiselle*! You look amazing!

- So, you were waiting for me? Any special reason?

- The greatest goal I have already achieved and I feel rewarded!

Pretending not to have understood, she insists:

- Do you want to tell me something?

- Yes, because, I have decided to present myself for the prize, I contradicted your uncle's first statement. I ask for your help to approve my decision.

- Then let's go to the people in charge of the list of contestants and there will do whatever you want.

- Thank you in advance for your kindness. I could never do without such a kind company!

- We are the ones who are grateful to those who come here, helping us to brighten up these celebrations, which are very special to us.

- I am flattered, *Mademoiselle*, to participate in this extraordinary event. I am sorry I waited so long to accept my friend Richard's invitation.

- As Ecclesiastes says, "There is a time for every purpose under heaven..."

- Indeed! Although... I don't know if I'm under it or in it anymore, *Mademoiselle*. - Charles fixed his gaze on hers, more and more fascinated, leaving no doubt about his intentions. She goes quiet and he continues:

- I salute you for your philanthropic ideals!

- I thank you on behalf of myself and my family.

This idea came to us when, gathered together, we were talking about the great difficulties people have in finding success in their professions.

At the same time, we wanted a different kind of Sunday, in which, together with those closest to us, we could share our joys and strengthen our hopes more. And to share the bread of the body and the spirit, we created these events that have made us very happy.

Gradually, these activities took on unexpected proportions. In this sense, we decided to choose more carefully who we invite, so that the objectives are not lost.

- I understand and admire you more!

- Don't be deceived about us, Monsieur Marquess! We are imperfect and, as such, fallible! We have ups and downs, despite our good intentions.

I would like to take this opportunity to apologize for my impetuous attitude of a moment ago. I am used to my dear uncle Richard's attitude, but today it was too much. I must have made a terrible impression to you.

- I'm the one who should apologize! What reassures me is that, despite everything, I have been sincere, believe me. I want to be your friend and a regular guest at these wonderful events. If this has your approval, of course!

Shocked, Madelaine responds:

- Let's leave it in peace and not apologize anymore, okay? We are already friends. Now let's hurry, otherwise the registrations will be closed.

Richard, who was arriving, was surprised to see them together and in good terms:

- Where are my young people going with such enthusiasm?

- Monsieur Marquess, must sign your presentation, replies Madelaine, without pausing.

Bettine, who had seen them, was delighted. She wisely concluded that he was the reason for her daughter's distant attitude. Walking away discreetly she went on her way. When she saw her husband, she realized that he came to the same conclusion, because he smiles amused, while his gaze accompanies the two young people. Hugging his wife, he accompanied her to her activities.

Shortly after signing his participation, Charles stops at the instrument kiosk and begins to tune his lute. Trying unsuccessfully to hold Madelaine. But she is overwhelmed by the commitments.

Away from her for a moment, he rehearses his different plays. Some women that look like they were in love stand in front of him and start to sigh for him and his music.

People gather around the various rooms and the colorful exuberant garden. People star grouping together according to the things they are interested in, like they were bouquet of flowers divided in colors and parfum.

When the guests come, they are received at the gates by the servants that are in charge to take everyone one of them to the right area according to their necessities and preferences.

The guest's joy increases, vanishing in the blue sky full of white clouds that try to copy the shapes that are in the land, but in the other hand the wind passes without problem between them.

An elegant carriage pulled over right in front of the gate and an eccentric and proud character descend from the vehicle.

He is a Russian Prince, Aleksei Nikolai Ivanovich.

He seems to be looking for someone. The crew is to him an insignificant stain that has fallen on the surface of some canvas that absolutely does not interest him.

As soon he is welcomed with the common manners, he shows indifference. Looking over his shoulder to everything and everyone, he continues looking for someone. From his dark eyes like the night come out sparkles of burning fire, when he found what he is looking for, Madelaine D'Or Alvarado!

And she, who already had seen the magnificent carriage, felt like she was touching hot iron in shock.

There are so many things that his manners and eyes had said about the Prince's intentions. She feels the urge to escape, but she controls herself. She already knows how the wealthy people act when someone disobey or refuse them. He is a noble, powerful, fierce, high-handed and tyrant by nature. He knows that she already knows his real personality. She must be careful.

Covering up, she continues with her activities. For now, she is organizing the last details of the "spinner" group that their looms choose and work with it.

Madelaine, feeling how this royal character was coming closer to her, couldn't avoid thinking in the stories about the mythological parkas that changes the strings of the life and death…

Making himself noticeable by his strong footsteps, he quickly approached her, leaving the distance between them behind, all thanks to his presence and medium complexion.

He is without discussion, a handsome man. His skin is white, his eyes are black and big, his face with impeccable marks, his mouth well made, and with a great remarkable intelligence that anyone can see.

There's still a fire in him that burns his surroundings and consume him inside, with a great passion for everything he wants and love. His fierce soul, submit everything; he likes to be in control, has never lost anything.

His artistic side has taken him to participate in those kinds of events in company of his two sponsors. But the real reason to be there, is Madelaine, and he never hide it.

Already close to her who, with every step of his shiny boots feels more threatened, he snapped his heels, arrogant, in his military uniform, with all the embellishments of his privileged position. On his uniform, the shiny gold buttons, the cape, neatly slung over his left shoulder. Facing Madelaine, with captivating smile, he bows, and says:

- *Mademoiselle* Madelaine, it gives me immense pleasure to see you again!

It seems to me that you are more beautiful each day. I think there is a great honor in getting a smile from you more than a victory against an enemy. My most cordial greetings!

Intimidatingly, she withdraws the hand he kissed, makes an elegant bow while, with delicacy, she responds:

- I thank you for the honor, Your Highness! Truly, I do not deserve so many praises!

- Well, well, always modest! Anyway, I admire you! The heaven has endowed you with sui generis qualities that I do not find in other mortals.

Perhaps the gods have them! Will you accompany me to see your parents?

I wish to greet them in your lovely company! - as he speaks, he offers his arm to Madelaine, who can't escape the imperative invitation.

From a distance, Charles watches them interested and curious. He cannot hear them, but in witnessing what he sees, he supposes that the royal character has rights over Madelaine.

When he saw him arrive, he was disturbed, without knowing why, fearing something indefinable. Seeing them now, together and apparently satisfied, he feels the urge to leave, but contains himself and decides to look for Richard.

Perhaps his friend can clarify this situation which, for him, has suddenly become of great importance to him.

As if guessing his thoughts, his friend appears in front of him:

- Charles, are you ready for the competition?

- Of course. Can you tell me if Prince Aleksei will also compete? His virtuosity is widely known!

- No, he wouldn't come down from his pedestal to compete in anything whatsoever! He only judges and rewards the winners, regally and, it must be said very proudly! Do you fear him?

- If I am being honest, not in the field of art!

- And in others?

- I have my doubts. We know this prince well and we know how arbitrary he is.

- How can this affect you, my friend? Is there any misunderstanding between you two?

- No, rest assured, I am speaking only in theory.

- I understand. Well, excuse me, Charles, but I've just seen a beautiful widow that interests me a lot! Ah, she has noticed me too!

See you later!

Very annoyed, Charles returns to the lute, strumming it absent-mindedly and almost without interest. Unable to concentrate, he goes in search of Madelaine. He finds her standing next to the Prince, talking to the Counts.

She answers the pleas of a maid and hurries away. Fabian had climbed a high and dangerous staircase, challenging anyone who tried to bring him down.

As she follows the maid, Madelaine assesses the dangers she is running, not responding to the Prince's amorous desires.

A few moments ago, he had succinctly and authoritatively stated his intention of receiving her and her family at his castle for a royal banquet.

She rightly concludes that this Sunday she will have no peace. With her gaze, she anxiously searches for the kindly figure of the Marquess.

A little distant, quietly, Charles is thinking on the new feelings that insinuate themselves powerful in his soul, previously so free and mistress of herself:

Madelaine, Madelaine! Who are you that touches so deeply the strings of my heart? What fate will this new reality hold for me? I feel overcome and so I wish to remain!

I will accept, without murmuring, any pain that life imposes on me out of affection for you, my dear... I seem to have waited for you for centuries...! What strange spell has befallen me in such a short time?... We exchanged only a few words...How should I understand this? It's impossible!

In a little while, I will loosen the bonds of my heart... I will play and I'll sing only for you... My reason at this moment is as far away from me as the moon from the earth...

After saving her brother from the dangerous prank, Madelaine gives up looking for Charles. The Sunday activities become more and more intense.

The family will open the festivities by playing in trio, solo, duo and quintet:

Madelaine and Bettine alternate on piano, Soraya on violin and Fabian on his flute. They will perform folk songs, madrigals and a symphony.

Then Bettine will accompany her husband in a beautiful operatic aria and, finally, they will all sing together the hymn (composed by a friend of the family) that officially opens the get-together.

At the starting of the *overture*, Charles was floating between heaven and earth during Madelaine's presentation.

He also admired the family in their artistic performances. This is also the reality for Charles.

At the moment of his presentation, he expressed his feelings towards Madelaine, making himself fully understood. Her look and her emotions are perceptible, especially for someone like him, an artist, a poet…

Pouring the last notes into the air, Charles wins everyone over unanimously. He receives frantic applauses.

Descending from the stage, he plunges his eyes into Madelaine's eyes, electrifying her.

But… not far away, a hard, hateful look reaches them. It is Prince Aleksei, vigilant and jealous. Facing him, audacious, Charles challenges him in silence.

To Madelaine's parents, the fact did not go unnoticed. With Charles' arrival, the certainty of tribulations and dangers for all. Approaching them, Madelaine declares:

– The Marquess Charles D'Alençon is the composer of this beautiful madrigal!

– So he is not only an instrumentalist, but also a composer?

– Yes. Uncle Richard had already informed me – she says.

Soraya comes looking for her to talk to her about the children's lunch, which is going to be in a separate large hall and is under her and Fabian's responsibility.

The Counts seek out the Marquess to congratulate him on the happy interpretation:

– I salute and congratulate you, Mr. Marquess, on your probable victory! – says the Count, kindly.

- Thank you, but I respect the competitors! I will await the final tally to then rejoice, or not!

- "Mr. Marquess, what direction will you take the prize, in case you win it? - the Countess wants to know.

- Madam Countess, I already have plans, I have held nothing back and I have played to make the competition more exciting! I would like to congratulate you for this beautiful party, and I would like to ask for your approval to include me as a regular guest on these Sundays!

Stepping forward, the Count declares:

- Will be an honor to have your presence. It will brighten up even more these activities that are dear to us! Madelaine sometimes also organizes exhibitions of the work of award-winning artists!

- I will attend these occasions as well! I will bring people who are interested in art and can afford to buy the artworks!

- Well done! So long, Marquess! We'll see each other again in a while!

- See you around! - bowing, Charles also walks away.

Intent on getting closer to Madelaine, he goes out to look for her. He walks among the guests and listens to their enthusiastic compliments. He thanks her and continues his anxious search.

He finds her on his arm with the prince. Aleksei monopolizes her, intentionally.

He feels a deafening irritation, his blood boils in his veins.

Struggling to control himself (he's not usually like this), emotionally disharmonized, he decides to go.

Another time, he will try to approach her.

With strides, he reaches them and, bowing slightly, addresses to both of them:

- Your Highness, *Mademoiselle*...

Turning to the marquis a furious look, almost covering Madelaine with his body, Aleksei retorts:

– It's not polite to interrupt someone else's conversation, Sir Marquess!

– Forgive me, Your Highness! That was not my intention! I wanted to say goodbye to *Mademoiselle* and inform her of my decision regarding the prize, should I win it, if I may...

Stepping back a little, he leaves Madelaine in sight.

Disappointed by what she has heard, she inquires:

– Are you leaving us already, dear Marquess? You have given us so much beauty and you rob us of the pleasure of crowning your victory? I am sorry...

– In fact, what I wanted was just to compete with so many talents! I have already received the legitimate prize, which was to be able to participate in such a beautiful event!

– Why don't you stay longer? Uncle Richard will be devastated!

– *Mademoiselle* is mistaken. He is in excellent company! And I must confess that someone is also waiting for me. It would not be polite to delay me!

Annoyed, Madelaine looks pale.

Realizing her disappointment, the Prince, outraged, crosses his arms across his chest, ostentatiously interposing himself between the two, while he waits for the Marquess to finish his explanations.

Charles thrills. He had hit the target. He acted this way to evaluate the conquered land. There is no date.

– What about the prize, Marquess? – she wants to know.

– Should I win it, as I said, I leave it to you to give it the most appropriate direction! This has been my intention from the beginning!

Out of control, possessed, the Prince explodes:

– Is that all, Sir Marquess? For someone who had no intention of interrupt us, you have already annoyed us too much! – thus saying, he hugs Madelaine by the shoulders, embarrassing her.

Charles reflects his obvious annoyance on his face. Nevertheless, he bows elegantly and leaves, followed by Madelaine's gaze.

At the attempt to free herself from the embrace to accompany the Marques, Madelaine receives a quick squeeze from that powerful hand that holds her back against her will. She feels the urge to cry with rage, but contains herself and delicately frees herself, claiming other commitments. Badly impressed by the Prince's attitude, she feels her blood run cold in her veins as she concludes that from now on, Charles will be seen by him as a mortal enemy.

Losing her ability to calm down, she goes to the castle chapel. On leaving the chapel, she runs into the prince who had followed her through the woods that separate the chapel from the castle.

Indignant, she confronts him:

– Are you looking for someone, Your Highness?

– Yes, you *Mademoiselle*. I followed and waited for you to make your prayers in peace.

– Forgive me, but I thought that in my own home I had freedom!

– Easy, easy! Don't worry, beautiful Madelaine! Actually, my care for your person is extreme! *Mademoiselle* is the most precious jewel that I know!

Great treasures must be well kept!

– I wonder, Your Highness, how I will manage when you are not around! – she exclaims wryly, to which he, smiling sinisterly, reports:

– As for that, I have well-designed plans, rest your heart! And I'll tell you something else: I will never be robbed of what I consider mine! Woe to him who crosses my path! It would have been better not had been born!

She understands the allusion to Charles. She takes a deep breath, controlling herself, when he rushes forward, trying to put his arm over her shoulder. Like being stung by a snake, she jumps back and retorts courageously:

– Your Highness, let me breathe, please! I don't recognize your authority over me! I am not part of your estate, nor of your empire! I am not at the disposal of Your Highness or any other!

Laughing heartily, he speaks to her as if to a child:

– Dear Madelaine, were someone else to speak to me in that tone, she would pay me dearly! But what do I see? A beautiful woman who becomes more beautiful when exalted, ready to defend herself!

I admire you so much that nothing you do or say will change my feelings!

We forgive beautiful women easily. After all, they are gifts from the gods that embellish the face of the planet! And in your case, dear Madelaine, they did it! Praise to them! – Giving more sweetness to his voice, leaning over, looking into her he pleads:

– Please don't be angry with me, okay?

At this point, he sounds more like a boy asking forgiveness for some mischief.

Ignoring his request, Madelaine remains quiet and with quick steps heads towards the castle; faces flushed, deeply disgusted.

He, apparently disconsolate, moves on in the same direction.

The Count, jealous, had followed the prince unnoticed and from afar followed their movements. He fears for his daughter's safety; he knows her intrepidity, which sometimes borders on recklessness.

Aleksei is a big threat.

Seeing them return, he returned to his duties as host.

The prince has decided to give Madelaine a truce in the hope that she will calm down. Feeling more secure in the absence of the Marquess, he joins his peers in a noisy conversation in which his voice stands out, imposing itself and monopolizing all the subjects. Every now and then he lets out a loud laugh.

Freed from the prince's harassment, Madelaine looks for her mother and gets it all off her chest, telling her everything.

Very worried, Bettine advises:

– Beware, dear child! We know of the almost unlimited power of this regal lord! The more intensely you react, the more he will be interested! Don't challenge him too much, because he is not kind of people you think he is, you don't want him as enemy! Be more rational and be more subtly when refuse his invitations! He will get tired, you will see!

And now, we have the Marquess who seems to bother him a lot!

Am I right?

Madelaine nods.

– But where is he? We haven't seen him since his presentation!

– He left soon after. He was in a hurry, so he said goodbye only to me. He said he had an appointment he couldn't postpone, you can imagine! – Bettine senses in her daughter's reproach a small amount of spite.

– You, my child, are already leaving reason aside a bit to be more sentimental! Thank goodness that the Marquis is worthy of you!

– Oh, come on, mom! He didn't interest me that much after all! But... in view of the joy you showed in being here with us, and the compliments you gave us, I thought he would stay until the end. I was wrong!

– Madelaine, are you a little jealous!

– Jealousy? Why? What reasons would I have for that? Well.., thank you for listening to me. I feel calmer! - kissing her mother, she rushes into the crowd.

The time of Nemesis, the Greek goddess of vengeance, arrives for the characters in this story of ours... They will meet and measure their forces, physical and spiritual.

After the denouement, on the return to the true homeland, the evaluation of each one and of the group as a whole will be made...

So praise God that everyone has grown in spiritual stature!

* * *

IN ENGLAND, HENRY prepares to meet Eugene, and together with Mr. Jaime goes to the school.

– "What a hassle! – he thinks. – Wasting my precious time in a school for girls! Nevertheless, I must do it... Dear Eugene, you can't imagine the plans I have for you!"

Mr. Jaime breaks the silence:

– Henry, I love Eugene too much. My daughter is the greatest reason for my life. I have amassed a fortune for her, guaranteeing her a comfortable and peaceful future.

She lost her mother very early and never got over it.

Trying to compensate her, overcoming my limits, I end up doing the least of her wishes. She, in turn, makes "good" use of this my weakness.

In this task I am marvelously supported by the sisters of the school. Especially by Sister Rosália, who loves her as a daughter.

Sometimes a vague feeling of guilt comes over me, but at a distance and burdened with my financial obligations, how can I show her my love? – Henry is strangely silent and moved. After a few moments, controlling himself, he continues:

– Excuse my emotion! I am opening my heart, without no strings attached! I don't do it to anyone else, only to you, dear son!

In a mellifluous voice, Henry replies:

– Oh, Mr. Jaime! This makes me admire you more and more! How lucky Eugene is! I envy you. To be the owner of so much love. – In this moment, in this realization, Henry is being sincere; love, in fact, he never had. And he adds: "I grew up alone, without anyone, as you yourself know...

– Yes, I know. With each new day I thank God for the opportunity I had to help you on that unfortunate occasion, when you were struggling like a fish out of water...

Today, thanks to your merits, you have grown a lot as a person and as a professional. In the constant exercise of a remarkable dedication, you conquered me forever! Today I feel a paternal affection for you.

I hope Eugene likes you! That would make me very happy! With her arrival, I feel our family has been enlarged.

– She will like me, you will see! I will spoil her so much that she will have no other choice!

Mr. Jaime, moved by the assertion of his most faithful administrator, now as his beloved son, reports him:

– Henry, don't worry about your future. I have plans in that regard!

– Now, Mr. Jaime, don't tell me such things, I don't need to hear them to judge your kindness and justice!

– Thank you, my son. My greatest wish is to see my daughter happy! I already feel worn out by the years of struggle, in the acquisition of the values! But don't think me distracted from things of the spirit! No...! I feel an uncontrollable longing to live them! Eugenia was a pious and faith-filled woman. At her side, I could countless times appreciate the Gospels of Jesus... How much I miss her, Henry! I loved her too much and I love her still!

Henry suddenly feels remorse. This man, worthy of much gratitude opens the floodgates of his good soul for him, just for him!

He disguises himself and looks out the window of the vehicle.

– Are you all right, my son? I hope I'm not boring you; I'm talking too much! I'm sorry!

– I am fine, thank you! Don't apologize! Your conversation doesn't tire me, quite the contrary! I'm just anxious to get there soon and finally meet Eugene!

Despite what he heard and believing in Henry's good will, Mr. Jaime followed the rest of the trip in silence.

At the school, Eugene dresses up neatly for the visit of his father and his companion. Patient, Marianne tolerates her bad mood and unreasonable demands. Eugene is already overdressed and remains unhappy. Marianne, despite being poor, has more refined taste, knows how to choose the pieces of clothing, but Eugene disagrees with everything; she likes to dress up exaggeratedly.

Just before reaching the destination, Henry asks:

– Dear Sir, I beg for your permission to keep my distance while you speak to Eugene. I don't want to disturb with my presence, rushing in.

– Don't worry, son. Everything will be fine!

Eugene, taking long walks, without explaining to her friend what she wants, goes to the Superior's office and asks:

– Reverend Mother, I ask your permission to not receive anyone but my dear father!

– And why do you say that? It has always been this way!

– Today, however, he is accompanied by someone, it seems to be an employee of his... I don't want him to have access to my person!

– Dear Eugene, replies the Superior with a sharp look, – My consent will depend first on your father's wishes.

He must have reasons to bring someone along. But first, tell the sister governess to keep your father's companion in the hall, until further notice!

- Thank you, mother! - she leaves to give the order, while thinks, "If it's up to me, this intruder won't even see me!"

She informs the sister preceptor and goes to the garden, where, from a strategic angle, she can see the gate without being seen.

After a while, which seemed interminable, she sees her father's carriage parked in front of the school.

She sees her father get out, then immediately she sees the elegant and refined man who seemed familiar to her. She sympathizes with him.

She runs through the corridors looking for the sister and gives her a countermanding-order:

- Sister, allow the two of them to enter, together! I've changed my mind! But wait a bit until I can reach the drawing room!

Without saying a word, the sister, already habituated to Eugene's temper tantrums, goes about her business, because the ordinance will fulfill her specific orders.

A few moments later, Mr. Jaime enters the room and takes his daughter in his arms, happy and emotional.

- Daddy, I miss you so much!

- Forgive me, daughter, for not being by your side more often! I missed you too!

- I wish I could go home with you!

- Let's wait, daughter. The time will pass quickly!

You look so beautiful! Come, I must greet the sisters! Besides the packages, I brought you many other gifts, Eugene!

- Did you come with someone else, like you said you would?

- Yes, he's waiting in the hall, he preferred to wait a bit. He will meet you.

They enter the office of the superior, who greets them with a smile:

- Welcome, dear friend! How are you?

- I am very well. And you, mother?

- As God allows me! The struggle is big. Educating is a very difficult task! On the other hand, we also have problems with employees, suppliers, teachers, and more!

- All this is part of a very important scenario, isn't it? Managing properly is one of the most difficult things! I can say that! What about Eugene?

- Well, as you know, she is very studious. She is always among the best in the school; and in this aspect, she deserves praises! However, in other aspects, Eugene does not control her temper, causing us a lot of problems! I am telling you this so that you will help us with your parental authority; we are counting on your words of admonition to our dear girl.

- I thank you for your sincerity and your warnings, which are more than opportune!

I promise, as always, to do my part. Sorry for the trouble Eugene gave you!

- No need to apologize, dear friend! Under the circumstances, make yourself comfortable and enjoy the visit! Your presence always cheers our hearts!

Eugene leaves the office with her head down, embarrassed.

Her father gently scolds her:

- Dear daughter, why can't you control your temper?

- Why are they always against me? - she asks in a mournful voice.

- If you are always transgressing school discipline, how can you expect anyone's approval, Eugene?

- Why can't you just leave me alone? How I'd like to get out of here once and for all!

- Eugene, you're behaving just like a spoiled child! You do the wrong thing and you don't want to be scolded! One day you'll find out that life itself teaches us, harshly, at every step!

We are not as important as you think, Eugene! And so, you will end up being very unhappy!

- Daddy, if you come to strengthen those who attack me, what defenses will I have? Not even during your visit will I have peace? - She is on the verge of tears. Regretfully, her father tells her:

- You see things in a twisted way, Eugene. I hope that next time I won't have to hear the same complaints! Help me in this matter, my child... Okay, I won't talk anymore for now... Come on, come on... No need to cry!

Wiping away her tears, she asks with curiosity:

- Where is your companion?

- Let's go to him, since you want to meet him so much!

- Not so much! What drives me is pure curiosity! - she says arrogantly.

At the sight of them, Henry stands up straight, elegant. He will capitalize on his natural charm. A lot will depend on that...

He brought her expensive and original gifts. She will be delighted!

Facing Henry, Eugene analyzes him silently. He holds her gaze, accepting the challenge.

She hears her father say:

- Eugene, this is my manager, Mr. Henry John Stanford. He is also my friend and a great collaborator.

I am glad you two finally meet!

Offering him her hand, she asks:

- How are you, Sir. Henry?

- Sir Henry? Well, I think I've grown old before my time!

- No, it's not that, I speak to you like this because, to me, you are a strange person...

- But, if we've been already introduced, Eugene! Just call me Henry, please! I want to be your friend! Look! I brought you gifts. I hope you like them!

Interested, she receives the packages and with each new surprise, she squeals with joy.

Moved by Henry's care and affection, Mr. Jaime admires his perspicacity.

When the surprises are over, he invites them over:

- Well, daughter, let's unload what we brought for the sisters and your friend Marianne.

The next few minutes were taken up by this task. Well impressed, Eugene did not see the strange sparkle in the eyes of Henry's. He continues in his care, supporting her in everything.

Enthusiastic, she decides to show him around the school, which she does, happily and cheerful, in an unusual way.

The father, stunned, concludes that he was in fact very happy to have brought Henry with him.

To Eugene's naive eyes, Henry appears like a hero. She is surprised, giving him the attention, she has always denied to strangers.

In his company, she smiles at everything, relaxed, different. He is all caring, a gentleman, helpful. He praises her smallest gestures, winning her over completely.

Sister Rosália, who had been busy since early in the morning, approaches to greet them. Smiling, she embraces her good friend.

When she is introduced to Henry, she stares at him, analyzing him, as she hears from Mr. Jaime:

- Dear sister, this is Henry John Stanford, a dear friend and my manager. He is now in charge of everything. In his competent performance, my assets have prospered considerably! Henry has come to me at a good time, when I have had enough of the business world!

- My respects, Sir Henry! - she says, extending her hand to him.

- Pleased to meet you, Sister! - he answers, without facing her head on.

- So, my friend, you've suddenly found yourself an administrator, huh? - to Henry the sentence sounded ironic.

- Not quite, sister. I've known him for some time. Now, he is taking over the management of my business in an admirable way, as I said. Extending his duties, he is also managing my own home.

Astonished, Eugene exclaims:

- Daddy, is he living in our house?!

Hearing this with deep displeasure, Henry tenses up his performance and suddenly shades of resentment appear in his dark eyes.

- Of course, child! - continues Mr. Jaime. - For some months now, he has been residing with us, at my invitation. I confess to be very happy with it.

Pretending not to have heard Eugene's declared reproach, Henry turns to Sister Rosália and lets it out:

- Sister, Mr. Jaime knows me well enough to evaluate my character and intentions! Under his generous protection, I have searched tenaciously the unstable financial world for the most advanced techniques, and applied them to the multiplication of his goods.

As you know, the machine overwhelms those who do not get up to modernization. New times are settling in, inviting us to modernize. This way, I preserve and multiply the goods of our dear girl as the sole heir of her father.

One day, Mr. Jaime gave me shelter and work, taking me off the streets where I lived and was very unhappy! - Henry almost bursts into tears.

- I will be eternally grateful to him for that! What would I be without his merciful help?

He turns his face the other way, apparently to disguise his emotion.

Eugene, saddened, concludes that once again she has followed her impulses. Her father reproaches her with his gaze.

Sister Rosalia has heard every word, yet she is not moved. She sees his dubious character and unbridled ambition.

She knows souls, and his is not one of the best...

Showing remorse, Eugene invites him to the arcade. Controlling himself, 'with effort', he accepts, following her in silence.

Turning to his friend, the sister insists:

- If I remember correctly, you told me several times that you did not trust your business to anyone. You have always been in charge of everything.

Have you changed your mind?

- Yes, Sister. The years are weighing on me...

- But you are still a beautiful man, in full physical and spiritual maturity! We all know you're not getting remarried because of Eugene. Surely you fear her jealousy. Beautiful women, however, must ask for it!

- Oh, come on, sister! It's not like that! Eugene has weighed in my decisions in this regard, but in truth I miss Eugênia so much that I can't even imagine being married to another. I've also decided that if Eugene doesn't have her mother anymore, let his father be only hers!

- I regret finding that our dear girl is encouraged to be more and more selfish.

Her life should follow the natural course, despite Eugene. One day, she will marry and you, my friend, will be left alone. And by this time, your heart would probably already be tired...

- I realize, dear sister, as always, the wisdom of your words. However, I beg you, don't worry. It is not worth it. I am well as I am!

- Are you okay or are you resigned?

- Resigned, perhaps... But, tell me, what do you think of my manager?

- I tell you that your confidence is reckless! Forgive my boldness! You should be more prudent, dear friend!

- Why do you say that?

- Intuition, perhaps, call it like you want.

- But if even Eugene sympathized with him to the point of forgetting us!

- This shows the strange power he wields over people.

- Don't you consider this a quality?

- It depends on the intentions that move him. But you will know how to lead him, won't you? After all, everything is fine if it seems that way to you! - she concludes, smiling kindly.

- So it is, my dear sister. While Eugene is distracted, I'm going to the chapel for a little prayer. If Eugene asks for me, please let her know where I am.

- I will!

After sometime of fervent prayers, the good man enriches the church vault with a large sum.

He goes to the garden and sits comfortably on one of the benches.

He breathes in the scent of jasmine, his favorite flower, while reflecting:

"For some time now, I feel excessively tired...

Am I ill, or does this despondency come from my unsatisfied soul?"

Meanwhile, Eugene and Henry chat excitedly:

- Eugene, your friends pass by us without greeting us! Do you know why?

- First of all, Henry, they are not my friends! They also don't approach me because they know I don't want them to do it!

- You don't like them?!

- No, I don't!

- And among them, there is none with whom you sympathize?

- No! Or rather Marianne, but... she bores me too much! She's very silly! She doesn't understand me!

- You must be very lonely!

- You are wrong! Soon I will leave this place and go to my home; to the life I wish for!

- May I apply for the position of your older brother?

- You are too bold, Henry! I don't usually accept people as I am doing with you! Be satisfied with that, for now! In fact, I never wanted brothers!

Very upset, Henry feels a certain deaf resentment.

Mr. Jaime and sister Rosália arrive, inviting them to lunch.

- Have you forgotten us, dear? – the father asks, smiling.

- No, daddy! We were playing different games, and I must confess that I am the completely loser!

- Come on, Eugene, if we were just playing, there is no winner and nor loser!

- Eugene, sister Rosália warns, beware of Sir Henry! He can crush you like an insect!

- No one will ever do that, sister! - she replies, irritated.

- Odd conversation, my dear! - Mr. Jaime intervenes. - It must be caused by hunger!

- Forgive us for being so late, Mr. Jaime! - explains sister Rosália. - While we were taking care of the various orders and gifts you brought, sister Berta forgot she had put the meat in the oven, and it got burned! But, finally we have another one ready!

- Unforgivable! Next time I will bring just fewer presents! Maybe then we'll have lunch earlier? - he exclaims, laughing pleasantly.

In the large dining room, the table is exquisitely set and lined with a rich, embroidered linen tablecloth. A floral arrangement sets a cheerful tone and the fine porcelain tableware has delicate patterns. The cutlery and crystal reflect the lights that come in changing colors through the changing colors through the stained-glass windows.

- Will you be joining us for lunch, sister Rosália?

- No, Sir Henry. I rise at sunrise. I eat frugally, and the foods that most people prefer, do not appeal to me. Bon appetite to you!

While they are eating, Mr. Jaime notices that his daughter is not very well:

- Why do you look so pale, Eugene? - he wants to know.

- I don't feel very well!

- You must have been playing too much, my child! Why do you put so much effort in everything you do?

- I like to feel victorious, papa!

Aware of everything, Henry enjoys a piece of lamb.

Wiping his mouth with his napkin, he smiles, showing perfect teeth, as he comments:

- Eugene will soon be fine!

Sister Rosalia, who had not yet left, invites her to go and rest a little. She agrees and goes to her room.

There, she finds her colleague, Marianne, bustling about with notebooks and books.

- Aren't you well, Eugene?

Without answering, she orders her:

- Close these windows! I need to rest before my father leaves!

Unwilling to answer, Marianne gathers her school materials and prepares to leave, watched by sister Rosalia's understanding gaze.

- Sister, asks Eugene, stay with me for a while!

- I will, Eugene. You've been too restless, dear!

- If you want to stay, sister, please be quiet!

Patiently, the sister exchanges glances with Marianne, who, after locking the windows, closes the bedroom door carefully. Taking her rosary, sitting by the bed, sister Rosália prays for Eugene.

She fears for her future.

Madelaine can't wait for Sunday to be over. She needs time for her meditations.

The Marquess, in the other hand, already at his home, feels the urge to return to the castle. He could say he did not find the person with whom he had arranged to meet... But, no! It would not be a good strategy!

Reclining in a luxurious lounge triclinium, still in his finery, he falls asleep.

In a familiar contrast, after the big event, some of the participants return home in rich carriages, while others follow on horseback or on foot.

Many live in Mansards, where cold and hunger are their companions. They face all sorts of difficulties in the name of their dreams. Travelers or not, they seek for a better position.

They chase after glory and fame, unstoppable. Some become famous; others, after great efforts, give up.

Because of the riches it has scattered, the Alvarado castle has become known as the Castle of the Sponsors.

In one of its halls, Bettine does beautiful work of charity, which, praised by the good people, generates skepticism, and displeasure in those who rule the unfortunate French people with an iron fist.

Count Luiz is a mature spirit, deeply affected by pain throughout his existences. At this moment, introspective, he doesn't notice Bettine is approaching:

- My dear, what has been troubling you for some time now?

- Nothing, Bettine. I'm just like that, you know!

- Nevertheless, I can see that you are feeling sad!

- Don't worry, my love! I am the happiest of mortals and that, perhaps, frightens me! However, I trust in the Creator! Whatever may have to happen, will be!

- Whatever happens in your life, don't forget to include me!

Do not underestimate my courage, Mr. Count Luiz Santiago de Alvarado! - Exalted, she is dazzling: her eyes illuminated, her voice vibrant, trembling with emotion. He smiles with pride at the woman that is his wife, embracing her in love.

- Heroine materialized of my dearest dreams, do not get upset! I was only wandering, speaking in general terms! You forget that your husband is born philosopher? As you know, I read and admire the free thinkers of our time and, as such, I am influenced by the negativity of some of them, about the future of this country! Forgive me if I worried you; I didn't mean to!

On the other hand, my dear, we live with the misery of this people, which distresses us greatly! If only the leaders would love them! No doubt history would be different! We all expect harsh pains for France!

- You are too pessimistic, my love! I don't like to see you like this.

- Forgive me! I will redeem myself: first with my kisses, and then by inviting you to the kitchen to taste Ignatia's sweets! I haven't had time for that yet!

Tightly bound, they kiss, lovingly.

Then, they leave, holding each other in their arms, in search of the sweets.

* * *

WAKING UP FEELING BETTER, EUGENE goes out to look for his father.

She surprises Henry, thoughtful, taking a walk in the garden. Without being seen by him, she follows him.

Her father is in the dining room, very cheerful, chatting with the sisters, discussing about the most diverse topics.

When he sees her, he asks with interest and love:

- Are you all right now, daughter?

- Yes, you don't have to worry! - she answers sharply, causing the disconcerted sisters to disperse, leaving them alone.

- From what I could see you were happy with the sisters! - she adds, still bitterly.

- Daughter, the sisters and I are old friends! We have similar ideas and goals! It is understandable that we talk pleasantly about different topics!

- For me, my universe is you and our life. Beyond that, nothing else matters to me! Living away from you is a pain!

I hate this school!

- My child! This is the best time of your life and one day you will miss this place!

- Oh, papa! What a stupid idea!

- Other girls, my dear, would like to be in your position!

- Only the foolish ones! I know what I'm missing! The real world outside and I, here, between these walls that look more like a prison!

- Before facing this 'world that is throbbing outside' that attracts you so much, Eugene, you must prepare yourself very well!

- But I have you. I won't be alone!

- Don't be so dependable, my child! I am not eternal! Think about life! Imagine the future, that you have problems, and they weigh you down, you must come back here and look for the dear sisters!

Promise me that you will!

- If I leave here, daddy, I will never come back!

- Please, Eugene! It's worrying me!

- It's all right! I promise because I know I won't have to! You are still too young and too wealthy!

- Eugene, remember this! We can lose everything from day to night, at any time! The business world is very unstable! Stop talking about material things and think about your immortal spirit too!

- Come on, dad! You are very annoying today! You keep repeating the same chatter of the sisters! Don't you think I hear enough every day? Ah! - she blows at the top of her lungs, irritated and impatient:

- Where is your manager, anyway? Or should I say, 'our' manager!

At least he's more amusing! - kissing her father on the cheek, she leaves quickly. She doesn't want to go on listening to her father.

When Henry sees her, he smiles and asks her kindly:

- Are you better now? You had us all worried!

- Well, it was only a matter of physical exhaustion! After all, I tried to beat you at every game! How reckless of me, wasn't it?

- I admire your courage and effort, Eugene. That's why you've already made me your most faithful servant! - bending down with an elegant and little smile on his lips, becoming even more charming.

A bit disconcerted by the compliments, she exclaims:

- Well, I'm starving, how about you?

- *Touché!* Well, me too!

- Then let's have a snack?

- With pleasure!

Side by side, happy and relaxed, they reach the dining room.

On the table, an exquisite snack composed of bread, cookies, milk, cheeses, fruit juices, and sweets.

During the conversation, Henry masterfully monopolizes all the topics, making the meal very pleasant.

Sister Rosália, however, seems to be the only one who is not deceived by the charms and qualities of Mr. Henry John Stanford.

However, the hours go by and they must return.

Eugene is very saddened. His father speaks to her in a broken voice:

- My child, I miss you already! Be a good student and take good care of your health, please! Obey the sisters, especially sister Rosália and Reverend Mother! - hugged by him, she cries softly, leaving him with a tight heart.

At a distance, Henry watches them, and in the same way, he is watched by sister Rosália.

Annoyed, he turns to her and says, ironically:

- Well, sister! I seem to have found in you my guardian angel!

- Don't deceive yourself, Sir Henry! I am very far from being an angel! I am a religious woman, still imperfect, lacking in virtues! If I were invested with this attribution, I would certainly protect Eugene, and not you!

Listening to them, Mr. Jaime concludes that the good sister definitely does not sympathize with her manager.

Saying goodbye, Henry goes ahead to put the baskets that had the gifts and sweets for Mr. Jaime; an act of kindness of the good sisters.

As he bids farewell to Sister Rosália, Mr. Jaime confesses:

- If I had a blood sister, I would not love her more than I do! I thank you from the bottom of my heart for your dedication to my Eugene! Whatever happens, I hope she will never be far from your providential care! Count on my friendship and gratitude forever!

- It's not that much, my dear friend! Within the limits of my life as a of my religious life, I promise to help you always! I love Eugene very much and I will do everything for her! Go in peace and may God be with you!

✳ ✳ ✳

STILL IN BED, MADELAINE thinks about the successes of the previous day.

Through the window, she hears the birds singing. She gives thanks to the heavens for another day of life.

Her sleep had been restless. In nightmares, she saw the Marquess and the Prince facing each other in a bloody duel.

Rising, she opens the curtains and the generous sun fills the room. She thinks about the parish house and the many activities that await her.

When she gets a chance, she tells Father Estanislau about her troubles.

Quickly, she goes downstairs to the dining room and eats her meal.

Bettine appears beautiful and refreshed.

- Madam, you look very well!

- I can't say the same for you, dear! I notice a certain sadness!

- I didn't sleep very well! I had nightmares! - she declares, biting a tasty apple, eagerly.

- Don't get too tired today, child!

- I'm used to it, don't worry!

- Before you leave, tell me: what will you do with the Marquess' prize?

- I have his authorization to use it as you wish, so it will be used for charity work!

- What a nice gesture! Worthy of this friend who has already won us all over! What about the trophy?

- He will come for it himself, in due time!

- To see you again, my child!

- Is that so, mama? Well, I don't have time for small talk!

Work is waiting for me!

- I have another guest for the wards of the Parish House.

Nestor will take him when he arrives. He went to his house to get a few items. He makes a point of taking them. The unfortunate man can barely walk, so weak!

And Salústio, how is he?

- He is very well! He is our main support in everything we do. He is always passionate about France and the poor. May God protect and bless our worthy friend!

Madelaine looks up, in her emotional prayer, and adds:

- I fear for him...!

- Me too, my child! May the Lord of us all protect him always! Take him with you, my dear, and if you come back too late, ask him to accompany you, okay?

- I'll do that!

- Our greetings to Father Estanislau and our dear doctor!

- I will send them for you, mama! See you there!

In the carriage, deeply interiorized, she thinks about the fascinating Marquess.

She sees on her mind: his refined elegance; his noble gestures; his sweet voice; his ardent gaze, full of promise...

In between thoughts, he realizes that the vehicle has already parked in front of a large and sober building with a front of red bricks decorated with white friezes. It is the Parish house, an extension of the church Our Lady of Mont' Serrat.

As she entered, she greeted cheerfully those he met along the corridors. She enters the room, removes her dresses, soaps her hands and forearms; she puts on a large white uniform with a pleated skirt and a large apron over it; she hides her full head of hair in a thick, starched cap, and wears white shoes.

She then goes to the medical wards, where many beds are lined up with very white sheets. Attached to the foot of the beds, slips of paper with medical observations.

At the top of a wide passageway in the shape of an arch, there is a portrait of Our Lady of Mont' Serrat, in shades of blue and gold.

A doctor, in a white lab coat, with gray hair, strong hands and reddish features, attends to a boy covered in sores. Without stopping what he's doing, he calls out:

- Dear Madelaine! You're just in time! Help me with these bandages!

- Of course, Dr. Sergei!

- How are you and your family?

- We're all fine, thank God.

- You know I don't believe in him.

- Speaking like that, you only confirm his existence.

- It's just a way of expressing it, my dear! And don't try to convert me. Father Estanislau has already given up!

- And can't I start where he left off?

- If you like lost causes...

- I embrace them every day, my dear doctor!

- I only believe in what I can see and touch! - he adds.

Without answering and very worried, Madelaine notices that the doctor's hands tremble slightly. She knows about his vodka habit. She admires his dedication to the unfortunate ones. Tireless and loving, he does good for the sake of doing good.. "Dear friend of God!", she thinks.

- We'll get to the evaluation of each patient in a moment, Madelaine. We have new

interns. The medical wards aren't enough anymore! How long can we help them?

- Always! We will find new resources!

- What about the new syndicates?

- They are scheduled for early tomorrow morning. Can we count on with you?

- Absolutely!

- Heaven help us, tomorrow we can ease the hunger, cold and thirst of those that, for now, we don't know!

- And besides those who are here, we will bring many others, as always!

- Trusting, above all, in God!

- You trust for both of us, right? - he asks, smiling, his blue eyes shining with tenderness.

- So be it! - she replies, smiling as well.

- Have you seen the baby they left at our door?

- Yes, doctor! I watched as he swallowed the milk furiously, poor thing! I wonder where the mother is?

- Somewhere, ashamed and full of problems, for her situation! We must find her and help her to keep her the baby.

- We will try! Salústio baptized her as Natalia. A beautiful name, don't you think?

While they walk among the beds, he examines the sick patients, informing her of the true condition of each one and the necessary steps to be taken in terms of treatment. She listens carefully and, from time to time, makes a comment about the cases she already knows. The interns show them deep gratitude.

A pause and he asks with curiosity

- Madelaine, don't you get tired of this? - Opening his arms in a wide gesture, he indicates the sad and desolate aspect that is around them. - After all, you are young and beautiful as few others! What are you doing here? When will you take care of yourself and your life as a woman? Are you seeing anyone, Madelaine?

Surprised, she answers with another question:

- What happened, Dr. Sergei? Did it occur to you today to make a full investigation of my life? You've known me for so long! You know about my ideals!

What have we here?

- Forgive me and answer me, if you want: isn't it dangerous to live like this? Are only suffers in your head? What makes you forget about yourself?

- The doctor's view of my life is distorted. I will answer you, naturally, but the Lord deserve me much more.

When I am here, I feel less sad about the misery that is spreading like an epidemic among our unfortunate people... In a kind of "spiritual politics", I strive to help them, the same way you do, feeling closer to God, because my conscience is clear!

Of course, it is easier and more comfortable to live among beauty and comfort! To mix with pain, suffering, dirt and revolt, is a great challenge!

The task of transforming evil into good is a priority and requires self-denial!

In their midst - Madelaine makes the same broad gesture as the doctor - Jesus lived like us! And more than that, he went out to meet them!

At his touch, wounds were healed; bleeding was stopped; lepers were cleansed; the apparently dead were raised; the guilty repented; the mistaken reorganized their minds, portraying themselves before God and before themselves; the ignorant learned; the blind saw and the cripples walked! What else could I tell you? There are so many lessons and experiences, that time, nor words would be enough!

If I strive to follow him, what should I do?

Outside, I live the so-called normal life, and you know how happy I am with my family!

In these two ways of living, I feel fulfilled and thankful to heaven!

- And what about your future, my child?

- My future is in God's hands! It is too soon to change anything in my life!

- But, Madelaine, at your age, women are already married and surrounded by children!

Becoming introspective, she answers almost in a whisper:

- Married? having children?... Perhaps this is not for me, doctor! I thought about it and no matter how hard I try, I don't see myself in this situation...

- Won't your Prince charming get tired of waiting for you?

- Maybe he doesn't exist! Who can know? Marrying me won't be an easy task for any man, doctor! I will never change my way of living!

- Whoever he is, he will be a chosen one of the gods! I hope he deserves you, Madelaine!

- We talk in theory, doctor, because, after all, this man doesn't exist!

At least for now... - but while she speaks, she cannot avoid the memory of the Marquess...

- But, after all, how much time does you have for yourself? - the doctor continues.

- Enough! I often ask myself if, when I dress up with luxurious clothes or sit in front of a bountiful table, how would I feel if I didn't do something for those who suffer and who have nothing? No! It is impossible to ignore all this, doctor! - she says, pointing to the large infirmary.

Moved to tears, the doctor hugs her by the shoulders, unable to speak. Pulling himself together, he takes a deep breath and exclaims softly, lovingly:

- In this 'your God', Madelaine, I believe!

Moved, she bends down and kisses his hands, while declaring:

- And he believes in you, dear doctor!

Surprising them, Father Stanislaus says, pretending to be angry:

- So, this is how you work? And my sick ones, how are they?

Smiling warmly, the three embrace, and walk out among the various beds.

✶ ✶ ✶

WITH THE MEAGER resources they manage to get, those people who need the most and live in poverty in Paris try to acquire some food to ease their hunger.

Relegated to the most complete abandonment, they feel fatigue and disillusionment.

Some, more daring or desperate, steal, being arrested and thrown into infected prisons to die amid physical and moral torture.

To come across a bad guy at night and lose your life is part of the normal risks in any city; so think the authorities (as long as it is not with them).

The paradox between wealth and misery is astonishing.

The king's retinue, wearing silks and lace, traveling in emblazoned carriages or and lace, traveling in emblazoned chariots or caged steeds, reeking of the most expensive perfumes, seems to glide in a private sky, distant and indifferent to all that may happen on the ground floor; the floor that belongs to all French people, regardless of social position. Ground watered by the blood of so many heroes!

The people speak softly, frightened; for any so-called slip of the tongue, one can disappear without a trace.

There are castles and castellans who turn their dark underground into other fortresses, in which they imprison those who bother them, to make them disappear, while their possessions are quickly attached to their own coats of arms.

Tributes are steep, in order to allow almost all the nobility to live a life of debauchery.

The various institutions are undermined, and often honesty hides or corrupts itself in order to survive.

And it will all collapse at any moment! Painful events will haunt everyone! Slowly at first, and then overflowing with raw passions. It will be life's hard demand for rebalancing through the imperfect attitudes of men who generally act with violence in the name of rights and freedom, leveling themselves in the cruelty of those who enslave them...

In a process of invigilance, societies throw themselves into the puddles of misery and pain, stimulated by selfishness, to later suffer in the midst of the purifying storm...

ON THE DAY SCHEDULED for the inquiry, Madelaine got up earlier than usual.

In front of the gate to the north side of the castle, a carriage is parked and the coachman, a stout, dark-haired, smiling boy, goes to the dining hall, where you can see skinniest, poorly dressed and suspicious people, eating heartily.

While he sips a delicious mug of hot milk and eats a piece of bread, he observes, respectful, those people who are in suffering and needy. When he finishes his meal, he hears a familiar noise.

The other vehicle, which will carry clothes, food, sheets and medicine, has just arrived. His companion, like him, tries to eat before they leave.

Madelaine arrives and boards the first vehicle, which is closely followed closely by the second. Once the group has gathered detailed information, they decide which route suits them best.

Together, they trace the most unusual places, helping and assisting many. After hours of exhausting work, they stop at a pleasant place and feed themselves happily. The lunch was lovingly prepared by Ignatia.

- Salústio, now we will go to the address of the cave. It is a place of difficult access and, pay attention: inhabited by a strange human mole. You can't be too careful! - warns Father Estanislau.

Somewhat refreshed, they head towards the cave.

Close to it, they see people that look more like the living dead that actual people: dirty, ragged, some covered with sores, with menacing expressions.

In the midst of this mob, children play grotesque games, amusing themselves at the expense of others. They, oh, God, already show malicious and cruel expressions! They are already experienced in vices and in crimes!

Accompanied by two policemen, they enter the cave, while two others stay outside to protect the vehicles.

Madelaine can't help but have serious thoughts:

"God! Evil is the child of misery, of ignorance, of pain and of contempt! Here they are, Lord, untrained for life and thrown into the pool of misery!

What to expect from them? When will all this finally change?"

He hears the noises of rats and distinguishes in the darkness, beings huddled here and there, amidst the rags and garbage. Food scraps stink and disturb.

Fumbling along the path, they hear groans. A few seconds more and they come across a man lying on a board as a bed. An old woman is trying to wrap him up with some rags from a bag.

Opening a large bag, Salústio distributes the food that they devour, greedily, asking for more.

Doctor Sergei examines the patient. Suspicious, a lady asks fearfully:

- Who are you? What do you want with my son?

- "Fear not, madam," advises Father Estanislau, "we only want to help you."

- If you say so, father... But why the police?

- Just to protect us; be at ease.

Madelaine approaches and reassures her with friendly words. And with a blanket, helps the doctor to wrap up the patient, who is coughing with extreme difficulty, clutching his chest with both hands. Between one spasm and another, he asks:

- What do you want from us?

- Nothing, sir, trust us. We are trying to help you!

- Help my poor mother, I beg you!

- We will, now take this medicine! You'll feel better! - advises the doctor, which is promptly answered.

Careful and saddened, he makes the group understand that he can't do much for the patient.

Madelaine feeds the old woman and she wants to know:

- Do you have food for my son, too?

- Ah, yes! We're just waiting for the doctor's orders to feed him!

With each sudden movement of someone, she shudders.

Being fed by Madelaine, the patient exclaims:

- You are good! May God reward you!

- What is your name, Sir?

- Baron André Brumel of Villefort! - he exclaims, as if at that moment he has recovered his identity.

Shocked, Madelaine looks at Salústio, who, as she, thinks. Proceeding, he confirms, disgusted:

- I am the legitimate Baron André Brumel of Villefort, betrayed, despoiled and thrown into prison to die! - Exalting himself, he coughs again.

He closes his eyes, his mouth dry, overcome by weakness.

Salústio gives him some fresh water, and while they wait for him to recover, they continue to attend to the other 'residents'...

After a few quarters of an hour, the patient, who seemed asleep, speaks up again:

- Father, I wish to speak to you.

- Here I am, my son.

- Father, help me to protect myself from me, in the name of God give me some peace!

- Why, my son?

- Because I hate, mortally, those who threw me into this disgraceful situation!

- Your feelings are understandable, but hatred is an unacceptable in a christian!

- I must confess to you; if I could, I would take revenge harshly! You cannot imagine what we have lived through! No! Only the one who has been through it can know!

- Forgive them, in the name of Jesus Christ!

- I can forgive what they did to me, but the pains imputed to my poor mother, never!

- If you do so, son, you will be devaluing her sacrifice; and consequently, taking away from her the peace she deserves! Think it over and, if you love her, forgive her tormentors!

- I can't, Father, help me, please! My heart is torn! - the unhappy man cries a convulsive weeping that aggravates his health, so precarious.

- My son, listen to me: Jesus suffered much more and did not deserve it, being the immaculate lamb! In the extreme moment, he asked his father forgiveness for us and, in a glorious and incomparable gesture gave us his most loving mother, in order not to leave us alone!

For him and for you, forgive! Only this will bring you peace!

- Father! What will be of her in this world? If I, young and powerful, was vilified, kidnapped and stripped of everything, without defenses? I know that in my present circumstances, I am of little value, but... she has only me!

- As for this, my son, we can reassure you! Your beloved mother will receive from us the protection she needs. We will make her remaining years a period of peace and security.

He stares at his mother, unable to speak any longer, overcome with emotion.

Approaching him, Madelaine takes his hand and says:

- I, my lord, promise you, before the faith that bathes my soul:

I will personally take care of your dear mother-in-law! Knowing her happy, you will have the peace you so longed for and deserved, after so many sufferings!

Struggling, he kisses her hand reverently; deeply grateful. He looks at the priest and concludes:

- Father, knowing my mother is protected, I will try to forgive my executioners!

- Thank God! - they all exclaim in unison.

Turning to the sick man's mother, Madelaine suggests:

- Come with us, madam. Your son is already medicated and he will be moved to a hospital.

Shaking off Madelaine's embrace, she replies:

- No! I wish to stay here with him! I will never leave him, not even for a minute!

Doctor Sergei looks meaningfully at Madelaine, making her understand that the patient will not be removed.

- "Father," calls the patient once again, "I want to receive from your hands the holy viaticum, please!"

- Of course, son. Salústio, help me, please!

- Yes, Father.

At the end of the ritual, the group bids farewell, promising to return early the next day, very early. He leaves them well fed and clothed.

Once in the vehicle, Father Stanislaus, exhausted, sits back and exclaims in a loud, voice and clear.

"-Love one to another as I had loved you. – then look to other place and continue the journey in silence.

- Madelaine - calls Salústio - do you really believe that the patient has the identity he has declared? Could he be delirious?

- We will find out, Salústio! We have before us an enigma!

- Careful, my dear! From the statements of the sick man, you can imagine the risks of this enterprise!

- I know, my dear Salústio, I will be careful, rest assured!

- Count on me!

- I always do! Thank you! Doctor Sergei, why won't the patient be removed?

- He couldn't stand it, Madelaine! Is important to wait for the medication make effect! I'm sorry to tell you, but he's probably living his last moments...

- Poor man! - Salústio says, while he remembers how he got to know this philanthropic group. He owes a lot to everyone and to each personally, especially to Madelaine...

Interned in the infirmaries of the Parish House, she took care of his wounds and his tortured soul. He was silently in love with her, until he transformed this feeling into fraternal love. Today he loves her like a sister, in a feeling that borders on adoration. He would do anything for her! Closing his eyes, tired, he thanks the heavens for the productive day.

Father Estanislau steps down of the carriage, and then, Dr. Sergei. Salústio accompanies Madelaine to the castle. After this, he returns in the same carriage to his home.

After some time, during which the vehicle has traveled through deserted and poor streets, the coachman stops the horses with a 'hoot! He waits for Salústio to come down and bid him farewell with a kind wave of the hand and a broad smile.

Salústio enters the wide doorway of the old building. He passes through a spacious hall, turns right, and steps onto a long staircase.

Reaching another floor, he overcomes more steps and continues up. At the end of a large hall, there is a spiral cast-iron staircase which he climbs in long, determined steps.

Finally, he reaches his humble quarters.

Along the front wall, we see a large bed covered with a beautiful bedspread. A little further away, a table and on it, some jugs with water, cutlery inside a porcelain mug, books, inkwells and feathers, bowls with bread and a basket with fruit.

All arranged on a white lace tablecloth. A chair of carved and aged noble wood completes this set.

On another small table, next to the bed, a wooden tray with some glasses.

Hanging behind the door are clothes and bath towels.

A small room, attached and barely lit, is used as the bathroom. Inside, on a stool: combs, soap, and a few bottles of perfume.

Without stopping, Salústio continues to climb, reaching the roof area of the building. He leans over the wall and takes a deep breath, introspective, in search of refreshment.

He suffers deeply from the conflicts that torment his people, revolting against the misfortunes that reach them at every new instant.

In this deplorable context, a painful perplexity is installed in good hearts, together with the realization of the impossibility of reacting against the ruling power. The constant exemplifications' take away the courage of many.

It seems to them like a bitter chalice that never ends, poisoning their insides, little by little...

The stars begin to appear...

Burning tears started coming down his dark, handsome and virile face.

With a strong shiver, he recalls the fateful day when, not far from there, he was attacked and nearly perished. The robbers took the few pennies he carried and began to beat him, mercilessly, while laughing devilishly. He still seems to feel the alcoholic breath that emanated from their mouths.

He defended himself bravely, strong as he is, but they had the numerical advantage and he succumbed to the pain, crumbling to the ground in the mud, in the rain, on that deserted street. There were three of them.

He kept in his retina the memory of their monstrous features.

He tried several times to get up, but could not.

Hours later, straining her swollen and bruised eyes, he saw through the mists of the night some noisy boys returning from a party. When they saw him in this state, they were sad. Together, they decided to carry him to the church of Our Lady of Mont'Serrat. They knew the good parish priest, who was the one and only Father Estanislau.

After they gave him the first aid, Salústio was between life and death. Pneumonia had set in and his condition was becoming more and more serious. Finally, his physical constitution overcame the challenge and he survived, sad and depressed. Nothing could drag him out of his intentional mutism...

Going back a little further in time, he remembers the tragic loss of his beloved father and brother in a terrible fire. One sad day, when he was returning from work, he saw a lot of people standing in the door of the house.

The flames enveloped everything, making it difficult for him to see anything through the black rolls of smoke. Desperate, he tried to fight the flames in a futile attempt to save them but was stopped by the neighbors so he could not continue his irrational actions. He fainted and, when he awoke, there was nothing left of what had once been his home, nor of those who were his only memories!

Since then, he had only the clothes on his back and a few pennies of louis in his pocket, the same ones that had been stolen that night (angry, walking through the streets to clear his head, in a vain attempt to alleviate the pain he harbored in his carelessly, he went on, in spite of the coming of night, without noticing that he was walking through deserted, dangerous places... And the result was almost fatal).

He spent months in hospital. More than his body, his soul was the one sick. The good priest did everything he could to bring him back, but could not achieved it.

Madelaine unveiled herself at his side and, with admirable abnegation managed to rescue him back to that life he hated.

He began to nurture an unsuspected adoration for her. Then came the overwhelming passion that made him suffer cruelly.

He remembers the mournful voice saying to him:

"Saulo, don't forget to eat something, please! Life is precious, my friend! You must overcome the tragedies and try to be happy! Have faith, Saulo! Come on, had some more of this soup...that's it! And now, some of this tasty candy made by Ignácia. She sends you a loving hug and best wishes for a speedy recovery!"

One day, entering the infirmary, Dr. Sergei exclaimed:

"How is it, Salústio? Are you better, my dear young man? Get well soon, because I need someone to help me in the office! And make it quick, because I can't wait too long!"

His name, said like that, pleased him more than he could have expected:

"Salústio," yes, it sounded great to him! It made sense, to be alive again with a different name, in a new stage of life.

Determined to live, he made an effort and in a short time, he was ready for work:

He arrives early at the doctor's small clinic, clean the place very carefully, arranges the various furniture and sterilizes the multiple surgical instruments. Then he opens the doors, welcoming the clients, keeping them calm and comfortable during the wait, between one appointment and the next.

He has become loved and admired by those who have enjoyed his company. He also began to work in the wards of the of the Parish House.

Today, with great pride, he is part of this fraternal group.

He loves France and its people with devotion...

Admiring the City of Light that begins to yawn, he emits a deafening whimper from the bottom of his patriotic heart... He sees no favorable prospects for his beloved country, nor for his people...

Misery is quickly approaching, and along with it, diseases, violence, fear and insecurity...

- France, my dear! - he exclaims ardently. - I love you so much that my chest seems to explode! I will do everything I can for your happiness! I will give you my own life if I have to! For this I survived: just to die for you and not for myself!

Why, my God, are men so insensitive? Why are there so many injustices in the society when we are all equal to you? Why does man create absurd differences? When this nonsense of a few people scarifying so many, in the name of their pride and ambitions will stop?

When, my God, will we have peace? Looking into the future, we can foresee great pain for all! Yes, the hand of fate will fall heavy, causing bloodshed, pain and panic in the terrible "gnashing of teeth"!

Oh, heavens, this kind of acts will take so many victims! Poor, unhappy people!

- Ecstatic, his eyes are wildly open.

Surrounding him, there are trellises of herbs and flowers that he had grown. A light, freezing rain begins to fall, inviting him to go inside.

Taking a deep breath, he runs his hands through his silky brown hair, wet from the drizzle. Feeling a little better after his introspection on the night that started out starry and became rainy, he goes down to his chambers.

After careful cleaning the place, he eats some bread, wine, roasted meat and fruit. A few more minutes later, he lies down and falls asleep deeply. When he gets up for a new day, the stars are still in the sky; the rain had passed during the night. Tensing his agile and muscular body, he stretches. He must be fast. He needs to get to the doctor's office early.

There, when everything is in order, the first patients begin to arrive.

Joyful, he greets them.

The doctor arrives hurriedly, passes through the waiting room, say hello to everyone and walk to his office where he lays down his briefcase on the desk. As soon as he puts on his sanitary gown, he calls Salústio, ordering him to go immediately to the cave to give a new dose of medicine for the patient. He will go there soon, he promises.

- Hurry up, Salústio! - he orders. - That unfortunate man must be agonizing! Also, take this tranquilizer for his mother, so weak, poor thing! Keep a close eye on her, I fear for her life. Go, my friend!

- Right away, doctor!

- The carriage is outside with Nestor and a policeman who will accompany you.

Arriving to the place, Salústio enters the cave, struggles to see in the darkness, and sees them in the same place.

The old woman is still sleeping, wrapped in the blanket that Madelaine had given her.

The patient breathes with extreme difficulty, but recognizes Salústio. Greeting him, Salústio gives him the medication and offers food and a tranquilizer to the lady, who gradually wakes up.

The sick man refuses to eat. His physical strength already abandoned him. From his chest come hissing and extremely painful sounds. He looks really pale, almost like a cadaver. Feeling a little better thanks to the effect of medication, he struggles to see his mother, who approaches anxious.

- My mother - he says - may God bless and protect you always! As well as our dear ones, wherever they are! Pray for me, dear mother, and never forget me! Forgive our torturers! I have finally managed to forgive them! I take to God a suffering but very light heart... In front of the balance of eternity, in the assessment of my sins, I have little to fear...

The poor woman weeps uncontrollably. She hugs her son and lays her head on his chest, in a loving and desperate way.

Hugging her, he looks at Salústio and says:

- May God reward you! You can count on my eternal gratitude! -

Thus saying, already with difficulty, his hug loose its force, while he tries to keep the dear image of his progenitor in his memory. In a deep sigh, his body shudders and quiets... He is dead.

With delicacy, Salústio pulls the poor woman away, and try to comfort her.

He settles the body and goes to the cave's entrance, to inform:

- Oh, Nestor! Tell the doctor that our sick man has given his soul to God! We must follow the next steps! Go!

Nestor obeys and leaves quickly. Salústio returns to the interior of the cave to watch over the body and console the poor mother. From the bottom of his heart, he says a prayer:

"Dear Lord who watch for all of us! Have mercy! Deliver us from evil! Have mercy on this man who, in this grave and right now is crossing the barrier of the livings! May his sins be light, Lord...".

A few hours later, Father Estanislau, Madelaine and Dr. Sergei arrive to the cave. The priest says the usual prayers, assisted by Salústio. The doctor made the legal examination and draws up the death certificate, preparing to go to the local police station and register the death of that "French citizen".

Madelaine tries to take the old woman with her but is rejected. Respecting her wishes, she gives up her attempt. The poor woman seems to have lost all condition of understanding in her understandable despair.

- Salústio, a mortician and two gravediggers will soon arrive! - says Dr. Sergei, before leaving.

A few more hours go by and in front of the cave, a wagon with three men stops. One of them, well dressed, addresses to Salústio:

- Where is the corpse?

- Over there, sir! - he answers, pointing the dead body.

- Strange place to die, eh?

- I think so too, sir! It's pitiful!

- What was his name?

- André of Villefort!

- That's what it says here on this document. I'll let the gravediggers arrange the burial! Farewell! - Thus saying, he turns around and disappears.

The two gravediggers' approach, enter hesitantly, looking around. They then lift the dead man by his shoulders and legs.

At that moment, Salústio hears a deafening thud. The unfortunate mother has fallen, a victim of pain. He bends down, listens to her heart that is still beating weakly. He lifts her in his arms, carries her to the entrance of the cave, and calls out to Nestor who, next to the policeman, waits. They go to carriage and quickly take her to the infirmary of the Parish House.

In one last look, Salústio sees the gravediggers throw the body, without any ceremony, throw the body into the wagon. A thought of reverence makes him pray, once again, to heaven, for that man who ended his life so unhappily.

He carefully holds the poor lady, protecting her from the rocking vehicle. He hopes she will make it to the infirmary alive.

The cart, with the gravediggers, drives along the streets, creaking, in a grim way.

After a while, it stops in front of an old, black, iron gate, half-open. They identify themselves and enter, driving for a few more minutes, passing luxurious mausoleums and funerary statues that seem to mourn all those who will, sooner or later, end their existence there...

They come to a halt in front of a dirt lot, where several open graves can be seen. In front of one of them, looking around, they strip the corpse naked and put the clothes in the vehicle, doing the same with the sheet. They take a large sack, put the corpse in it, and, without any nobler feeling, they intensify the pace of the rhythm until, with force, they throw it to the bottom of the hole. You can hear the deafening sound of the body. One of them, mockingly, exclaims:

- He must be giving an account to the devil by now! If he was good, he would not have died in that horrible place! Now, you will be eaten by worms, you bastard!

The other arrives limping while carrying two shovels and a bucket with a good amount of lime:

- Speak less, Attilio, and help me with this! You're not on stage to be representing Shakespeare! My throat is dry and I'm in a hurry!

- When your time comes, I'll be glad to do the same to you, you cripple!

An ominous bird hoots. Crossing himself, as he throws the lime to the corpse, he advises:

- Let's hurry, Atílio! The weather is getting worse with every minute! Let's sell his clothes and cap, and let's drink! Don't forget my Delilah's gifts!

- God, what an insatiable woman you have! Did you ever tell her where the things she wears so proudly come from?

- Shut up, you stupid man! Someone can hear us! Do you want to report us?

You know we'll be arrested!

- Get some rest, man! The only witnesses besides us can't talk! Ah, those rich idiots, who think they can take their wealth and vanities to the other world! Why should we let the worms destroy what is so valuable out here? Without those resources, what would this profession be worth? Let's move quickly and store the chariot for today, because we have had enough!

Hours later, they are sitting at the table of an infected tavern, getting drunk...

* * *

AT THE SCHOOL, Eugene, unhappy, creates all sorts of problems, and goes so far that the sisters decide to call her father. This has never happened before.

Henry, informed, recomfort his boss, defending his daughter.

He offered to accompany him, but he heard how his kind offer was declined.

Eugene had lost a very rich pair of earrings and accused Marianne.

Marianne denied everything, pretty upset. Eugene, furious, tackle her and hit her; she threw her belongings at her, scattering them all over the floor in an attempt to find the earrings among her belongings.

Sister Rosália came to help, scolded Eugene, and consoled Marianne, then handed her over to the care of her loving sister Berta.

Eugene, exasperated, burst into tears and finally fell asleep amidst all the disorder in the room.

Hours later, Mr. Jaime goes to the office of the sister preceptor, hearing from her:

- Mr. Jaime, this time Eugene has crossed all the limits! She had has gone so far, rebasing the limits that we've been obliged to call you in. Excuse us, but there are occasions when is important to have the presence of the person in charge of the students, like now!

Perhaps we can no longer allow your daughter's presence here in this institute. She is unbearable! Forgive us for our rude frankness! It seems to us that, with Eugene, all disciplines flatly fail! And believe me, we have tried everything!

- I know you are doing your duty, sister. Don't worry! I apologize for her! Perhaps my fierce love has spoiled my dear daughter. Truly I try to change myself, but believe me, it is difficult not to try to bribe my conscience!

- Out of consideration for you, we have often turned a blind eye to some of your little girl's misdeeds. But today, we need to stay strong, demonstrating to her our authority; authority that she deliberately ignores!

The Reverend Mother did not want us to call you; however, Sister Rosália and I managed to convince her, and here we are in this educational proposal! – While they were speaking, they see Eugene, who seeing his father, throws herself into his arms, weeping and crying out loudly:

- Daddy, take me home, please! I don't want to stay here anymore!

I hate this place!

- My child, what is this? - he asks, looking her face and pointing to the mess.

- I was looking for my earrings! Marianne must have stolen them!

- How can you, Eugene, say such nonsense? I am ashamed of your behavior!

Turning away from her father, she exclaims, lamenting:

- Even you, papa? Instead of consoling me, you scold me?

- How can you expect my support when you are totally wrong?

Don't you realize the risk of your actions?

- Of being expelled from the convent? Well, that's all I want! I've already told you that I want to go back home!

- This time I won't listen to your pleas, Eugene! And I won't even be moved by your tears! If you can't stay here, you will go to another school!

- Very well then! At least I will be free of this one! With your money, I can study wherever I want!

- And you will continue annoying the people that is around you and become more and more lonely. Don't you realize that you embarrass me in front of everyone? -

Inside of him, he thanks the kindness of the sister, who, had leave the office, and could not hear his daughter's rantings.

Energetic, he orders:

- Stop this crying and tidy up! Then, clean up everything! - Eugene had never seen his father so angry. Turning his back, he goes to the chapel, attempting to calm himself through prayers.

Sister Rosália saw him go in there and, passing by, respected his time for think and refreshment. She goes to Eugene and surprises her with an unexpected cleaning. Who gives her a pleading look. In silence, she continues on her way. She goes to the kitchen to check the menu for the day. Perhaps Mr. Jaime will agree to dine at the school before returning home.

Half an hour later, in the middle of his prayers, he hears her say softly:

- Dear friend, the superior is calling for us!

- Well! First, if you don't mind, I'll go get Eugene.

- Of course! Make yourself at home!

A little later, the group enters the superior's room, looking at them, she bows her head slightly. Greeting them, she shows them the chairs where they should sit, and kindly says:

- Dear Sir. Jaime, I apologize to you in advance! For me, this situation is deeply unpleasant!

- Calm down, Mother Eulalia! I know that the administration is acting with the best of intentions! I am the one who should apologize!

- We have decided that Eugene will participate in our decisions, so that she will know what we think of her arbitrary behavior!

She challenges and despises every person that approach her, that's how we ended up in that embarrassing situation we are today!

The decision to accommodate them in the same chambers was just another attempt to control her bad temper, by living with Marianne, a docile student.

Today, Sister Rosália and the governess asked my permission to call you. At first, I refused, trying to protect you from these annoyances. Now I see that, in a way, your presence eases the discomforts that Eugene is going through at this moment, a consequence for her behavior! Do you have something to tell us, dear friend?

- Yes, that I am at the disposal of the school's management! At enrolling Eugene here, I became aware of the statutes and the intern regiments. I never transgressed them!

Eugene, however, immature, ignores them, and it is only right and necessary that she must be grounded. I am embarrassed by this situation, because parents expect just a minimum of consideration and respect from their children, and when they disregard important disciplines, knowing the consequences beforehand, they forget the duty to honor their father and mother!

I am in a very uncomfortable position, but these setbacks are part of the greater role I must play in guiding my beloved dear daughter! I will accept the decisions that result from a proper evaluation, but I also expect indulgence for Eugene. We all know how much she needs to stay here! I thank you in advance for anything that you decide having in mind our situation.

- Sister Rosália, could you get the afternoon shift inspector for us here? says the superior.

- Right away, madam!

Sister Rosália returns accompanied by a tall, thin woman, dressed in a gray habit, hair tied up in a braided bun, firm gaze.

- Hildegard, how would you describe our student, Eugene Sartorelli? - asks the superior.

Looking at father and daughter, she clears her throat and says:

- Miss Eugene is very solitary! She doesn't interact with her classmates and sometimes spends the break time looking down at them!

Contrary to my orders, she is in the habit of taking things into the yard, which she did two days ago when she left an embroidered bag on one of the benches. A student found it and handed it to me.

I waited for Eugene to claim it before admonishing her. Since this didn't happen, I gave it to the sister preceptor.

- Thank you, Hildegard! You may go now!

- Excuse me, Mother! And Hildegard leaves with firm steps in the noise of her thick-soled, heavily lace-up shoes.

You can still hear them for some time, the sounds echoing in the corridor.

- As you can see, everything was duly clarified! – says Mother Eulalia, turning to see Eugene. What we wanted, Eugene, was to teach you a lesson! Maybe if you got scared by the probable loss of your earrings, perhaps you would be more careful and obey Hildegard's orders! We didn't expect from you such a violent behavior! Our dear Marianne, informed of everything, promised to wait for the director's order to speak! Even having in mind that she was assaulted by you, she kept silent, obeying the rules that exist and that must be followed, my dear girl! A good education is not made without good discipline!

Raising his eyes, Eugene sees the superior handing his father the aforementioned bag. It is a very rich piece of Egyptian handicraft, which his father brought him from one of his trips.

- My bag! she exclaims, taking it from her father's hands. Then, she proceeds to opens it, saying in a disconcerted voice:

- The earrings... they're here!

- Where they've always been, Eugene! You accused your companion and assaulted her without reason! You owe her an apology! It's the least you can do!

Next time, control your impulses, because above you, are your father and the school board, and above all of us is God!

As you can conclude from all this, you are not the center of the universe, as you think!

We sincerely condemn this situation, Eugene!

Sister governess, speak up!

- Reverend Mother, we think the student should be suspended for one week, so that she can decide whether if she really wants to continue her studies here.

We want her to evaluate not only what happened today, but the unruly behavior that is part of her.

- Do you have something to say, Eugene? - asks the mother.

Clutching her purse to her chest, she stubbornly shuts up. Her father touches her arm lightly and she, understanding, asks:

- I'm sorry! I will also apologize to Marianne!

- Thank you, and once again I apologize! - concludes Mr. Jaime.

- Don't apologize, Mr. Jaime! – mention sister Rosália.

You are for us a valuable friend and benefactor of this home.

We will be eternally grateful for what you grant us in your boundless kindness!

The decisions we took hurt us deeply, but you must agree that if we don't correct Eugene, we will lose our authority in front the other pupils!

We will wait for a different Eugene to come back, a more mature and more friendly.

- But, sister, this week we have tests!

- Dear girl, think about that before you act so clumsily! - interjects the superior, energetically. -You'll have to do it on the second call, with all the difficulties that implies!

- It will have to be that way, Eugene! - adds Sister Rosália. – Pack your things, because you're going with your father.

Eugene goes out to look for Marianne. She finds her sitting in the garden, saddened. She takes a deep breath and declares:

- Marianne, I'm sorry for everything! My earrings were stored here in this bag!

- Eugene, I would never take your things! You should know better!

- I said I was sorry. I've been suspended for a week.

- What about the exams?

- I'll take them on the second call. I'm going home now. Will you help me pack?

- Yes! You're not very good at that! Come on! – answers Marianne who has already forgotten everything.

After talking for a few more minutes, Mr. Jaime shows his desire to return. Declining the invitation to join to the dinner, he looks for Eugene and hurries away. He is very upset. He confirms Marianne's apologies and embraces her, kindly. He says goodbye to everyone and leaves with Eugene.

They board the vehicle and travel in silence.

After a few quarters of an hour, Eugene, coming out from his mutism asks:

- Are you very tired, daddy?

- Yes! - he replies angrily.

To her, the answer seemed too broad. If only she could take her actions back.

Almost in a whisper, she asks:

- Forgive me, daddy!

- Why ask for forgiveness without the intention of making things right? By asking for it, do you commit to change yourself?

- I promise to try! You know how difficult is for me to act passively when it comes to things that are important for me!

- Daughter, you seem to me to be really worried about trivial things! Why do you waste so much time on it?

- It's just the way I am!

- It's a sad way to be!

- I'll make an effort to change, I promise! Now, stop scolding me, please!

- All right, Eugene. I ask God to protect you and change you; after all, you are still very young!

- Look, we're getting closer to home! Is your manager there?

- Yes, Henry is there! He is extremely dedicated, dealing with almost all the responsibilities and taking care of me, which you don't do, Eugene... My health is not good!

- Are you sick, daddy? That worries me!

- I don't know, could be just tiredness...

- So, you leave everything in the hands of a stranger?

- He's not a stranger, my child! I've known him for a long time!

- Daddy, you're as good as naive!

- I don't get it, you even get along with him!

- He is fun! But to hand him the direction of our business on a silver plate... I would never do that!

But tell me: did you see a doctor?

- Yes! He examined me carefully and recommended that I should rest.

- I will take care of you, papa! In a few years I will oversee everything! I can't wait! - exclaims Eugene, with shining eyes as she lovingly hugs her father tightly.

When they arrive, she descends from the carriage, fast and eager. Through her eyes a glint of anger passes through her as she remembers why she is there out of time. She crosses the gardens without stopping. She enters the hall and several rooms, surprising the displeased employees.

Climbing the luxurious staircase, she enters her chambers and slams the door. With a furious look, she analyzes everything around her. Grumbling, he opens cabinets and drawers frenetically, checking everything sloppily. She stares for a long time at the portrait of his mother and bursts into tears.

Approaching, her father hears her weeping and is torn between comforting or leaving her to her own devices. He chooses the second alternative and goes downstairs.

When Henry is informed that his boss has arrived, he goes to look for him:

- Did you have a good trip?

- Yes, thank you!

- Is everything all right with Eugene?

- No, Henry. She was suspended and came with me.

Henry bravely controls himself not to burst into a loud laugh. Disguising himself, he asks:

- And now, where is she? I would like to see her and be supportive!

- She is in her room, but... I don't think this is a good time to talk to her! Shall we go to work?

- Yes, I'll see Eugene later. We are friends after all.

- If you say so! - replies the boss, doubting of his words.

After having been informed of the day's activities, Mr. Jaime goes up to take a bath and rest from so many emotions. The day had been quite unpleasant, thanks to Eugene.

While he relaxes, he remembers the kindness of the sisters, especially Sister Rosália, who knows how to understand Eugene's heart like no one else. He thanks the heavens that Eugene was only suspended and not expelled from the student body of that school...

* * *

IN CHARLES, THE ENTHUSIASM of the first moment was replaced by a more measured behavior since it was based on reason. Never before he had ever loved. He had courtships and flirts in abundance. He just had a relationship based in passion with a famous artist of the time. She was elegant, beautiful and sensual, but, little by little, he lost interest; the fire was completely extinguished...

He is romantic, talented and requested. Even though he is part of the nobility, he lives from his work as a teacher and musician. Will he have finally found in Madelaine his dream muse?

He needs to understand himself before he meets her again.

She, in the other hand, was focus on the routine of the castle that demands a lot from her and in the infirmaries of the Parish House, she had exchanged her love concerns for others more urgent. However, a festive Sunday is coming and she has to make up her mind about it. She fears the prince's threats; he is not the kind of person that you can reject!

At home, hearing the maid's footsteps, she calls out:

- Corine, come here, please!

- What do you want, *Mademoiselle*?

- Answer me: what is Baron André's full name?

- Baron André Brumel of Villefort! He is immensely rich! In addition to his title, he owns valuable properties, among which is the Portal da Luz, and numerous servants. He lives in Vila Francesa, which is part of this complex of houses, gardens and orchards!

- What is the origin of so much wealth and power? Do you know?

- He says he was born in Romania. His parents owned a rich lumber company that prospered well.

When he was still a child, he came to live in Paris and, very early, he had to take over the family business because his parents died in an accident.

He was educated in the best schools and has a military rank in addition to his baronetcy.

He married a beautiful woman but lost her and became a widower.

He is just waiting for a single glance from you to throw himself at your feet, *Mademoiselle*!

- Does he live alone?

- No, his sister Louíse lives with him.

- Thank you, Corine. I hope the person we were talking about will not be informed of my questions.

- Rest assured, I won't say anything.

Bowing, Corine walks away, sure that Madelaine has finally taken an interest in the Baron.

Looking for her mother, Madelaine finds her checking the sterilization of clothes. Solange, one of the maids, sings a beautiful Andalusian song, enchanting the Countess.

Seeing her daughter, she asks her:

- Wait a minute, Madelaine. I'm going to the greenhouse to do some pruning and we could talk more freely there. - picks up gardening tools, puts on a large apron with large pockets, and, humming the tune she heard, heads off in the direction she intends to go, followed by her daughter.

- So, daughter, what's up? I understand that you have something to tell me!

- Yes! - she tells her briefly what happened in the cave, without omitting anything. Her mother wants to know:

- Did Father Estanislau give the holy viaticum to the dying man?

- Yes, mum. At his own request.

- And what about the poor lady?

- She is in the infirmary of the Parish House. She needs urgent medical treatment!

- I sense in this narrative some greater intention, am I right?

- Yes, very sure! Guess what name the patient gave us!

- I can't imagine, tell me what it was!

- Baron André Brumel of Villefort!

Letting go the twigs off her hands, Bettine takes off her gloves and exclaims in astonishment:

- Did I hear you right, child?

- Yes!

- Are they homonyms?

- I don't think so, because the sick man has made serious accusations to the one who currently uses his name and title, as well as his fortune!

- My God! Do you know anything about the Baron?

Madelaine transmits the information gathered from Corine.

- We conclude then that he is an extremely dangerous person! If only the poor woman wasn't in that state of delirious!

- Let's go to the point, Madame! We must find out. In the throes of agony, disgusted with his executioner, he only calmed down when we promised to take his unfortunate mother into our hands! I, in particular, told her that I would bring her to my home, personally watching over her protection and happiness!

- Count on me, daughter!

- Thank you, mama. Returning to our concern, I am thinking of making some inquiries about the Baron's life, using Corine's versatility!

- Promise me that you will be prudent and talk to your father before make anything about this matter!

- I promise! Don't forget, I always count on the solicitude and protection of Salústio.

- Yes, I know, daughter! Good and brave friend! I trust you. Tell me, how are you solving your own problems?

- I still don't know exactly what to do, next Sunday I intend to go away. That way I'll have more time to think! What do you think?

- So many things will depend on your decision, my child!

- I will take care of them all, rest assured!

- Who knows if the two gentlemen in question will be absent?

- Do you believe that?

- No!

- Mother, I will not endure another suffocating day like that! Do you remember the prince's impositions? I even disrespect him!

On that day, I will go to the Parish House and stay there the whole day. Naturally, you will say that I left for only a few hours and that I'll be back in time! That way we won't arouse suspicion.

- All right, my child. We will support you, rest assured.

- And I will leave everything so well planned that no one will miss me in my absence!

- Of that I doubt, dear!

- Well, thank you for everything, mama! - giving her mother a loud kiss on the cheek, she leaves quickly, coming across Fabian doing somersaults, imitating circus performers. Seeing her, he throws himself into Madelaine arms, warning her:

- Madelaine, you can put my flute away!

- Why?

- Because I won't need it anymore! Now I'm going to be a circus performer!

Kissing him lovingly, she replies:

- Oh, come on, Fabian! They also need musicians in the circus, do you know?

- Really? Then I'll be one of them! Can I be a circus performer and a musician too?

- Yes, my love!

- That's great! I'll go up and tell Soraya! See you later, Madelaine!

- See you, Fabian! - As he runs off, she admires him, proud of his beautiful and healthy brother.

Her ears delight in the sounds of Soraya's violin, who is now studying. She concludes, courageously, that if their happiness ever depends on hers, she will renounce her own happiness without any questions on their behalf.

Noticing her introspection, Corine asks:

- Are you sad, *Mademoiselle*? Fabian will soon change his mind!

He already wanted to be a king, a swordsman, and many other things!

- What did you say, Corine?

- That Fabian will change!

- I hope not, Corine.

- Then why are you sad?

- I'm not sad, Corine! I'm just thinking about how much we have to do!

- This must not be the reason for your discontent, *Mademoiselle*!

- No, it's not! I really like to work!

Shrugging her shoulders, Corine follows her without understanding. Seeing her father again, Madelaine asks:

- Papa, how is the case of poor Pierre?

- I am finding it unexpectedly difficult to defend him, my child! He is deeply depressed and speaking of suicide!

- My God!

- He is young, he has a small child, and above all, life is sacred in any circumstance! His wife, as you know, has come to me for help. She is the picture of pain! She looks old for her age, screaming thinness, nerves on the edge! With the help that she has received from your mother, she now has time to eat, as does the baby.

She told us that, on the fateful day, she and Pierre were fighting for lack of resources. With the baby on her lap, she scolded him for not having a job.

Disgusted with his own situation, he was lying down, looking for some rest after a strenuous walk. Desperate for her complaints, he went outside again, returning minutes later with a basket of fruit.

After a while, the owner of the emporium and a policeman knocked on the door. The pain of the misery that reigned there and her explanations were useless. Indifferent, the policeman took Pierre away amidst blows and insults. Thus, ashamed, he made his way to the local police station.

In tears, she added:

- Count, as long as I live, I'll never forget this scene! My poor Pierre tried to feed us, harassed by my incomprehension, and was arrested like a common criminal! God, how can such things happen?!

- Poor woman, my father! This story is depressing!

- I am convincing the greengrocer to drop the charges. I have already paid a generous amount for the fruit consumed, because the rest he thrown away in the rush.

- How can the heart of man be so insensitive?

- In the defense of what he considers his own, he acts by instinct, as if he were still in cave times, in a primitive way! Well,

I'm off! See you, my child! Keep praying for them! Will do everything what we can! I hope soon to see this family reunited and happy again!

- May the angels say amen, papa! - replies Madelaine, standing on her tiptoes to kiss him.

Meanwhile, Corine comes into the kitchen:

- Oh, Ignácia, you good and hardworking woman! Is there anything new around here?

- Looking for news here in the kitchen, Corine? - Ignácia replies, surprised.

- Places don't matter! Why not look right here for something to get me out of this boredom?

- Despite everything you have to do, Corine?

- Never mind, Ignácia! You really can't understand! – she answers, annoyed, and goes off to look for Solange:

- Solange, do you have any news?

- And since when do I collect news for you?

- Come on, Solange, aren't you my friend?

- I'm not so sure! But if I know you well, you must know something! Come on, spit it out!

- Oh, yes! - and she lets Solange know about Madelaine's questions about the Baron, adding:

- Know that I, too, will soon find a good match.

- Such pretension, eh?

- It's not pretension, Solange! I actually have plans! I am young, beautiful and in the latest fashion! Men want me, but I won't belong to just anyone! I swear that I won't die poor and that my children will have different fortunes than mine! I need to rise in social status! - Thus saying, she walks away almost talking to herself, since her friend is not very interested in her babblings.

AT VILA FRANCESCA, Portal da Luz, André attends to his private servant:

- What do you want, Mateus? Be brief!

- I will! You don't know, Baron, but my cousin is an official at the local police station. Amid papers and documents, he had access to information about the death of Baron André of Villefort!

- How can this be possible?

- I don't know, Sir, but from what I have heard, I believe it is "the same person" that we both know.

- What could it be? - André speaks to himself - How many dangers we are exposed to by the incompetence of those we trust? Scoundrels! Indeed...! - thumping loudly on his desk full of papers, he orders: Go ahead, Mateus!

- Yes, Sir! Knowing that I work exactly for the aforementioned Baron, I was wondering if my boss had died. What most intrigued me was the fact that his death had taken place in such a strange place; in an infected cave. Imagine what thoughts must not have passed through his head! I informed him, very surprised, that the dead man was not, thanks God, my boss, who is in very good health!

Pale and perplexed, André thinks: "How and why did 'he' die so far from prison? - He sits down, devastated. Mateus laughs nervously. He enjoys the terror stamped on his boss's features. He goes on vainly:

- I told him a great story; the most convincing one possible.

- What did you tell him?

- I told him that the dead man was your servant. That he disappeared some years ago and that we never saw him again. Intentionally, I told him that his devotion was so great that, foolish by birth, he thought he had the same name! Deeply moved, lamenting the fate of the unfortunate man, I almost wept. I promised to reward him for the charitable information. I asked the address where the poor man was buried, telling him that the Baron, would be grateful for so many years of dedication, and will reverence him with many prayers. Telling me that he was waiting for the reward, he promised not to speak of it again.

- Is that all, Mateus? - André asks thoughtfully.

- No, Sir! I went further; I got him to promise to 'get' the death certificate of the unfortunate man and give it to me.

Obviously, for a good sum of money. I know that the Baron likes to surround himself with a lot of security.

- Very well! Stay tuned to the development of these arrangements! And watch your language, Mateus!

- Don't worry, boss, I'll be a tomb! - he smiles at the reference. He leaves slowly, hiding from André a debauched laugh.

The Baron gets up, annoyed by everything he has heard. He opens a door that leads to an exuberant garden and there takes a deep breath, reflecting. Full of anger, anger that shines darkly in his eyes, he raises his head to the sky, stares at the moon, clenches his fists and explodes:

- Good thing you've already gone to hell! May you stay there and leave me in peace! - The wind blows hard; he thought he heard a strange groan. He looks around; he is all alone. He shivers and crosses himself, in an unusual behavior. He goes inside and looks for the bed, trying to sleep, but unable to do it. He thinks of Madelaine, with passion... One day, very happily, he will marry her! He strongly believes so.

The next day, he takes his silver-handled cane and his elegant hat, the complements of his rich attire, and walks aimlessly, restless and lonely.

Hoping to see Madelaine again, he approaches the castle and he can hear her singing. Completely focus, he listens until the end, and then goes on his way again, dreamy and in love.

On Sunday, Madelaine is torn between the desire to see the Marquess and to protect herself from the Prince. Longing for Charles, she almost decides to stay, but finally, reason wins...

Once in the wards, she comes across the mother of the unfortunate dead man of the cave. Cheerful, she goes to her:

- How are you, ma'am? Are you better?

- Yes, I'm better! If it weren't for the fact that I miss my son...

- Just think that he is all right now! God is just, and no doubt blessed him!

- What is your name, my child?

- My name is Madelaine. And you, madam?

- Gotuza... I think... So many things are confused in my head... I'm not even sure who I really am. But that doesn't matter anymore... May God the father has received my dear André into his bosom! - Thus, speaking almost alone, ignoring Madelaine's presence, she sits back again and closes her eyes.

Madelaine, respecting her need to rest, takes a step back and joins in the work. Between one occupation and another, she goes to see her.

On one of these occasions, she thinks:

"Poor thing! How much she suffered! But, despite everything, Gotuza, you lived and were happy, fulfilling yourself as a woman and a mother! Will I have this chance? I don't know..."

After a few hours, she goes to breathe in the garden and comes across with Salústio, who arrives. Surprised, he asks:

- What are you doing here today, Madelaine?

- I'm here for private reasons. I wouldn't know how to behave safely in the castle, under certain circumstances, arising from the previous festive Sunday, my friend! - they chat animatedly for a few minutes.

Then, while she works, Salústio watches her with a sweet smile on her lips: with a plate soup in her hands, she convinces an old man, who is showing his toothless mouth while laughing at the jokes she makes to relax him, to eat. Sometimes, you can hear his crystalline, sonorous laughter over something funny he says.

The starry night comes, warning her that she must return. Salústio will accompany her, as always.

- See you, Father! At the next opportunity, I must speak to you!

- Whenever you want, my daughter! Goodbye! May God be with you!

Seeing them arrive, Bettine hugs Salústio tenderly and when he leaves, she takes her daughter's hands in hers and asks her:

- Tell me how your Sunday was, Madelaine!

- I had a great day, Mom! And around here, how the things were going?

- Well, let's get the report! - exclaims Bettine, smiling. – The normal activities lived up to our expectations! But a certain lute player was the picture of desolation itself!

Madelaine's heart soars. Her mother continues:

- When he performed, he did so in such a melancholy way that it even affected the audience!

- Do you think he missed me?

- Sadly, not only him! The prince arrived very early, arrogant as always, and knowing you were not there, he watched the entrances. After the performance of the Marquess, which seemed to contradict him, he angrily left, without saying goodbye.

- Um... I was right to leave! Now I'm going to take a comforting bath! I'm exhausted! Good night, Mom!

- Good night, my child! Sleep well!

At home, the Marquess can't concentrate.

The Count told him that Madelaine had justifiable reasons for her absence, but that she would return in time. In this expectation, he waited for her anxiously.

He had almost lost his savoir-faire; he presented himself without stimulus. Everything seemed grey and aimless to him.

Facing each other, he and the Prince fought over the same thing. Sometimes they looked at the same door...

***

REELING FROM HER EMOTIONS, Eugene stands up for herself, arrogant.

Intentionally pampering her, Henry supports her.

The poor father corrects his daughter's mistakes here and there. Hard tempered, Eugene is a stubborn spirit. When he loses control of the situation, Henry takes the reins, dominating her, without, however, accusing her. Thus, the boss becomes more and more grateful to him. Finally, time passes, and Eugene must return to the nursery school.

Letting his real intentions take control, Henry has already tampered with several documents, keeping them hidden. He has surrounded himself with accomplices in several public departments, and periodically disburses large sums of money to silence those who live by these expedients. He needs to use a lot of much intelligence to create the desired opportunity and put his plans into practice.

His permanent restlessness arouses Sir. Jaime's curiosity:

- Henry, are you by any chance ill?

Involved in paradoxical feelings, he stares at him, a little sad by such naivety, and his heart sways... But it is too late! He has already committed himself too much! Out of control, he bumps into a chair and walks out into the street without answering.

Perplexed, the boss concludes that somehow his daughter has offended him and he, to hide it, remains in silent.

Henry, almost absent-mindedly, walks on aimlessly. Hours later, he decides to return. He must somehow keep his boss away from his home and business.

- Have you returned from your walk, my son? - asks an interested Sir. Jaime. - Has Eugene offended you?

- No, Sir! She's done nothing to me! Despite her temperament, she treats me very well! I even think I like her! This gratifies me!

- I'll hand it to you, Henry! You seem to win her over more every day! But you are worrying me! What's the matter? Are you, by any chance sick or tired, my son? Maybe you need a vacation! Do you want to take a trip? I will give you the time and money for this!

- In fact, I think it is a great idea! - Henry smacks his forehead. How could this had not occurred to him? Without wanting to, Sir. Jaime himself gives him the solution. - But not for me! – he declares, enthusiastically.

- Not for you? What do you mean is not for you?

- I mean that you need to rest! I have observed that sometimes you feel sick and hide it! Now that Eugene is back from the school, you can take some time away from business and get back on your feet.

I'll oversee everything! You must take care of yourself so Eugene has you for a long time! And I must tell you that I also wish to preserve you, dear boss and unconditional friend!

Listening to him, surprised and thoughtful, Sir. Jaime comments:

- This idea is tempting...! Once again, I admire your competence! I haven't been able to relax for years! When I travel, it's either for business, or I take my beloved daughter with me! Because of it, I am always involved in multiple concerns! Besides, time passes... I feel tired already!

- Well, you will return rejuvenated then! Perhaps you will marry again? You have everything to make a woman happy!

- Don't be delirious, my son! This is out of discussion!

- I respect your wishes, but you should think of yourself!

One of these days, Eugene will get married and you will be alone!

- I'm tempted to take your suggestion and travel! I really need this!

To find a nice and peaceful place and hide there for a while...

But how will Eugene react when he finds out?

- Do you forget that I have influence over her? I will tell her that you went for business, and then that you'll have to stay longer than you expected! Trust me and you won't regret it!

- You really care about me, son! May God bless you!

- I don't believe in God, Sir. Jaime!

- Why not, Henry? He is our creator and he leads us in life!

- I disagree! We make our own fate!

- Under his power and his permission!

- Well, in these matters, we will never understand each other, sorry!

However, if you believe, may he protect you and give you much health!

- So be it!

* * *

THE MARQUESS DECIDES to visit Madelaine again. He already sent a message announcing himself.

While visiting Richard, he was so excited to talk about her that his friend, as thieving as anyone, told him that he would be very happy if he married his niece. He confessed an old desire to have great-nieces and nephews to brighten his old age:

"- When she arrives, of course!" - he exclaimed laughing.

In the note he wrote to the Count, the Marquess requests the opportunity to hear them at a re-presentation of the artistic part of the festive Sundays.

Dusting off his clothes, he is pleased with his own image reflected in the mirror.

On the way, he rehearses what to say to Madelaine, but he knows that when it comes down to her, his heart will take over.

Arriving at the gate, he makes himself announced and the Count himself comes to welcome him:

- How great to see you, Monsieur Marquess! You are very welcome!

- The pleasure and the honor are mine, dear Count! - he replies, returning the kindness with nobility.

- Let's sit here and talk for a while! Do you have any news about my brother?

- We were together only a few days ago! He is very well!

- Although we are brothers, we are opposite in temperament. He is outgoing, while I am more reflective without being sad.

We love him very much and miss him when he takes time to show up. We know how much he love us too!

- Yes, he doesn't hide the enormous affection he feels for everyone, especially for Madelaine!

- And she, like no other, knows how to conquer hearts, don't you think I'm right dear Marquess?

Disconcerted, like a child caught red handed, he loses his spontaneity, causing the Count to burst into a loud laughter.

Inviting him up to meet the family, side by side, they reach the desired place. Bettine, smiling, receives him with undisguised joy.

The children graciously greet him.

Looking around in silence, he looks for Madelaine. He hears footsteps and looking up to the spiral staircase, he sees her descending, splendidly dressed in pink velvet, captivating smile, with some sheet music in her hands. Seeing the Marquess, she asks interested and gentle:

- How are you? Nice to see you again!

- I am very well! And *Mademoiselle*, how are you? - he says, kissing her fingertips and dipping his insinuating gaze into her eyes.

Clutching her sheet music, she disguises her emotion. Fabian laughs loudly. Soraya reproaches him with her gaze and he pulls himself together.

Madelaine asks:

- Does the dear Marquess want to grace us first with his incomparable talent?

- Thanks for the compliment, but I'd like to hear you first!

Embraced, the Counts go to the piano and the performance goes on admirably.

The Marquess applauds enthusiastically. His eyes and Madelaine's seek each other irresistibly.

When she plays and sings, he thinks he is in nirvana.

At the last chords, he can't help himself and, rushing towards her, kisses her hands, while exclaiming warmly:

- Bravo, bravissimo, *Mademoiselle*!

- Thank you, now we want to hear you! - she replies.

- With pleasure! Today, I have brought new music. Results of my latest inspirations!

Thus saying, he takes his lute and plays it masterfully, being applauded with enormous enthusiasm.

As he performs, Madelaine closes her eyes, sweetly lulled by that voice, so familiar to her heart...

Bettine asks the Marquess for copies of some of his compositions and he promises to send them.

The Count invites him to go to the library. While they are on their way there, he automatically recalls the Prince's threats:

"Monsieur Count Luiz, be sure that the absence of your daughter Madelaine was not intentional! What a pity for those who conspire behind my back! You Sir, as head of this family, must protect her! - and then, tapping his shiny boots against each other, bowed slightly, went downstairs and stayed a few hours in the castle waiting for Madelaine. When he left, without even saying good-bye, he was very upset."

How will he react when he learns of Charles and Madelaine's closeness? At the thought of this, the Count feels a chill run down his spine.

- Is something troubling you, Sir? Perhaps you have other engagements! - the Marquess remarks.

- No, I don't. I won't be going to the forum today and the office work is already advanced. Your presence is extremely pleasant!

- Hoping to be worthy of this honor, I thank you!

- Here we are, Marquess! Men of letters that we are, we will have much to talk about!

Charles admires the aesthetics of the environment while the Count is explaining:

- We have here some very rare works that I am acquiring from famous booksellers. Madelaine assists me in this task. She has good taste and is very cultured. I encourage her, vain and happy for her privileged intelligence.

Picking up a few tomes, Charles examines them, analyzing them in depth, leaving the Count pleasantly surprised.

For several minutes, they exchange ideas on a variety of subjects, until the host invites ask him:

- Shall we meet the others? I have monopolized you more than I should have, Marquess!

- Would you do me the honor of calling me by my first name only?

- Certainly! We like to treat intimately those who are nice to us.

- Thank you! - They rejoin the family group and in no time at all, Charles feels as if he has known them for a long time.

Approaching Madelaine he asks - *Mademoiselle*, I would like to know where you take refuge while you play and forgotten about us miserable mortals!

- The Marquess is certainly exaggerating! - she defends herself. - But I can tell him that, at these moments, I feel strangely happy and a little unaware to what is going on around me.

- If you could just call me Charles, it would give me great pleasure!

- Well, no, Charles, then do the same for me. - they are close and rapt. Charles dares:

- Madelaine, why did you go away last Sunday?

Surprised, she hesitates to answer:

- Well, I work in the wards of the Parish House, in the church Our Lady of Mont'Serrat. This Sunday, I had unpostponable commitments. I thought I would be able to return in time, but it was not possible. I am part of a philanthropic group led by the good parish priest, Father Estanislau.

- I admire them! Would you allow me to visit them? Perhaps I can help in some way!

- It will be an honor to receive you! We need all the help we can get.

- Then I request the right to join these ranks!

- So be it! Consider yourself invested in this work of helping to the unfortunate, Mister Marquess Charles D'Alençon!

- My dear, if I close my eyes, I can feel a sword over my head, consecrating me, through your hands! - he says, bowing his head respectfully.

Resuming his previous posture, he continues:

- Madelaine, I would like to arrange a day for us to play several pieces of music together, what do you think?

- I think that's a great idea! And by the way, did you arrive in time for your meeting that Sunday? - Charles smiled satisfied, and Madelaine blushed.

- Imagine that a friend of mine promised to lend me a musical score that interests me a lot, but he didn't show up for the meeting! How irresponsible of him! - lied Charles.

After hours of delightful relaxation, Charles leaves, promising to come back again.

✱ ✱ ✱

AS EXPECTED, Eugene studies hard and has not created trouble at school. She respects her classmate, Marianne, she surprises herself by confiding in her about her dreams and willingly participates in the tidying up of her rooms.

Observing them, the sisters confirm, more and more, that the discipline is the predominant factor.

Henry pressures his boss in such a way that, in a few days, he leaves for his dreamed-of journey.

Getting permission, he goes to visit Eugene.

He gives the mother superior the power of attorney signed by his boss, sacramentalizing his responsibility to Eugene.

He spends a few hours at the girl's side, he is very polite, explaining to her about her father's business trip and, between expensive gifts and a lot of relaxation, he leaves her happy when had to go.

* * *

CHOOSING FRANCE, Sir. Jaime stayed at a pleasant inn on the outskirts of Paris, run by a nice Russian family: the Korsanikovs. Of exuberant nature, comfortable accommodations and first-class service. Breathing eagerly, he concludes that he has put this day off too long.

At night, he hears a noise accompanied by traditional Russian music. He reaches the window and distinguishes a group of people around a huge bonfire.

He goes downstairs and approaches them. Some boys are playing traditional instruments, while others dance frantically, jumping and spinning on their own bodies. The others clap their hands to set the rhythm. He watches fascinated.

After a while, he notices, a few meters away, sitting on a wooden trunk, a beautiful girl dressed in the Slavic style.

She admires the stars and seems to be dreaming. Going up to her, he asked her, politely:

- May I sit here or does my presence disturb you?

- Not at all, sir, make yourself comfortable!

- Then, allow me: my name is Jaime Sartorelli and I'm from England.

- I like the English; they are orderly people!

- To tell you the truth, not all of them!

- My name is Natacha Korsanikov. I am the daughter of the hosts.

- Nice to meet you!

- Nice to meet you too!

- Your family is very cheerful! You don't come to the party?

- I don't feel like it! I'm not always cheerful, sometimes I become very introspective.

- And why, if you are so young and beautiful?

- Thank you! But I am aware of my "weirdness" and I learned to live with them...

- Could you be more clear, young lady?

- Yes, but I'm afraid I'll bore you...

- You won't bore me. If you want to talk, feel free.

- Well, I live normally like everyone else, but sometimes I get so internalized myself in such a way that I cut my ties with life, being 'absent' for hours, scaring everyone, especially my parents.

At other times, my thoughts are directed at me in my own in my absence. So, I express myself correctly, clearly, expressing knowledge that is beyond my studies and experiences... I speak unknown languages and often create problems for people, revealing their thoughts and intentions, unknown to me until that moment.

I often go to the woods and there I dance for hours, barefoot, adorned with flowers, as if I were living an enchanted dream! And many other things I do without understanding the reasons, following my impulses...

\- Have you ever been to the doctor?

\- Many times! They prescribe me soothing teas and cold baths as if I were hysterical!

I pray daily in front of icons and I become quiet, but even now I have visions.

\- And the specialists in nervous diseases, what do they say?

\- Some have tried to have me committed for further study. As if I were some kinds of laboratory guinea pig, imagine!

\- You are right, Natacha. Certain treatments are scary! After all, you look great! I wouldn't say you are sick.

Intellectually, you look very well endowed!

\- Thank you. After all, I live well and work hard.

\- *Mens sana in corpore sano*, dear girl!

\- I agree! And did you have a good trip?

\- A very good one!

\- Did you come alone?

\- Yes, I'm looking for rest! If I had brought my daughter, I wouldn't have it.

\- What is she like and how old is she?

\- She is fourteen years old; she is studious and intelligent.

\- You must be a great father!

\- I try, but I don't always succeed. Eugene is impulsive and willful. The last setback she created brought me here.

\- So, in a way, you are our ally! Welcome, Sir. Jaime!

\- Thank you. In fairness, I owe this opportunity to Henry.

\- Who is he?

\- My administrator and great friend!

Suddenly, Natacha exclaims:

\- He is not what he seems! He will cause you serious problems!

Taken aback, he asks:

- What did you say, Natacha?

- Me? I don't know, I think I got lost in myself again, sorry... How long will you stay with us?

- I don't know yet. That will depend on many circumstances.

Two stubby, red-headed boys, with small, blue eyes, are watching her, insistent. Curious, Sir. Jaime asks her:

- Who are those boys? Strange, aren't they?

- They are my cousins: Rupert and Nikolai. A few months ago, they arrived from Russia. They work with us, but...

- But?

- They chase me with nasty jokes and they threaten me! I'm afraid of them!

- Why do your parents allow them to stay here?

- Out of pity! After all, they are relatives and do their jobs well!

- Be careful, my little one! They are scary!

- Yes, I know... But you said you owe this trip to someone...

- It's true, I owe this rare opportunity to my administrator, Henry John Stanford. He oversees everything, so that I could travel.

- Aren't you afraid that in his absence he will be dishonest?

My friend would never do that!

- Why, that's extraordinary! You talk like Sister Rosália! If you knew him better, they would have no doubts as to his loyalty!

Even after hearing Sir. Jaime's statement, Natacha confirms her first idea:

- One can never trust too much!

- In him, I trust, Natacha!

- So, what can be done? Let's wait! - she exclaims, discouraged.

- Dear girl, instead of standing here talking to me, why don't you go dancing?

- I don't feel like it! Tell me about your daughter!

- Eugene has a difficult temperament, but I can tell she has a beautiful soul. She seems to defend herself all the time; but from what? Poor girl! I fear she will bring herself so much suffering!

- That question made you are sad! Forgive me!

- Don't worry, Natacha!

- Rest, for her sake! It is our destiny to be good. That is what we will reach it sooner or later!

- And how did you come to this conclusion, being so young?

- By observing the world and people, and by reading good books!

- And what do you like to read?

- Philosophy, novels, poetry, biographies...

- I have brought excellent books on these subjects. Look me up in the following days! Now, see you later, beautiful and wise girl! I am really tired! I'm not your age and I've traveled a lot!

- Farewell, Sir. Jaime. Thank you for your attention!

- Thank you. I think we'll be good friends!

- We already are! - she declares, smiling.

The next morning, he wakes up, goes to the window, is dazzled by the exuberant green and the polychrome of the flowers. Breathing in, he thanks the creator.

Hearing an argument, he looks down and finds the two cousins of Natacha fighting, almost at punching each other. Their faces are congested with anger.

He wants to approach Natacha's father about them and the risk they represent.

He goes down to the dining room and there serves himself a delicious breakfast. He then requests a carriage. He wants to go to the surrounding area, enjoying the balmy morning air.

As he walks around, he says, "I've only been here a few hours and it seems to me that I have never lived anywhere else!" His home, England, his business, are becoming more and more distant... Stopping the horses, with open arms, as if he wanted to embrace the whole world, he looks up at the sky and exclaims excited:

- God be glorified, for making us part of this greatness! Oh, men! Let us open our eyes, and especially our hearts, to all that is good and beautiful! Let us love one another to be really happy! - He sits down again and from his chest bursts uncontained sobs. He lets his tears flow freely. After a few minutes, with his soul refreshed, he returns.

As promised, Natacha asks him to borrow the books that interest her.

In this way they both began serious and profound studies.

A little time later, on one of their usual walks, in a green glade of greenery, dotted with flowers, birdsong and streams that reflect the sunlight in the restful movements of their waters, he comes across Natacha.

She doesn't even notice his presence. He avoids being seen so as not to disturb her. Sitting on the grass, she made garlands of flowers that she places on her head, arms and ankles, while she is humming an old madrigal.

Sir Jaime can almost feel the magical presences of the elements: small, light, and irreverent. Already adorned with the flowers, she gets up, crosses lightly the large green space and stands still. She raises her arms to the heavens and bows to the ground in deep reverence. Then she dances; first in a soft rhythm, then a gentle one, then intensifying, she volutes frantically. There is music in the air? Sir Jaime believes so. Natacha continues dancing.

She turns on herself, kneels and stands up again with amazing agility and technique.

He had never seen such beauty, not even on the great stages of England. Places that Natacha has probably never been. Finally, she falls exhausted, arms outstretched, staring the sky, ecstatic.

Trying to not disconcert her, he returns to the inn in silence.

Half an hour later she arrives, bare feet, hair undone with the shoes in her hands. She still wears the flower crown over her blonde hair that reflects the sunlight. On her face, you can see an indescribable peace.

Unaware of everything, she passes by without noticing her surroundings.

Sir Jaime concludes that he has never seen such a pure and crystalline soul: "What a beautiful figure you would make on the world stage, Natacha! But nowhere else would you be happier than here! God bless you!"

Getting used to their studies, the two go deeper and deeper into metaphysical subjects. They have already talked about most of the works chosen.

Fascinated, he spends hours investigating the world of philosophers, inventors, musicians, painters, theatrologists, magicians, scientists, great missionaries, statesmen, and so many others, identifying himself with many of them.

He takes a deep dive into the appreciation of ancient religions in their historical contexts, principles, rituals, and empirical processes.

His old feelings of concern and anxiety are being replaced by a great peace. If it were not concern for his daughter.

Thoughtful, he misses her... He worries. But she must be very well. Henry is very devoted and has promised to take care of her while he stays in this pleasant country... At this instant, Natacha comes up to her room with a bunch of flowers:

- Sir Jaime, may I?

- Come in, my child, come in!

- I brought these flowers to decorate your room.

- You are very kind! Thank you.

- Don't thank me. Since you arrived, I feel happier and calmer. Have you read a lot today?

- Yes, look how many notes I've separated for you! Subjects that speak to us of human aspirations; of experiences that prove the survival of our individuality and the possibility of its appearance after 'death'. It is what we call ghosts. They ask for prayers, give warnings, or simply they appear to us. Remember the play by the brilliant English bard, Shakespeare, called Hamlet? Already told you that the ghost of the king appears to his son, Hamlet, Prince of Denmark, to point out his murderer, remember?

- Yes! When I visit England, we will go to the theater?

- We'll see all the seasons! Eugene will go too. I miss her so much! She hasn't answered my letters.

- She must be angry!

- She probably is. But let's get on with our studies! Take that book there, with the black cover, with the markings I made, and you can read everything.

Obediently, Natacha sits down comfortably after taking the book. Between readings and researching they ignore that in the sky the stars warn that another night has come...

LET'S GO BACK NOW to our Madelaine, who doesn't walk, she flies! She doesn't speak, sings! She doesn't think, she dreams!

Inside her soul, the seductive image of the Marquess. She had never experienced feelings like these! Her feelings are obvious, making everyone happy. And so, she spent some time forgetting of the inquiry about Baron André of Villefort.

For his part, Charles lives airy, dreamy. The lute is his confidant. At this moment, the sounds still hover in the room while he puts the instrument away, pensive:

"Madelaine, Madelaine! Your presence in my life is as solemn as the presence of God himself! I want your love, just as Moses longed for the promised land! I have lost my mind and I am happy! Sweet and torturous madness!"

Amid these reveries, he hears the servant announce the arrival of a student. Coming back to the reality, he let him in and gets down to work.

* * *

HENRY ORGANIZES, EXASPERATED and impatient, his new life.

Servants are being fired and exchanged for new ones. After his plan, he will leave England without a trace. He is excessively thin, with pale cheeks, undernourished and emotionally unbalanced.

When he visits Eugene, he explains that he is recovering from a scam caused by the burden of taking on the business alone.

Comforting, she asks him:

- Henry, work less! My father isn't worth the effort!

After the business trip, he decided to go to Paris! There, he is now in a pleasant country house and, imagine, he writes to me his joys with his new Russian friends. He even talks about his typical parties! Oh, how I hate him! I am not answering his letters!

- Calm down, Eugene, he'll be back soon! Maybe with a new woman? After all, he is still a good-looking man and you need a mother! - he says, with a certain irony, waiting for her reaction.

As if stung by a thousand bees, Eugene jumps up:

- Have you gone mad, Henry? My mother is irreplaceable! Let him dare he! Let's see if he dares to even think of such a possibility! Did he consider this possibility?

- No, Eugene, I am only speaking in theory! Your father, being a widower, may marry again! – he says, adding another dose of his poison.

Sister Rosalia arrives, surprised by the expression of anger on Eugene's face:

- Eugene, what happened?

- Eugene: Nothing, sister. Don't worry, doesn't matter!

And turning to Henry, she dismisses him and warns him:

- Goodbye, Henry! Go back to your duties and be careful in our business ventures; mine and my father's! Very soon, I will be in charge of everything! - thus saying, she turns her back on him without looking back.

Accompanying Henry to the exit, sister Rosália asks him why Eugene is so upset, and he answers sharply.

- Spoiled Child stuffs! See you!

Sister Rosália caught a strange glint in his eye and a thin, sarcastic smile on his lips. Never before had she seen someone to change his mood so quickly.

"What risks will Eugene and his father be exposed to? May God help them!" - she thinks.

Arriving at his chamber, Eugene surprises Marianne tidying up some drawers. Without preamble, she orders:

- Let's study some more, Marianne!

- We've studied enough today, Eugene!

- I want to try my best, Marianne. I have serious reasons to do it!

- Okay, Eugene, agrees the other, patiently.

- Marianne, in the next vacations I intend to start managing the business with my father. Maybe we can even fire his manager!

- And when you return to school?

- I might not! I'll hire private teachers. I can't stand being stuck here while things are happening outside! My father's money will open all doors for me! If you want, you can live with me. What do you say?

- I don't know, Eugene, I must think about it.

- Aren't we friends?

- Yes, we are! But our fates might be different!

- You can choose! In my house you will be happy and you will continue to help me in everything, as you always do! Your relatives are not in conditions to offer you much!

- I don't want anything, Eugene! I just want to be happy!

- And poor people can be happy? Come on, Marianne, what a silly idea!

- Eugene, we are friends, but we have different aspirations! I long to live with my family!

- Then go and share with the rabble, you fool!

- Eugene! You are offending me!

- You think like a pauper, but act like a queen? – Forgive me! I didn't mean to insult you, your majesty! - she says, bowing mockingly.

Fearing her friend's unbridled ambition, Marianne dares to ask her:

- Eugene, what if your father would lose everything he owns?

- Have you gone mad, Marianne? Today, you have decided to take away my peace and quiet, right? I wouldn't accept that, believe me! The simple thought of it makes me furious.

- I'm sorry, Eugene. I'm such a fool as you say!

- Only nonsense can come out of this head of yours, Marianne! Enough of this talk and let's study!

With resignation, Marianne picks up the books and gets ready to assist her.

NOT PAYING ATTENTION TO THE TIME, focus in his research, Sir Jaime little by little, discovers an invisible, transcendent world, full of mysteries and surprises, satisfying his old thirst for knowledge, finally.

Natacha, docile and happy, follows his steps, focus and accustomed to this fascinating culture that enlightens her about so many things. She is dazzled by each new discovery, stimulated to make new ones, which seem to have no end.

- Sir Jaime, although I feel grateful to heaven for this opportunity, I must confess to you that I fear to lift so many veils...

- You said it very well, my child! Knowledge frightens us! We have lived accommodated, forgetful of these truths that are part of us intrinsically! For this reason, "we do not learn, but we remember", as Socrates told us!

- Yes, Socrates set an example of honesty and courage!

- His disciple, Plato, followed his teachings, but he could not reveal them without the diverse allegories out of fear of the pressures and risks of the time. The persecution of the legitimate defenders of the truth was fierce.

- Sir Jaime, Greek mythology fascinates me! In front of it I am not so strange!

- In fact, daughter, she is the portrait of our exercised passions, resulting from our feelings and desires! It also points us, our great intellectual and spiritual potential. Jesus told us that we are gods! These myths, usually tragic, resalt our humanity which Jesus called us adulterous and perverse, alerting us to the urgent need for inner transformation!

- Jesus loved us, even though he knows about our multiple imperfections.

His love fills my soul in such a way that I feel my heart explode! Because of this love I understand humanity, made of ups and downs, of good and bad!

I can appreciate, just a little, the immense love that took him to the cross, and the courage of the all-time martyrs!

The power of true love is unstoppable, life-changing! I want to feel it and keep it in me, amplifying it, making it unconditional!

Exited, Sir. Jaime waits until the last word rings out in the room.

- My dearest daughter! I am happy to see someone so young understand life and therefore understand God! You get to the very essence of metaphysical knowledge! That is the safe path: that if reason and love! Deeply moved, Natacha asks:

- If we understand each other so well, if we love each other in the purest love, have we met in other lives? Studying the process of multiple existences, I am curious about our past. What do you think?

- No doubt we have lived together before. This had connected us since the first time we met.

We don't know who we were, but we know that real affection has crossed forms and times, surviving everything, throughout the centuries.

Would you like to know who you were? See what you are now! We are the same for quite a long time. Our progress drags on.

We evolve very slowly, by unexpected impulses, most of the time dominated by pain. As for what we used to do, it is enough to see and feel our impulses and aptitudes.

- Ah, I see. I, for example, love to dance! I never learned, but I know how to do it! I need to exercise myself constantly, creating choreographies that I have never seen, and yet I know how to do it! I can conclude that I was a dancer, is that it?

- Exactly. We are the result of the sum of all our incarnations.

- And what about my weirdness?

- Well, this is another matter. What seems strange to us may be just a lack of knowledge about certain issues, facts and phenomena not yet very well explored scientifically.

In your specific case, they may be individual acquisitions, marks of the exercise in mediumship, in space and time, correctly or not. Only God knows in what way we have been using our talents for centuries. What we don't have now is what is the proper support and guidance.

Give yourself to God, keep praying and studying. Your life is harmonious, your steps, must be correct and secure. You will be able to control yourself, dominating the phenomena that, for now, surprise you, because you will be enlightened and will be the rider of your own life.

The mind enlightened in Jesus leads to a safe harbor.

- Oh, how good it is to hear and understand! I gain a new soul, thanks to the heavens and to Saint Sophia!

- Let's thank God? - he says a warm prayer. Natacha joins him and at the end of the gratefulness, moved, her eyes clouded with tears.

Changing the line of the conversation, Sir. Jaime wants to know:

- Natacha, why don't you think about getting married? I notice so many boys interested in you!

- I'm not interested at the moment. Until now no one has really gotten my attention.

- Be careful, my child. Life goes by too fast!

- I'm sure it does. I must think about it, don't I?

- Yes! I pray to heaven that he'll make you very happy!

- Thank you.

Sir. Jaime has been receiving regular correspondence from Henry, reassuring him about Eugene and advising him to make the most of the rare opportunity for physical and spiritual recovery.

Among other things, he confesses that with each new day he gets attached to Eugene. He describes her behavior, which he says is milder and more docile.

He tells him that his business is prospering admirably, and that everything in his house is going well.

Despite the news he has received, Sir. Jaime feels a squeeze in his heart. After all, Eugene continues not answering his letters!

Meanwhile, Henry has recovered his good looks, rebalancing his health through consultations with the best doctors, therapeutic baths, tonics, and methodical exposure to the sun. Visiting Eugene, he asks him:

- Dear Eugene, how are you? You are getting more beautiful every day!

- Do you really think so, Henry?

Come on, anybody can confirm it! I can just imagine you in the halls of nobility, seductive and elegant, driving the best matches crazy!

Enraptured, she asks, vainly:

- Henry, will you marry me?

Caught by surprise, he almost bursts into loud laughter.

But he restrains himself and answers, seductively:

- If I were not your brother at heart! Know that I would be honored, dear princess! The other men would die of envy!

Eugene shuts up, happy. Her gaze distant, dreamy. If she could read in Henry's soul, she would see the hellish abysses, hidden by physical beauty and manly fascination.

In her office, the Mother Superior looks imploringly at Jesus crucified, consults her pocket watch and confirms that it is time to leave to visit sister Berta, who is in the hospital recovering from a minor surgery.

Distant from her father, with bad ideas in her head inspired by Henry about the possibility of a stepmother in his life, Eugene becomes withdrawn and taciturn. She no longer disguises her dissatisfaction. Sister Rosália fears for her health.

At the inn, Sir Jaime speaks to Natacha:

- Daughter, I feel very well among books and nature, which benefit me visibly. In a relatively short time, I have reached surprising stages of my soul! Nevertheless, I must think to return. I fear that Eugene will not understand my long absence.

- You are right... As a teaching, can you tell me about these stages of the soul?

- Yes, they are unique experiences, sui generis!

When I pray, fervently, if I get to focus a lot, I surprise myself loose in an unknown space! On the outside, I am limited, but deep inside, I am an immeasurable cosmic, luminescent, grand and frightening universe!

- Wouldn't this be the integration with the absolute whole?

- Yes and no, because this theory only makes sense on an allegorical level. When we speak of the absorption of spirits into a whole, we must consider the progress acquired over the millennia through reincarnations and in our reincarnations and in our individuality, which is unique, indivisible and non-transferable! These acquisitions cannot be lost, they are sacred!

We will always be ourselves, a little improved at each new stage.

Well instructed in truth and morals, we will be highly evolved! We will then have great civilizations, based on love, freedom and true justice!

Natacha listens, surprised.

Amused, admiring her curious expression, he declares:

- That's enough for today, Natacha! Rest your pretty head and go enjoy nature, because it misses you!

Before leaving, she comes up to him and kisses him on the cheek, pleasantly surprising him. He smiles appreciatively.

Being alone, he thinks about Eugene and the pressing need to return. In this state of mind, he gets up to put his books away, when Natacha returns with an envelope in her hands.

- Correspondence for me, Natacha?

- Yes, it has just arrived!

- Thank you, my child!

Anxiously he reads the name of the sender: sister Rosália of the Espírito Santo.

With his heart pounding, he opens the letter:

"*Dearest friend, Sir Jaime.*

Greetings of peace!

I sincerely hope that this one will find you in good health. And that your stay there is fully corresponding to your desires.

Our regards to your new friends, the Korsanikovs!

We miss your kind presence! Your periodic visits are already part of the life of this school.

Sister Berta is in the hospital, because she has had a minor surgery.

We are praying so she will heal soon and return to us. For now, we have dear sister Mary in the kitchen, who works hard to prepare the different menus and the delicious delicacies that the girls enjoy so much.

Everything else continues the same.

Well, now I'll get to the point that made me write to you in the first place.

Our dear Eugene is ill. She refuses normal health care, and food, is depressed and withdrawn. She causes us concern because, from time to time, she has a fever and falls ill at the first sight.

We call the doctor, but she also refuses to take the prescribed medication.

We decided to call you to help us in this difficult situation.

Sorry to disturb you, but we are distressed. The Mother Superior has given me permission to send you this letter, calling you for a meeting.

Please don't take long!

May God keep you safe and accompany you on your return trip!

Fraternal hugs!

Sister Rosália".

Running his hand through his thick black hair, Sir. Jaime despairs. Tears come quickly to his eyes; he gives vent to his tears. He clasps the letter in his trembling hands and thinks:

"Dear daughter, forgive me my selfishness! This time, you are right, I am being mean and careless! I will do everything to repair my mistake!

And what about the news that Henry sent me, saying that you were well? That's why I have these hunches! That's the reason for your silence... I should have known.

God bless you, Sister Rosália. You must be reproaching me, and rightly so!

Natacha, who had not gone very far, returned and asked interested:

Was there something serious, Sir Jaime?

- Yes, dear child. Eugene is sick!

- Oh my God!

- I'll be back tomorrow! I'll make the arrangements!

Noticing that the girl has become sad, he asks:

- Will your parents allow you to go to England? If you don't come now, with me, I can arrange for someone to come and get you, if you wish!

- They strictly forbid it! - she replies, dejected.

- Well, daughter, I'm stunned by the news from Eugene!

I'll think about it in due course, I promise! - he leans over, opens a drawer, puts away the missive and looks for some documents.

Natacha becomes silent. Sir. Jaime senses something.

He turns around and is surprised: she is motionless, pale and transfigured.

He helps her by sitting her down on a chair.

Straightening up, she raises her right hand and exclaims with authority:

"- *You will go together! It must be this way!*

Get ready, because you will have difficult battles ahead of you! However, don't rebel because it will be worse! Trust in God, because you will have to experience great pain! Your testimony awaits you! Be strong and show your faith! Your protectors will be watching over you, strengthen them!

Don't let it get you down! Remember my words and my warnings, be alert!

May God protect you! Peace!"

Natacha drops her head, breathing deeply; then she looks around, as if she were returning from a long trip away.

Curious, she asks her good friend:

- Why am I sitting down? What happened?

- You had a brief faint, Natacha, and I supported you - he said, not knowing what else to say (he was stunned). - Are you better now?

- Come on, I am fine! How strange, isn't it? - Getting up, she says: If you need help, let me know, and I'll help you to prepare your bags.

- Thank you, Natacha.

She goes downstairs and he remembers everything, without being able to understand the warnings.

He feels confused and depressed; he thinks about his beloved daughter. At this moment this thought dominates all the others.

The next day, tickets in hand, luggage ready, he informs the hosts that he needs to anticipate his return. He pays them, tips the servants and is ready to leave. Asking for Natacha, they tell him that she has been in her room since the night before. They conclude that she doesn't want to say goodbye to him. It would also be extremely painful for her to face the separation.

Better this way, he thinks.

Getting into the carriage that will take him most of the way, he tries to keep all that beauty in his mind. He regrets having to leave.

Will he return? Only God knows! What will he find in England? At this thought he shudders; he remembers the warnings he heard from Natacha's mouth. They were decisive! Where will this testimony come from? And the great pain?

He leans back, closes his eyes and prays to heaven that the journey be fast and safe. I wish I had wings...

A few hours later, the vehicle stops at the signal of a passenger who pays and continue the journey, being looked at suspiciously because of his of medium height, wears a wide cape that goes down to his feet. A hood falls over his face, hiding his face. He sits down, eyes downcast, carrying a briefcase in his hand. He remains motionless and silent. Finally, the others relax and leave him alone.

Two hours later and they arrive at the lodge. Everyone gets ready to get off.

The hooded passenger politely approaches Sir Jaime:

- Dear friend...

Astonished, he doubts. He recognizes that dear, unmistakable voice! Revealing her face, Natacha pleads with gentleness:

- Don't force me to return, I beg you! My heart has led my steps! I must go with you! - On the verge of tears, she silently waits for him to recover from the fright.

He doesn't know what to do. Deeply concerned about the situation, he asks:

- Daughter, do your parents know?...!

- They must have already found the note I left in my room, stating that you ignore my decision and that I will return soon. I left before dawn with my brother to wait for you on the way.

Sacha praised my courage and did not reproach me, as she always does. She understood and helped me. We are already a long way from home!

Distressed, Sir Jaime ran his hands through his hair. Time is pressing. We need to eat a meal and then continue the journey.

As he thinks about it, he watches the horses being replaced by others.

The new animals growl heavily, digging the ground with their paws, impatient. They are black, strong, luminous.

He asks God for inspiration and finally, turning to Natacha declares:

- Let's eat, daughter. The trip will still be long.

Let's stretch our legs a little. And may God help us!

I know this lovable heart that must have good reasons to do what it does.

Many people descended from the various carriages in a great fuss. Everyone is looking for refreshments and food.

Diligent and solicitous, the tavern keepers attend to the many requests of the travelers.

Steaming plates pass through the hands of the servants. Meats are placed on rustic tables. Wine and bread are consumed. Sweets and fruit complete the meals.

An hour later everyone returns to their vehicles.

Once settled in, Sir Jaime and Natacha lay back, already refreshed and well feed. For him the trip had taken surprising turns.

Resigned, trusting in God over all, talking to himself, he says in French:

- *Alea jacta est*...! which mean that the die has been casted - Looking at Natacha, he realizes that she has fallen asleep.

HAPPY AND ANXIOUS, Madelaine awaits another visit from Charles.

Careful, she takes care of the smallest details: from decoration to rehearsals, from menus to clothing. And she runs from there to there, in a feverish agitation that makes her parents and siblings smile benevolently.

In the music room, Soraya and Fabian exercise the *ouverture* of the musical programming. Once again, at Charles' request, the family will play. This time, new and different songs from the ones that open the festive Sunday.

On top of the piano, a beautiful corbeille of exotic and scented flowers shares the space with statuettes of famous composers.

Moments after the rehearsal, Soraya looks for her sister:

- Madelaine, I wish I didn't play today! I'm very nervous!

I shudder to think that, once again, I'll be under the Marquess's competent assessment!

Fabian, thrilled by his sister's attitude, decides to rebel too:

- I don't want to play either, Madelaine!

Faced with the picture that presents itself, she smiles:

- What do we have here? Is it perhaps a revolt?

- Yes, a revolt! - exclaims Fabian, jumping in the same, excited.

Hugging them, one on each side, she replies:

- My loves, why don't you think about how you are an important part of the program? If we take one star out of a constellation, it will be incomplete and less bright! Think that: If Charles appreciate your interpretations once again, he will be able to evaluate the great virtuosos that you will be in the future! Do you understand?

Taking a deep, convinced breath, Soraya replies:

- Forgive me, Madelaine, you are right. I will try to reassure myself; I promise...

Aware and restless, Fabian decides:

- Since Soraya ended the revolt, I'll end it too! I'm going to play and that's it! Is that right, Madelaine?

- That's fine with me, my loves! Thank you! - she kisses them effusively, while asking smiling:

- And now, how about if we go to the kitchen, and help Ignatia to taste the sweets? - at the last words, the two are already far apart, making her laugh heartily.

At the appointed time, in a beautiful toilette, heart racing, she waits for the Marquess.

Her parents look at each other in sweet complicity.

The bell rings and Madelaine's heart seems to want to come out of her mouth, beating violently. She tries to control herself. Seeing him coming, she steps forward, smiles radiantly, and holds out her hand.

Bending down, very elegantly, he kisses her fingertips, while asking with loving inflection:

- How are you, my dear friend? Am I late?

Blushing slightly, she answers:

- I am well and, as expected, you were punctual!

Approaching, effusive, the Counts greet him. Fabian, cunning, confides in Soraya:

- See how Madelaine and Charles look at each other!

- Shut up, Fabian! - Soraya orders in a whisper and he obeys.

Charles takes a sheet of paper out of his pocket, unties the ribbon that holds it together, and addresses Soraya:

- Dear Soraya, I bring you a small violin piece. A composition by an unknown author from the last century. It is a rarity!

- For me?!

- Yes. The interpretation is a little different than usual. I have a student who does it masterfully! There are strategic repetitions, demanding redoubled attention to the positions of the violin bow.

Excited, Soraya exclaims:

- I will be delighted to study it! Should I come to your school for this?

- That won't be necessary, Soraya; I will come here in due course. If your parents allow it, I can bring the student with me. He is a good boy, from a good family.

- Of course we will allow it, Charles. And we thank you in advance, replies the Count.

Interested, Fabian rushes forward:

- And for me, what have you brought?

- I ask you to wait, Fabian. I am composing a country tune for you to play on your flute. Next time, I will bring it.

- I'll wait! Thank you very much! Will it be as beautiful as Soraya's?

- Yes! I am inspired by the melodies that shepherds play to soothe their sheep.

- Will I play it like a shepherd?

- You will, Fabian.

- I like that! I will get some sheep and play for them! - he exclaims enthusiastically.

Everyone laughs heartily, making the boy embarrassed. Charles hugs him, smiling.

Looking at them, Madelaine realizes that Charles has completely won them over. She delicately places his lute on a large cushion, while she comments:

- I feared your burdens would not allow you to come!

- Only death, Madelaine, could prevent me from coming! - he replies, looking her firmly in the eyes, excited, exposing himself.

She is sure; his heart fully corresponds to hers...

Next to Soraya, the Counts examine the score, while Bettine solves the melody:

- What a beautiful sound, my child! When you learn how to play it, we will be able to appreciate it better!

Disguising himself, the Count observes his daughter and the Marquess, who are irresistibly attracted to each other. He recalls once again the threats of the Prince Aleksei Nikolai Ivanovich. He fears for this love that is barely beginning.

Bettine notices his introspection:

- Do you feel sad, my love?

- No, Bettine.

- Your eyes are on Madelaine and the Marquess. Is something bothering you about them?

- I think, Bettine, that heaven has sent us this boy! He seems to be everything we want for our daughter! I feel that we will lose her, very soon...

- You haven't convinced me, Luiz! Don't you trust me anymore?

Looking at her with infinite tenderness, he answers:

- Don't worry, my life! If I have any worries, they are those of the Forum. Some things seem impossible to me! As to your question: I trust you more than I trust myself. You know that.

Look, Madelaine is calling us.

- My dears, we would like to hear from you in the first instance! Do you agree? While they introduce themselves, Soraya and Fabian relax into their performances.

- With pleasure, my daughter! - replies the Count, noticing Bettine's approval. Hand in hand, they make their way to the piano. Bettine, elegant, sits down and opens the previously chosen sheet music.

They sing a beautiful madrigal. Their educated voices combine admirably while their souls surrender. The last notes still hang in the air as they softly close the performance.

The applause began. Madelaine plays on, accompanied by Soraya and Fabian.

Listening to them, the Count, distressed, puts his hand to his chest. Happy with the presentation of his children, Bettine doesn't notice anything, however Charles is surprised by the gesture.

Finally, Madelaine invites Charles and both play and sing, exceedingly talented. From one song, they move on to another and another. The hours pass quickly without them realizing it.

Gradually everyone leaves, leaving them alone in their sweet conversation.

Hours later, they go downstairs for a snack.

Every now and then, Corine looks at Charles with resentment. Without understanding the maid's reasons, he ignores her and eagerly enjoys those moments.

Alone with the Count, she decides to ask him:

- Dear Count, forgive me for daring to ask, but are you in some kind of trouble?

- My Lord Marquess, in general, we all have problems in these times of insecurity.

- I am not talking about that, dear Count. Is something troubling you, anything in particular?

- Actually, yes... Lately, I have been surrounded by bad omens...

- About what? Can you tell me?

- They are the cares of a family man, that's all.

Tell me: how will you face the probable adversaries regarding your friendship with my daughter? You have gained the attention she has denied to many! They will certainly feel uncomfortable.

- I will do anything to stand by Madelaine's side. I am aware of this opportunity! But your question seems to have some intention; what do you fear, in fact?

- The iron hand of absolutist power!

- I see... You mean Czaréviche Aleksei, am I right?

- Yes. You, as I, have already understood his intentions regarding Madelaine, and he is no rival to be ignored!

- Rest assured. If need be, I will defend your daughter with my own life!

- In the face of this enthusiasm, should I conclude that you love Madelaine?

- With the sincerity of my soul, my dear Count! She doesn't know it yet.

- And how did you discover that you were in love?

- After having a talking with myself, I surrendered. I threw myself into the clutches of love! Soon I will declare my love to her!

- We owe it to Richard to have known you.

- He was my oratory student and we became friends. He is kind of witty and outgoing! A beautiful soul!

- Madelaine adores him!

With that saying, the Count hugs him by the shoulders and they head towards the group, who now are laughing with Fabian because of his antics: sometimes he pretends to be a sheepherder and sometimes a circus juggler.

TIRED, PALE, AND WITH DARK CIRCLES under his eyes, wandering in the house, Henry awaits the decisive moment of his life. He fears to be surprised by unfavorable circumstances, before the conclusion of his plans.

And... on a rainy afternoon, as cold and dark as his thoughts, he hears the characteristic noise of a carriage pulling up to the main entrance. He stands at the window and sees a beautiful young woman getting out from the carriage, being helped by a man who he recognizes as his boss.

- Who is this girl? - he thinks, and hurries down. He puts his clothes and stops in front of the door.

Then he sees Sir Jaime's inquiring face in front of him.

Jaime, who, despite his astonishment, still manages to say:

- Henry, my son, what happened here? Did I get wrong the address? What are these changes?

Silent, hands folded across his chest, he answers nothing. Behold, the curtain opens for the grand finale!

- Henry? - insists the poor man. - For God's sake, enlighten me! Tell me something that will make me understand what's going on, calm my heart! Could I be the victim of a nightmare? Why are all the furniture had been disassembled and packed?

- There is nothing to explain! Think it over and you will understand! While you were strolling along, enjoying yourself in very good company, he says looking at Natacha. Who pale and terrified, can see that in that moment, in her friend's house, a strange duel is starting... -, here I became the owner of everything that used to belong to you!

- Everything that used to belong to me?! What do you mean?

You must have gone mad, Henry! Have you been through trauma, my son? You're unrecognizable! - Walking, he tries to touch Henry, who jumps back, vociferating:

- By all the devils! Don't you understand yet? I am now the owner of all the goods that once belonged to you!

I was afraid that you would still find me here; which has happened! Waiting for some documents delayed me, regrettably! Anyway, "so be it", as you, religious people say!

Sir Jaime puts his hands to his head in despair. As absurd it may seem, Henry had betrayed him, in the most sordid way possible! In a hoarse voice, he exclaims, regretting:

- Henry, is this how you acted behind my back? How could you? What about the trust I placed in you? What have you done with the power delegated to you to take care of Eugene while I was gone?

Bursting into a raspy laugh, he replies:

- Well, Eugene will be happy to know that you have returned very well accompanied! She's in that boarding school where the sisters spoil her for her money! Well, now the pampering won't exist anymore! The income has been transferred out of her hands! And the sisters will not get a single nickel from me, I assure you!

Sir Jaime is on the verge of tears. Courageously, he still tries to control himself. He believes that Henry has gone mad. Seeking balance, takes a deep breath and asks:

- Show me the documents you say you have, please!

- Follow me to the office! You know the way!

With faltering steps, he walks toward his office.

Natacha, deeply frightened, not knowing what to do calls out to him:

- Sir Jaime... What's going on?

Turning around, he answers:

- I don't know, daughter. I'm as surprised as you are. Wait for me here and pray. I think I'm dreaming!

Between the tears falling from his eyes, he sees Natacha's pallor and he hears her trembling voice:

- Courage, God will help you, my dear friend!

His legs tremble, his head throbs and his heart beats uncontrollably, his sight dims from time to time. He knows he won't resist the pressure that Henry is putting on him for a long time.

They both enter the office, and Henry shows him the various legal documents, recognized by different notaries.

Handling them with trembling hands, Sir Jaime realizes, appalled, that everything he owned before, now has a new owner: Henry John Stanford!

Getting out of control, he closes his fists and advances on him:

- Scoundrel! Viper that I have cradled to my breast! I'll take you to the courts! I'll prove that you are a skillful forger and a refined thief!

Henry, like a bronze statue, arms folded, receives his blows impassively. In an authoritative voice, he threatens:

- Accuse me and I will destroy Eugene! She will be happy to know that she already has a stepmother! What did you expect? You've left her alone for so long that she now believes more in me than in her father! If I know her well, she'll love that blonde girl downstairs!

What a beautiful girl! Any man would linger beside such a beautiful gift! God, how lucky you are!

The poor man goes on, trying to hit him to no avail. He, stronger in complexion, defends himself with ease, exhausting him finally.

Suddenly, Sir. Jaime's face turns purple; at the corners of his mouth a whitish froth appears, and, putting his hand to his chest, uttering inarticulate sounds, he falls to the ground in convulsions. Indifferent, Henry stands watching him, when Natacha appears and pleads:

- Lord, help him, by God! Call a doctor!

Ignoring her request, he jumps over his former boss's body, thinking that if he died, it would save him further embarrassment.

Natacha kneels, takes off the manteaux, folds it and accommodates her friend's head. She goes out into the street and there she comes across a pale man who asks her a question:

- Miss, Sir Jaime is there, isn't he? I saw them come in. I've been lurking out here for several days! Don't be afraid of me! I'm a former employee of the house. Are you a relative of his?

Listening to him, confused, she asks him:

- Good man, if you know him, help him! He is in a very bad way! He had a stroke! Call a carriage and help me take him to a good hospital! Please, let's make it quick!

- Yes, yes, I will do that! - replies the man, shocked, while he left to look for the carriage.

Natacha goes back inside and puts her ear to her friend's chest.

His heart is still beating. She breathes with relief and returns to the street. She sees the carriage arrive. With the help of the driver and the ex-employee, they hold Sir Jaime. Inside the vehicle, the man asks:

- Have you seen Miss Eugene yet?

- No. We had just arrived.

- I will tell the girl and sister Rosalia!

Taking some money from her purse, Natacha gives it to the man:

- Here, Sir. For the trip and for whatever else you need.

- Thank you, Miss!

When he arrives at the hospital, rescued and installed in one of the beds, Sir Jaime is struggling between life and death. Next to him, Natacha, is vigilant and solicitous.

Nervous and exhausted, she cries copiously. What seemed an adventure is now something bigger. Asserting her heart, she fervently prays for the recovery of her dear friend. It is already evening and Natacha lies down to rest.

The next day the sun's rays awaken her. She remembers the facts and look at the sick man, who is still inert. Her heart constricted. She approaches him and speaks softly:

- Dear friend! Don't leave us! Wake up and come back to life! Your daughter needs you very much! – she kisses her hand reverently and goes away for a few minutes to wash and eat.

Meanwhile, Eugene and sister Rosália arrive at the hospital.

After identifying themselves, they give access to the patient. Hugging the girl, sister Rosália advises:

- Dear Eugene, try to control yourself! We have been informed that his condition is delicate!

Trembling, she replies nothing. She had never seen her father sick. They arrive at the infirmary and see him: motionless, seraphic, breathing with difficulty. Putting his hand to his mouth, Eugene cries. Rushing to him, she begs:

- Daddy, wake up! - Realizing that he cannot hear her, she cries more. Sister Rosália, hugging her, reminds her:

- Remember what I asked you, Eugene! Don't torment him! He needs peace! Be understanding! Let's trust in God!

Shaken, she accedes to the sister's request and controls herself. Observing her dear friend's so changed features, sister Rosália thinks:

"Has he received my letter? Why, after assuring us that he was well, does he show up here in this state? Where is Henry?

Who brought him to this hospital? God of mercy, what a mystery!

- Sister Rosália, he was really sick! That's why he must have lingered! When he said he was fine, it was to reassure us!

I didn't believe him and now he's dying!

- No, Eugene, he's not dying! He's just sick! Trust in divine providence, child!

After a quarter of an hour, sister Rosália says:

- Say goodbye to him, dear. Trust in his recovery. That is all we can do right now! We'll be back tomorrow.

- I don't want to leave here! I'm staying with him!

- You can't and you mustn't, Eugene! You're not very well. Who knows if tomorrow we'll find you better? Let's go!

Kissing her father on the forehead, she tearfully leaves.

Finding a doctor, sister Rosália asks him:

- Doctor, how did Sir Jaime get here?

- He was brought here by a pretty girl and a very thin man.

They must have helped him on the public road.

"Very strange!" - she thinks.

Inattentive, dejected, Eugene did not listen to the doctor's explanations.

A few minutes later, Natacha resumes her position beside her friend. She does not even imagine that Eugene and sister Rosália were there.

She carefully arranges the sheets for him, makes him more comfortable, and sits down beside him. In the inside, she prays for him.

Days and days go by, without any change.

Eugene was no longer able to visit. Her physical condition, already precarious, became worse, pinning her to her bed and worrying the sisters.

Sister Rosália remained at his bedside, fearing the worst. Mother Superior began to receive news of Sir Jaime through the gardener, who, living near the hospital, passes by every day.

Natacha has never seen him. Wondering about, , Eugene and sister Rosália delay, she concluded that perhaps the man who had helped her had not kept his promise.

A few days later Eugene finally shows great improvement.

Obedient, she makes an effort to heal herself. Sister Rosália tells her that his father is still in the hospital.

Feeling stronger, she asks to visit her father. As always, sister Rosália will accompany her.

Meanwhile, in the hospital, Natacha, untiring, encourages him to back to life:

- Dear friend! We love you! We need your loving and harmonious presence! Don't be cowardly, don't run away disappointed and frightened!

Don't rush your steps towards that Amenti that will weigh down your heart, condemning you! Give yourself time to redeem yourself from this and other faults that perhaps your spirit carries!

Don't let go because it's not time yet! For Eugene, for me, for yourself, for the new knowledge, come back!

You can't cut the thread of life! That is not for you to do! After won so many battles, don't lose the war! Use our love, live in it, and react! How much remorse you will feel, coming into God's world with empty hands, a bitter heart, a rebellious mind and unsubmissive spirit! - No longer able to bear it, Natacha bursts into sobs. Her tears fall on him.

The nurse arrives, turns him over in bed, while declaring pessimistically - If he continues like this, he will have other aggravations, no doubt!

I don't think he wants to live! I've seen it other times, I'm sorry! - After the terrible prediction, he leaves, shaking his head negatively.

Silent, Natacha dives into deep prayer. After a few minutes she can be heard snoring softly. Her face still bathed in tears, her hands in her lap, her head resting on her back. Time slips away.

The doctor comes to see the patient. Seeing her asleep, he moves away carefully. Just over an hour has passed.

A light breeze comes through the window, bringing the scent of flowers from the garden.

Only those with a "sensitive soul" will be able to pick up the soft dialogues, inaudible to the common people.

Over there, present, a "different" team of doctors and nurses, diligent and caring.

Let's sharpen our ears to identify the patient's polite and resonant voice, explaining himself with difficulty.

Then, a larger, conciliatory voice rises fraternally.

The sobs of a deeply disappointed man are heard.

Then, among all the others, a feminine and affectionate voice stands out:

- Dear friend, listen to us! Change the course of your thoughts!

This is a decisive moment! There will not be another! Come, come back to us... For your daughter. For me. So, come!

Asleep, Natacha stirs and exclaims loudly:

- Come back, my friend, be brave! We love you very much!

Awakening, she looked around, trying to understand herself. She lies back again, strangely sleepy. She continues this way for several minutes when, watching the patient's face, she notices slight movements in his facial expression. Then she hears a sigh.

Unable to believe it, she kneels and kisses his hands, emotional:

- Praise be God!

She runs to call the doctor, who comes immediately:

- Finally, the answer to our prays, miss! The reflexes return! He will live if God allows it and he wants it! But I think he has decided to live.

And you, try to rest, I don't want another sick person here! That's an order! Go with sister Clarencia and tell her to show you the bedroom! Go!

With no other alternative, Natacha obeys. The doctor's orders fulfill her great need for physical renewal.

Once again sister Rosália and Eugene arrived. At the reception desk they are informed of Sir Jaime's sudden improvement.

Hugging his father, Eugene lays his head on his chest. Affectionately, speaks words of comfort to him. Sister Rosália satisfied, exclaims:

"That is the real Eugene! What she shows to the world is just a mask! Otherwise, why is that little soul so scared?"

Sir Jaime opens his eyes, takes a deep breath, feeling their presence. His countenance gains expression. He tries to raise his arms, but can't. Unable to articulate sounds, he looks at his daughter, whom he recognizes is moved. Surprised, she exclaims effusively:

- Dear daddy, let's go home! - At his daughter's plea, his face hardens.

Sister Rosália did not miss his reaction. Eugene continues:

- Daddy, get well soon so we can go home!

With a sense of providence, sister Rosália warns:

- Eugene, be careful. He can't manage strong emotions! Don't ask for things that are impossible for the moment! Thank God for his improvement and strengthen him with your affection!

Agreeing, she restrains herself and asks lovingly:

- Forgive me, papa. I'll come here every day and help you get better, okay?

He essays a smile that looks more like a rictus of pain. He looks at sister Rosália, who, coming closer, declares:

- Rest your heart! There is a cure for everything, as long as there is a will to live and a lot of faith in God!

Fixing his gaze on Eugene, without saying a word, he asks for her. Once again, with perspicacity, she states categorically:

- Don't worry! We will take care of her as always, my friend! Calm down!

Unable to contain herself, Eugene suddenly asks:

- Where is Henry, daddy? Why did he forgot me? He never visited me! He's taking care of your expenses here, isn't he?

At hearing the question, the sick man's hands clenched in the sheets. And sister Rosália confirms her suspicions: "Ah, that's the explanation!"

That snake must have struck! What will come next? I'm scared just by thinking on it! May God protect them!"

Eugene recounts her successes at the school and her plans for the future. In a few moments he falls asleep. She stands examining his features as if she had never seen him before. She caresses his face disfigured by thinness and kisses his hands repeatedly. He breathes noisily in his sleep. Looking at the sister, not knowing what to do, she listens to him:

- Kiss him and let's go, Eugene! We'll be back tomorrow! Embraced, the two of them leave the place.

MEANWHILE, ARRIVING in Paris, dramatic and euphoric, Henry exclaims, his arms open:

- Paris, receive me and enlighten me in your greatness and brilliance!

Make true my limitless dreams of power and glory!

I am now a new Creso! I bow at your feet, a servant of the power that you represent and the beauty that emanates from you! I want to live and die in your bosom, golden Paris! - he breathes in hisses, with eyes dazzled, admiring the city that begins to emerge from behind the mist. Finally, tired of his own raptures, he stops, sighs, and pulls himself together.

LET'S TAKE NOW, dear readers, an incursion into the heart of Sir Jaime, who with narrowed eyes reflects:

"How did I end up here? How did Eugene and Sister Rosália know?

Where is Natacha? - he tried to remember little by little everything he has lived through; the cynical image of Henry facing him, insensible! - How could I trust that scoundrel? I was too naive!

Ah, you poisonous viper! I'll take you to court, you won't see it coming! I'll prove your felony, you scoundrel! May the heaven curse you! May your days be black, hellish! May you, Henry, never have peace!

Why didn't I listen to sister Rosália and Natacha's warnings? I should foresee and realize the danger he always represented! What power blinded me? I should never have given him the position of my administrator!

My own daughter, though almost as dazzled by him as I, saw farther, and put him in his rightful place! Now I must recover to leave this hospital and see what I can do about it. God forbid I should be left without a nickel! How will we survive? How will Eugene react when she finds out?"

Internalized, he is unaware of Natacha's approach.

Opening his eyes, he is surprised by her smile. Feeling his doubts, she says:

- A former employee assisted me in bringing you here. You, sir, had a sudden illness and spent days between life and death! You still can't speak?

Making a vague gesture he indicates that he doesn't know. She continues:

- My dear friend, thank heaven you survived!

Forget the evils that have befallen you and try to recover as soon as possible. Calm down and trust in God! Your daughter will be your greatest strength to overcome the difficulties that may arise in the face of the new reality! You can also count on me!

Looking at her tenderly, struggling, he stammered:

- Thank you... daughter... Eugene... she was here...

- Ah, finally! You must heal, quickly, for her sake!

- She came... with... sister Rosália...

- That's great! Next time I'll be attentive! I want to meet them!

Exhausted, trying to smile, showing his gratitude, he got quiet and, in a few minutes, he is asleep again.

At the broad school, Eugene turns fifteen years old. With no other demands, she celebrated with a beautiful cake that sister Mary lovingly made her. She received a few gifts and the solidarity of her classmates, who were sad because of his father's illness.

She was surprised by Henry's absence, but thought he was too busy with the business...

MADELAINE AND CARLOS, seeing each other often, feel the powerfully attraction. Unable to contain himself, he decides to declare to her.

Finishing playing and singing, he removes the lute from his shoulder, stands up to put it away, and returns.

He delicately takes Madelaine's hands in his and asks, tenderly:

- My dear, return from these heavenly moors where I cannot enter! Though my heart is in heaven, I want to stand on firm ground, to be rational and practical. Listen to me!

- Speak, Charles. I am listening.

- My dear, from the first moment, you awakened in me strong and unexpected feelings! I thought that true love existed only in our lyrics, as music, or in our romantic verses! And yet, here I am, in love with you, hopelessly!

I love you, beautiful Madelaine, deeply and ardently!

Look in my eyes, be conscious of the sacred adoration that you inspire in me, my dear! Feel the flames of my passion, devouring me, longing to have you for myself! In the morning when awakening, my first thought is for you! At night, dominated by sleep, I still retain in my mind your idolized image until I lose consciousness of myself! I can no longer live without your company! I am doomed to be half of myself without you! My love, I will be the happiest of mortals if I can confirm what I read in your eyes, which for me are the stars in the sky! You are the love, the greatest inspiration, the hope of happiness, the light of my soul! I want to ask your parents and marry you as soon as possible. I offer you love and happiness in this life and the perpetuation of this feeling in eternity! On your lips, my happiness, or my misery!

What do you say? – staring at her, he waits for her answer.

Madelaine thinks she is dreaming. She feels the warmth of his refined velvety hands. Her heart beats so strongly that anyone can hear it. How many previously unknown emotions visit her soul! Her small hands disappear into his.

- Charles, she answers emotionally, your love finds an echo in my heart! I love you the same way and with the same intensity!

When I saw you for the first time, my heart recognized you!

Only you possess the keys that open the floodgates of my soul! Your love is the promise of bliss! Yes, I want to share your destiny! God will bless us!

Enraptured, Charles seals the commitment with a long kiss.

Thus, entwined they remain like that for a long time, hidden of the world.

Corine, who goes upstairs pretending to do her choirs, sees the scene and turns red with rage. She goes downstairs and looks for Solange in the laundry room.

- Oh, Solange, are you there?

- And where could I be, Corine? In the Versailles palace? - answers the maid, stirring the clothes in the boiling cauldron.

- And what happened, woman?

- I'll tell you! It's our dear *Mademoiselle* Madelaine, she is upstairs kissing and hugging with that Marquess!

- What? - shouts Solange, burning herself with steam. If I were you, I wouldn't be surprised!

- Have you by any chance ever seen me hugging someone, Solange?

- I have never go out with you! But where there's smoke, there's fire!

- How sordid you are, Solange!

- Me? I'm here working and you come to me with intrigues. Mind your own business, Corine, and let the bosses live!

They can do whatever they want!

- Gosh, what a mood, huh? I thought I would find a friend to tell what I see!

- Friend, Corine? Do you remember being my friend? How many times could I count on your solicitude? The Countess pays me right and treats me well, so let me work! As for you, go embitter your envy far away from here! What do you expect? *Mademoiselle* is beautiful, single and rich. It was supposed to happen one day! May she be happy, because she well deserves it, and you know it!

- But, Solange, she needs to be happy with "someone else"!

- You're fool! Wake up, Corine! You want to decide who your mistress should marry? You must see a doctor... for craziness!

- Oh, you're too stupid to understand me!

- I'm the stupid one? Well then, let me work in peace, because I´m burning myself in this infernal heat! - Thus saying, she turns her back on her and begins to hum an Andalusian song.

Solange is disgusted with Corine. The day before, with her old mother sick, she had asked Corine for money and Corine had denied her. The Countess helped her with the doctor and the medicines. Her mother is already recovering well.

* * *

LET'S GO TO THE PORTAL of Light, the property and residence of Baron André of Villefort, where he walks restlessly.

Time is ticking and, despite Corine's help, he has not yet managed to win Madelaine over... He decides to put a new plan into action.

In the garden, we see a beautiful blonde girl, with rosy skin and big blue eyes. Her bound hair reflects the brightness of the sun.

She is sitting on a chair, reading a novel, entertained and dreamy.

- Louise! - he shouts, startling her.

- What do you want?

- I need your help!

- Aren't you tired of tormenting me? - she asks bitterly. - Your cruelty has made me what I am. And what about my people? Where are they?

- I didn't come here to listen to your whining; stop this nonsense!

You already know what can happen if you go against me!

- What do you want from me? - she asks, hoping that he will reveal his intention and then finally leave.

- That you get a friendship and trust of someone who interests me. You will be my business card! You must commit yourself to this!

- I will not do this!

- Well, you must, otherwise...

- No, by God, I beg you!

- Then obey me! You need a good friend! I'm giving you this opportunity!

- Is a woman then?

- And what a woman! She'll be mine, no matter what!

- If she loved you, you wouldn't need any tricks!

- You fool! How can she want me when she won't even allow me to approach her?

- Maybe she already knows who she's dealing with. She must know your qualities!

- Don't challenge me, Louise! You may regret it bitterly!

She got quiet, fearful. And he goes on:

- If you become her friend, I may have her close to me.

- I can't do that! It's against my principles.

- Your principles must be my principles!

- Do you have them, by any chance?

- If I had them, I wouldn't be who I am, you fool! Obey, or else or I'll throw you in the stinking cellars of some prison, where you'll die in a short time. You will have rats for company, and not those scented flowers!

Knowing beforehand that he will keep his promise, she shakes her head affirmatively, devastated.

- Corine will help us! - he informs, walking away.

Louise concludes that he is talking about Madelaine's mistress.

And, at the Alvarado castle, Madelaine, faced with Corine, calls her:

She answers facetiously and covertly:

- You called for me, *Mademoiselle*?

- Yes, Corine, once again I must question you about the same problems! Why do you neglect your responsibilities so much? And why do you go out so often? Could you explain it to me?

- I go out to fulfill orders! Whether it is sunny or rainy, hot or cold, I go out in search of what is asked of me! And I also go out for other reasons and these I would like to keep secret!

- Are you dating someone?

- No, not yet! - she replies, defending herself.

- Corine, please be clearer! We both have a lot to do! How can I understand if you don't explain?

- Well, I'll try... - she says, rolling her eyes. - I follow the examples of my employers and, as such, I also have my protégé! - she is silent, for a moment, to feel the effect of her statements.

- Very well, so what?

- At Baron de Villefort...

- It's been a long time coming! I will not listen to this conversation, Corine!

- Please, *Mademoiselle*! It's very important! Listen to it! On hearing of the soirees that are held here, his sister, who is paralyzed, took an interest. She's so lonely, poor thing. Her brother is very busy and she lives very lonely!

- Do you know her, then?

- Yes, I like to help people too! *Mademoiselle* could invite you to the next Sunday party!

- And who says I wish such a thing?

- Please, *Mademoiselle*! It might gladden the heart of the Baron's sister!

Madelaine suspects that Corine is lying. However, an idea occurs to her that this could be an opportunity to get to know her lair.

Without knowing it, Corine is offering him the means... He doesn't want them there, but she will be able to visit her sister... If she really exists – with that thought, a shudder a shiver runs down her spine.

– Let's see, Corine. I'll think it over and give you an answer later.

But if you continue this path of irresponsibility, you will be able to pass permanently to the Gate of Light, and there you will be the servant's girl. What do you think? Perhaps this is the best solution for you!

– No, *Mademoiselle*! I wish to stay here. I will do as you wish!

– All right, then, fulfill your obligations!

– Yes, *Mademoiselle*! - she leaves without Madelaine being able to see the gleam of victory in her eyes. At last, she had managed to extract from her a promise concerning the Baron.

Madelaine can't measure how aware Corine is of what she is doing, listening to the Baron's pleas.

IN BETTER CONDITION, physically and spiritually, and out of danger, Sir Jaime is transferred from the hospital to a small house, by the kindness of a friend of his who is a doctor.

Natacha writes to her parents asking them for a little more time.

She already knows Eugene and sister Rosália.

She remembers how it happened:

"Sitting by the bedside in the infirmary she saw a nun come in next to a very thin and weak young woman who, questioning her with her gaze approached, torn between the desire to question her and the desire to ignore her, she finally asks:

- What are you doing here and who are you?

Cautiously, Natacha answers her with another question:

- You must be Eugene Sartorelli, Sir Jaime's daughter, right?

- Yes, that's me. And who are you? - she insists.

- I am Natacha Korsanikov. I live and work at the Estancia Santa Sofia, where your father stayed. We traveled together because I wanted to meet you and England.

Fate, however, prepared this unpleasant surprise for us. Your father fell ill and had to be urgently hospitalized. I stayed here by his side, as his companion.

- In the place that belongs to me! - exclaims Eugene, angrily. - I beg you to leave!

- I will, dear Eugene, as soon as you can stay by his side. Right now, you look sick to me, am I wrong?

- No. However, I reaffirm; this place that you pretentiously occupy is mine by right! I demand it!

- I'm not competing with you, Eugene. I know about you through his love, and that's why I had a great desire to meet you! I deeply respect your father, admiring his character and good heart. Do not fear my presence. My parents are waiting for me, and as soon as I can, I will return home. Do you believe me?

- Well, you seem sincere to me!

Sister Rosália heard everything and could see Natacha's great power of persuasion. She had the urge to applaud, but this would have provoked Eugene's jealousy even more. Smiling, she approached her:

- I am sister Rosália. How are you? What a pleasure to meet you!

- I'm fine and I'm also happy! It feels like from what Sir Jaime told me about you, I already know you. He praises you a lot!

Our patient, as you can see, is finally better, and is now on the road to recovery! He sleeps under the effect of tranquilizers but will soon wake up! - the two hug, effusive, like old friends. Intimately Sister Rosália concludes: 'What a pearl of a little creature!

Approaching her father, Eugene calls out:

- Daddy... - noticing the impossibility of waking him up, she sat down beside him, forgetting everything around her.

A little distant from her, Natacha and the good religious woman chat. In a low, careful tone, Natacha summarizes the events that took place at Sir Jaime's house, between him and Henry, leaving her speechless.

Indignant, she recalls:

- I warned him! Poor friend, he let himself be clumsily betrayed! He was reckless and innocent! But what can we do? Pray to God for both of them: for him to be healed and forgiven, and for Henry to regret it and save his so disoriented soul!

- I think so too, sister.

- For now, Eugene must not know, right? I must prepare her, first. She doesn't have the emotional structure to withstand blows; she gets sick very easy! She is extremely proud and very impulsive! She dreams of a life of luxury and wealth, do you understand?

- Poor thing!

- May God help me to clarify this misguided heart about the true values of life! I love her as if she were my own daughter! I was with her during her childhood. I know her very well!

- Sir Jaime will soon be transferred to a house located next to one of the doctor's. His friend, aware of his situation, decided to help him.

- Thank God!

- I will go with him, and there, of course, Eugene will be able to stay with him more often, whenever she can.

- Dear Natacha! I seem to have known you for a long time! As if my heart is longing for you and is happy to see you again!

- I feel the same way, dear sister!

- Tell me about Estancia Santa Sofia!

They talk for a long time, until she and Eugene say goodbye to return.

Natacha locks herself in her memories when she sees the sick man approaching, with steps faltering, still weak. She runs to support him and asks:

- Do you want your breakfast now?

- Yes, daughter - he answered with extreme affection, bathed in deep gratitude.

She makes him sit up in bed and offers him the food.

Tasting the food slowly, he watches the birds singing through the window. He takes a deep, silent breath. The girl senses in him some decision. Finishing his meal, he wipes his mouth with his napkin and continues thinking.

She removes the tray, arranges the pillows, and smiles, encouraging him to speak. Looking at her longingly, he tells her, finally:

- It's about time for you got back, Natacha! Your parents must be missing you and worried. I am hurt too much by the grief I have unintentionally caused you! I will miss you a lot, but I cannot be selfish!

Listening to him, she approves his arguments. She will miss everything, but she must come back. He wriggles in bed to cover himself and gasps. Natacha cannot express herself and two thick tears speak for her. Helpfully, he comes to her:

- We will see each other soon, daughter. If I get better, I will go back to Santa Sofia. Although...

- Although you don't know if you'll be able to pay! That won't be an obstacle, I assure you! Shall we read the Gospel of Jesus?

- Very good thinking! We both need comfort! How much I miss our studies, Natacha!

- We will return to them!

- Will it be possible?

- Yes, God will allow it!

After the reading and the prayers, he asks her - Daughter, write to your family and organize your return. If it is necessary, I will provide someone to accompany you on the trip.

- I accept the offer and thank you. It would be scary to travel alone!

There is a knock at the door. Eugene and sister Rosália arrive. Discreetly greeting Natacha, Eugene throws himself into his father's arms, while complaining:

- Why, papa! Is this where you are living? Without any comforts? Ah, it must be to be near the doctor!

Sister Rosália, who had been hugging Natacha for a long time, comes to her friend's rescue:

- So it is, Eugene. Don't forget that despite appearances, your father needs rest. Soften your impulses, darling!

- Okay, sister...

- Come on, Eugene, said Natacha, as a daughter, your outbursts are only natural! Are you entering your free term at school?

- Yes, and I will resume the place you have occupied at his side!

- A place that I am leaving at your disposal, dear Eugene!

I'll be back in France in a few days!

- Good, then things will be back on track!

At a reproachful look from sister Rosália, she makes amends:

- I'm sorry, Natacha. I will never be able to thank you for what you did for my father, which must not have been easy, I must admit!

- Why don't we all go to Santa Sofia, Eugene?

- Not this time, Natacha, answered Sir Jaime.

- Why, the weather is great and would help you in your recovery!

- I insist that not for now, child. Thank you - he confirms determined.

- All right. I'll wait for you.

- Natacha, shall we go to the garden? While Eugene does her weekly report, we can talk! - invites sister Rosália.

- Look, sister, said Natacha, pointing to the flowerbeds, our dear Dr. William, besides being a great doctor and an excellent friend, is also a competent gardener!

- Sir Jaime is right when he says he has great friends. In them I put my hopes for his future. His financial situation is quite complicated!

While listening to her, Natacha, on an impulse, leaned over and kisses her hands. Surprised, the sister takes her in her arms and squeezes against her heart. From the bedroom window, Eugene is surprised by the scene and thinks: "Go away soon, Natacha! Even her love you take it from me!"

- We have so much to thank God for, sister! Despite the circumstances, we know each other!

- I agree with you!

- It is like we have already knew each other from other lives.

- Do you believe that, Natacha?

- With my whole soul!

- When will you come home, child?

- Soon.

- And how did you come? Did your parents' consent?

- Actually, no. I planned myself. My brother helped me.

- Was all this about wanting to come here?

- In part, yes. On the other hand, I knew he shouldn't travel alone!

- Why is that? Are you trying to tell me that you foresaw what happen to him?

- That's right, sister!

- And how was that?

- Intuition, or a little more than that.

- Explain it to me, please!

- I have feelings that usually come true! If he had been alone, he would certainly have died without help! His administrator left him on the floor in gasps! - and Natacha tells in more detail the drama experienced by Sir Jaime. The sister listens, in shock. At the end of the narrative, she comments:

- Good Lord! It was worse than I could have imagined! And Eugene will have to know everything! What a disappointment awaits her!

- Yes, somehow, she must defend herself and her father.

Maybe she will get back what belongs to them!

- It belonged, Natacha! If I can judge Henry's character, any saving action will come too late! He had the time execute everything calmly! Our good friend was deaf and blind to our warnings! In truth, I have never seen him so trusting! Henry seems to have a strange power of fascination! Well, Sir Jaime and his daughter need urgent help! I will do everything I can for them!

- Me too, sister! When I go back to home, I'll be expecting your visit. I'll miss you!

- Who knows, right? I am very grateful to God for this 'reunion'!

- God! It even looks like you study with us, dear sister!

- Do you study?

- Yes, we study; we try to illustrate ourselves to understand life and its mysteries. As subjects, we chose philosophy, religion, science...

- And what have you learned?

- Well, I will try to summarize:

God is infinitely just, wise and powerful.

We are souls on redemptive journeys, purifying ourselves and learning more and more, exercising ourselves in the life of relationship. We are eternal and on the way to perfection! We are one big and unique universal family! To live is to try to be happy, to learn and to evolve!

After we return this body of flesh to dust, we will return to the real world. And there we will make an evaluation of our successes and mistakes, to then return in new opportunities, when God allows us to do it.

When we have achieved all the progress that the earth can offer us, we will ascend to better worlds, and so we will continue evolving, unceasingly! Jesus told us: *"There are many mansions in my father's house..."*

We are interdependent and we must love each other as Jesus loved us and we must forgive our enemies in order to be equally forgiven by the Father!

The bad ones are imperfect and mistaken spirits on a learning journey. We were once like them; that is why we are here, struggling for our transformation, which is made according to our greater or lesser effort! Evil is fleeting and good is eternal!

Natacha is silent, introspective, thinking of Henry. Sister Rosália, perplexed, asks:

- Natacha, my dear, and where is these: heaven and hell?!

- Ah, sister, these are states of mind! Feelings, emotions, anguish, that are independent of place, because they are inside us!

- God, Natacha! It scares me! How can someone so young can speak about the most varied subjects in such an objectively way?

- This is a small part of what I have assimilated in the studies I told you about. We study based on our faith and strengthened by fervent prayers!

- Dear girl, while you were speaking, I was surprised with a wonderful light and beauty!

- When I talk about these subjects, I feel filled with a strange strength and full joy!

- What a beautiful soul you are! Nevertheless, keep this knowledge in your intimacy. It can be dangerous to talk about it like this!

- Don't worry. I will be careful!

- I am stunned by all that information! I promise to think about it! Tell me, if you can: Why, when I hear you, does the image of Joan d'Arc come to mind?

- Well, sister, I worship her memory with devotion! Along with Santa Sofia, she is part of my life!

- And she ended up living in the land of the 'intrepid servant'!

- Yes, as a newborn baby I went from Russia to France.

- Well, dear Natacha, I am taking Eugene back. Don't travel without saying goodbye to us!

- I promise it! - the two hug each other.

Back at the school, Eugene realizes that sister Rosália has something on her mind. In fact, the sister has decided to tell her the truth about her father. She must hurry, because other people might do it in a disastrously.

At the first opportunity, she calls Eugene for a talk.

Sitting in the parlour, Eugene moves, uncomfortable and expectant. She senses that what she is about to hear will mark the path of her life. Sister Rosália still holds the breviary and the rosary in her hands. She takes a deep breath, looks at the restless girl and begins:

- Eugene, what I am about to tell you has to do with your present and your future.

- I knew it! - she bursts out, already despairing.

- Calm down and listen to me carefully! Don't interrupt me and have great faith in God!

Sister Rosália reveals everything to her: since her father's arrival to England to the saving lodging in the doctor's house.

Deeply surprised, pale, eyes shining almost to tears, biting her lips, she hears everything.

While the sister's last words still ring out in the room, she stands up quietly, looks through the window and walks across the room.

She sighs deeply as she stares at the image of Jesus, bloodied on the cross, and babbles:

- I will not forgive!

- What did you say, Eugene?

- Nothing, I was talking to myself!

- I thought you were talking to Jesus!

- I'm in no condition to do that at the moment.

She sits down again and bursts into sobs. Her whole body shakes. Sister Rosália, hugging her, advises:

- Cry, dear, you must!

After the hour of despair, Eugene wipes his eyes, takes a deep breath, and explodes:

- Coward, infamous, traitor! That's why, sister, I have always had a strange feeling of friendship and rejection! He will pay me dearly!

- Eugene, at this moment you are moved by emotion and revolt. Later, upon reflection, you will understand that you must not harbor revenge in your heart; we teach you this every day!

- And I, sister, certainly haven't learn!

- Eugene, try to calm your heart!

- It is in chaos, sister. But I won't make trouble, don't worry!

- How can I not worry, Eugene? Don't forget that suffering makes us grow!

- Right now, I'm small and petty! And what about my situation here at the school?

- Don't worry. Before traveling, your father paid us for the rest of the year – lied the sister, clasping the breviary in her hands and looking imploringly at the image of Jesus.

- That's good! I have some time, then. Soon I will be at my father's side and will decide my life! Thank you for everything, sister! - saying this, she goes to her room, where she spends the rest of the day introspective. Not even Marianne can bring her out of her mutism.

Now she understands why Henry has disappeared from the nursery school. "He must be a refined scum, used to rob those who trust him! My God! Our house has been sold! He already has other residents! We had no defenses! Everything is consummated, irreversibly!

Henry, your nights will be filled with nightmares! Your black soul will face mine, innocent victim of your cruelty! I will take the law into my own hands! I will follow your tracks to hell!"

With these thoughts she falls asleep, exhausted by her emotions.

Marianne carefully closes the door and informs sister Rosália that she is finally resting.

Sister Rosália asks her:

- Dear, don't leave her, I beg you!

- Rest assured, sister. I will be by her side, constantly!

- God bless you, Marianne!

Natacha is already at the ranch. Her parents wanted to know all the details. They are very sad for Sir Jaime.

She is going back to her usual duties.

She works hard, dances in the woods, studies the subjects that interest her and does not forget to pray for her good friend and for Eugene.

She has won a small library from him.

**

HENRY BENEFITS from his new situation.

Elegantly dressed, leaning on his cane encased in silver; with unnormal gestures, he walks along the banks of the Seine River.

Breathing in a huff, he declares, impatiently:

- This is my place in the world! Here I am happy!

He continues his stroll, when suddenly he sees a carriage run over a little boy and disappear around the corner. He continues walking when he sees another carriage that stops and helps the child.

A priest, another man, and a woman get off. And... what a woman! He stares in astonishment.

Without delay, he sets off in the direction of the group. He wants to meet her and the moment is providential.

- Well, what a bunch of bastards! They must have come out of hell! - he vociferates, wanting to impress. - Let me take care of this poor child!

I hope he's still alive! - Thus speaking, he advances toward the boy, who is already in Salústio's arms. Who, looking at Henry immediately feels a sudden aversion.

As he acts, Henry devours Madelaine with his eyes, embarrassing everyone. Father Estanislau rushes in:

- Excuse us, sir, but we can take care of the boy. We are used to!

Recovering from his refusal, Henry insists:

- If you allow me, I will go with you! I can help too!

Besides, if I don't do anything, I won't sleep tonight!

- As you wish, but let's hurry! - agreed the priest.

They get into the carriage and leave, quickly, for the nearest hospital. In the vehicle, Henry tries to start a conversation. In a gently voice, he complains:

- Poor child! How can things like this happen? We must find the responsible and punish them severely!

- For now, sir, let us do our duty and take care of this little victim and let's not judge in haste! - Madelaine advises.

He drinks in every word: "What an admirable voice! In heaven, by the way, the angels are not more harmonious! It's a goddess!" - thinks. -

Understanding what kind of person he has in front of him, he changes his strategy:

- You are right! I am outraged to see this child suffering and I forget my most loyal duties of charity! My heart speaks for me! Only the creator can judge us! We cannot do it because we are equally susceptible to mistakes! I find you a beautiful soul, *Mademoiselle*!

- Thank you, Sir...

- Henry John Stanford, your humble servant.

- Sir Henry, I am Father Estanislau from the church Our Lady of Mont'Serrat; this is Salústio, our friend and work partner and this is *Mademoiselle* Madelaine D'Or Alvarado.

Salústio feels the urge to ask him to come down, to stay right there but he restrains himself.

Henry continues:

- I'm happy to meet you! Having friends nowadays is rare and dangerous!

Not containing himself, Salústio declares:

- Indeed! We cannot accept the friendship of anyone who approach us at the street! Friendship requires trust!

Pretending not to understand, Henry continues:

- By the way Priest, you must have philanthropic movements in your Parish, am I right?

- Yes, Sir Henry. We have numerous activities in favor of the needy people, of which there are a great number! We were on our way there when the accident happened. We will be late for today, but the cause is noble!

- I ask because, for some time now, I have been looking for a suitable place to exercise charity. I have considerable possessions and I can help your protégés. Our meeting was providential!

Salústio looks significantly at the Priest. It will be difficult for them to get rid of that infatuated Mr. Juan.

They arrive at the hospital and Henry rushes down, takes the boy in his arms, and steps in front of them, loudly demanding help for the child, standing up and leaving everyone bewildered.

Respectful, the Priest hurries up and conducts the usual procedures.

Finding a doctor friend, he tells him the facts, and receives urgent care for the boy.

- We haven't seen who ran him over, Dr. Joseph. The expenses are on our account!

- Not at all! - exclaims Henry. - I will not allow you to use proceeds that certainly belong to your asylees! I will pay for everything today and the resulting expenses! I will not give up this opportunity! And I'll tell you something else! I will go to your parish and there I will see how I can help!

Disarmed, the priest leaves him free to act as he sees fit.

Finally, the child is released, he is out of danger, and the group proposes to send him back home. She is handed over to her parents, they recommend the prescribed medication, say goodbye, and promise to visit her later.

Then, they all go to the Parish House, followed by Henry.

Upon arrival, Madelaine thanks her 'new friend' and disappears.

After donating a large sum, he says goodbye, promising to return many more times.

Back in the carriage, he sits back vibrant: "Finally, I have found the woman of my life! It was about time! How beautiful, luminous, elegant! And her moral qualities are obvious! Madelaine, Madelaine! - repeats her name several times, delighted with each syllable.

After this date, Father Estanislau's parish and his protégés began to be lavished with generous contributions donated by Henry.

With much persistence, he has become a regular person in the departments of the Parish House, and it is not unusual to see him praying in the church, kneeling and apparently devout.

Increasingly fascinated, he searches insistently for Madelaine. She, in the other hand, treats him with consideration, but keeps him at a distance.

Nevertheless, Henry does not give up. Gifted with a brilliant brain, very experienced in society, he ends up making himself dear and useful. Since then, even for Madelaine, his presence has become pleasant.

Gradually leaving aside his artificiality, he showed his better side, and not infrequently, they talk at length, discussing the most varied subjects. Finally, Madelaine is surprised by her friend. She learned to admire him in his stoicism to win her over.

Untiring, influencing his diners, he leads them to the church pews and the coffers of the needy. In this way, Father Estanislau now has fewer financial difficulties.

At this point we find them in a friendly dialogue.

They smile relaxedly, sitting side by side in the garden, in a rare opportunity to rest.

Restless, he takes a deep breath and dares:

- Madelaine, I would like you to listen to me; I have something important to tell you.

- Speak up, Henry! - she answers, breathing in the perfume of the flowers on the beautiful spring morning.

- I want to open my heart and confess my feelings to you!

Madelaine shudders. She didn't expect that. Nevertheless, she respects the right to express herself.

- Since the first time we met, on that memorable day, despite the fright and the embarrassment about that boy, my soul has been in suspense, because you, for me, Madelaine, are the materialization of my ideal of womanhood! And I'll tell you more, without false modesty; I know how to tread on this mysterious, fascinating, and almost very deceptive! Oh, what great abysses they offer us, my dear!

You, pure and good, would be scandalized, if you knew of the fantasies and the traps that surprise us at every new angle of this path! We almost all live wrapped up in anxieties and great affective needs! How many mistakes we make on this life!

How many disappointments we cause and how many we suffer! – Henry takes a deep, abstracted breath, as if remembering something painful...

Taking advantage of the hiatus, Madelaine asks:

- Henry, don't go on, I beg you...

Looking at her, pleading, he insists:

- I beg you to let me go on, Madelaine... For God's sake, don't stop me from speaking! I need to get this off my chest and try to make myself understood.

Let me speak to you with an open heart, will you? This is a new experience for me... Give me a few more minutes...

She is silent, yet distressed by the situation. Intimately, she prays to heaven for him. She doesn't want to hurt him...

Taking advantage of her indecision, he takes up the thread of his statements:

- To see you was to recognize the most dreamed of image, dearest!

You combine physical beauty with spiritual beauty, in a wonderful harmony! For sure, the angels of God accompany you wherever you go! Your luminous soul must be fed by them, who must be missing you, seeing her exiled among us!

As I got to know you, I began to observe you, and with each new facet of your character, I was enraptured!

In resume, Madelaine: you have awakened in me a love that I have never believed in before; combined with a great passion that makes me live in heaven and hell at the same time, because I don't know if I will be victorious among others!

I love you, Madelaine! As I never imagined I could love anyone!

This strong and glorious feeling torments me daily in the great need that reaches me to have you by my side forever! Without you I will never be happy! I want to be your husband, to the heavens and to the world! What do you say to me? Your lips hold my happiness or my misfortune!

Madelaine senses his sincerity. Silently, she ponders how express herself without hurting him... He is, in fact, opening his heart, with great trust and honesty... Pausingly, she begins to answer him:

- Henry, I would never wish to possess such power! I am sure that I have done nothing to arouse in you the feelings you speak of. I have, therefore, a clear conscience about your statement. You know that I am almost engaged to be married. This fact would be enough to avoid such embarrassment between us.

Exalted, ardent, wrapped up in the emotion of the moment, he exclaims:

- You can break this bond, Madelaine!

- No, Henry, I can't, because I don't want to! I am engaged to the only man I love, and I intend to marry him!

I thank you for your kind remarks about me, but I must tell you that you see me with an optic distorted by the raptures of your heart! You have not cited my faults, my dear friend! I am a person like any other. You have fantasized me out of an excess of friendship, idealizing me!

- I didn't say friendship, Madelaine, I said love! - he corrects, pale with emotion.

- Whatever, Henry, I will not contradict you. But, with the sincerity that characterizes me, I want to warn you: my fiancé is everything I love! Forgive my rude frankness, but I don't want you to get your hopes up!

In this healthy coexistence, I have learned to admire your qualities.

You have won in me a true and everlasting affection, Henry. Today, you are for me a very dear friend; with this affection you can always count on.

- I am honored by your friendship, Madelaine. And I know that I have been worthy of it, but I don't want only this! I want to be happy by your side, as a man, and I will not give up realizing my dream! I will fight for it with all possible and imaginable weapons! Your fiancé will have in me, a worthy rival!

- I hope, Henry, you won't make trouble for me! - Madelaine tells him, showing contrariness.

Strongly, he says:

- I will never harm you in any way! But, also, I will not give up the right to fight for you! I want you for myself, and only the future can tell who will win, him or me! - His dark eyes shine, illuminated, speaking more than words, of his decision. Henry releases his pent-up emotions. Despite Madelaine's refuses, he feels happy for the rare occasion to declare himself...

She, showing surprise, asks him:

- Are you ignorant of my feelings or are they unimportant to you?! And yet, you call yourself my friend, Henry?

- Don't misunderstand me, Madelaine, I beg you! The heart is a mysterious terrain! As I have already told you, I have much experience in things of the heart; precisely because I have searched, untiringly, for the woman of my dreams! I hope that favorable circumstances will catch up with me! New things can arise in my favor!

We often change the course of our feelings from this person to that person, surprisingly! We are naturally fickle, Madelaine. I must reach for your heart, or I'll never be happy...!

- Henry, I have never loved before, and I am sure I will never love again after this love that bathes my soul! You, my dear friend, are deluding yourself into a useless wait!

- We shall see, Madelaine! I know the resources I possess! – he exclaims, with a very deep sigh, showing sorrow; expressing a lot of sadness. I thought I could convince you to at least give me hope... But not even that...

Madelaine decides to be more incisive than him:

- Henry, today I listened to you out of necessity to explain ourselves.

From now on, if you want to continue being my friend, restrain your impulses because I am faithful to my love and I must not listen to seductive statements from other men; you must agree! You must know that I allow few such closeness, as I have done with you.

- I know this and I repeat: I will try to be worthy of this prerogative, always. I thank you for your understanding!

My constant presence will be the certainty of my hope and my fidelity to my feelings for you. I beg you, don't stop me from dreaming! I will live waiting for the fulfillment of this love! I will love you forever, Madelaine!

- I reaffirm my friendship with you and regret your persistence!

I hope that your philosophy about our natural inconstancy will also be true for you! Otherwise, you will be wasting your precious time, Henry!

- I don't think so. I love you more than life itself, and the time that I spent trying to be happy with you will always be worth it!

- Friends? - she asks him, holding out her hand and ending the conversation.

- Yes, always and above all! - stooping down, he kisses her hand, reverently, and then leaves a Madelaine very thoughtful.

Minutes later, she has already resumed her activities with the unfortunate ones in the wards.

She is excited to see Gotuza again. She is very well; flushed, red, her hair was tied up on top of her head, framing a beautiful face. "Does she have any connection with the Baron André's sister? What haunting facts might come to light?" - she thinks.

Remembering her in the cave: aged, suffering and untreated, she can't relate her with this nice lady.

After greeting her affectionately and exchanging a few kind words with her, she fixes her own hair, which insists getting over her eyes and realizes that it is time to return home. Her family are waiting for her.

Next Sunday, Gotuza will be installed in the castle, in chambers rooms previously prepared for her, away from prying eyes. On the day of the event, she will arrive among the guests, so as not to arouse suspicion.

At home, Madelaine discusses with Ignácia the idea of going to visit the Baron's sister. She, very frightened, exclaims:

- Daughter, what temerity! Have you made up your mind?

- Yes, but I need to consider the idea and plan it better.

- You're doing this because of Gotuza, aren't you?

- Yes, Ignácia. You must see her; she's rejuvenated! She doesn't even look the same!

- I'm happy for her, poor thing! After so much suffering!

Madelaine, please be very careful! I shudder to imagine you in an adventure like this! Oh, my goodness, I shudder!

- Rest assured, my good Ignatia! - says the girl hugging her by the shoulders - If I go, I won't go alone. I'll take Corine, Salústio and you too with me!

- Me too? And for what, my child?

- Under the pretext of bringing you sweets! In fact, I'm afraid of a trap; together we'll be stronger!

- Have you consulted your parents about this? Will they allow it?

- I have told them of my intention, but we are going to talk definitively, when everything is better planned. For their approval will depend on the greater or lesser security that this company offers us. We don't know much about the aforementioned Baron.

- Let me know first, so that I can make the sweets!

- Okay, Ignatia! It would be great to gladden Gotuza's heart and rescue her to a new life! Who knows, we might just succeed, right?

- Yes, daughter. Let's trust in God! And what about Charles?

- I will tell him nothing! I don't want to involve him in this! It would be to demand too much of his understanding and tolerance!

- The truth is that you are being imprudent; there is no doubt about it!

- As you said, let's trust in God, Ignácia!

- I fear for you, my daughter. You are so young and full of life.

- My dear Ignácia, the life we choose involves a lot of risks, you know! Our journey is almost always insecure! We live to challenge the absolutist powers that massacre the people we help!

We go to the caves where they throw the disinherited French and we pull them out, rescuing them back to life!

That, Ignatia, is constant danger! I know we won't go unpunished!

When will we be persecuted? At any moment and under any pretext! But what can we do? I tell you: trust in the divine protection and wait for the facts, with an open heart, because we, otherwise we do not know how to live! We are a like-minded and determined group! Do you agree?

- I completely agree, but... what about your future, my dear?

You love and are loved; you need to think about your love and be happy!

- Our true happiness is, in fact, in the hands of the Creator!

Let us do good, thus fulfilling our first duty. The rest, dear Ignácia, will happen by sheer force of things. Whatever will be!

While Ignatia, unable to speak, has her eyes filled with tears, Madelaine tells her with immense affection:

- Thank you for this zeal! I love you, my good Ignatia! Be calm this wonderful heart! We'll all be "happily ever after", like in fairy tales! - Kissing her, she heard her mother exclaim, amused:

- Madelaine and Ignácia, always together and accomplices, eh?

The Countess approaches and the three share a hug.

They chat happily about some subjects when Charles arrives and greets them, elegant and jovial.

He walks away with Madelaine and, alone, wrapping his arms around her waist, kisses her ardently, completely in love.

- How I miss you, Madelaine! It's hard, if not impossible, to be away from you!

- I feel the same way about you, my love!

- I know that you are very busy with the preparations for the Sunday festive, and instead of getting in your way, I intend to help you. I am at your disposal!

- Thank you very much, Charles, I accept your offer! - suddenly, Madelaine remembers the probable presence of Prince Aleksei.

Charles notices her introspection and asks, solicitously:

- What happened, Madelaine? You seem to have become sad!

- Don't worry, Charles, I'm fine!

- The allusion to the coming Sunday holiday has changed your state of mind...Something wrong?

- The usual, Charles. I fear for both of us, in our just yearning to be happy...

- Put these thoughts away, my dear, because I will face the world, if necessary, to be happy with you!

- Charles, I am aware of the great happiness we feel when we are together, but the future is unknown!

Charles recalls the Count's apparent distress, on another occasion.

"Are you being pressured by someone?" - he thinks. Squeezing her against his chest, he insists:

- Is there any real danger, Madelaine?

- Oh, no, Charles! This insecure context in which we live is bringing us down, causing us bad omens! I love you too much! I fear for us; I fear for you!

Taking her hands in love, he exclaims:

- Fear not, my life! I will face any danger to defend you and our love! And even after death, Madelaine, I will go on loving you for eternity!

- For God's sake, don't talk about death, Charles!

- Forgive my exaggerations, I beg you! Instead of reassuring you, what do I do? Oh God... I am an artist, and as such, extreme in my feelings! Calm down, my love, I want to live many years to make you happy!

Exchanging affection, they remain embraced for a long time, happy to be in each other's company.; forgetting for a moment, at last, their fears. They hope that the future will be propitious for them to realize the just desires of their hearts...

May no shadows put on their blue sky, now full of joy and peace...

* * *

MEANWHILE, IN A DIFFERENT castle, dark and luxurious, where the sun seems to refuse to enter, another passionate heart suffers.

We are talking about his real highness, Prince Aleksei Nikolai Ivanovich. Richly dressed in dark tones, reinforced by the brilliant black of silks and velvets, he inspects his domains by tormenting all those who cross his path and owe him satisfaction.

He demands, shouts, assaults, punishes one or the other, for this or that. He takes out on them his frustration with Madelaine. The more she resists him, the more determined he is to win her over. Surprised, he finds himself loving her, desperate; he will not live without her.

In front of a precious, carved chalice full of wine, he meditates, while savoring the captivating drink.

His strangely shining eyes reflect his torments:

"Madelaine, Madelaine! Woman of incomparable beauty!

A thousand times dear and desired by my loving heart! I despair, to imagine that you might escape me!

That someone might took you from me! I will never allow such a thing!

I'll use all my weapons, Madelaine, without qualms! I have no limits if you are the final price!

If you are not mine, you will not be anyone else's! I swear it!" – he slams his vigorous fist on the table, bouncing the falling bottle, spilling over.

In torment, he cries out for the servant. The unfortunate, one-legged trough, rushes over, doing it with extreme difficulty, frightened and servile.

- Oh, you wretch! Walk faster! I can't wait all time! Damn, I should have broken both your legs and not just one! Hurry up man, I left you live and now I regret it! I'll kill you right now! I don't lack the desire!

- I'm coming, your highness!

- Shut up! I don't want to hear your voice! Just do it!

Trembling, the servant changes the bottle and cleans the table. He pours it again and drags himself out; with a rancorous expression, he mutters angrily, to himself as he heads outside:

- One day, 'Highness' - and he spits sideways - you will pay me dearly!

I'll have a good opportunity to take revenge!

- He goes to the stable and sits there, ruminating his anger.

While he drinks, Aleksei resumes his sinister and Machiavellian conjectures...

He recalls Charles and Madelaine talking. He saw the Marquess's interest and was surprised when saw the displeasure at Madelaine's eyes seeing him leave before the party was over.

"I must see her again! I have already caught up on several matters and now I'm going to fight for you with tooth and nail!

You, Madelaine, do not know it yet, but you will love me! For you, I will move heaven and earth! You will be my wife! I love you and will live with you the rest of my life! A love like this can only take me to life or to death!" - Out of control, he greedily drinks the entire contents of the bottle.

He decides to settle the marriage with Madelaine. He will present his propose to Count Luiz Santiago de Alvarado as soon as possible.

* * *

INSIDE THE SACRISTY OF THE Church Our Lady of Mont'Serrat, Henry and father Estanislau are talking:

- Dear friend, I hear that next Sunday will be one of remarkable festivities at the Château des Patrons! I would like to be present!

- Do you practice any form of art, Henry? - asks the priest, wanting to gain time to know how to conduct the conversation and defend Madelaine from Henry's patent amorous 'persecution'.

- No, father! Although, if I could, I will use it to win Madelaine's heart. I would illustrate myself in this regard in an unbeatable way! But I can be one of the patrons! Father Stanislaus decides to be honest; the occasion demands it:

- Henry, our friendship allows us sincerity on both sides! I must remind you that Madelaine is almost engaged! If we love her, we must contribute to her happiness!

She is a free spirit, determined and free to act according to her own will. She is one of those creatures who, at an early age, acquire the full use of free will, because of her irreproachable behavior! I hope you understand me, and that you don't get hurt yourself.

Shifting uneasily, Henry understood very well the priest's intention. Taking a deep breath, he answers:

-I thank you for your sincerity, and as usual, I confess that I will not give up on my dreams. My dear friend will be surprised at my obstinacy! Rest assured; I will never hurt Madelaine! If it is impossible to be happy with her, I will be just happy to be her friend! But I will do everything to win her. I have never loved before and I'm not a boy anymore! I have known many women, but in them I have never found such beauty, fascination, or the rare qualities that possess Madelaine!

- I advise you at least to be honest with her.

Don't use more strategies, Henry!

- Do you think I am capable of that, father?!

- Forgive me, but in truth I do not know you as well as I should! The image you give us it not real. I know well the human being, Henry, and I can tell you that by the brightness of your eyes, I see more than your words can say!

I respect you and thank you for helping our parish, but don't see it as a springboard to reach Madelaine, I hope you understand me!

Surprised and embarrassed to find himself discovered, Henry stutters and stands up. He walks through the sacristy, restless and silent.

The priest realizes that he has discovered him.

Henry looks out the window and stays that way for a while. Father Estanislau respects his introspection and waits.

Finally, he returns, sits down again, and takes a deep breath. He seems to have remove the mask he has been wearing since he arrived there.

He got relaxed and begins to talk:

- Father Estanislau, it is very hard for me to agree with you! I wish that won't be this way. One day, when I feel ready, I will confess, trusting in your priestly secrecy. I can assure you, that I have no evil intentions towards Madelaine. I love her, but I will not stand in the way of her dreams coming true! I swear to you in the name of God!

- Do you believe in him, to swear in his name, as you do now? - the priest decides to go further.

- I don't know, maybe... I've been denying it since I was a child!

- So, you have been pretending all this time, in order to belong with us! We are getting to know each other, eh, Henry?

The question goes directly to Henry's soul. He reacts quickly, defending himself:

- Father, you are being ruthless with me...!

Your faith demands mercy! Don't throw my spiritual misery in my face! Try to understand that I only use the resources I know to reach my goals, I have been doing it for a long time, all because of suffering and disorientation! If you grant me your pity and your understanding, maybe I will find myself! As a stray sheep, I deserve to be rescued with love and tolerance! I am right?

- In part, Henry! When you artificialize a personality, you take away the resources that spontaneity could offer us! How can we consider ourselves friends without revealing ourselves at all?

I must, in all truth, confess my admiration for your effort and talent to maintain the image you have created!

I'm not condemning you at all, because not even Jesus would do that. What I want is for you to come clean. And from now on, everything will be easier.

Certainly, you had helped us in a valuable way, sparing neither efforts nor expenses. We are grateful for everything you gave us, but we cannot mix things up, especially when Madelaine's happiness is at stake!

- I agree with you! I am the first to defend her and her happiness, even if it's not by my side. I am sincere in this love that has bound me, irretrievably! Never doubt my true feelings. It is the most beautiful and powerful love I have ever felt, in my whole life, Father!

As for myself and my past life, for the moment I do not want to make a confession, but because of the confidence awakens in me and for the true friendship that I have months of living together, I will be able to do it soon, relieving at last my heart! As for Madelaine, I repeat, have no fear. I would never harm her in any way!

- And what about the others, Henry, would you harm them?

- Dear friend, do not make such a cruel and debasing examination! Trust me a little more, I beg you! Don't be so defensive now, please; I need your friendship and your support!

- You have had my friendship for a long time; as for trust, it will depend on the circumstances and on your behavior!

Henry is silent, takes a deep breath and internalizes himself. He is emotional, almost in tears (something unusual for him).

Looking at the priest with respect and admiration, he vents in a voice:

- Father Estanislau, I don't know what power Madelaine, you and this group of selfless people have that you manage to invade all my being, sensitizing me so deeply, in loving appeals that seemed dead inside me!

- It is the power of love, Henry, the great power of love!

Henry continues, loosening the bonds of his heart:

- I thought I was strong and untouched by any feeling, but I find myself fallen, caught in the mist of this love, and thankful for it!

Let me paraphrase you, precious friend of the creator and his creatures, let's thank God!

Surprised, the priest can notice the sincerity of his exclamation.

He regrets having been so direct; but to speak to Henry and to reach him, this is the only way: with energy, sincere as a true friend, and severe as a father who loves his son very much.

Emotionally tired, Henry says good-bye and leaves; not before extracting a promise from the priest to guarantee him access to the festive Sunday at the Alvarado castle.

Unfortunately for Madelaine, Baron André also suffers Amenti's torture, because despite Corine's information and their machinations, he is unable to get closer to her.

He concludes that he must act quickly, before she marries the Marquess. Choleric, he walks through the streets, trying to calm down.

Insane, he walks aimlessly, crossing streets, bridges, and avenues.

A few hours later, he is surprised to find himself in front of an old barracks, in which he has a friend, legal authority, and a guaranteed (and mysterious) connection between the various prisons. This friend and old acquaintance move with ease through the various departments of the absolutist government. Slapping his forehead, André exclaims:

- Why, my own feet brought me here! That old fox will be useful to me! - He shrugs his well-groomed beard and his devilish eyes gleams.

He approaches the front. He identifies himself and requests for General Antoine Belfort.

After a while, he is led to the interior of the barracks.

Passing through corridors that seem like labyrinths, he arrives at a large room with open doors that seem to be waiting for him. He speaks to the General.

As he rises from his comfortable chair, the General clanks the weapons he carries while he theatrically steps with his large, heavy boots on the grimy floor. He looks like a giant. Red-haired; middle age, small eyes, bright like snake, reflecting coldness; freckled skin; semi-long beard; thin hair on his forehead and thick at the nape of his neck. Elegant in his uniform, he is arrogant and heavy of movement.

- Welcome, 'Baron' André of Villefort! - he exclaims, loud and ironic. - What brings you here? It can't be good!

- Calm down, General! Let me at least greet you!

- Ah, yes! You must have missed me! - he bursts into loud and stupid laughter.

Pretending not to understand, André, flattering, asks:

- Tell me, General, how is your career going?

- Very well, as you can see! The uniform and I complete each other! But you, as far as I can see, are not well!

- Not that well off, General...

- Really? And what do you need? Or rather, what reasons brought you here?

- I went out walking, tormented by my conflicts and I ended up here, without any premeditated intention.

- Okay, so, what conflicts are these?

- Love issues, General! I am madly in love with a beautiful woman! A true angel...- An angel? You must be mad! Heaven is not compatible with hell, André! - he smiles, debauched, looking sarcastically at his interlocutor.

- Don't make me despair, Antoine! I love her and I'm going crazy because another has approached her! I'm afraid that he will conquer her once and for all!

- So, stay away, because this game is already lost! Or is it not?...! If you came to see me, it's because you have something on mind.

- Yes, when I recognized the barracks, I decided to ask you for help.

I have been trying to win her over, but to no avail. She won't even allow me to come close to her! I am desperate! For her, I would kill or die!

- Kill! You're too selfish to sacrifice yourself!

- You know me well! After all, I have been under your orders for a long time!

- It's true. As a soldier, you were never much, but as an instrument of my will...

- Antoine, I am fascinated by this woman and I trust in my resources!

- And in mine, I conclude! We can do anything, can't we, André? We have no heart, remember!

- Once again, I am forced to agree with you!

- And how can we love?

- With our brains, our nerves, the blood that boils in our veins, I guess!

- What do you expect from me?

- I count on those 'expedients' that you manipulate so well!

- Be careful, André! I am still your superior, don't forget! Be careful with your words when you speak to me!

- Calm down, Antoine! Aren't we friends?

- No, we are not! We are accomplices, without fidelity and without honor!

- Which is the same for me!

- I know that! Answer me: what can you offer me in this new business that for you is a matter of life and death?

- The Alvarado's castle, her residence, I have an accomplice.

At home, I count on Louise, whom you already know.

- Ah, the beautiful Louise... She makes me sigh! And who is your rival?

- The Marquess Charles D'Alençon!

Antoine explodes in surprise:

- The Marquess? Oh, come on! He is my son's music teacher and his friend!

- But he is my greatest enemy! I don't care if he is a friend of your son or anyone else's! He is the barrier that prevents me from being happy! In the old days, you were more liberal! You are getting older, Antoine?

- André, he warns, don't forget who you are talking to!

Don't challenge me or disrespect me! You may not return to your good life as a "Baron"!

- I'm sorry! That woman drives me crazy!

- Well, go get crazy far away from here! I've wasted enough time with you! I'll think about everything we've talked about! We'll see each other later!

- When, Antoine?

- I don't know, André. Now leave, my time is precious! - Thus saying, he pushes André outside and returns to his papers.

André, on the street, realizes the scandal he is causing by walking on foot in luxurious attire.

He calls for a carriage and boards it, telling the driver his address. He makes the trip worried about the conversation. He knows Antoine's power but doesn't trust him.

At the Alvarado's castle, the stage is ready and waiting for the guests.

In the family, it is agreed that Madelaine's engagement with the Marquess will be announced during the festivities.

Now, with the powers vested in us, let us pry into General Antoine's intimacy:

In the dead of night, in his rich mansion, he admires a portrait of a woman on the bedside table. Suddenly, he begins to weep. Clenching his fists, he exclaims loudly:

- Finally, André! You have come to me on your own two feet ignoring what I feel here! - and he beats his chest violently. - I will make you the most disgraced of men! For a long time now, I have cherished this desire!

Turning again to the portrait, he laments:

- Jeannete, my love! Why did you leave me alone? Ah, André, you cannot even imagine what awaits you! - Antoine, in tears, is the portrait of pain and failure.

Meanwhile, André rolls around in the silk sheets, as if he were sleeping on hot coals, amidst terrible nightmares.

In the castle, when the first guests arrive, the Count enters the hall, majestically dressed; haughty and arrogant, Prince Aleksei enters the hall and requests:

- I ask you for an urgent audience, dear Count!

- Your highness, as you can see, I am receiving the guests.

- And I am one of them! I demand your attention and cannot wait. Time is short and what I have to tell you can no longer be postponed. I have been absent because of my multiple occupations.

Realizing the risks, the Count agrees upset:

- Whatever you want, your highness! Let's go up to my office and there we can talk! - guessing his intentions, he feels his blood run cold in his veins. Their footsteps sound ominous in the corridors. He puts his hand to his forehead and a profuse sweat bathe his forehead.

- Are you ill, Count? - asks the Prince.

- No, your highness. It is because these Sunday demand too much of us! It may be fatigue.

- You must take care of yourself! Health is a precious commodity!

- No doubt about it. Look, here we are! Come in, please.

Comfortably settled in, the Prince tells:

- I will be direct, my dear Count. The matter is serious, though but it's a good thing for my compromised heart! Your opinion will decide my future, your daughter's, and consequently, that of your family! I love Madelaine! I never intend to have it as a secret, and today I come to ask her to marry me.

Unable to speak, faced with the Prince's declaration and request, the Count falls silent.

Disguising his great distress, however, he looks to God for strength and asks:

- Have you asked my daughter about this?

- Why, my dear Count, what nonsense! Since when do we ask women such things? Since when do their thoughts are important for our decisions?

- Madelaine is free to decide her own life, your Highness!

- And will she dare to refuse me, my dear Count?

- I have serious reasons to think so!

- Is she engaged to another man?

- Yes, your Highness!

Pale with hatred, he explodes:

- Does she act guided by her own free will, ignoring the Constitutional Powers? Do you look disrespectfully down on them, Count? Or are you doing this on purpose? I am completely unaware of this engagement. Therefore, I repeat my request and I will not accept any negative answer!

- Forgive me, but we will honor our first word!

- You dare defy me?

- Not at all, your Highness! I am just honest, as a gentleman should be. Madelaine is free to decide her own life.

- Do you approve Madelaine's choice over me? I will not let this offense pass!

- Do not misunderstand me, your Highness, I beg you!

- Am I a fool who does not understand what he hears?

- Your Highness distorts my words!

- Am I a sell-out now? You leave me no choice, my Lord Count! I must impose myself and make you understand with whom you are dealing! I have already request and I'll wait for your answer for three days. If you refuse, we will fight a duel! But, listen carefully, in any case, I will not give up on Madelaine! She will be mine above everything and everyone! And now, have a good day!

Giving a slight bow of his head and noisily tapping his shiny boots against each other, Aleksei leaves the room.

The Count feels like he was about to faint. Still, he hears his strong footsteps searching for the exit without being escorted. He touches his head with both hands, feeling it throbbing. He takes a deep breath, trying to calm himself, settles his heart, and goes down toward the guests.

He sees Soraya, happy, chatting enthusiastically with her little friends. Fabian runs frantically through the garden, competing with other boys for a sporting prize.

His heart squeezes; he might be saying goodbye...

He is a man of law and letters; he has never been a fighter. Peaceful by nature, he will never kill; rather, he will let himself be slaughtered!

For the moment, he should shut up and let the festivities take their normal course.

The Prince, coming down the stairs without being seen, spots the Marquess. Angry, he imagines that the Marquess is Madelaine's suitor. He leaves quickly. Few people notice his presence.

Meanwhile, Madelaine and Salústio were busy hiding Gotuza, who arrived at the agreed time, elegant and beautiful. Blending in with the guests, she passed herself off as one of them. She was taken by unknown pupils to meet the others, and then was comfortably installed in the rooms already prepared to receive her. Then, Salústio and Madelaine returned by opposite routes.

Back in his domains, the Prince, furious, goes to his office and begins to seriously think on his own actions. He concludes that once again he had acted hastily. He had not even seen Madelaine!

He should have sought her out, made himself present, solicitous, seductive! In his absence, the other suitors will be able to get close to her, especially, him, the Marquess!

He regrets his impulses. What if he hurts her father? What will she do? She is strong and fearless! She will surely face him, even if she has to die! He could lose her...He despairs. He must rethink his own attitude. The threats made to the Count are difficult to be carried out. The Count is older, not given to arms or fights! He will certainly be ridiculed by his peers!

In haste, he grabs some letterheads and writes a letter.

He calls a messenger and orders him to go, urgently, to deliver it to Count Luiz. Before sealing it, he adds a very rich jewel for Madelaine.

In short time, the Count holds the missive and the gift in his hands.

Opening the seal, in awe, he reads:

"Dear Mr. Count Luiz Santiago Alvarado, my respects!

I hope you have understood me and will forgive my impetus, the one that came from a passionate man! I just don't want you to worry in what I said earlier and forget my threats, as well as the alleged duel between us.

I never intended to assault or harm you in any way!

However, my proposal of marriage to Madelaine, I stand by it. Everyone will see, she will be immensely happy with me!

I count, for this, on your consent and your discretion. Nothing you can say or do will change my feelings and my determination!

Here is a treat for the one we love so much; I hope that she will appreciate it and forgive my absence!

At the next festivities I will be present. I greet you with nobility and admiration!

Prince Aleksei Nikolai Ivanovich"

Surprised, the Count thanks the heavens for the turn the event has taken. He is relieved to be rid of a situation that would undoubtedly be fatal to him. He puts the paper away when he sees Bettine approaching:

- What's the matter, Luiz? You look upset!

- Don't worry, my love! I have faced some problems that have solved!

- Can you explain them to me?

- Later, Bettine, now we are too busy!

- I can see that you are very upset.

- Yes, indeed! When we can talk calmly, I'll tell you. Now, my love, allow me, I will deliver this package to Madelaine! - kissing her lightly on the forehead, he leaves to find his daughter.

Opening the small package, Madelaine shudders as she reads the card:

"*Dearest,*

Forgive my absence! Unexpected setbacks have prevented me from being at your side today! I will come visit you soon.

Accept this present, from a loving and longing heart!

I hug you, affectionately!

Eternally yours,

Prince Aleksei Nikolai Ivanovich"

Tearing discreetly at the card, she calls Corine. Willing, the maid answers and receives from her hands a very rich hair clip made of tiny, pink pearls.

- Take this to mama, Corine! Tell her we'll get more bread for the hungry!

- Yes, *Mademoiselle*! How precious! - she replies, dazzled by the rich ornament.

Charles has arrived in time to witness Madelaine's actions.

He controls his jealousy and curiosity. Hugging her by the waist, he drags her to the musicians' kiosk. They pass happily through the guests and for a few minutes they rehearse several songs together.

A few hours later, with a great display of apparel, overflowing with packages and flowers, accompanied by several servants, who in their turn carry other volumes, Mr. Henry John Stanford - elegant, handsome and overdressed - makes his triumphal entry into the castle.

As he approaches Madelaine, he blatantly ignores the presence of Charles. Noisy and infatuated, he exclaims loudly:

- Dear Madelaine, seeing you is always a renewed pleasure! I bring you presents! Where is your family? I want to meet them!

Delicate and providential, she tells him:

- Dear Henry, I want to introduce you to the Marquess Charles D'Alençon!

Bowing, elegant and indifferent, he greets him and continues:

- Madelaine, I beg you to introduce me to your family!

- Yes, come this way! They will be pleased to meet you! - she answers, polite but confused.

On his own, Charles understands the situation, "Another rival! And how much ostentation!"

After introducing her parents to him, Madelaine tries to get rid of Henry, but he persistently tries to propose her, telling her in a soft voice:

- Madelaine, this is a rare opportunity for me! I have brought you many gifts, I hope you like them. They were specially chosen by me with extreme care!

- Thank you, Henry! I'm sure we'll like them; you shouldn't have done that!

- Oh, Madelaine, it was a pleasure!

Charles, resolute, approaches, excuses himself and takes Madelaine with him. She finally breathes in relief.

Resigned, after a quick chat with the hosts, Henry walks through the castle, always trying to get closer to Madelaine. When find her, he complains:

- Madelaine, I cannot disguise my disappointment at seeing you so insensitive to my presence! You don't know how much effort I have made to finally get here! And, with how much anticipation I came! ... I can bear anyone's indifference but you...! Don't hurt me, my dear.

Kind but resolute, she replies:

- Henry, I thank you with all my heart for your kindness and brotherly affection; however, we have already understood each other regarding my commitment to Charles! I beg you, in God's name: don't create troubles for me!

- I won't, rest assured! But please be indulgent with me, by giving me a little of your attention!

- Henry", she said very patiently, - you shouldn't have come. Today, I will officially announce my engagement with the Marquess! My dear friend, save yourself the suffering of a broken heart, find someone else! We're already talked about this!

- You speak like a truly lawyer's daughter, Madelaine! The heart, however, doesn't understand laws! It simply loves and that's all! Besides, who says I wish to change the course of my feelings?

- Excuse me, but I must insist; save yourself the trouble and leave while there's still time! - Madelaine already has tears in her eyes. She suffers for him. His good friend will be very disappointed... Henry, moved to see her worried about his fate, has the urge to take her in his arms and leave her again. However, this is not the way things happen... It is hard for him to remain calm in this touching moment, even though they are surrounded by so many people... And at this moment he is aware that he loves her too much; much more than he could ever imagine... Controlling his impulses, he replied committed:

- Not at all, my dear. Whatever happens, I will stay. I have this right as any other guest, let me tell you!

- Well, Henry, I give up! Don't forget, I warned you! So, don't count on my complacency! Good-bye! - Nimbly, she leaves, with her stubbornness.

He ecstatically admires her, until she disappears among the alleys... His heart tightens into a tourniquet; from then on, nothing interests him anymore. He has lost all condition to rejoice, to benefit from the beauty of the place and the joyful excitement of the event...

Joining Charles, Madelaine continues welcoming and attending to the various participants of the event.

Tournaments take place repeatedly. There is the effort to surpass themselves with the intention of winning. Those who pay for the competitions make fiery cheering crowds.

The coloring is intense through the diversity of the costumes, the decorations, the polychrome of the flowers. Part of the day has already passed. There is a happy and productive buzz.

Hope intensifies at the end of every painting, at the finishing of a beautiful touch in a beautiful carpet, in the arrangement of natural or artificial flowers, fruit that would fool anyone by pretending to be real, in the woven baskets, in the flower arrangements real ones, in the woven baskets of reeds or thin strips of wood and resin. Pots and jars of baked clay in the most bizarre shapes, raw leather garments, fine lace imitating spider webs, shoes handcrafted with care and whimsy jewelry of all colors and shapes, metal mesh quotas, painted plates, painted dishes, bowls decorated with delicate designs, luxurious harnesses for horses, richly crafted saddles, and more things.

Sonorous and seductive verses, praising love and beauty or the deeds of heroes; religious elegies, hymns to nature, Greek tragedies and the mysteries of Eleusis.

Compositions of enchanting madrigals, light and uncompromising music to the people in their spontaneous knowledge; odes made for the goods and to the idyll that move couples of all times.

Sculptures in wood, stone or clay emerge as if were made by the skilled hands of the sculptors who, with their chisels, transform inexpressive materials into sublime imitations of life.

In the air there is an inaudible sound of praise for work and progress.

The sun, enchanted and smiling, watches and illuminates from above, without warming God's creatures.

Irreverent, the clouds pass quickly, copying the artistic forms below.

People mumbles, in harmony with the melodies.

And the forgetfulness of the world and its sorrows is a natural consequence...

These hours are an elevated congealing of art and culture, of solidarity and faith in a better future.

Bravo, bravissimo!

NOW RECOVERED, MR. JAIME accepts the life that fate had reserved for him in a bitter way. He does account services for former companions of fortune. With his new work, he rents a modest house where he lives with her daughter.

She has said goodbye to school and to her life as a rich and carefree girl. She rejected the Board of Directors' offer to continue studying there until the end of the course. She finished her studies, with much sacrifice, in a different school. She would never accept to live without the luxurious things she had always been accustomed, because she was used to be center of everything because of her wellness and proud self. So, she then entered the world of fighting for her own survival, employing herself in a boutique, as well as giving private lessons. Despite giving the appearance of being calmer, inside she is a volcano of pain and revolt. Along with the bitter memory of the good life before, the decision is made to pursue Henry for revenge.

How often she is humiliated by rich ladies who think they are as important as she once thought she was!

Her father forgave Henry and bravely accept his new reality. She, however, is far from forgiving! She will make him pay for every tear, every sleepless night, every hour of tiredness at work to earn a little bit of the money she uses to had so much of! She feeds this constant hatred, directing her thoughts of revenge toward Henry.

Sometimes she goes to the boarding school and there she talks for a long time with Sister Rosália, but she hides her intentions of revenge.

When she can find the time and the permission of the Mother Superior, the good sister goes to Mr. Jaime's house. He continues his studies, the ones he began at the Estancia with Natacha.

Sister Rosália is delighted with so much knowledge and kindness. At this moment we can visualize them talking:

- Dear friend, where is our Eugene? I don't see her here today!

- She is giving private lessons to two children, the daughters of one of her customers in the boutique. Then she will go to work. Today, she'll be back home very late.

- So, I can talk freely. I have questions that I would like to clarify with my good friend. For example; what do you think about our dear Eugene's state of mind? She worries me!

He stifles a breath before answering:

- Your concern meets mine, sister. I don't believe she is doing well. No matter how much she disguises it, I can see her dejection and her eyes often red from crying! Sometimes, she comes home disgusted by the un-Christian behavior of the ladies who humiliate her for this or that. I conclude that she is not resigned to or oblivious of the great blow that has been our life. I fear for her future, sister! Not the material future, because that comes to us from God, but the spiritual, which has a price that she seems to ignore!

- And my friend, how do you feel now, in this period of adaptation to a new reality?

- Me, sister? - he sighs deeply, looking through the window at the birds singing and building their nest. He thinks they are so beautiful, so confident! Turning to his good friend, he continues: I often feel angry too! You must agree that seeing my daughter paying with her sweat and tears for all the things I used to give her lavishly thanks to the fruit of my honest and hard work! ... That in an evil move by someone more unfortunate than us, the fortunate ones, everything was taken from us! Oh, sister! I must be very strong to not get off balance! Even though I blame myself many times for my absence in those days, judging myself the only responsible for the great loss, I sense that, through those luminous and incomparable days, I was preparing myself for this hard teaching of life! Today, despite everything, I try to keep my feet firmly on the ground and my hearth turned to the heavens; giving to the Creator what I am and what I still have, thankful, always! I am conscious that in this world everything is given to us on loan! For this, and for something else that I never understood, but that must have its reasons, I worked so hard and ended up in this situation! Remembering him, in his multiple torments, I identify with his pain and indignation, but above all with his strength, courage and faith!

I know that I must forgive, I do it every new day, so that God will also forgive me! Little by little, the wounds will heal, as I free myself from my wounds... - his last words echo in the room, when sister Rosalia, eyes filled with tears of respect and admiration, declares:

- Dearest friend! From this well-formed heart, God expects a lot! Heaven help Eugene to follow your example! The tears that you both have been crying will wash your souls, purifying them. Jesus suffered much more! Who are we? Imperfect creatures, bankrupt, in need of mercy!

May God strengthen you in your purposes and sustain you in the struggle you need to survive, giving you the health and the means, you need! Little by little, as you said, your heart, strengthened, will conquer the desired peace! You can always count on my prayers and my friendship.

As you know, mi family died very soon, leaving me alone. After the orphanage, very young, I entered the religious life to which I felt strongly inclined, and in it I am more and more fulfilled, in fact, I believe it is my true path.

You, my dear friend, and your daughter have become a family for me! I am grateful of the affection that unites us and I thank the father every day of my life!

Deeply moved, he confirms:

For us, sister, you are more than a relative! We love you so much!

- I am sure of it, thank you! Have you had any news from our dear Natacha?

- Yes, she writes to us regularly! I dream of being able to return to the ranch one day!

- Frankly, if God wanted to give me a gift, I would like to accompany you! To see Natacha again would gladden my heart, besides the great pleasure I would feel in getting to know the famous Estancia Santa Sofia!

- Let's trust in God! The time and the opportunities are in his hands! Ah, sister! What a beautiful day I lived there! I may never have others like them!

- Well, who knows? Life's surprises are not always bad!

Well, I must return. Kiss Eugene goodbye for me!

- Yes, sister. Thank dear sister Berta for the delicious peach compotes! We'll be visiting her soon! Ask her to pray for us! And especially for Eugene, who now faces serious conflicts.

- Dear friend, in life we take the bitter medicine that will cure our sick soul. Everything is part of our growth. I know you know this! Our dear girl will grow stronger through the difficulties she faces!

- I fear for her future, sister!

- Rest easy! God knows the way to our hearts! I feel that Eugene will still be very happy! And maybe in a quite surprisingly way!

- Why do you say that, sister?

- Intuition, perhaps, my friend! Farewell!

- Farewell, dear sister Rosália!

* * *

AT THE END OF THE festivities a delicious supper is served, right after the prize-giving, starting at eighteen o'clock, traditionally. After a two-hour meal, the hosts bid farewell to the guests letting them know that the program has been fulfilled. In this disciplined organization excesses of any kind are prevented.

As this moment draws near, the Count, full of fatherly satisfaction, invites everyone into the great hall and asks for silence. Being heard, he exclaims in a loud and clear voice:

— Dear gentlemen, noble and brotherly people who share with us the bread of good coexistence! Today, as at other times, we drink the captious wine of solidarity! Imbued with the same ideals we welcome with open arms as many as brought us their purposes of life purposes, yearning to realize their dearest dreams!

Bathed in their own talents, they displayed their work with responsibility, demonstrating the best of what they know how to do, making their best efforts and, not infrequently to the point of sacrifice! Happy are we in this unity that unites us, emulating us in the search for true brotherhood!

Today, several personalities have entered these portals, each with their own individual characteristics: honest, respectful and worthy! Those who are not in harmony have arrived here by mistake and, certainly, if they have not already left, they felt displaced!

We know that the real purpose of these meetings is to stimulate the incessant progress of the arts and culture, most especially giving support to those who, possessing the talent and the will, lack the amassed resources!

Above all, we intend to make them feel supported in this fight for the victory that beckons, when effort is allied to vocation! May they be crowned with laurels, on their own merits!

Finally, we come to the end of the various competitions, and it is necessary to crown the victors, with ever-renewed pleasure!

We want to thank each and every one, who in some way contributed to the success of this endeavor! In a moment we will raise our cups, saluting life, the opportunity to be together, and today's winners!

Bravo, bravissimo! To those who strove to reach the goal, best wishes for health, peace and glory!

We are grateful to the sponsors who invest generously in artists, with the goal of enjoying the good and the beautiful, in a thirst for real progress! This is what you will talk about in the future, grateful to receive the blessed inheritance of enlightened minds, in the concert of hearts! They will be praised for allowing the survival of the history of peoples in their various particularities, through the art of all times! They are the divine presence on Earth for the fraternal exchange of means and gifts that every one of you possess, in benefit of the world's balance! To the various participants and competitors, we will call "God's builders"!

Enthusiastic applause explodes and he elegantly asks for silence to continue:

- Today, in a particular way, we bring our hearts in celebration because we have an important announcement to make! – Trying to control the emotions that betrays him, he continues. - I am the messenger of the family in the happy announcement that our beloved daughter Madelaine will today officiate with us, her engagement to the noble Marquess Charles D'Alençon! As of today, we can consider him as a member of our family!

He comes to extend the ideals of life in which we believe!

I give you my permission and my blessing, hoping that soon we will be here together celebrating the wedding!

Joyful sounds explode in the hall.

Thrilled, Madelaine and Charles are the target of all eyes and comments.

In the eyes of Countess Bettine, tears of joy shine like pearls.

With the first enthusiasms, the women bow down, elegant, greeting them and their family. In their graceful movements one can hear the friction of the lace and brocade.

Bowing, this time the men approach in formation, and disciplined; they click their heels, raise their right hand with a closed fist, while the left is held over the chest, and exclaim in unison:

- *Bravo, bravo, bravissimo!* Health, peace and the blessings of heaven to the future bride and groom!

Next, the same 'contingent', hats in hand, bows in deep reverence, stands up again, and burst into applauses.

The greetings keep coming. The friends are thrilled with the event that they had already expected.

Then you hear the noises of the servants arriving with the various and finest wines for the toast.

But... at the end of the immense room, livid, Henry John watched it all, pale like death. He feels like he is in a terrible nightmare. After all, hadn't Madelaine warned him? Why did he insist on staying?

Seeing the faces of some other guests, he concludes that he is not the only one disappointed; in him, however, the moral pain has become physical.

Feels like he is stuck to the ground, unable to move. Direct eyes like daggers to his heart. And not even a glance from the one who is the reason of his life!

He wishes something terrible would happen that would strike everyone down!

He feels the most unfortunate of mortals. On the verge of weakening because tears are announcing themselves treacherously, he rushes forward, gathers his entourage, climbs into his luxurious carriage, and returns to Ruede-La-Chapelle, painfully disappointed...

To his ears still sound the harmonic and vibrant:

"*Bravo, bravo, bravissimo...!*"

Without the slightest modesty, alone in the cabin of the vehicle, he cries, opening the floodgates of his soul...

Slowly, while crying, he closes the curtains of the vehicle. His tears fall abundantly on the silks and lace of his elegant and fine garment... His whole body shakes convulsively...

He feels an unbearable pain; the urge to scream to alleviate the anguish that dominates him crucially ...

It's been a long time since Henry cried...

After the guests leave, Madelaine and Charles go to see Gotuza.

They find her in a good mood and comfortably settled in.

After greeting her warmly, Charles drags his fiancée outside; they hardly had time to be alone, so many greetings and celebrations.

They are walking together when they encounter Corine.

Madelaine is surprised and, scolding her, leads her away from Gotuza's chambers.

Under the perceptive gaze of her fiancé, she realizes she has been imprudent.

He takes the opportunity to ask her what she fears; why she hides Gotuza and why she has driven Corine away. Striving to be as convincing as possible, she argues:

- Dr. Sergei has recommended absolute care for Gotuza's tranquility and Corine is very agitated! We are protecting her, just to get her back on her feet soon.

Standing in front of her, looking to her eyes, he insists:

- Tell me, why do I have the impression that you are hiding something from me?

Laying her head on his shoulder, she expresses herself lovingly, asking him:

- Trust me, Charles!

Squeezing her tightly against his chest, kissing her perfumed hair, he says:

- I trust you, Madelaine! But the thought that you might be in some danger, I shudder! I have no right to question you, still, but I know your courage and dedication! I also know that if you choose to hide something from me, it will always be for the good of others! But, by God, protect yourself! If something happens to you, I won't survive! I will always and above all respect everything you consider most sacred: your freedom! However, I love you too much, to not to be afraid!

Promise me that you will take care of yourself, for God's sake!

- I promise, Charles!

- If you weren't you, I wouldn't love you, Madelaine! At most, I'd give you an ardent passion for your beauty, but what I feel for you is an immense love, physical and spiritual! This feeling embraces heaven and earth, in a cosmic integration!

Madelaine, happy, smiles gratefully and advises:

- Now let's go, otherwise they'll think we've run away!

- And that's not a bad idea! We'd certainly put up a hell of a fight!

Impetuous, he snatches her to his breast and kisses her, ardently.

She, immerse in happiness, fully respond to him.

FLAWLESS IN HIS UNIFORM, General Antoine Belfort performs his duties, while planning to destroy André, thinking in destroy his dreams and... maybe even his life!

It will be an "eye for an eye" in his own way. He must be careful and act in the shadows. He doesn't want to take any risks. His dark thoughts torment him:

"If you only knew, you scoundrel, the great feeling I harbored in my heart for her! No, she was not like the others we knew! You know no limits, André! For I will be a barrier in your way! I want to see you suffering at my feet!

Ah, Jeannete! My idolized and unforgettable love! Where are you now? I think I hear you calling me sweetly! Why didn't you choose me? I really loved you! He destroyed you...!" – Thick tears come to his eyes, small and cruel, but he, resolute wipes them away and hurries out into the street. The strong wind whips his face, ruffling his thin red hair. Against the windows, he imposes his body in wide, noisy strides. His feet know twisting paths, the paths of traps, of torture, of mercilessness...

A few days later, André of Villefort, at the Portal of Light, receives a letter to appear at the Royal Prison of Paris, which he does between perplexed and terrified.

On this date, his private tragedy began for him.

Everything had been done with full knowledge of the facts and highly competent in a context of which André himself was a part of.

Now, isolated, far from home (he had been violently put in a closed carriage in the middle of the night), he doesn't know where he is. After days and days of hunger, thirst, and mistreatment, he is broken. He rightly concludes that he will never emerge from this strange nightmare into which he has been thrown.

Let's go back a few days, to the Portal da Luz, Vila Francesa, to understand how it all happened:

Corine is received by André, who hopes to hear something interesting about the woman of his dreams.

- So, Corine? I'm looking forward for the news!

Counterfeited, she fears what she has to say and stutters:

- News?...! Well, Baron... I don't know what to tell you.

I came on my own...

- Come on, Corine, speak up! I don't have much time. Besides, this way you're a nuisance to me! What have you come for, anyway?

- I came to ask you...

- More money? Well, you're insatiable, eh, little one?

- No, it's not that! I've decided to work here, under your orders! - she exclaims, finally, all at once.

Choleric, he explodes:

- And who told you I wish this? You work for Madelaine and need you to stay there!

- Yes, I know, but... at the moment, I feel insecure there! Madelaine charges me with responsibilities because, in order to serve you, Baron, I'm always contradicting her! I make up a lot of lies and fail with my obligations in the castle. There, everyone has his or her roles, even the family! The success of all the enterprises, of which there are many, depends on it! They are tireless and dedicated! Madelaine is very energetic and will fire me at any moment! My heart warns me!

— I already have too many servants! Besides, I need you there! What good use would you do to me here?

— I'll be able to lure her here! The Baron will think of how to do it and I will obey, as always! To prove to you my fidelity, I will tell you something very important.

— Yes, and what is it? Tell me, Corine!

— Do you realize that Madelaine, right now, is always asking me about you! It seems to me that she is finally interested in you!

— Are you sure about this, Corine? Oh, at last she notices me! I knew it! — he stands up suddenly, eyes shining, a wide smile on his lips.

— Of your inquiries I am sure, but... It's hard to understand *Mademoiselle* Madelaine! — exclaims Corine, frightened.

— Why do you say that?

— So, the Baron doesn't know yet?

— What should I know, Corine? If I was expecting your visit and only today you showed up! Did something very important happen? Stop being so reticent!

— Well, the Baron won't like what I have to tell you. That's why I'm so confused by the behavior of *Mademoiselle*!

— You make me despair, Corine! I end up losing patience with you! Say it all at once! — he bangs heavily on the table, causing Corine to startle.

Already regretting talking about the subject that is sure going to exasperate him, she babbles fearfully:

— Get ready, Baron, because... *Mademoiselle* Madelaine has made official her engagement to the Marquess!

Pale, his hands shaking, he falls heavily into his desk chair. Angry, he runs his tapered fingers through his hair, full of hatred and revolt. Between his teeth, he speaks to himself:

- Where have you been, Antoine? Treacherous snake! This meddlesome Marquess must disappear!

Corine moves, restless. With a wave of his hand, he orders her to leave his office, without defining himself as to his situation.

He calls for Mateus, he needs to do something. He doesn't know what yet. The servant appears, but comes to warn him:

- Baron, someone is waiting to see you!

- I'm not here for anyone, Mateus! Except for the general!

- But the person in question is an officer!

- Well, what does he want here?

- I don't know, sir! According to him, the matter is confidential!

Beating his forehead, André exclaims:

- Why, I've been so distracted! He must be a messenger from Antoine! Bring him in! And then leave!

- Yes, sir!

The servant leaves and returns accompanied by an elegant man, with hard, indecipherable features.

André waits for Mateus to step aside and then exclaims, holding out his hand to the stranger:

- To what do I owe your visit?

Ignoring his gesture, he replies harshly:

- I am not a visitor. I am the bearer of a court summons for Baron André Brumel of Villefort!

In shock, André replies:

- Now, from whom do I receive orders like that?

- From the Royal Prison; from the department of affairs directly connected with his majesty the King!

Feeling sick, André feels his legs weaken. He understands the risk he is running. Trembling, he asks:

- Isn't it possible that there is some mistake? I fear nothing! My life is an open book! I am a nobleman, faithful to his majesty!

- If you are the person in question, there is no mistake!

If you do not present yourself within two days, you will be arrested where you are and taken by force!

- Please, sir, can you tell me something in advance?

- No, sir! I am simply the bearer of the summons! Anything else?

- No, thank you, sir. I will be there on the appointed day and time!

- Wise decision! Have a good day!

He answers the courtesy with a slight inclination of his head, André watches him disappear through his office door. He thinks he is dreaming. He decides to go look for Antoine. Only he can help him in these circumstances.

In his luxurious carriage, he makes a real journey to all possible and imaginable places, without, however, finding him.

The only information he receives is that he has traveled on a special mission, in the service of his majesty, to a distant place, with no date of return.

Desperate, André sees the time running out, without being able to find anything concrete to help or defend him.

His own lawyers seem confused and unstable.

Accompanied by them, he went to the police station and was questioned about unconnected facts that disturbed him considerably, this shows him the true intention of confusing him and his defenders.

The aim of incriminating him at all costs was clear. His powers, titles, name, all in vain. Equally involved in a biased manner, his lawyers quickly tried to save their own skin, leaving him by his own! ...

Overwhelmed, he returned home, more unhappy and unprotected than any sewer rat! He was ordered not to leave the house because he would be questioned again. Silent, he arrived at his palace, gloomy and downcast. He decides to get organized.

He must anticipate the probable events; dark prognoses reach his anxious, restless mind. After a comforting bath, he lies down and sleeps. The next day, he calls his private servant:

- Mateus, for the next few days I must go away! I must travel! At my absence you must control everything as if I were here!

I demand fidelity above all else!

In the great hall are some of my employees. Call them because I must organize my goods. Send them in!

While I work with them, prepare my luggage with everything I am used to take with me. Do your best, because I don't know how long I can stay!

After interminable hours, the employees leave André's office, overflowing with large, bulky folders.

Next, he requests again the presence of the servant:

- Listen, Mateus, when I return, I will hold you accountable for everything that falls under your purview! Keep strong hand with the servants. These people only work under your responsibility! Watch Louise! When I come back, I want an account of everything!

Corine will come to work here. Bring her under strict surveillance! Let her with Louise, both will be useful to me; I have plans for them! Now, go!

André could not see the evil glint in Mateus eyes, nor could he see his malefic smile.

He retired to his bed, trying to rest, but failing to do so.

He spent a few days feverishly agitated.

On a mild night, he went out to breathe, near his house, under a sky full of stars and was violently approached, gagged and subdued. He was thrown into a closed carriage, with black curtains, which took an unknown route. Arriving at an almost inhospitable place, he was pushed into a shadowy fortress and thrown into a cubicle, without any kind of comfort, from which he desperately cries for help and freedom in vain.

IN ESTANCIA SANTA SOFIA, Natacha suffers the harassment of her cousins. Her parents doubt her fears, which they think are unfounded, but in truth, they also seem to fear their nephews.

Despite this, she goes on with her normal life. Whenever she wishes, she goes to the woods to dance and, on her return, faces aflutter shoes in her hands, tired by the effort, she feels refreshed. In these moments, the world seems like a simple background to her. It is like only she and nature were real.

In her studies, she unveils each new day the inconclusive truth that comes from God. She reaches levels of consciousness that most creatures cannot reach. Not rarely, she participates in beautiful phenomena that move her to tears of emotion. Her heart is closer and closer to the Divinity.

Her brother Sacha has traveled to Russia. After marrying Olga, his fiancée, he will be the manager of his in-laws' business in that country.

Even though she is overburdened with her many duties, Natacha finds time for her studies, meditation and the reverent observation of beings and things.

One of her favorite places is the main square. There, amused, she watches the arrival and departure of the various carriages at their usual schedules.

Silent, she is sometimes surprised by scenes and facts from the past interpenetrating the present. They are, in fact, two different dimensions, in an ignored coexistence: "ghosts"

wearing ancient robes, beautifully caged steeds, the clang of fighting weapons, and not infrequently, she hears moans, imprecations and cries of pain...

At these moments, she shakes her beautiful head and everything disappears.

Upon seeing her, two men comment:

- Look, Terence, there she is again! Does she remember anything? How beautiful and kind!

- Indeed, Carrel, agrees the other, when she is here, the air becomes lighter and there's a certain happiness!

And when we need to stay at the ranch, she makes generous concessions! Some find her eccentric. I wish they were all like that!

- God bless her! Come on, Terence, duty calls!

Let's leave her alone! Look, the carriages are coming!

From one of them, a young man hurries to get off after making sure of something. His elegance and beauty are remarkable. He cannot pass unnoticed. Taller than average, he wears practical, luxurious clothes. His face is perfect, his eyes the color of the sky, his lips are flushed and smiling, showing pearly white teeth. As he passes, admiring glances accompany his proud and sure steps.

Carrying a small suitcase, he walks toward Natacha.

Distracted, she doesn't notice his approach, and when he touches her lightly on her shoulder, she is startled. Looking reproachfully at him, she hears:

- Forgive me, but I needed to touch you to make sure you are not a mirage!

Surprised at him and his attitude, she protests:

- Now, who are you? Since when do you go around touching people to make sure they exist?

- It's not a habit, *Mademoiselle* - he defends himself. - I only did it because of you!

- And why with me? Can't one be at peace? How dare you?

Fascinated by her beauty, which is even more accentuated in that exaltation, he makes a wide gesture of reverence in front of her:

- Forgive me, Majesty! I had no intention of offending you.

Crossing her arms and looking even more serious, she inquires:

- Do you amuse yourself like this, at people's expense, all the time?

- No! Nevertheless, I am tempted to continue, if my daring has resulted in these wonderful colors on your face, beautiful young lady! I thought that only I had the power to see you sitting there, as I have done at other times!

You seemed magical, and I was tempted to accept the challenge of find out whether you were an enchanted fairy! If I have offended you, forgive me, and if I can do penance, I will spare no effort! I would like to redeem myself before you!

She, hands on her waist, like a child defending herself, answer:

- All right! I apologize for the outbursts, but you can't go around scaring people!

- I don't do that, believe me! Today I decided to talk to you, and here I am! You really exist! But I still find you magical, unreal!

- And we are back where we started? And speaking of starting, look! Your carriage is gone! Great punishment!

- What better penance could I want? As you can see, all that I need is with me. I had already intended to stay and get to know you better!

- And how will you do that?

- I don't know yet, but I will find a way! Since you are normal, you will not require me to make reckless forays into the realm of fantasy!

To Natacha, he seems to have emerged from the mists of some distant and mysterious past, part of her visions?

And she can almost see him: dressed in shining armor, shield with carved coat of arms, helmet of fluttering white feathers, spear in hand, white fiery horse covered with a saddle embroidered with his heraldry and silver harness, eyes looking to the horizon, dreamy...What do you seek? The Holy Grail? Who can know? - Ecstatic, her eyes seem to cross him with ease, unraveling his past...

He, fascinated, while waiting for her to return from her ramblings, declares:

- Well, returning to the ground we walk on, mortals that we are, I need to tell you that I have various needs, and not all of them are romantic! How about helping me, indicating a place where I can stay? I intend to stay here for a few days!

Seeming not to have heard him, she goes on analyzing him, carefully. She realizes that she has never met anyone so beautiful, elegant, and intelligent! He's a real fairy tale Prince! Refined in the smallest trappings of his attire, noble gestures, luminous eyes that rival the color of the sky. His long, brown, curly, silky hair reflects the sunlight and falls over his shoulders like waterfalls...

Delighted, he lets himself be admired. He is confident; he knows his own attributes.

- Do you always travel like this, with all this elegance? - she doesn't hold back.

- No! The true is, I wanted to impress you! For this reason, I put on my best clothes! - he clarifies, letting out a hearty laugh.

- Do you take anything serious? At some point can you do it?

- Yes, my dear...

- Natacha!

- Natacha. Like just now, when I asked you to show me a good hostel!

- Well, you are talking to the right person, Sir...

- Marcel!

- Mr. Marcel, I live in the best one in the region!

- Can you take me there?

- Certainly! Do you want to go on foot or by carriage?

- On foot, without a doubt! Besides enjoying the region, we will have more time to talk. If I passed the test, he says, bending down and looking into her eyes, seductively.

Blushing strongly, she sharply replies:

- I don't know what you're talking about! Nevertheless, for now I will give you a vote of confidence! I'll wait for the near future to evaluate you better!

He bursts into a loud laugh, leaving her disconcerted.

Noticing her embarrassment, he stops and asks, conciliatorily:

- Don't be upset! I just found it amusing to be under trial as effective as it is desirable! You can judge my character or whatever you wish! Be my guest!

Even more confused, she concludes that with him she needs to be more subtle.

A local family approaches and greets Natacha with affectionate words before going on their way. He observes. They continue through beautiful green forests, enjoying the balmy air and listening to the birds singing. When crossing paths with other people, she smiles at them and, occasionally, makes some pleasant comment. He can see how much she is loved in that community. He makes remarks about the natural exuberance of the place and, on the other hand, he sees her knowledge and love for nature.

Breathing in hustle and bustle, he concludes that it was a great idea to walk.

Some distance away he glimpses a large stately building, all white and surrounded by flowers.

- That's the housing I told you about, Natacha explained.

- That wonderful postcard? My goodness! Is it real?

- Do you often doubt your own eyes?

- Often, because I am a great dreamer! If what I see is a dream, I will wake up very disappointed!

- I also never get tired of praising all this beauty! Well, Mr. Marcel, here we are!

Stopping in front of the beautiful house, he pauses in reverent observation.

At the reception desk, Natacha leaves him and goes to get her father to introduce him.

She returns and surprises Marcel with his luggage at his side, keys in hand, waiting.

Mr. Korsanikov, with the tact and practice that are peculiar to him, greets him:

- Welcome, sir! We hope you feel very well here! I am Konstantin Korsanikov, Natacha's father and the owner of this resort! We are at your disposal!

Shaking the hand offered to him, he declares:

- Thank you! My name is Marcel, and from what I can see, I conclude that I will stay less time than I would like!

- Thank you!

In a rush, Natacha asks him for the keys and returns them to the counter. Then she invites him to follow her. Arriving on the second floor, she opens the rooms that Mr. Jaime had occupied.

The father, surprised, sees her opening doors and windows, settling the boy in.

The boy, satisfied, looks around, nods his head in approval, and goes to the window to see what he can see from there.

- Excuse me, sir! I have other things to do. Natacha, will do you the honors of the house! - declares Mr. Korsanikov kindly.

- Thank you for everything, Mr. Korsanikov!

- We are here to serve you, Mr. Marcel! - so saying, he comes down.

He goes to the big dining-room and calls his wife.

- What do you want, Kostia? - she says as she answers him.

- Have you seen the new guest who arrived with our daughter?

- I couldn't. I was and am too busy. Why?

- He's nice and our daughter seems to like him!

Imagine, she's installed him in Mr. Jaime's quarters, which she preserves so much! Do you understand what I mean?

- No, in fact I don't understand what you mean! - she replies, impatient.

- Oh, woman, think! She is single, beautiful, and has never dated!

Who knows if this guy has interested her?

- I don't believe it. She must have gotten tired of guarding those quarters, that's all!

- No, she would not rent those quarters to just anyone. It was, in fact, a special way to treat this guest! And he is quite handsome, by the way! Very elegant too! You, as a mother, should ask about the feelings of our daughter!

- No, Kostia, I won't do this! She is independent and sincere; she knows what she does and what she wants! Nevertheless, I will be attentive, rest assured!

- At least that much, woman! Farewell!

- See you, Kostia! - she continues working. For the moment, she is in charge of the menus, according to the variety of fruits, vegetables of the season.

Stopping for a moment, she goes to one of the windows and looks up at the intense blue sky. Raising his hand to his chest, she sighs and almost in a whisper exclaims to herself:

- Our dear Natacha doesn't seem to have been born for marriage! She's so strange... she frightens men!

Meanwhile, Natacha helps Marcel to settle in comfortably.

After she leaves, the boy concludes that he will be able to enjoy the best comfort. The rooms are airy and clean; on the bed, spotless sheets scented with air of the forest. In the bathroom, the set of towels is exquisite.

On the bedroom floor, rich carpeting and comfortable pillows. By the window, padded seats in thick, brightly colored checkered fabric.

Curtains allow the room some darkened.

- A king could live here without boredom! - he exclaims, happily.

After a comforting bath, he throws himself on the soft bed and sleeps heavily...

* * *

AT THE PORTAL DA LUZ, Vila Francesa, in André's absence, the days pass by very strange.

With a fist of steel, Mateus commands in his peculiar arrogance.

He waits for the boss to stay away longer; he has own plans to execute in his absence.

"The Baron didn't even say goodbye! He told me to prepare his luggage, and he didn't even take it! He must have left in a hurry!" - he thinks.

He watches Corine very closely and gives Louise special treatment - he is madly in love with her. He intends to conquer her and make her his wife.

At this very moment he is investigating André's chambers.

In the garden, Louise, alone, thinks on the latest events:

"I wonder what is happening? André disappears and Mateus controls everything now?...! I feel in danger! His glances show his intentions towards my person!"

Corine appears and she calls out:

- Please, Corine, come here!

- I don't think so, *Mademoiselle*!

- Tell me, do you know where André is?

- No, *Mademoiselle*. We were told he was going on a trip! - In Corine's eyes you could see the strangeness of the question. After all, Louise, being his sister, is not informed?

And Louise goes on:

- But none of us saw him leave! He even left his luggage! How can he be traveling without them?

- Indeed... Very strange, isn't it?

- Yes, indeed! It all intrigues me, Corine!

- When he returns, we will know everything!

- You're right, Corine! But... listen to me: What is the possibility that we bring Madelaine here? You say she's sensible, charitable and above all courageous! I need a friend like that, especially now... Although Mateus will try to stop us... But if he does, I'll be harsh with him!

- Well, what a coincidence! *Mademoiselle* Madelaine is planning to come and see you! She told me so.

- Ah, thank God! And you, how do you feel, away from the Alvarado castle?

- Very bad! Mateus torments me too much! I'll get out of here when I had the first opportunity. I can work somewhere else.

- Don't leave me, Corine, for God's sake! I'm afraid of Mateus!

- He threatens you?...! Isn't he afraid of the boss? Your brother will defend you, *Mademoiselle*.

- Of course, Corine. But only when he's here. For now, don't leave here, I beg you!

- Alright, you can count on me.

Today, I must go to the Alvarado castle to get some things that were left with my friend Solange! I will take the opportunity to confirm the visit of *Mademoiselle* Madelaine!

- You do that Corine, and may God bless you!

Hours later, well dressed as always, Corine leaves.

Mateus asks for her and Louise tells him that she sent her to do some shopping. He, annoyed, keeps quiet.

* * *

ONE DAY, Eugene comes across a former employee of his father's, named Gualberto, on the street. Equally surprised, he stops to greet her:

- Dear Miss Eugene! How are you? Is Sir. Jaime doing well?

- I can say we're fine, thank you, Gualberto!

- I hardly recognize you! What a transformation!

- How long has it been since we've seen each other?

- Since I started a new job!

- So, you don't know!

- Don't know what, Miss Eugene?

- What happened to us. Listen to this:

She tells the ex-employee everything. Him, with a certain amount of astonishment, listens attentively. At the end, he gets it off his chest:

- What a disaster! Yet this was to be expected! The manager's ambition was visible since the start. For a long time, he had been creating serious problems for everyone! Many of us left because of him... Now everything has sense. His behavior was sordid!

Indeed, what a scoundrel, eh?

- Please, Gualberto, search your memory for something that might help me! Have you ever heard information about certain places or addresses, that we didn't know about it? I need some reference point!

- Let me see... As you know, I left to join an import-export company, where your father was dispatching according to his needs.

I remember something that intrigued me greatly in that time: a company, while checking several goods, I found, among them, Henry's address on the sender. They were precious works of art, and utensils of the most varied kinds; all packed with great care. I thought they were his father's commercial transactions, dispatched by him. Now, listening everything that you have told me...

Oh, God! These were your things! That were your goods, part of your house!

- No doubt about it, Gualberto. Do you remember the customer? For God's sake, make an effort! - Eugene begs, pale as death, showing great anxiety.

- Let me see... the customer's name was that of a company in Paris... Yes, that's right... at Paris center...

- Ah, finally! Thank you, Gualberto! Asking for the address would be too much, isn't it?

- Yes, it's been a while! I can't remember...

- Thank you, you've helped me a lot!

- You're welcome! My regards to your father.

- Thank you, sir. Farewell.

- Farewell, Miss Eugene! - Gualberto stands there, thinking in everything he's heard, lamenting his former boss.

A few minutes later, Eugene, flushed and restless, knocks on the door of a luxurious mansion. They answered, she enters quickly and, crossing several halls, reaches a garden surrounded by rooms, with a refreshing fountain in the center.

Among the flowers, she catches a glimpse of her friend Marianne playing with her two beautiful children, two-year-old chubby twins. The little ones jump and evade her attempts to grab them. Their laughs are music to Eugene, who loves them very much. She has become too attached to these children.

She admires them, tenderly, without being seen.

That good friend had been endowed with every happiness a woman can aspire to: a deeply loving and devoted husband, two beautiful children, incalculable possessions, and the longed-for peace.

Marianne looks stunning in her white gauze dress. Her silky brown hair, pinned high on her head, stubbornly falling over her eyes in cascades.

Blushing, bright eyes, happy, she runs into Eugene:

- Ah, how nice to have arrived! Help me, these little demons have already tire me out!

After kissing Marianne, Eugene calls out:

- Come here, my loves!

Running towards her, the two of them collide with her, heavily, almost knocking her over. Effusive, she kisses them, receiving in return other kisses and hugs.

The nanny arrives and takes them to the bath. Reluctantly, they leave in a whimper.

Destroying the calmed air of moments before, Eugene takes a deep breath.

Perspicacious, Marianne comments:

- Let's sit down! I notice you're tense! What's wrong, my friend?

Sighing, Eugene replies, exalted:

- Coming here, I ran into an ex-employee of my father's. His name is Gualberto and he was unaware of the sad events that involving us. He works in an import-export firm.

She briefly recounts the conversation she had with Gualberto and, at the end, bursts out angrily:

- Indeed, Henry! I take my hat off to you, my father's administrator! You were as sordid and thieving as anyone! - The tears come to her eyes.

- Calm down, Eugene! It's all over now! - her friend asks.

- You are wrong, Marianne! It's happening "here" inside, every instant, feeding my hatred and my revolt! - she explodes, beating her chest.

- Eugene, Eugene, forget it! We love you! Your father's dedication is worthy of praise! My children adore you! My husband is your friend! And our dear sister Rosália keeps snuggling us, as if we were still fragile adolescents!

- I recognize all this, Marianne! I am not ungrateful! I love you all equally! I am deeply grateful for your kindness in opening the doors of your home to me as if it belonged to me too...

- And so it does, Eugene!

- Thank you! However, nothing you can do or say will change my desire for revenge!

- I'm sorry, dear friend...

- Don't be sorry, help me find him! Don't weaken me; I must be strong and determined to collect, hard, all that he owes me!

- No, Eugene, don't ask that kind of help! You must be protected from yourself! When you wake up from this lethargy, life will have pass! You don't live...

- You are wrong again, Marianne! I live this revenge minute by minute! I enjoy, in anticipation, the pleasure I will feel when I see with that scoundrel!

- Don't do this! Build yourself another life!

Change those feelings that make you suffer!

You hide from everything and everyone! The brother of my dear Hans is always sighing for you! He's a great guy and a great catch! But you shut yourself away, just like an oyster! Forgive Henry, Eugene, and think of yourself!

- Forgive? - she replies, standing up, exalted. - Do you know how many nights I stay awake, despite the physical fatigue? The effort I make to hide from my father the abundant tears I shed on my pillow? Of the Amenti torments experienced by my spirit thirsting for revenge? The great disappointment that I carry, for having been robbed of a future I cherished? How can you understand me? You are and always been good, Marianne!

- You are too, Eugene! I know your essence! The one you insist on hiding!

Letting go of her friend who tries to hug her, she continues unyielding:

- You are wrong, Marianne, I am not as you think! You forgive me because you are my friend, my sister! I must remain vigilant!

Ready for the decisive confrontation! I feel like a general who doesn't sleep before the final battle!

- God, my friend, how can you talk like that? And after all this, will you have peace?

- I don't know! I don't want to know! Let me go, Marianne! Let me follow my impulses! - Out of control, she bursts into a convulsive weeping.

Drawing closer again, Marianne hugs her, trying to calm her. She asks the maid for some tea and helps her sip it down to the last drop.

Slowly, Eugene calms herself. Taking a deep breath, she looks around, without much interest, tired of her outbursts. Turning to her friend, she apologizes:

- Forgive me! I have no right to come to your house and steal your peace...

- No one can steal the peace we build within ourselves, dear Eugene. One day I will see you like this, too. I have faith in God!

- Who knows, right? - she exclaims - Why are you so patient with me? When I have been so bad with you...!

- Oh, Eugene! Girlish nonsense! I knew you needed my friendship! Sister Rosalia gambled on this affection! And she was right, my dear!

Today we are adults, we have matured! Forget the mistakes and don't commit yourself to others!

- I will never be grateful enough, Marianne!

- Our friendship is true and needs no thanks, Eugene!

- You are right! I thank God for this!

- In his name, I must tell you, everything you will do, good or bad, will reach our hearts! Think on your father, Eugene!

- I will spare them, rest assured!

- Maybe you can't! Often, the consequences of our actions are beyond our control. Careful, I beg you...! - The twins already returning, request the attention of both of them. Matters... closed, everyone goes for a snack...

Sometime later, determined and unable to continue pretending, Eugene leaves for Paris, foolish and lonely.

Her father already tried to dissuade her, but it was in vain.

Arriving in Paris, Eugene rented a room in a modest hostel. During the trip, she had the urge to return and forget everything, following the advice of those who love her, but imprisoned by her own passions, she decides to do the opposite. She writes to her father, reassuring and informing him where she is.

At this moment, looking at the ceiling, lying down, she remembers the conversation she had with her father. His energetic and loving voice still rings in her ears:

- Think, Eugene! Your life may become a never-ending search! You'll miss the best years of your life! Bury the past and live the present! Be rational and not impulsive!

- I can't, my father! I swore to myself that I would go all the way! Don't know if I will achieve what I want; however, I will made an effort to exorcise the ghosts that haunt me, charging me to make amends with Henry! I can see that you are getting stronger every day and in good health. This has led me to this sincerity and to the decision to follow the trail of that serpent! Forgive me for doing exactly what you have forbidden me! Pray to God for me and give me your blessing, my father!

- I give you my blessing, dear daughter, but I do not support your intentions; have great faith in God! He will avenge us! If you really loved me, you wouldn't go!

- Though you doubt it, I love you, above all else!

- Know that I will not stay here, alone and waiting for you. I'm going to Estancia Santa Sofia. With the savings I've managed to amass, I intend to spend some time there, while you insist on this madness!

In case you give up these purposes that I condemn and want to meet me, I'll be there. You know the address and have the right direction. Some days, I will come here, to keep our house in order.

- This makes me happy! You will find peace there!

- How, if I'm constantly worried about you? Ah, stubborn daughter! May God keep you safe!

A few days later, amid tears and difficult goodbyes, she traveled to Paris.

Sir. Jaime, on the other hand, before leaving, went to the school to invite Sister Rosália:

- Dear Sister, now that Eugene has decided, against my will, to go to Paris, I'm going to spend some time at the Estancia!

- I applaud you for the idea! Too bad I can't go. A trip like this would do me a lot of good!

- Can't you request permission from your superiors?

- Not at the moment! Sister Berta is sick again and Mother Eulalia, our superior, will go to Rome in a few days. I must remain here, in charge of almost everything that concerns the school, my friend.

- I am sorry! Maybe another time, right, sister?

- Yes, without a doubt! I hope that God will allow me, someday, to visit this ranch! And to see our dear Natacha again! Tell her how much I miss her! Hug her affectionately for me!

- Yes, I will! Before travel I will visit dear sister Berta in the hospital.

- She will be very happy to see you! This dear sister worries us too much! Her case seems to be very serious, poor thing! Pray for her, dear friend!

- She can always count on my prayers. May God help her in this difficult situation!

He visits the dear sister, gets organized and, a few days later, he arrives at the ranch, pleasantly surprising Natacha:

- Dear friend! I dreamed about you! Now I know why! – she exclaims, hugging him lovingly.

Squeezing her to his heart, he can hardly express himself, with such emotions:

- How are you, daughter? It seems like we haven't seen each other for ages!

- I am very well! And you seem fine to me! Why didn't Eugene come with you?

- Right now, she is here, in the center of Paris. But her intentions are quite different from mines. I will tell you everything later. First, I must get rid of this dust!

- Let me help you with the luggage!

Hours later, sitting in the large reception hall, they are chatting:

- Imagine, Natacha, Eugene has decided to go after Henry!

- Oh my God! – she exclaims, shaking her head negatively.

- That's right, I couldn't talk her out of it. Neither I, nor Marianne and the dear sister Rosalia, who, by the way, misses you, and send you regards!

- Dear Sister Rosalia... I miss her so much! May God keep her safe! But tell me, what will Eugene do, alone and fragile, if she manages to find him?!

- Dear God! I don't even want to think about it!

- Then don't! We'll pray a lot for her!

- Now, daughter, I want to arrange chambers for myself.

- Yours are in order and waiting for you!

- No, Natacha. I can't pay that much. I require simpler ones!

- Not at all! We will be even happier to have you with us when we see you well installed as always!

- And your parents, what will they say?

- They will agree with me, don't worry.

- Still, I prefer to go according to my principles and my conscience. Thank you for your generosity. We will see how things will work out. In any case, I am very happy to be here and that is all what matters.

- I respect your wishes, dear friend. My parents already know everything, and no doubt they will know how to convince you to accept our best chambers. My father will certainly talk to you.

But I must confess to you: I have made use of your chambers for a guest... as special as you!

- But, my child, these rooms must be at the disposal of the other guests, just as I, one day, very happily, was able to occupy them!

Your extreme care, in a way, embarrasses me! I do not want to be a nuisance or a motive of prejudice!

- Don't worry, my friend; we know what we are doing! No harm done! We have many other spaces, and yours have been preserved in the hope that you would return at any moment! But, to get back to the point, the one who stayed in your chambers, for a few days, was someone very, very special! I can go further, saying that he is a Prince charming!

- Well, well! I hope it's yours! And where is he now?

- In Belgium, where he lives. He courted me, unabashedly, and promised to return. In fact, he really came looking for me, imagine! He promptly won us over with his bonhomie and his verve! He is well polite and elegant!

- I conclude from everything I'm hearing that you are fascinated! I'm glad about that! It's about time, my child!

- I'll tell you the details, listen...

As she recounts how it all happened, Sir. Jaime bursts into loud laughter. At the end, she sighs:

- I miss him already!

- Do you love him, Natacha?

- I don't know, maybe!

- Good luck, daughter! You deserve to be happy! Now, excuse me! I'm going to greet your parents! Farewell!

Natacha did not hear, she is oblivious, distant... She remembers Marcel and his seductive figure. Talking about him increased her nostalgia...

Happy to see Sir. Jaime again, Mr. Korsanikov smiles and exclaims:

- Welcome again, dear Sir Jaime!

They hug each other, friendly. Sir Jaime expresses his joy for being back at the resort.

- We've been informed about everything that happened to you, comments Mr. Korsanikov - We are very sorry!

As for your accommodation, we know that our daughter wishes the best for you, and so do we.

However, knowing you, we can imagine your scruples in accepting the chambers that you used before, because of the price. But we can find a way for everything, except death, when it comes, we have a suggestion that will accommodate everything, if you I need help with the accounting records. I am overwhelmed; my best employee in this sector died a few days ago.

I know his competence in the world of finance, and if you wish, we will take mutual advantage: the costs of your lodging will become an integral part of your earnings as our employee. What do you say?

- Well, the proposal is undeniably irrefusable! I accept and thank you for the offer. You are giving me a great opportunity! I hope that you will be satisfied with my work.

- We certainly will! I am just as grateful to you, Sir. Jaime!

The next day, surprised by Rupert and Nikolai, he asks Natacha:

- Daughter, are your cousins still here?

- Yes! My parents want them here.

- And how are they behaving? Are they better?

- Not at all! They are the same as always.

- So bad! Everyone is at risks!

- And speaking of risks, I shudder to imagine the ones Eugene might be facing, Sir. Jaime!

- I'm losing my mind, Natacha! I hope she gives up and come here to meet me!

- Will depend on God! I would like that very much!

- What is the name of your Prince charming?

- Marcel!

- I'd like to meet him! Are you going to get married?

- I don't know, my friend! He does me good! When we are together, I am happy! I seem to have waited for him all these years!

Yet marriage doesn't seem to be part of my destiny.

- Oh, Natacha! And why is that?

- I don't know! I feel something strange about it!

- You have been surprised by a new reality. Later, you will think different. There will be time for an adaptation, no doubt. You reveal joy and hope when you speak of him. Your eyes shine differently! He must be someone very special to win this little heart!

- Yes! He's wonderful! - she exclaims, dreamily, making Sir. Jaime smile.

- What do your parents think about him?

- They are delighted.

- Well, young lady, I must go down and check the accounting with your father.

- That makes me very happy! Seeing you focus on this new function with my father, who knows, maybe you can consider stay here permanently?

- We cannot be sure about the future. Let's live day by day.

Let us work and trust in God, the greatest provider of our real needs.

While I'm here, daughter, I want to find a way to help those who suffer hunger and cold!

Clapping her hands like a child, she approves:

- Yes, this is exactly what my heart desires, dear friend! Together we can do so much!

- By joining forces, we will be strong, Natacha! Praise God!

* * *

LIKE A POISONOUS SNAKE, André crawls in a dark cell. There, days and nights are the same. He has given up reacting because is useless and exhausting. He has no points of reference to know where he is and why. He feels on the verge of madness.

The jailer, whenever he goes to see him, is accompanied by a brute, almost two meters tall, with muscles of bronze, who, at any reaction, attacks, violent, sometimes leaving him unconscious.

André decided to make the jailer, whose name is Joubert, aware of the situation, but was in vain. He is cold, impassive.

At this moment, he remembers the brief conversation he had with him while the giant looked at him, ready to jump at his neck:

- Mister Joubert, listen to me, I beg you!

- Listen to you, what for? I am neither a lawyer nor a judge!

- But you are the only authority I can see! I need your help!

- Above me, I have superiors who do not admit favors to anyone!

- Then, please, take me to them!

Joubert bursts into laughs as he starts to leave.

André, in despair, continues:

- I don't know why I'm here! Enlighten me, so that I may defend myself!

- And for what do you want to defend himself?

- In the name of what you love the most, help me, I beg you!

- Can we help him, Gothardo? - the attendant shakes his head in denial.

Supplicant, hands folded, André kneels at Joubert's feet. From out of his chest burst uncontrollable sobs. Turning his back on him, the jailer heads for the exit. André rushes forward and, clutching to him, prevents him from leaving. Gothardo holds him tightly by the neck and throws him against the wall. After the thud, André's body slips to the floor. There, he cringes in pain, clutching his head with both hands. He feels hungry, cold, and afraid. He imagines himself in hell.

When he receives a plate of meager food through the hatch, he eats to stay alive. He gets weaker every day.

He reaches a pile of straw, lies down and struggles to stay lucid. Panicking, he thinks:

"- Why isn't Antoine looking for me? Who kidnapped me that night? What am I complaining about? Isn't that how it was done with the legitimate Baron de Villefort? Didn't I know, from long ago, about this sordid and cruel context? Surely, "he" also went through this, and much more, which I do not yet know, but which I shall find out at my own expense! I have no defenses, no salvation!"

Deeply downcast, he hears a childish humming. He runs to the tiny window and sees a boy of about ten years old.

Desperate, he cries out:

- Come here, boy!

- You called for me, sir? - asks the boy.

- Yes! Who are you?

- I'm the jailer's adoptive son. I live here!

- Help me, please!

- How can I help you, sir?

- In any way!

- Are you hungry?

- Yes, very hungry!

- Then wait for me, I'll be right back!

While waiting, André sits at the bottom of the cell.

Passing through countless corridors, the boy reaches a grimy room where Joubert is getting drunk next to his defender.

- Mister Joubert...

- What do you want, Francois? Can't you see that I'm resting?

- I want to go to the new prisoner's cell... You haven't allowed me to do that yet...

- Because he's dangerous! He can kill you, stupid boy!

- He won't hurt me! Besides some dry straw, I want to bring him some clothes, the Turkish woman has washed a lot of clothes and he needs to warm up! Please, Sir. Joubert!

- I already know that when you want something, it's useless to deny it! Go and leave me in peace! Gothardo, go with him. Take care of this boy! Maybe I'll be held accountable for him one day!

- Why do you always say that? - François wants to know.

Pretending not to hear, Joubert fills another glass.

Francois comes out with the big man and asks him:

- Wait for me, Gothardo. I'll get the clothes!

In awe, staring at the boy like a dog in adoration for its master, he obeys. He loves François and defends him against everything. François returns, clutching straw and clothes. They follow in silence through the dark and sinister corridors, full of imprecations and painful lamentations. The tinkling of keys on Gothardo's bulky waist accompanies the rhythm of his huge, heavy steps. He opens the cubicle and stares at André, challenging him.

- Come out, my friend. Wait for me outside. - says François, pushing him.

Quiet, he answers and sits down outside, leaning against the heavy, dark old oak door.

- Here, sir –says the boy, offering him the straw and the clothes. From inside his shirt, he takes out a small package with a slice of roast beef and a piece of bread.

Eagerly, André eats it all and wipes his mouth with the back of his hands.

Then he wants to know:

- Where did this food come from?

- From my house. The Turkish woman made it!

- Who is she?

- My adoptive mother. She does everything for me, while Mr. Joubert, even though, he says he's my adoptive father, mistreats me too much. Her name is Betbara, but we call her Turkish. Her husband, who is dead now, protected me and was my friend!

- For me, my boy, what I have just eaten is a delicacy of the gods! Thank you!

- Keep your voice down! Gothardo must not know!

André feels weakened by the food he has hastily devoured.

His head is spinning.

- Put on these clothes and lie down to recover, Sir!

- What is your name, good boy?

- Francois!

- What about you, Sir?

- Baron André of Villefort. I am rich and powerful! Or was, I don't know...

While André is trying to think, François says good-bye:

- Farewell, Baron!

- Farewell and thank you very much!

André changes his clothes and warms up. He fixes the new straw and lies down on it. In a few minutes he snores heavily. François comes back again and again, and whenever he can, he helps him, hidden and as he does with most of the prisoners, from cell to cell, in a selfless pilgrimage.

On one occasion André asks him:

- Francois, help me to escape! I will reward you lavishly!

I can even take you with me, would you help me?

Staring at him with his clear blue eyes, he fixes his hair, the color of ripe wheat that falls across his forehead and declares:

- It is impossible, sir! No one has ever escaped from this fortress! I am constantly under vigilance! I tried to escape several times and I was beaten! Many times, the Turkish woman cried with pity as she healed my wounds! Gothardo, not infrequently, took me from the hands of Mr. Joubert before he beat me to death!

I can only live with the Turkish woman in a house in the back of the prison.

There, fortunately, I have sun and rain! There is also a small garden where we grow flowers. I am happy and amazed when a beautiful flower manages to bloom or the birds come to sing next to us!

When I came here, at very young age, from I don't know where, the baby of the Turkish had died of a pernicious fever. She and her husband adopt me. He protected me until he died, and she continues caring for me, loving and good.

Give up running away! If you try, they will execute you right here! I have seen it and it's terrible!

- Francois, the same way you bring me hidden food, you can bring me a gun!

-I have no access to them!

- Get it out of sight!

- No, forgive me... But sometimes, sir, I myself doubt that I'm alive! I feel like I'm in an endless nightmare and I wonder who brought me here and why... I would like to live like any other boy!

- So, you don't know where do you come from, do you, François?

- No, sir!

- I'm very sorry... As for me, if I don't return in time, the woman I love, will marry someone else.

- God will help you, Baron! Pray!

Bored with this advice, André hesitates:

- If you will not help me, get out of here with this nagging! You sound like a priest!

Disconcerted, François obeys. It is already late at night and, together with Gothardo, walks through the corridors. He passes by

Joubert, who sleeps intoxicated. Once again, he hears the cries and groans of those who are slowly dying there. His heart squeezes painfully.

The Turkish woman prepares him a mug of warm milk, hugs him and wraps him up, carefully.

Feeling his body settling down on the heap of straw, François thanks the Creator for the bed, the milk and the care of a mother like the Turkish woman. He falls deeply asleep.

The Turkish woman, a middle-aged, sturdy, hardworking woman, goes to check on him. She fixes the covers, kisses him, and goes to bed.

She is exhausted. The next day, they will have to wake up very early.

***

OBSESSED BY HER REVENGE, Eugene continues with her plans. At every step of the path, she thinks she will discover Henry, only to be disappointed. Her resources are already running short.

She fears returning without achieving her goals. For more than a month, she has been on an exhausting pilgrimage through the streets of Paris.

He goes to public and well-known places. She knows the city well. She has been there several times with her father.

Today she woke up feeling nervous, as if she sensed something. It's still too early, she walks along the boulevards of the Champs-Elysées.

Suddenly, she feels her blood run cold in her veins.

Yes, it's him! Who else has that arrogant walk, that swagger? From a short distance she watches him without being seen.

He, unsuspecting, strolls along, leaning elegantly on his silver-handled cane. Rich, impeccable clothes; in the latest fashionable clothes. Fine lace appears under the sleeves of the long, perfectly tailored, dark colored overcoat. Shiny shoes, polished. His gait is studied, seductive. Women sigh at he walks by.

Eugene's heart beats unbearably. She crunches his hands, angry, full of hate. She feels the urge to throw herself at him.

Like an animal watching its prey, she follows him stealthily. For a long time, he enjoys his morning stroll.

Paris emerges from the mists, at that hour, under the mild heat of a shy sun.

To Eugene, those minutes seemed like centuries!

Finally tired, he decides to return home, call a carriage and boards it.

Crossing streets and avenues, the vehicle stops in front of a very rich mansion on Rue-de-La-Chapelle.

Eugene gives the driver a supposed address and climbs out, then returns to the boarding house. She is excited. What to do now?

The truth is, she didn't think she'd find him. She has no plans...

She spends the night very agitated. Amidst conflicts and nightmares, she decides to face him in "his own game".

The next morning, she dresses quickly and goes to the mansion.

She knocks on the door and a man with a grave face comes to meet her:

- What do you want, *Mademoiselle*?

- To speak to your boss!

- Have you made an appointment?

- No, I haven't.

- Then he cannot see you!

Quietly, she thinks and dares:

- Listen to me, what I really need is work!

- Do you have any references?

- Not now! I worked in England, and just get here. I need a job, please!

Looking at her, compassionate, the man with the long coat, white gloves, voluminous whiskers, and blue eyes, is thoughtful. After a few moments, he decides:

- You seem like a nice girl! Clean, well dressed, you express yourself correctly... But for the moment, we can only offer you manual labor.

- I accept! I need to pay the rent for the boarding house and feed myself!

Opening the door, the man lets Eugene in while he calls a maid:

- Clara, take *Mademoiselle* to the housekeeper!

Obeying, she shows Eugene the way. They pass through rooms and polished corridors, and then they go to another wing in the back, where a tall, blonde woman can be seen guiding the gardeners.

Elegant, soberly dressed, hair made, haughty, she turns to see who arrives. Stiff-faced, she stares at Eugene as she asks:

- What do you want?

- Just work!

Looking at her from top to bottom, she declares:

- You don't strike me as the type who seeks servile occupation!

- Appearances can be deceiving! Far from home, I need to take care of myself!

- Where do you come from?

- From England.

- And what were you doing there?

- I was teaching and making fine clothes for ladies in a boutique.

- You've wasted your time! We don't have this kind of work here! We don't have children and the costumes of the master of this house are ordered from the most famous dressmakers and tailors in Paris!

- I'll take any other job!

- Would you like to be a maid?

- Yes, I can.

- Then come back tomorrow. Come early, I'm very demanding!

- Yes, ma'am! See you tomorrow.

- See you tomorrow!

Eugene reaches the street and takes a deep breath. She feels electrified. What if Henry showed up? What would she do?

At this thought, she panics.

The next day, early in the morning, she is instructed by the housekeeper and assumes her duties. Wearing an impeccable uniform, she walks through the mansion.

Days and days go by and he doesn't show up. She heard that he is traveling. His maid falls ill and she is asked to replace her. Anxious, she continues with the farse and takes over the activity.

She is astonished when she enters Henry's luxurious chambers. The luxury dazzles: marbles of every tone and different qualities cover floors, walls, capitals, consoles ...

Valuable curtains and carpets recall the West and its stories. The gold, white and red furniture, is upholstered in soft and luminous velvet. The bathrooms are worthy of the Caesars of Rome!

And in one of the galleries, Eugene's heart seems to explode... There, on luxurious granite pedestals, the works of art that his father took years to collect!

A few hours later, tired and sweaty, she is about to leave when she hears familiar footsteps. Paralyzed with horror, she lets herself stay. Still holds the silver polishing tools in her hands.

His voice thunders in the middle of the hall:

- Lucrecia, prepare my bath! Go, I'm exhausted!

When he sees Eugene, he doesn't recognize her immediately and asks, annoyed:

- Who are you? Where is Lucrecia?

Unable to answer, she tries not to look weak. The decisive moment comes suddenly.

Getting rid of his wool overcoat and gloves, without looking at her, he asks, sarcastically:

- Are you mute, by any chance?

And she, with her characteristic courage, which sometimes borders on rashness, she replies incisively:

- I wish I was, for your own good, Mr. Henry John Stanford!

- What does that mean? You are not mute, but you are crazy! - he vociferates.

- No, Henry, I'm not crazy! Don't you recognize me? You thief! - inflamed, angry, she confronts him.

Staring at her, not wanting to believe what he sees, he explodes:

- By all the gods! How did you get in my private chambers? How did you find me?

- One thing at a time, Henry! I've searched for you, obsessively, for all these years! I employed myself here and watch for myself everything that once belongs to us, in this luxurious lair!

- You remain foolish! - he comments wryly.

- For someone who had me for a sister, you have changed a lot, huh? Have you stolen from many others too? Yes, because that seems to be your profession!

- Shut up, you fool! I will give you no satisfaction, and between your word and mine, guess who will be right!

Such decadence! Have you become a housekeeper? Where are your dreams of greatness, Eugene Sartorelli?

- How mean you are, Henry! I work in another trade that doesn't concern you! And along with everything else, you have stolen "my" dreams of greatness too!

- In the face of this new, irreversible reality, what do you want, Eugene?

- Take you to the competent authorities! Demoralize you, naturally!

- It's useless, you won't succeed! Be content with your fate!

- What fate, Henry? You must have lost your reason, if you ever had one!

- Eugene, listen: I can give you a good amount of money, with which you will live well and in peace! Forget about me!

- Forget you? Do you have any idea, Henry, of all we have suffered because of you?

Eugene is on the verge of a nervous breakdown.

Henry feels sorry for her. He is moved by his righteous despair...

He runs his hands through his black hair and, softening his features, he concludes:

- It's too late, Eugene! If you want to accept my money, fine, otherwise...

- Or else what? What more can you do to me?

- You can't even imagine, Eugene. Now, I can do more than ever!

I'm no longer your father's servant.

Go away and forget we ever met!

No matter what means I used to get here, my fate is already decided! I will not back down!

I'll walk all over you if I have to!

- Will you do it again, Henry?

- Yes! Again and again, Eugene! If you don't make up your mind, I will ring this bell and, in a few minutes, you will be arrested!

- Will you do that?

- Without a blink of an eye! Don't doubt it! I would go through hell if I had to defend what I own!

Eugene's sight dims, her legs weaken, and she collapses heavily on the beautiful floor, only to awaken in a hospital.

Wondering how she got there, she is told that a burly, well-dressed, thick-suited man came to her aid in the street, out of pity. On the occasion, he had said, saddened: "Poor thing, she must be starving! Take care of her! I don't know who she is or where she came from!" – then disappeared.

Deeply disappointed, Eugene cries. She is treated with tranquilizers and sleeps for hours. Refreshed, she returns to the boarding house.

She goes through several days of depression. So many days of tiredness for nothing! She feels like the little ant sister Rosalia, very wisely, had told her about. From sadness to angry, her emotions change quickly.

Walking around the room like a caged animal, without feeding nor thinking, she decides:

"I will kill you, Henry! In a desperate and definitive way, I will take revenge! I will destroy you, without mercy! You wanted it that way!"

With this intention, she organizes herself to execute her sinister plan...

***

IN A BLINDLESS AUDACITY, Antoine Belfort goes to the Portal da Luz, to speak to Louise:

- What a pleasure, to see you again, beautiful Louise! - he says, vainly, in a thunderous voice, holding out his hand.

- How are you, General?

Getting her visible displeasure, he restrains himself and declares:

- *Mademoiselle*, I come to sympathize with your pain, for the absence of André, my dear friend! I have made unheard-of efforts to find him, without success! It seems to me that the earth has opened and swallowed him up! I am already discouraged because of this fruitless search! This has already cost me time, expenses and annoyances!

Surprised, Louise replies:

- But, General, he is traveling! Your statements amaze me!

- You are wrong! We, the police, suspect that he was kidnapped and probably murdered!

- Do you have reason to believe what you say?

- Yes! We are friends, and knowing his habits, I know that he wouldn't leave the house or his business for so long!

- However, he informed Mateus that he was going on a trip! What makes you think differently?

- We both had pending appointments regarding matters that interested him. He didn't even give me an answer! I conclude something very serious must have happened to him. Thanks to my experience in these matters, I know he has disappeared.

And there is more; agents of the King have discovered that André has usurped the identity of a disappeared nobleman, having used, until now, his property and titles!

- Who made this discovery, General?

- As I told you, the King's officials.

- And what actions have been taken?

- Until now, none. Nevertheless, his majesty, the King, will confiscate everything!

- And the rightful owners?

With a laugh, Antoine answers:

- Do you think that his majesty, the King, is interested in them?

Silently, Louise concludes that the General knows more than he says, and that he must be responsible for André's disappearance. She feels the urge to shout at him that everything André wears belongs to his family, and not to the King. But she is afraid of the man with the cruel eyes.

Annoyed, she lets him know that she's finished with the interview:

- I thank you for your sympathy, take care!

- Farewell, beautiful Louise!

The General leaves, stepping heavily, elegant in his luxurious uniform.

Louise rightly concludes that he knows where André is.

However, she cares little for the two of them; she hates them!

Corine returns from the Alvarado castle with the promise that in two days Madelaine will come to the Portal da Luz, to visit Louíse.

Happy, she presents Corine with a rich medal.

IN THE PARISH HOUSE, Madelaine talks to Father Estanislau:

- Father, I am going to the Portal da Luz, to discover if Louise is indeed Gotuza's daughter!

- Beware, child! Don't rule out the possibility of a trap.

- Fear not. I'll take Ignatia and Salústio. Pray for us!

- I will! May God be with you!

- So be it!

A few days later, we can see Madelaine, Ignácia, carrying a basket of sweets and the good Salústio, serene and vigilant, heading towards the Portal da Luz.

Casually, Salústio asks:

- How is Charles, Madelaine?

- Very well, Salústio!

Between one conversation and another, they arrive at the address.

Salústio announces himself to the doorman:

- Dear Sir, *Mademoiselle* Madelaine and friends present themselves for the visit previously arranged with *Mademoiselle* Louise!

The man goes to call Mateus, who arrives looking displeased:

- Who are you and what do you want?

- I am *Mademoiselle* Madelaine D'Or Alvarado, and this is Saulo Venturo from the Parish House Our Lady of Mont'Serrat, and this one here, is Ignácia, my servant. *Mademoiselle* Louise is waiting for us.

Looking frowning, Mateus warns:

- Sir. André is traveling and has forbidden any visitors in his absence!

Bravely, Madelaine bluffs:

- For if he finds out that you prevented my entry, you will lose your job, sir! I assure you!

Mateus feels confused, and behind his back, he hears Louise:

- Let them in, Mateus! They are my guests!

- But, *Mademoiselle*, your brother...

- In his absence, I give the orders! You dare disobey me, Mateus?

He leaves feeling humiliated. Louise invites them in.

- Corine, how are you? - asks Ignácia..

- I'm fine, thank you, Ignácia.

- Take these sweets to the kitchen, they're for *Mademoiselle* Louise!

- Yes, Ignácia, excuse me!

- Thank you, for the sweets and for coming! You can't imagine how pleased I am to receive you! Let's go in, please.

- It's our pleasure, Louise! I didn't come earlier because more urgent occupations prevented me, declares Madelaine.

Attentive and suspicious, Salústio walks, restless. Louise clarifies:

- "Get some rest, sir! The owner of this house is out of town! For us, he is traveling; but for the police, he is missing. Either way, we don't have to endure his presence in a while!

- I don't understand you, Louise! - comments Madelaine. - Isn't he your brother?

- No, Madelaine. That is a long story...

- We would like to hear it, if that is your wish. Ignácia and Salústio are completely trustworthy. Nevertheless, keep an eye on Corine.

Thinking of Mateus, Louise recommends that they lock the door.

Then, she tells them everything, from the beginning.

At the end, she bursts into tears:

- I am alone! My brother, had disappeared, must be dead by now!

I have lost track of my mother and my younger brother!

- God of mercy! - exclaims Madelaine, saddened.

Meanwhile, Ignácia wipes away her tears.

- Louise, does the name Gotuza mean anything to you?

- Gotuza? For God's sake, Madelaine. You... said... Gotuza?

- Yes, Louise, I said Gotuza. Answer my question, please!

- Yes! That's my dear mother's affectionate nickname! Her real name is Caterine Brumel of Villefort!

- Very good! So, I was right!

Louise, listen carefully to what I have to tell you and control your emotions.

Louise listens as Madelaine recounts the events in the cave that culminated with the death of the lawful Baron de Villefort and the presence Gotuza in the castle.

She bursts into tears. At times causing desperate moans coming from her chest, which causes Madelaine to pause the story, so that she can calm down.

Ignácia rises and hugs Louise, wiping away her tears, tender and serene, although she was also crying.

- So, my dear mother is safe? Thank God! I wish to be able to hug her again! When will I be able to see her, Madelaine? I wish I could be with her now!

- Calm down, Louise. We must be careful!

After so many setbacks, we can't afford to take any chances! We still don't know where your enemy is! On the other hand, Gotuza needs medical care constantly! She keeps recovering from the torments she has experienced. She must be preserved from great emotions.

We have already taken a big step towards the rescue of her life. The rest will come therefore.

I beg your pardon for my delay. I have serious reasons to fear your false brother.

- You are right. He was always trying to rule with his tyranny, by threatening to death my little brother that you claim to have in your power. And he would also use me to attract and conquer you definitively, because he loves you with madness!

When he disappeared, I asked Corine to invite you to come here because I am frightened; I need a good friend.

I feel alone and helpless. Mateus pursues me with love proposals!

- Is that still going on? Order Corine to not stay away from you! We will figure out a way to protect you, trust me. God will help us, have faith and courage! I feel the worst is over!

- May the angels say amen! How can I thank you, Madelaine?

I ask heaven to make you very happy!

- I'll try to be, Louise, thank you! Soon I will marry the man I love, and I will certainly be very happy! It will be the fulfillment of my dream as a woman!

And so, the conversation takes a happier turn.

Salústio, dignified and brotherly, speaks little, but is fascinated by the beauty and the gifts of Louise. Seeing her crying, he felt like to hold her close to his heart, comforting her, tenderly. She is so beautiful and so delicate... And what eyes! Blue like the color of the sky...! In the time she remained there, he was in mute adoration.

To Madelaine and Ignácia, these feelings, so spontaneous in the dear friend did not go unnoticed.

Salústio is transparent like crystal clear water.

After a few hours of relaxation and joy, the group returns with encouraging news for those who remained.

Mateus had tried several times to approach the group, without success.

Deeply upset, in the mysterious absence of André, he feels insecure and now, threatened by those Louíse's new friends.

Salústio confronts him in an ostentatious manner, in a silent, challenging posture.

✲ ✲ ✲

IN SANTA SOFIA, Marcel and Natacha made their courtship official with the assent and joy of her parents.

Marcel became friends with Mr. Jaime and so, between happy pleasant conversations and walks with Natacha, he watched the time go by, seen his soon return to a life of work and responsibilities. He gave a sad farewell to Natacha and left, leaving her longing and dreaming.

In conversation with Natacha, Mr. Jaime praises Marcel's gifts.

She seems to hear him, but suddenly changes. She shakes herself, breathes heavily and looks around. In a proud and dignified posture, she exclaims:

- I greet you in the name of divine peace!

Understanding that it is not the girl who is speaking to him, he replies:

- Welcome, in the name of the Creator!

- My presence here is due to several factors:

One is that I follow the steps of this dear spirit who now allows me to speak!

Your affection, presence and solicitude, have given her more security and tranquility.

You are old companions who, in recognizing each other, are resuming relationships of mutual help, in space and time to an ever more intense spiritual growth!

In the task of leading you, I joyfully involve myself in your life context as well.

In this sense, I want to clarify and support your paternal heart about the dear daughter who is presently fighting a fierce battle of good against evil.

Have strength and much faith! Prepare your heart for sufferings that may shake her still weakened physical body!

Painfully recalling the previous time, when he had heard a similar warning, Mr. Jaime asks:

- Enlighten me, by God, whatever it is! I will have courage!

- Well then: Coming across the person she was looking for, confronting him, unable to use balanced resources, desperate by the injunction of recent events that you don't know about, she behaves in an insane manner!

Her late mother and I have made efforts to modify her vibratory pattern, but to no avail! Therefore, she will suffer the consequences of her desperate and violent acts!

She is in error when she tries to take back what she thinks belongs to her by birthright.

"Him", ambitious and vigilant, has not forgiven them and instinctively charged you harshly, in a vile way, for what, in the distant past you two, now father and daughter, stole from him.

As you can see, situations are reversed according to circumstances on this unstable and suffering planet, where you learn, with great difficulty, the hard to learn the path of good!

What often seems to us as injustices are the reckoning of life!

We certainly do not approve the "eye for an eye and a tooth for a tooth", but in truth, this is what usually happens, because of the spiritual imperfection of those who, for the most part, well here!

You are still a long way from the progress that we would like to see.

However, you keep learning and working to become wiser and happier! "To each according to his work!"

- And what about my daughter? - he asks, distressed.

- Calm your heart, because out of apparent evil, anything good will come out! Your dear daughter, after drinking the bitter medicine that she imposed on herself, will learn to respect God's will, and submit to his just and wise laws! Have faith when pain overtakes you because of your daughter's impulsiveness!

- My God! I'll go look for her wherever she is!

- Yes, you must! After consummating her foolish plan, blinded by the hatred that consumes her, she will suffer harshly. Also know that in the future they will be reconciled!

- You mean her and Henry?

- Yes! He will surprise you!

You and her, he continued, pointing to Natacha's chest, a few years later you will return, together! You will have completed your earthly journey! So do all the good you can!

Another person, like the one you are allowing us to speak to now, and whom you don't know yet, is passing through the fortunately path of father and daughter to help them in a competent way. And, dear sir, in the not-too-distant future, those who will selflessly help you, will also need your solidarity, in the painful passage of their ordeals! I pledge, right now to be with you in this moment that will be decisive for many!

This is how we grow in the eyes of God! Helping each other in a universal exchange, enlarging the sacred resources that God grants us in his infinite mercy!

I have, in turn, affectionate ties with those who soon are going to cross favorably the paths of you and your daughter!

Now I must say goodbye, wishing you peace! May our creator enlighten you today and always!

Natacha is silent and sighs deeply.

Unable to hold back any longer, Mr. Jaime burst into sobs.

- What happened? - she asks, frightened.

With difficulty he asks:

- Hold on a moment, daughter! I need to recover! - While he regains his equilibrium, he analyzes what kind of information he will pass on to her.

Calmer, he tells her what happened, leaving out what might distress her.

- I'm going to meet Eugene. Pray for us, Natacha!

- I will be praying fervently! God keep you safe!

* * *

MEANWHILE, IN PRISON, André realizes that a great friendship between him and François is creating.

At this moment, François has once again brought him bread and pieces of roasted meat. In silence, respectful and deeply saddened, he waits for André to finish eating.

It is difficult to recognize in this person, the André who arrived here haughty and elegant, strong and well groomed. Now, scrawny and sickly, he clearly shows that he will soon leave the world... In these conditions, François observes him.

After the small meal, André shows his gratitude:

- Thank you, François! Why do you help me?

- I don't help only you. I do what I can for those who live here. I don't care who you are or what you have done!

- And you, François? How did you end up here?

- According to Mr. Joubert, my mother left me here and disappeared. Out of pity, he let me stay. The Turkish woman and her husband, as I've already told you, have looked after me lovingly.

- When will you leave here, Francois?

- When I am grown up and can decide my life. I look forward to do it!

- And when that time comes, will you have somewhere to go?

- No, sir.

- And what about the Turkish woman?

- We'll leave here together!

- I hope you succeed! I, for one, have already lost hope...

- Don't be discouraged, God will help you, one way or another!

- I don't believe in him! And if he exists, he won't help me because I don't deserve it!

- I will pray for you!

- Do it for me, François... Maybe he will listen to you! - André's voice sounds sad, desolate.

When François leaves, he cries freely. He regrets his past mistakes...

* * *

GOING WITH MADELAINE TO THE wards of the Parish House, Charles sees on the spot the charity exercised by this loving group.

Happy with his presence, she introduces him:

- This is Luciano; he has lost his legs, but not the will to live! And here we have Piotr, advanced in age and with multiple health problems, a consequence of the lack of food. He lived amid rats and filth, poor thing!

And look, they put this little baby here at the door a few days ago, almost without clothes and malnourished. He seems to want to live, because he improves every day!

The parade of unfortunates is endless...

The task is thorny: children barely out of childhood and mothers who have given birth in extreme poverty; young people mutilated by hunger, violent entertainments; wounds, ulcers, depressions; children marked by the savagery of their fathers; beautiful, poor young girls raped by cruel masters and thrown into the street without mercy; old people deformed by rheumatism...

They gather there, in a great appeal to the good hearts: the human junk, the outcasts, the disillusioned, the crippled, the maddened by pain and suffering continued without help.

Charles, perplexed, encourages them with words of respect and fraternity.

Salústio accompanies them in their presentations and in the various providences. Distancing himself a little from Charles, whom he admires and shares a sincere friendship with, he says:

- Charles, as you can see, there is a lot to do here!

- Now I understand, Salústio, why Madelaine is torn between my love and theirs!

- She, Charles, has the gift of quieting and healing them, rescuing them to life!

- Salústio, sometimes, I think she belongs more to them than to me! I wish I had her all to myself!

Don't blame me for this, I beg you. I am aware that this is a selfish feeling that reflects an unjust jealousy, but you can be sure, my friend, I would never take her away from them!

- I can understand your feelings as a man in love, Charles. She, however, is a kindred spirit with transcendent responsibilities!

- And you, Salústio, how do you feel, involved in this blessed work?

- I suffer for them, Charles! While the wretched ones lay in the streets and sewers, the powerful are fed up with food and drink, they dress in silks and lace; they sing and dance in the salons!

I even hate them!

- Beware, my friend! You know the risk you run by speaking or acting against the regime!

- How long will we put up with it? Will God not hear the cries of France?

- He certainly will, Salústio!

- Charles, I want to join the liberation groups. Father Estanislau advises me to be calm. How can I be calm? See, Charles, in every face the outline of a larger, real and sinister picture!

- Yes, you are right! But be careful not to lose your life and the opportunity to help them.

- No, Charles, I can't hold back for long! My heart bleeds for all those who suffer the painful injunctions of the current system!

Approaching, Madelaine interrupts them, inviting Charles to other wards. In one of them, Salústio says goodbye and goes to the sacristy of the church, where other activities await him.

Charles, to himself, says softly:

- Dear friend! Good and brave! May God protect you, because I see in your eyes the brilliance of the martyrs of great causes!

I admire you, and I fear for your future...

- Talking to yourself, Charles? - Madelaine wants to know.

- Yes, I was talking to myself, my love...

- I'm sure you're too tired! You are not in the habit of these walks in the midst of pain and misery!

- No, rest assured, I'm fine, Madelaine. I want to thank you for this unique opportunity!

Within the emotion that I feel and the pity that bathes my heart, coming closer to our Creator, I want to declare to you, my great and only love, that if you are not destined for me, may it be for them! - Extending his arms in a wide gesture, Charles shows them to her.

Surprised, Madelaine replies, enlightened and affectionate:

- Charles, I love them in a different way. For you, my love is unique and eternal!

Hugging her tenderly, he answers:

- I know, Madelaine! Forgive my insecurity!

Eyes shining, hair undone, face sweaty, smelling like medicine, she concludes, smiling disconcerted:

- I must look awful!

- I've never seen you looking so beautiful! If we were alone, I would kiss you. I burn with the desire to take you in my arms!

Saying this in a low, caressing voice, he hears Father Estanislau exclaim, shrewd and amused:

- Has our diligent Marquess comes today to steal the time of our most competent collaborator?

Accepting the friendly remark, Charles greets him and start chatting.

* * *

AT THE CURRENT TIME, HENRY LIVES many conflicts; between what he is and what he wishes to be. Deeply disappointed with the direction his life is taking, he desperately wants to be happy; to win Madelaine urgently. He is aware of the distance that separates both.

He rightly concludes that he could have taken the chance that Eugene had granted him in her anger to exercise a little kindness and, above all, to try to be fair. However, she was too aggressive, just like him, and the shock was fatal...

What if I tell Madelaine everything?

Father Estanislau, intelligent as he is, searched his soul in an unusual way.

If your transformation is not remarkable, you can forget Madelaine once and for all... She's marrying the Marquess you liked or not...

Why had he failed, why did he suffer the incompetence and lack of love of his parents? - With these and other reflections he spent sleepless nights: "I need to do something, real fast! The Marquess is gaining ground every minute! I must grow and he must shrink... But how? What strategy can I use?

Heavens! So much practice with women throughout my life and I know nothing of true love!

I'm going to put on a great show! - the idea suddenly comes to him.

- And I will be the main character, even if I have to dance, act, sing, I will use all the

resources I possess to make myself irresistible, and she, once in love with me will be happy to lead me back to the good path, from which I have strayed so long ago! And I, under her care, will be the most docile little lamb that ever was seen upon the face of the earth!

Ah, Madelaine, may I be able to realize my plans for the future by your side?

Eugene, however, without him being able to suspect it, plans to destroy his life.

While shopping on the street, she comes across with an old former co-worker at Henry's mansion, and get subtly information about a great event, planned by him to receive the most important people of society.

It was just what she had hoped for, an opportunity like this; the mansion full of people and a lot of noise.

Thinking in kill him, she goes to streets where she can get all kinds of illegal things and there, she acquires a small pistol.

She asks for recommendation to use it well, try to get accustomed to the pistol and even practice there, to then returns to the boarding house, frightened not only by what she has just done, but by what she intends to do...

She takes her uniform out of the drawer, leaving it impeccable for wear it later.

In the days leading up to the monumental festivities, she spends sleepless nights, unable to get rest. She is disfigured by lack of food and insomnia.

On the arranged day, early in the morning, dressed in her bright white apron, frilly bonnet on her head, she rented a carriage and goes to Henry's mansion.

As she approaches, the sun is already beginning to show its first rays. She asks the coachman to stop, pays him, and gets off.

She stands nearby, not knowing how to go inside the mansion without being noticed. There is great bustle in the house.

A carriage, filled with fruit, stops at the front door and she quickly takes the opportunity to mingle with the servants who leave to unload it. She lowers her head, and when she asks for permission to enter with the things in her hand, the housekeeper shouts at her:

- What are you doing here? And where do you think you are going?

Who gave you the authorization to return without telling me about it?

That's not how things work here! Go away right now! Get lost! Go! - With a wave of her hand, the housekeeper expels her, taking her out to the street.

Pale with fright and shame, Eugene acts out the kind of servility that knows how to please the housekeeper:

- Fräulein Isolde, please! I've been very ill, that's why I've disappeared! I was going to look for you on my way back today, but then I thought it would be best to help first in this service which certainly requires a lot of people...

I need the money, help me by taking me back, for everything you love most! As you must remember, I do my service very well!

Measuring her from top to bottom, she comments:

- Yeah, I can see you look pale and haggard!

Stay, but just for today! I'll let you work, but only because we need assistance. Listen to me, when the day is over, I will pay you, and you won't come back! That is one of my most important rules! - without waiting any longer, she turns her back and giving orders to those unloading the fruit, she leaves, stamping her feet hard in the entrance hall.

- Thank you, Fräulein! - babbles Eugene, and concludes that everything will be easier now. She can move around at will and wait for the right moment...

In the large, beautifully lit halls, the glitter and the gold can even be hurtful for the eyes. Flowers, in profusion, perfume the place...

The nobility is noted for its brocades, lace, silks, jewelry and fine ornaments.

In the courtyard, the most bizarre carriages speak about their owners' habits and eccentricities.

Henry makes himself wait. The guests are already murmuring about his delay.

Finally, he appears, triumphant, luxuriously dressed in black, clothes made especially for his statuesque body; seductive gait, arousing general admiration. Even the more ardent women hide malicious smiles behind their fans... Henry completely destroyed anyone's illusion of being the most elegant or the most beautiful in 'his party and his domains'.

In his gloved left hand, he carries an exotic bird, which in front of everyone, let free towards the great open arch of the garden, which means that officially begins the festivities, symbolically implying that freedom is the greatest gift of life.

A range of perfumes intoxicates the minds.

Theatrically, he slowly makes his way to the middle of the hall, feeling the eyes and listening a few whispers which helps to grow his pride; he claps his hands loudly, beginning the great spectacle.

Buffoons appear from the most unusual places, inviting the guests to taste the various delicacies. And thanks to their hilarious quips, they fulfill their role.

Huge boxes, set up at various points in the halls, open with a bang, scattering a cloud of white dust, flower petals, little birds, balls, and colorful ribbons. From there also jump, nimbly, trumpeters characterized in a comic mockery of the characters of the plays that will be performed there, and musicians playing their instruments; all amid the disconcerting jokes that they play among themselves. Then they leap at the guests, noisy and irreverent, eliciting cries of fright and exclamations of surprise.

In the extravagant staging, the clear intention is to mix reality with fantasy. Expansive, they spread out, sometimes joking with a guest, or involving someone in their performance, drawing applause and much laughter.

In another hall, a corps de ballet, composed by beautiful young people of both sexes, dance, while clowns in colorful costumes play with the audience and famous magicians, to the sound of the same music, amaze with their seemingly impossible tricks.

Ah, the delicacies! ... They are worthy of the gods! Just like the wines, chosen among the most expensive and finest in the world!

Abundance of all, offered by the bunches... Eat! Drink! Have fun...!

Those are the only things you will take from life, friends and diners!

Young and beautiful servants, dressed in Greek fashion, offer the guests water with rose petals in silver basins, in which they wash their fingertips after eating, and then wipe them on soft, colorful towels.

Overjoyed with the results of this strenuous and expensive event, Henry only has eyes for the various entrances and ears for the herald who beats his staff announcing the names and titles of those arriving.

He fears that Madelaine will not attend...She doesn't like parties, he knows. Nevertheless, he earnestly asks her to come; did he say that her presence was indispensable? He promised her surprises... Why are she delaying?

Finally, after much anxiety, he heard, excited and happy, the herald announces:

- Mister Count Luiz Santiago de Alvarado, Countess Bettine D'Or Alvarado and *Mademoiselle* Madelaine D'Or Alvarado!

His heart starts to race; it wants to jump out of her mouth. His blood start boiling, his cheeks reddening like he was a teenager, overcome by passion, he has the urge to rush towards her and hug her...

Trying to calm himself, stoic, he welcomes them, elegant and jovial:

- Welcome, dear ones! My humble house and everything I own are at your service! - he exclaims, vibrating with joy.

Smiling, amused at such exaggeration, and shaking his hand, the Count replies, affectionately:

- We thank you, Sir Henry John! Sorry for the hour! I was at the Forum today!

- Well, we know you are a very busy man, dear Count! There is no need to apologize!

I want to express my happiness to have you here! I was looking forward to seeing you!

Smiling, kind and patient with her friend's outbursts, Madelaine asks, pleasantly surprised:

- Well, well, Henry! What have we here? It's unbelievable! You transferred to your house the world of make-believe, my friend?

Madelaine's rather intentional "my friend" hurt his ears and his vanity; nevertheless, Henry must be patient, like a good player... Vain and prissy, he answers with another question, and then promises her:

- So, I managed to surprise you?...! I feel very proud, I am aware of your intellectual power and knowing your good taste, dear Madelaine! But get ready! We will have much, much more!

- I'll do that, Henry, I'll look forward to the other surprises! In advance, allow me to congratulate you on such a beautiful event!

One can see here the clear intention of encouraging arts and culture! Bravo! I bring you a message from my fiancé, the Marquess Charles D'Alençon. He apologizes for not attending your party.

Professional engagements prevented him from coming! He went to Bavaria with his pupils to take part in a summer concert.

Henry listened, with a radiant smile, until the: Bravo! From then on, he showed a sudden concern for what was happening around him, and even answered some questions and certain compliments from the guests. Pleased with the Marquess' providential absence, he invites Madelaine and her family to the various halls, to appreciate it all. Being called for something related to the party, he excuses himself and momentarily steps aside.

The Count takes advantage of the opportunity and, approaching his daughter discreetly remarks:

- Madelaine, we should not have come. It's pretty obvious what are the host's intention in regard to you! He doesn't even respect the fact that you are engaged to Charles! He deliberately ignores it and doesn't even slightly disguise his interest in you! I don't know why, but I have a feeling, my daughter, that this party will not end well!

- Stay calm, my father! - she answers as discreetly as he does, while Bettine, next to them, listens to both, visibly uneasy and alert like her husband.

- Our host and I are, above any circumstances, friends and companions of ideal. I feel secure at his side. Henry is, above all, a gentleman! Actually, I am not here for the festivities, although I am very happy with what I am seeing! Henry had the remarkable intention to please those who, like us, admire art and culture!

I accepted his invitation to observe him more closely, in the intimacy of his home. For us, for the Parish House of the church Our Lady of Mont'Serrat, he is still a stranger.

But he serves us lavishly, helping us with financial resources, thus benefiting many unfortunate people! First of all, Henry deserves our gratitude and respect. At certain aspects of his life, he is worthy of praise, there is no doubt about it! If problems arise, we will solve them the best we can, with courage and common sense, as we always do! Do you agree?

- And how can I not agree with you, daughter? You always have great arguments to defend what you believe! I admire your intelligence and the love that illuminates your good heart! So, we are reassured, aren't we, Bettine? - he asks his wife, and she, breathing with relief, declares:

- You always know where you are stepping, dear daughter. When you wish, we will return. We came only to accompany you. But since we are here, let's enjoy this unusual spectacle!

I am also enjoying it very much!

- Thank you, my dears!

Eager, Henry returns and approaches her again. Together they walk through the halls, chatting like the good friends they are.

Tense, Eugene waits for the opportunity to commit her criminal plan. Among so many servants, dressed as one of them, avoiding confrontation with Henry, she goes unnoticed.

She has hidden the gun, in a strategic position, between the large folds of her apron.

Enthusiastic, Henry invites Madelaine to visit the rest of the mansion. She nods, and they go away from the other guests.

Attentive to his slightest movements, sneaking around, Eugene follows them.

Going through corridors of shining floors, immense halls, lush inner gardens, Madelaine and Henry walk side by side.

He, happy and hopeful, tries to hug her, insinuating, forgetting the natural caution that usually characterizes him.

Taking from his pocket a medium-sized golden key with the shape of a buffoon, he opens an artfully carved door in dark, varnished oak, which gives direct them to the art gallery. They go inside. Proud, he points out to Madelaine's competent eyes the rare pieces.

The door is slammed, lightly. Eugene pushes it open and sneaks in.

Focus, Madelaine finds his behavior very strange. Watching him hate-filled countenance and extreme pallor, she senses something and alerts Henry, touching him lightly, indicating the maid approaching.

Surprised, he turns to her and gives her a warning, when he sees her taking out a gun and point it in his direction.

For Madelaine, the scenes unfolded like a nightmare...

She watched it all, terrified, petrified:

Henry opens his hands trying to defend himself, advancing towards the maid to take the gun, when he is shot in the abdomen.

The gunshot echoed, adding to his screams:

- Stop, Eugene! - suddenly, he recognized her.

Henry collapses on the floor, pressing on his wound, while blood goes through his fingers. He groans in pain and exclaims, in a state of both regret and anger:

- This is crazy, Eugene!

Madelaine helps him, holding his head, distressed.

Eugene shakes like a reed in the wind. Eyes squinted; she seems to be sleepwalking.

Servants and guests rush in, advancing towards her and disarming her, assaulting her, violently.

In a superhuman effort, Henry pleads:

- Madelaine, by God, don't let them hurt her! Protect her, I beg you! Use any arguments you wish, or any necessary resources - then faints, hanging his head back, bathed in blood.

Madelaine hands him over to a doctor who arrives and addresses the ones who are pressing Eugene, freeing her from them:

- Stop! Leave her alone! It was an unfortunate incident! Henry asked her to bring the gun, and she clumsily tripped, causing to be fired! He, who was approaching to receive the pistol, was shot!

Doubting this assertion, those who assaulted Eugene menacingly challenge Madelaine,; but, courageously, she goes on:

- Before being unconscious, Henry ordered for her to be protected, free from all suspicion!

Daring and reckless, Eugene goes to retort, but Madelaine does not give her a chance:

- This girl is innocent and I will take responsibility for her!

An officer, elegant, retorts peremptorily:

- *Mademoiselle*, this is the law's assignment! It is not up to you to take responsibility for anyone! I am taking this criminal under arrest!

Before to the right authorities, she will be able to explain herself and, according to that, she will receive what she deserved!

Madelaine understood his intention and shivered in horror.

She looks around for her father, whom appears, providentially.

Then she declares:

- Count Luiz Santiago de Alvarado, as lawyer, will from now on assume the defense of this girl, unjustly accused! He will accompany her and take the necessary measures!

- Have you forgotten the flagrante, *Mademoiselle*? - replies the officer, not giving up.

- From whom? - inquires the Count, taking the lead, dignified and haughty.

- From the wounded man himself, and from *Mademoiselle* here present!

- I have already told you what I saw and what Henry declared, loud and clear!

It seems to me that you have not heard correctly, or you insist on ignoring my statements, as a witness and friend of the victim that I am!

Be careful, officer! You could lose, your insignias and your rank, for such rashness and tactlessness!

Madelaine looks stunning in her defense. Bright eyes, fluent and persuasive speech, haughty and defiant demeanor.

Smiling slightly, satisfied with his daughter's courage and determination, the Count stands beside Eugene, leaving no doubt as to his intention to defend her. A few minutes later, he and Madelaine accompany Eugene to the local police station.

VERY EARLY, FRANCOIS awoke, tired and restless.

Amidst nightmares he saw André being swallowed up, sometimes by waves of a raging sea, sometimes by dark and heavy clouds...

He felt a strange feeling for him, a mixture of affection and pity.

Heading towards André's cell, he feels like a painfully hurt direct on his heart...

Gothardo, as always, remains outside the door.

François enters and, in the darkness, tries to see him. He is still sleeping on a heap of straw. Gently, François calls him:

- Monsieur André, wake up! Look, I brought you a mug of warm milk!

Groaning weakly, André struggles to see the boy.

He reaches out his hands and picks up the mug, but, trembling, feels unable to hold it up. Francois helps him, and he drinks it all. Gasping for breath, he leans back against the wall, in silent.

- Monsieur André, hold on! Perhaps your friends will still come to your rescue, as I had hoped!

- It was "my friends", François, who threw me here! Now, I can see everything and understand clearly! How could I think I was above the dangers of this criminal world if even I was part of it?

- Do you consider yourself a criminal, sir? - asks François, astonished.

- Yes, and I don't deserve your pity, Francois!

His voice begins to become pasty, slow, slurred, almost inaudible.

Filled with pity, Francois declares:

- Monsieur, André, Jesus Christ has forgiven even those who crucified him!

- Ah, Francois... I am so afraid of death... What awaits me on the other side? Is there something else? Forgive me for the trouble I've caused you. Soon, you will be rid of me, my dear boy... This is no life for you. You must run away from here, once and for all...!

- And how could I? I'm tired of trying! I've given up, there's no other way...

In André's tormented mind a saving idea emerges:

- Listen, I have a plan... A good idea is slowly forming in my mind..

Gasping for breath, he stops talking. Gothardo snores.

Partly recovering, he continues:

- Francois, when I die... and this will not take long, come to my funeral! How frightening it is to talk like that...!

- Then don't talk! You, Monsieur are not going to die! Hang in there a little longer! I will continue to help you as much as I can.

- Don't fool yourself, we are both too intelligent for that...!

Well, listen to me carefully: Take the chance, with courage, using all possible and imaginable resources, the chance to accompany the coffin. When you get to the cemetery, run away! Do this, strengthened in your faith, do you understand? I have a feeling you'll make it! – breathing with difficulty, he shuts up again. A moment later, in broken sentences, he asks:

- Bring me paper and ink! Don't let them see you! I will send through you a note to Louise. I really need to advise her about other matters that concern her property... If I do not do it, his majesty, the king, will confiscate almost everything that belongs to her and what the general's scoundrel will certainly take from him! Poor Louise! Her unhappy family...! May I, at least at the moment of my death, do something good, something praiseworthy... She will understand my regret, even if it's late... Francois, I am going to put you under her protection. Trust her, she is good. When you get there, take care of yourself, hide!

You have been my friend like no one has ever been before...Don't forget to pray for me! - André is slipping on the straw, exhausted.

Francois goes to fetch him fresh water and brings him the required material.

While Joubert drinks non-stop in another part of the prison, and Gothardo sleeps (after a big meal), they speed up the arrangements suggested by André.

Once the note and the address are ready, François tucks them carefully into his shirt. Feeling sorry for him, he keeps watch over his strange friend.

He laments his sad end... He can't stop the tears that fall abundantly from his eyes...

Soon, as he already says, he will die... François prays, reverent and silent.

André, moved by such concern, looks at the boy, deeply grateful. In shorter and shorter periods of time, he moans and emit spasmodic cough. After these actions, he becomes paler and shows an abundant and cold sweat... He feels how life fades away, like fine sand in an hourglass...

The next day, Joubert senses that André is on the verge of death. So, he sends a messenger to General Antoine, warning him.

Hours later, he enters the fortress, with an unusual glint in his cruel eyes. After a few minutes of talking with Joubert, he exclaims, laughing:

- What a joke! So, André and the boy are friends?

I didn't expect that! Things turned out better than expected...! Take me to him. I don't want him to die without seeing me.

Oh, no, he won't!

Dragging his sick leg, Joubert walks through the corridors, followed closely by the General, who replies just as violently to the imprecations he hears, passing through the cells, threatening and spitting, disgusted and insensitive.

Waking up Gothardo with kicks, Joubert opens the door, giving access to the General.

Hearing the noises and voices, André struggles to see who enters and groans painfully when he recognizes Antoine. His disenchantment has no limits. He faces the General's ironic smile and pretends to be unconscious. He wants to avoid a painful confrontation.

Antoine, however, gives him a strong kick in the ribs, causing him to twitch in pain.

François cries, saddened. He has been there, since early in the morning, he knows that his friend will not survive long enough... Not knowing what to do, he stays by his side, praying. He asks Joubert to call the doctor, since André got worse, but was in vain. Out of control, Joubert slaps him a few times for his insistence. His face is still red and swollen. Unable to do anything else, he stands there like a faithful little animal.

- Have you had enough of the "good life" that I have lavished on you, André? And look, I manage to do it twice! You must agree! Naturally, this one has nothing to do with the other, which you must miss a lot! It was necessary, André, for you to know both sides, for you to suffer more, do you understand? All that you have accomplished was only part of my revenge plan! What a joyful life you had, eh, "Baron André"? Has your black soul already bought a passport to hell? How funny, it was you, who walked with your own feet to my revenge dream! I would do it anyway, anywhere and at any time! You would never manage to escape from me!

In a superhuman effort, André asks:

- Revenge, Antoine? What are talking about?! We have always acted by mutual agreement!

- Can you still talk? Good, because that means you can still understand me! Why? You still dare to ask me? You are too stupid! More than I could ever know! You, André de Montmar, stole from me the only love of my life! The only woman that I have truly loved, with all the strength of my being! I wish that you had a thousand lives and that all of them were in my in my hands! - the general spits at André.

Rushing forward, Francois takes his place and begs him:

- Have mercy, sir, by God!

- You stupid boy! He does not deserve your pity! You shouldn't ask me to do that! You don't know what he did to you!

In a state between lucidity and trying to put his ideas together, André understood, unfortunately! If a lightning had struck his head, it would have done no more harm!

- The victim and the executioner, living together as friends! Life plays tricks on us, doesn't it, André? I couldn't have done better myself! - the General continues, enjoying his cruel revenge.

While coughing, tears come down his face, André pleads:

- No, Antoine, don't do this! Please!

- And let the best for later? Never! Look, François! This "friend of yours" is the cause of your disgrace! He threw you here into this infamous life! Out of ambition and sheer cruelty!

Looking pleadingly at François, already in the throes of agony, André stammered:

- Forgive me, Francois... In the name of your faith... If I had time, I'd change everything, I swear to you. I love you very much! May your God keep you safe and help you to forgive me!

Fearless and understanding, Francois drags him to himself, hold his head on his own legs, places a kiss on his sweaty, cold forehead, while comments:

- I forgive you, Monsieur, André! Jesus Christ will receive you into his kingdom as he did for the good thief! Go in peace; I will always pray for your soul! – Bending over him and hugging him, Francois, unable to continue speaking, falls into convulsive weeping.

- Antoine is taken aback by such behavior, coming from such a suffering child; actions like this find no echo in the heart of this cruel man, but for a moment he seems to be moved.

Looking at Francois, deeply grateful, André benefits from this sincere affection and calms down a little. Soon after, he is shaken by convulsions. There, under the hard gaze of Antoine, who had already recovered from his fleeting "weakness", and his satisfaction in a victorious smile, proudly admiring his own work, he breaks down...

Out of control, in a guttural voice, Antoine explodes:

- Hurrah! I am avenged, André! - and rushes out, almost running. He rides his fiery steed and, in a few moments, he gallops swiftly through the streets, like a typhoon...

Joubert, who had tried to accompany him to the exit, exercising his usual servility, returns on his own feet, grumbling.

He concludes, rightly, that he will have to face alone the arrangements that the situation demands.

Weakened, François stayed there. He prays for his friend who has just departed. Amid the tears that still wash over his face, he recalls the long conversation they had:

"- François, my friend, I would like to confess! There is so much to redeem! I need to relieve my conscience!

- We will call a priest, Monsieur André! I will ask Mr. Joubert's permission! Gothardo will call for the chaplain!

- It is not necessary; I never liked them, Francois. I wouldn't trust them! I name you as my confessor! Listen to me, in the name that powerful faith that guides your steps and the mercy that I need, my little friend.

Hear me out, in the name of the heaven that I do not know and which must be your place of origin! I beg you... - André is sincere. Not knowing what to do, intimidated, François shuts up and he begins:

- Francois, I am a fake! An abortion of nature! I am not the person everybody think I am! I got so used to lying...

I had no luck in life, although that doesn't justify anyone's mistakes. You are an example of this.

I had a very suffering childhood; I don't remember my parents.

I grew up in a slum, with relatives that I didn't love and who despised me, making me feel the weight of rejection... As soon as I could, I ran away from them.

Growing up on the streets, I went through every kind of hardship you can imagine... The years went by and when I was already a boy, on my wanderings without a destination, I discovered a barracks and I got used to admiring the soldiers in their daily exercises.

I was fascinated by their uniforms. I made myself so present that the Commander decided to use me in his work.

Despite the difficulties and the greater efforts than I could bear, I was too young, too exhausted, I was happy with the hope that I would become in a military man, like them.

In this coexistence, ah! Francois! I was chased off, exploited and abused, by ruthless, cruel men... These memories make me disgust and shame... However, overcoming everything, I stayed; above circumstances, I wanted to wear the uniform that fascinated me so much! And I did it!

I tried very hard to stand out in front of eyes of the Commander, General Antoine Belfort...

Absurdly servile, I became intimate with him, and he, in the other hand, discovered in me a faithful instrument for his criminal actions. I made myself useful, more and more; becoming indispensable.

In almost everything, we were accomplices.

Once, we imprisoned a nobleman, a Baron.

Full of ambition, tired of crumbs, I requisitioned for myself the unfortunate man's goods. I asked so much that Antoine, even against his will, allowed me such a fortune (until today, I still don't understand why he agreed, because he is stingy as anyone). And so, I took everything that belonged to him, including the title of nobility, changing my identity. I ceased to be, in a flash, a simple military, to assume the personality and wealth of the aforementioned Baron.

Naturally, this nobleman had to disappear forever. These practices were routine in our lives. We used the ways of dishonesty and crime...

Before arresting him, we surprised him and his family, in one of his many properties, overpowering them. I directed everything, authorized by my General. Then, I drove the Baron and his mother away from the family group; they were four in all. Poor, unfortunate woman, begged me for mercy, on her knees...! Her eldest son was imprisoned; she was carried away and thrown into the street... Ah, if only I had known I would pass through the law of Talion, so quickly! Even if I wouldn't have acted like that, if only out of selfishness or fear... But it's too late for me. One day, judged dead, he was thrown in a pile of garbage... However, surprisingly, he was still alive, and survived for some time, in a dark cave, a dwelling place of wretches and thieves. By that time, he was no longer even able to walk or defend himself; he was considered crazy when he said he was the Baron André Brumel of Villefort! At this time, his mother found him again, I was told. But they also said that she had gone mad, poor wretch!...

I kept the Baron's sister and his younger brother with me. She was beautiful, and I tried to seduce her. Strong and determined, she end up exhausting me. To put more pressure on her, I snatched her little brother from her.

That day, in a rage, she threw herself at me, like a lioness defending her cub. I pushed her violently. She fell from the top of a staircase where we were arguing and hit her back on the ground. Never was ever able to walk normally again. Today, she still walks with extreme difficulty.

As for the boy, I gave him to the General and never heard from him again. However, I threatened Louise, telling her that I had him in my power. In this way I keep her silence. I started to pretend that she was my sister. This gave me a certain pride. She is very beautiful, noble, refined, you know?

Well, my friend, the same way I always acted with those I wanted to keep out of my way, they did to me. So, I ended up thrown in here to disappear, far from everything and without defenses!

How ironic...!

Francois listened to his story, in a mixture of pity and anger.

Showing great desolation, André asks:

- François, if I die, will you be sad?

- Certainly, sir!

- There's more, Francois: The General was engaged to a very beautiful woman who enchanted me! Her name was Jeannette. Overcome with passion, and in a short time, I married her. She came from a good family, educated and elegant.

- Sir, what did the General do?

- He became possessed. He threatened me, but we were accomplices, remember?

I know too much about him. Then he calmed down and never said anything about it. He must have forgotten his former fiancée!

Well, I, frivolous and insensitive, quickly got tired of Jeannette and threw myself into the life of pleasure to which I was already accustomed to. I left her aside, and she, poor wretch, loving me in fact, withered away and died a short time later.

I finally could breathe! I was free again!

A few years went by, and during a musical concert in the theater, I saw Madelaine! Sweet, beautiful Madelaine! I was hallucinating!

I was walking blind. I could only feel life if I could see her, and I began systematically pursued her. I found out her name, her address, her family...

- And what about her, sir?

- She clearly showed me how much she abhorred my pursuit. Coming up against me at every angle of the road, she fled as if I were the devil himself!

Insistent, I sent her flowers, cards with loving verses.

I would walk around her castle to hear her sing...

Yes, she sings like a nightingale! Just by hear her, my soul was enraptured in love! The more she fled, the more I want her.

- Sir, where is the lawful Baron?

- He is dead! I will now experience the same fate! Ah, Francois, If I had known it would be like this, I would never have done everything I did...

I have told you only two cases, the ones that are most engraved in my memory... But I come from so many faults...! And what importance have now, all that I have lived? All that I have done? All the power I've achieved? From absolutely nothing!

- Seeing your sorrow, God will forgive you!

- My friend, I am sorry for what I did, because I am in pain and not because I feel regret!

- Even so, God understands our difficulties! Little by little you will discover that it is better to be good!

Ashamed and upset, André listens and accepts the child's wisdom.

Francois had heard everything, but did not know whether to believe it or not.

After all, André was feverish, one step away from death...

Focus, thinking in how to escape, he shudders at Joubert's shrill, rude voice that pulls him out of his recent memories.

- Get up, you scumbag! There's so much to do! Every time a prisoner dies, it's a nuisance! Everything is left for me! Notify my intendente to arrange for a doctor to come for the death and a priest to commend the body! Lieutenant André de Montmar lived and died like a thief!

Joubert's words ring in François' ears like thunder:

"André told the truth?...! Who am I, after all? What did the General wanted to tell me? Do the statements of both men refer to the same things, don't they? If I ask Mr. Joubert any questions..., I'll abort my escape plan... Then I'll think about it! God will help me!

I need to talk to the Turkish woman. Joubert is in a serious crisis of gout. In a few hours, he will be totally drunk in an attempt to escape from the pain that torments him...

With his narrow mind, Gothardo will be easy to manipulate... Those in charge of other functions will not understand my intentions...".

Obeyed the jailer's orders, Francois leaves to look for the Turkish woman. Washing clothes, she sees the boy arrive. She wipes the sweat on her apron and, smiling, asks:

- Was there something, habib? - she sometimes calls him that.

In a confiding tone, he answers:

- Turkish woman, finally we will be able to escape from here forever!

- And what gives you this certainty?

He explains to her the plans drawn up by André. Carefully, he takes out from inside his rustic shirt the piece of paper with the address and the note to Louise. There is also a small map indicating the way to Portal da Luz, made by André.

- Do you have any money? - he whispers.

- Yes, I have some savings, why?

- To pay for the rental of a vehicle. André thought that we are too far from his house.

- What if those who are there kick us out?

- He said that Louise is a very good woman! Anything is better than to stay here! May God forgive me, Turkish woman, but sometimes I want to die to get rid of this life! - Francois begins to cry. His emotions surprise him in a borderline situation.

- Son, it will be very dangerous!

- I know! Listen: I love you very, very much! But, if you don't come with me, I'll go alone! If you die, it's okay! It's worth it!

Hugging him, loving, with tears in her eyes, she tries to reason with him:

- Dear son, I fear for the risks we will take! You still a child!

- I am not, Turkish woman! I have matured too much for the life I lead, you say so yourself, remember?

I want to live like all the boys! I have dreams in my head, Turkish woman! With you and Rachid, I learned to read and write, but I want much more!

I will have a profession that will support us and who knows one day, as an adult and fulfilled, I will return to continue helping those who suffer here? – he looks in the distance, toward the blue sky, full of white clouds, as if he could see the future.

Impressed and moved, squeezing him against her heart she agrees:

- Okay, my great conqueror, we will go! And may be whatever God has planned to us! Explain the plan to me, so that we can put it into practice.

He hugs the good woman's neck and whispers the details in her ear. She nods her head affirmatively.

Soon after, Francois goes to his quarters and there, he wraps some objects in a tiny package that he hides in his clothes.

The Turkish woman, in turn, makes a small package and puts it in her breast. In the folds of the turban, she hides some jewelry.

After the quick arrangements, carried out without any respect or reverence, André's body is placed in a thick cloth bag and left on the ground, awaiting burial.

Disguisedly, Francois and the Turkish woman are ready.

Joubert has already lost track of everything.

Francois talks to Gothardo:

- My big friend, the Turkish woman and I are going to the cemetery and we'll be back soon!

- No, Francois! No way! Mr. Joubert will kill us! – he replies in a frightened, slurred voice and concludes:

- I'll ask him, wait here, Francois, my little friend!

- Gothardo, if you wake him up, he will punish you very much! And me too!

The brute shakes his head affirmatively.

- But, I won't let you leave! That's it!

- Gothardo, listen: André was my friend, just like you, do you understand? How could I leave him without my prayers? If you had died, even if I were punished, I would pray in the cemetery in front of your grave!

The Turkish woman will bring me back in the blink of an eye. She is keeping an eye on me, you know.

And there's more! Listen, get down here, I don't want them to hear us... And if André, angry with you, comes to haunt you, eh? You used to beat him, remember? – Gothardo's eyes widen. He is terrified of ghosts. – Do you want him to walk the halls every night?

- No! I am afraid, Francois! – he covers his eyes with his big, rough hands.

- Well then? Let us go and don't worry! We'll be back before Mr. Joubert wakes up, okay?

Swinging his body, he falters, grimacing as he thinks and decides. Finally, taking a long sigh and shaking his arms, he exclaims:

- That's right! You can go, my little friend! I'll let you go! But come back quickly, okay?

- Okay, Gothardo!

Pretending to appear at that moment, the Turkish woman exclaims:

- Let's hurry, my son, because the body is already stinking to high heaven!

Look, I'm taking our Bible. We must reassure André's soul that he will never come back here again!

Gothardo shudders at every word he listens. He fears the dead with a horror that borders on unbalance.

Deeply moved, Francois asks:

- My big man, give me a hug, I want to thank you!

Deeply moved, he bends down. Francois hugs his tawny neck and places a kiss on his forehead while saying:

- Thank you for everything, my dear friend. May God keep you safe!

As Joubert's right arm twitches, the Turkish woman pulls Francois by the shirt, hurried and nervous.

Finally, they settle down on the cart, next to the body.

Grinding on the treadmills, the wheels seem to weep for the unfortunate who lived deluded and died fearing the wrath of God.

The two gravediggers look at each other, suspicious of those unexpected passengers.

François sees the gloomy Fortress falling behind him. His heart beats wildly.

They arrive at the cemetery. The vehicle stops and everyone gets out. Silent, the gravediggers begin their work of digging the hole. It is horrible to hear the sound of shovels in that sepulchral silence.

Apparently distracted, they work when Francois and the Turkish woman, foot by foot, begin to distance themselves, but, startled they hear:

- Where do you think you are going?

Francois shudders. Keeping calm, the Turkish woman replies:

- We move a little away to pray for the dead man!

Dropping what they do, they approach and one of them threatens:

- Do you think we are idiots? You will come back with us! We don't want any trouble with Mr. Joubert!

Faced with great danger, she asks:

- What are you afraid of? Where could we go? We'll be there, look! - she points to a large cross buried on a mound of earth.

- Hum... you look suspicious to me... - Turning to his partner, he asks softly:

- Teodoro, what shall we do with these two?

- Well, what do we care where they go? Mr. Joubert is very stingy with us! But if they are running away, they may have money!

Nodding a deaf laugh, the other concludes:

- We can have something from the living customers this time, huh? Ah!

Ah... I didn't expect that!

- Yes, that's it! If you don't have any money, maybe you can carry something valuable! Look, they are terrified!

While they are talking, François prays and the Turkish woman waits, trying to exude a serenity that she is far from feeling.

Determined and malevolent, they approach:

- Well... we can let them go, if they pay us! Otherwise, they'll come back with us!

Resigned, Betbara removes two precious gems from her turban (gifts from her dearly missed Rachid) and places them on a nearby mausoleum.

While they run over each other and advance toward the small treasure, Francois and her, quickly walk away, disappearing without looking back.

Gasping for breath, after a mad dash, they board a hired carriage. Giving the driver the address and coordinates, she places Francois in the cabin.

The vehicle keeps rocking and his eyes start feeling heavy...

Finally, he gives himself up to a restful sleep, while, loving and solicitous, the Turkish woman watches over him. Calmer, she concludes that they are far from the fortress, and thanks God for that.

* * *

AT RUE DE LA CHAPELLE, in Henry's mansion, the situation is one of commotion and amazement. The guests make comments disparaging remarks as to Eugene's criminal daring, and then leave in their pompous carriages, back to their homes. A party had been finished, to the disappointment of many or, in truth, almost everyone. That day was going well!

Bettine returned to the castle, while the Count and Madelaine take care of Eugene.

At the police station they try to protect her as much as possible.

Warning her of the risk she runs, they try to get her out of the mutism, in which she has walled herself up.

- Listen to me, Eugene, and try to understand me! With my experience I can tell you with confidence: by being silent, by rejecting the help we offer you, you cannot even imagine the danger you are running. Don't be imprudent, and let us help you get out of this situation unharmed or you could live a real hell! – the Count advises.

Taking her frozen hands, Madelaine reinforces her father's warning:

- Eugene, if you do not speak out, we will lose the chance to defend you!

In a thread of voice, she replies:

- I must fulfill my destiny, paying for my criminal plan! That's what I want! Go away and leave me alone, please...!

- What did Henry do to you, Eugene, that you want to hurt him so badly? What is tormenting you to the point of making you lose your balance and your survival instinct? And even more, to punish yourself, as you are doing? – Madelaine inquires, looking into her eyes; eyes that she turns away, intentionally.

She is aware of the act she has committed. Despite all the rebellion she has harbored in her heart for so many years, and the desire to destroy Henry, she knows that she has transgressed the laws of God and men.

Amid the disparate and confused thoughts, the memory of everything she has learned, love and misfortune, coming from his father and sister Rosalia, as well as the entire educational institute, where she lived for so many years, since she was a little girl...

She betrayed everyone!

The seed of good, despite appearances, struggles to sprout in Eugene's soul...

Regretful, she would like to be living a nightmare and awakening... She had so much time to reconsider it, but she didn't...!

For years she had harbored thoughts of hatred, resentment, desires for revenge...

Now everything seems useless, empty, without purpose. Where is the joy she imagined she would feel when she saw him fallen, defeated, at her feet?

She is the only one defeated; her life, her future, the joy and peace of her beloved father! How will he live now having a criminal daughter?...!

His good and sensitive heart will not stand it...! What will he think of her, her good friend, Marianne? And her beloved twins? Such sweet children. She'll have to stay away from them forever...

Yes, she must pay for what she has done. She 'doesn't deserve help from anyone...

Eugene, in his foolishness, ignores that the justice she hopes for is far away; that her existence will now turn into chaos; that she will lose, suddenly or slowly, everything she values and life itself, in the cruel involvement of the situation itself; especially without the legal and competent help of the Count.

While Eugene thinks, father and daughter wait. They fear that she, inadvertently take on such an ominous fate. Finally, she takes a deep breath and asks them, between doubt and reproach:

- Why are you interested in me? If you are Henry's friends, why do you try to defend me?

- Calm down, Eugene. I am a friend of Henry's, but my friendship with him does not prevent me from acting freely according to my conscience! We do want to defend you, believe me. We have some idea what will happen to you, if you are charged, alone and obstinate in this revolt. Henry himself, before fainting from his wound, asked me to protect you. We don't know what happened between the two of you, leading to this act of madness; but pray heaven help him not to die, Eugene! Your situation will become much more complicated! Besides, as his friends, we wish him survive! May God help him!

Finally, Eugene can no longer bear the emotions that invade her soul, breaking her heart. She begins to cry, while she says:

- Henry has put us into misery! He is a vile thief!

- Young lady, let's see. Tell us what really happened.

Tell us everything, from the beginning, please, intervenes the Count.

Opening the floodgates of her soul, Eugene unburdens herself, telling them everything.

Father and daughter listen in dismay to the painful story that involved the lives of Eugene, his father, and Henry.

Madelaine feels a painful tightness in her heart; she deplores the unfortunate confirmation of Henry's bad character. She had accepted his invitation to probe his soul, and behold, she has access to a true spiritual autopsy.

At the end of the narrative, Eugene, in Madelaine's arms, weeps that seems to have been dammed for a long, long time... And so, it is.

Guiding her as to the most appropriate behavior in that place and following the legal processes, the Count surrounds Eugene with protection. For now, she will be detained.

Once alone, she gives herself over to despair. She asks Madelaine to warn her father at the ranch. She fervently hopes that Henry do not to die, lest she be condemned, and in a belated repentance pleads to heaven for help.

She remembers that she left a note for her father in the room at the boarding house, confessing to him what she intended to do and asking his forgiveness. On the little missive, she wrote down Henry's address.

Curled up on a rustic bed, Eugene wishes uselessly to return home and throw herself into her father's arms.

"My dear mother, wherever you are, forgive me and help me to get out of here!

God! What have I done? Oh, how embarrassing, when sister Rosália finds out! Why didn't I listen to the advice of all those who love me?! What would I do? Will the Count and his daughter really be able to help me?..."

The door opens and she is startled. A burly woman with hard features gave her a bowl of food. Even hungry as she is, she rejects it. Shrugging her shoulders, the woman leaves, closing the door behind her.

The hours pass mournfully... Sometimes sleep imposes itself and she loses her sense of reality to awaken frightened, feeling in danger. She tries to remain vigilant, but she longs to rest; she is exhausted and very weak. A lassitude takes over her body and she sleep soundly for many hours...

Madelaine goes to the hospital and is told that Henry is still in danger of death. Operated and medicated, he still sleeps. The next day, she returns and the doctor tells him that, luckily, the wound was not mortal.

Three days later, he can receive visitors and she is present.

He is sleepy and disfigured.

- Henry, thank God you are out of danger! We were worried!

- Thank you, Madelaine. I escaped this one. And Eugene?

- She's in custody, Henry. We've got to help her.

- If there's anything I can do, I'm here.

- We were waiting for you to be able to sign a statement, exonerating her.

- I will do that, Madelaine, give me the document.

- Thank you. My father sends you regards. We are at Eugene's side, comforting her and giving her all the support she needs.

Signing the papers, Henry grimaces in pain. The doctor, nearby, orders him to rest.

- Thank you, Henry!

Disconcerted, he wants to know:

- Did you talk to Eugene? Do you know... everything?

- Yes, and I can't hide my great disappointment, Henry.

- I'm sorry and I understand... So disappointed, you despise me, Madelaine? Have I lost your affection? Too bad Eugene did not succeed.

- Don't be dramatic, Henry! You know I'll never despise you.

- You're still my friend, after all?! – he is surprised.

- Certainly! Rest and get better, my friend! I will come back to visit you tomorrow.

- I'll be waiting for you, looking forward to it! Thank you, for your indulgence!

- We are friends, Henry. See you tomorrow!

– See you tomorrow, Madelaine! – she leaves. He, in a whisper, alone, begs, as if she could hear him: Forgiveness...! – Turning his face to the side, hiding it, cries... It is a painful cry of anticipated loss. His theater has collapsed; he has lost the condition to reach his star!

In possession of the required documents, the Count goes to the competent authorities, and in a few hours, taking responsibility for Eugene, he manages to free her.

She thanks him, humiliated.

Madelaine hugs her, moved and happy with one more victory of her father's over the law. She admires his beloved father.

She reveres his dedication to those who depend on his knowledge and competence and, above all, his abnegation to help those who need and cannot pay. He always defends the cause with true passion when it is just.

Eugene shows intention of returning to the boarding house, but they manage to persuade her to stay at the Castle; they fear to leave her alone in the face of such fragility.

Without resisting, she accompanies them, and once there, following Madelaine's advice, she takes a comforting bath, eats well, and falls asleep peacefully, feeling protected. She needs to get back on her feet.

The next day, Sir. Jaime arrives in Paris. He goes straight to the boarding house. There, he asks for the key to her room and finds the revealing note.

Trembling, he reads it to the end. His head spins and his legs shake.

He sits down on a chair, opens the floodgates of his soul, and weeps. From the date on the note, he concludes that she must have already done what she intended.

With Henry's address, he goes there without delay. Arriving, he identifies himself at the front desk. He is informed that the master of that mansion had suffered an attempt on his life and is still in the hospital.

He thought he was going crazy, when he was astonished to hear one of the servants' versions about what had happened:

- Imagine, Sir, one of the maids shot him with a pistol! She probably had other intentions towards him, do you know what I mean? - this, he says, winking, full of malice.

Ah, those gold-diggers! This is already common in our boss's life, but this time, it could be fatal to him!

She is already under arrest, and before she was arrested, she was slapped with a loud slap that she will never forget as long as she lives! Well, if she gets out of prison, of course! We know how things are done in there, don't we?

In Sir. Jaime's mind, the past settles in and he sees Henry verbally abusing him, insensitive, throwing in his face all his financial tragedy caused by his infamous betrayal ... He relives that cruel and decisive moment that almost took his life...

At this moment, however, his despair is much greater! His daughter's dignity and safety are being threatened!

Without answering, he turns his back on the man who, without responsibility says so much nonsense and walks slowly trying to organize his own ideas. A little far away, he leans against a wall so as not to fall.

Unable to bear it any longer, he collapses in a desperate weeping, in the middle of the street, unaware of the scandal he is causing.

He asks the hospital's address and goes there.

On the way, he prays to the heavens for help for Eugene.

When he arrives, he hurries to the reception desk:

- Please, I am coming from a trip and I need to see Mr. Henry John Stanford! My name is Jaime Sartorelli!

Madelaine, who at that moment arrives to visit Henry, hears the poor man's exclamations and concludes that he is Eugene's father.

She is surprised by his presence. Surely, he had not yet had time to receive his call.

- Are you Eugene Sartorelli's father?

- Yes, *Mademoiselle*! Why? – he answers, intrigued by the question.

- Calm down! I can see that you are not well! Your daughter is in my house, rest!

- Praise God! – he exclaims, leaning on the counter.

His pallor is extreme. – And *Mademoiselle*, who are you?

- A friend of Eugene's. Come, let's go with her.

They leave for the Castle. On the way, they chat:

- Sir Jaime, how did you know?

- Forgive me for not being able to answer this question. We will say I came by intuition!

- Of course, don't apologize. Do you live here in Paris?

- No. I am from England, but now I live and work in a resort in Reims. Well, I left my luggage at Eugene's boarding house!

- The coachman will take us there and you can pick them up.

- No, *Mademoiselle*, on second thought, instead, I will bring Eugene with me and we'll stay at the boarding house. We've caused you enough troubles!

- I insist, sir! You must be with us for the next steps in favor of Eugene's definitive freedom.

My father pleads her cause. She will surely be acquitted of attempted murder.

- What were you doing at the hospital, *Mademoiselle*?

- I was going to visit Henry, we are friends!

- You are friends? And why are you defending my daughter?

- Monsieur Jaime, Henry has won my friendship, but he has not taken my sense of justice. And speaking of justice, although defend your daughter and know the motives that moved her, I do not agree, absolutely, with her criminal plans!

- Nor do I, *Mademoiselle*! I tried uselessly to dissuade you from this obsessive pursuit of Henry. I never thought she would go that far. I could never have imagined her in a situation like this.

- When passions run high, the brakes are lost!

- I agree, *Mademoiselle*.

- God will help us and all will be well!

As she speaks, he remembers what he heard through Natacha: that the angel who crossed his path to help him, would need, later, competent help in a dramatic situation... "what does the future hold for her? Poor girl!" – he thinks, saddened.

Giving him time for his thoughts, Madelaine thinks about how to proceed with Louise and Gotuza; she must organize to promote the reunion of the two, probably mother and daughter.

They arrive at the boarding house. He goes downstairs, pays the landlady, informs her that Eugene will return with him to England, and in addition to his luggage, he also takes the daughter's belongings with him.

On the way to the Castle, he and Madelaine chat like they were old friends.

- *Mademoiselle*, I am surprised to think that I take great pleasure in meeting you, despite the unfortunate circumstances!

- Thank you, I can tell you the same, sincerely.

I believe that Henry, in time, will change the course of his thoughts and attitudes. The act of defending Eugene, already demonstrates it.

If wasn't for him, the process of proving her innocence would be more difficult and even doubtful. He signed the papers, releasing her from the charges. In this way, my father is already trying to get the satisfactory conclusion in the Courts.

- And so, we will always have to be grateful with you.

- Yes, Sir. Jaime. But you and your daughter will be very happy!

- How can we pay everything you are doing for us?

- Don't even think about it! The joy of seeing them well will be our reward, mine and my father's. In a little while, you and your daughter will be together; we are near the house.

When they arrive, she leads him to Eugene's room. He knocks on the door and walks away before she answers, leaving them alone.

As she walks away, she hears the rumble of voices and Eugene's cry.

She concludes, grateful to the heavens, that Eugene is letting off steam in his father's arms...

She goes on her way and, in other rooms, far from those where Eugene is, she tells Gotuza:

- Dear Gotuza, in a few days someone will come to see you. In a way, this will be a test for your memory. I hope that this event will gladden your heart and fill a gap in your life.

In a short time, Sir. Jaime and Eugene have become fraternally accustomed to living together with the Alvarados.

Right now, we can see them at the table:

- Would you like some more cookies, Miss Eugene? - asks Ignácia, serving them to her.

- Thank you, Ignácia! They're delicious! I can't thank you enough for everything! - she declares, touched.

- Promise to be more prudent, Eugene! - Bettine advises.

- Yes, Countess. I've learned that we can't play with destiny! I almost destroyed my life and my father's!

- And Henry's, Eugene, especially Henry's! Don't forget that!

- You're right, Madelaine. And how is he?

- He is recovering very well. He spent several days between life and death. Yet he never accused you! In the last few weeks, Henry had a change of moral!

- Praise God! - exclaims Sir. Jaime - Also for the help we have received from all of you, I don't know how to pay you or how to express my gratitude! I put at your disposal my most humble services! And, above all, I offer you my respect and my admiration! May God bless you!

While everyone is talking happily, Madelaine thinks about the possibility of arranging a reconciliation between Henry, Sir. Jaime and Eugene.

IN THE GARDEN, LOUISE breaths the scent of flowers as she remembers Madelaine's statements about Gotuza. She is almost sure that is her beloved mother. And Lucien, where is he? - she thinks.

Corine brings a letter:

- A servant of Madelaine's brought it and awaits the answer, *Mademoiselle*.

She opens it and reads:

"Dear Louise,

Kindest greetings!

Unexpected and serious issues have taken up precious time for me.

Now we can schedule your visit to see Gotuza. If you can come tomorrow, Salústio will pick you up.

Wishing you peace and health, I bid farewell while waiting for your answer.

Best regards!

Your friend,

Madelaine D'Or Alvarado"

Louise quickly writes back and dispatches the messenger, confirming her presence for the next day at the Alvarado Castle.

On her mind appears the beautiful and manly figure of Salústio and her heart beats strongly. He will come for her! She picks a rose and admiring it, introspective. On her knees, the book of poems that she has been reading. Looking up at the sky of intense blue, she gives thanks for the hope that now bathes her heart. Mateus approaches and she warns:

- Mateus, tomorrow I have an appointment. I'll leave early.

- *Mademoiselle* knows the orders I had received from the Baron!

- Don't worry, I take responsibility for my actions.

He pretends annoyance to cover his real emotions. He will escape in a few days, carrying everything he can. He has given up on winning her.

He will surely find another beautiful woman who will love him. Soon, very soon, he will be rich...

Planning for the following day, Salústio shudders at the thought that he will take Louise; that he will be close to her? After the feelings that Madelaine awakened in him, he never loved again. Now, the beautiful Louise makes him live like he was dreaming... But, between them, there is a great distance. She is noble, and he is just a very humble man...

Going around the garden, with her usual difficulty, Louise approaches the big main gate.

She sits down on one of the benches, hidden behind a bower, and watches the movement of the street. The burning sun seems to warm those who move along the sidewalk.

"I feel strange... – thinks. – I sense something... Why am I so upset? It must be anxiety about tomorrow's visit..."

A sound of voices arouses her attention and she stands up, holding on to the bench. She struggles to see better.

On the sidewalk, a policeman shakes the arm of a woman in a red turban who is holding a beautiful boy by the hand.

– Officer, what's going on? – she asks, curious and annoyed by his aggressiveness.

– *Mademoiselle*, I surprised these two looking in there.

They must be thieves!

The woman hugs the boy and defends herself:

– No, sir, we are not thieves! We are looking for someone and this is the address we have! Isn't this the house of Baron André of Villefort?

Louise shudders.

– And if it is, Madame? Why are you looking for him?

– It is not him we are looking for, but *Mademoiselle* Louise!

The policeman, impatient, tries to drag her away, but Louise intervenes:

– Wait! This woman is telling the truth! Louise is me!

- Praise God! – exclaims the boy, pale and hardly impressed by the distressing situation.

Louise orders a servant to open the gate for them.

Leaning in, hugging each other, they enter scared.

Mateus appears and rushes toward them, trying to push them out:

- *Mademoiselle*, what recklessness! Can't you see they're beggars?

Before they can reply, Louise declares, making Mateus turn pale:

- They're looking for the Baron! I will deal with them! The two are certainly unaware that he is traveling! – At the woman's explanation, she demands her to be quiet and waits for Mateus to move away.

By mutual agreement, the two, looking at each other meaningfully, pulling out a piece of paper from his rustic shirt, François, shows it to Louise. She reads, much to her surprise. There, in André's handwriting and with his signature, is the request to protect François. Whispering softly, she wants to know:

- And him, where is he?

- He is dead, *Mademoiselle*! We went to his funeral. He told me that we could trust your good heart. My name is François!

- And mine, *Mademoiselle*, is Betbara, your servant! Thank you for defending us! – adds the Turkish woman, holding the boy tightly by the hand.

- Come in, please! We need to talk! – Louise is in shock. They cross the large reception hall, slowly, due to her difficulty to move around, they reach the office and lock themselves in.

- Please, sit down! – she asks.

The two sit down next to each other, intimidated.

- Have no fear! – she advises, reassuring them.

- We're simply tired! – justifies the Turkish woman.

- Besides, Mr. André has assured us that *Mademoiselle* is good! - adds François, smiling.

- Tell me everything, please, from the beginning. We are alone!

He tells how he met André. He details the sufferings he experienced in prison, his death, and his plan to free François from the depressing and desperate situation in which he had always lived.

As she listens to him, Louise concludes that Lucien must be his age, and must have his physiognomic features as well. She feels a painful longing.

- How old are you, François?

- Ten years old, *Mademoiselle*.

- Who are your parents?

- I don't know. The dear Turkish woman, who is here, raised me.

Louise notices that they are exhausted and hungry.

She calls Corine, ordering her to take care of them.

A few hours later, General Antoine announces himself.

Welcoming him, Louise asks him:

- What do you want, General? Be brief, please! - she exclaims, not hiding the displeasure his presence causes her.

- By the devils, *Mademoiselle*! Can't you put your weapons away?

- What weapons are you talking about, General? I confess that I am very busy at the moment, so tell me what you have come for!

Without giving up, intentionally, he plunges his eyes into Louise's and speaks to her in a sweet, romantic voice:

- I wish I could create pleasant preambles, recite to you, beautiful madrigals, prepare myself better! But, *Mademoiselle*, make it difficult! Not everything can be said in haste! Let me get ready, please!

Louise, impatient, takes a deep breath and waits.

- Well! I have come to tell you, beautiful Louise, that I have decided to get married again!

- Really? And why can this matter be important to me?

- Come on, beautiful Louise! Don't play dumb! I have never hidden my interest in *Mademoiselle*!

- Could you be clearer, please? I can't understand what you are saying!

- I certainly will, that's why I came! I'm asking you to marry me!

What do you say? I will make you very happy!

She thinks about the note written by André and Francois' story...

Can you imagine what this cruel man would do if he knew how much she knows about him. She wishes him gone, definitively. Without preamble, she answers categorically:

- I don't intend to get married, for now.

- You are missing a great opportunity to be happy by my side, beautiful Louise! Think about it!

- I thank you for the proposal and the honor you do me, but I'm not interested. Anything else, General?

Controlling his great disappointment, he informs him in a contrite manner:

- Yes! André's death has been confirmed.

- And how did you get this "confirmation"?

- *Mademoiselle* forgets my position?

- Not at all! Even if I wanted to, it would be impossible! You remind us of it all the time!

- Often, *Mademoiselle*, I do much more than that. There are some people who are very stubborn and reckless! – she senses his subtle threat. He continues: - Before he died, André confessed his true identity. Just imagine! Something we could never guess! We concluded that he was not your brother, right?

Outraged at such insolence, she answers, ironically:

- How clever, General!

- I also assume that *Mademoiselle* has been taken hostage by the fake André! And, furthermore, that she must be the real owner of everything!

- Right again! If you had known, would you have done something to help me?

- Of course! Well, now, *Mademoiselle* can get part of his goods.

- Why part and not all?

- Because the absolutist regime will take, as it always does, the largest share! Don't you know that, *Mademoiselle*? I feel bad for you! Sick and alone, it will be difficult for you to defend yourself! But if you accept my proposal of marriage... You know my power! I assure you that you will not regret it!

- I thank you, once again, and I assure you that I am never alone! I do not need your pity, because I have God, General!

- Then, may "he" help you, *Mademoiselle*! – he replies with a musty smile.

- Did André report the whereabouts of Lucien, my little brother? – she risks.

- He disappeared? I never knew! What a pity, isn't it? Well, dear Louíse, I've just remembered that I have an urgent appointment! *Mademoiselle* is not the only woman who interests me! Farewell!

Bending down, he slaps one boot against the other and leaves, promising himself that he will never look for her again.

François, who was approaching the salon, spots the General and steps back. Trembling, making signs to the Turkish woman, he also prevents her from to appear. Hidden, they wait for Louíse.

On the way out, Antoine's eyes cross with Corine's. She passed on, indifferent, but she felt her heart soar. Dreamily, she continues with her duties. A few moments ago, supervising Francois' hygiene at the toilette, she declared:

- What a beautiful boy you are! Your features resemble those of *Mademoiselle* Louíse!

Quietly, analyzing François, the Turkish woman agrees with the talkative Corine.

That night, Betbara and François rest peacefully and safely in a comfortable bed, clean and soft.

With his eyes open, measuring the luxury that surrounds him, François understands why André missed it all. After his prayers, grateful to heaven, he falls deeply asleep.

* * *

THE FOLLOWING MORNING, in an elegant *toilette*, hair tied high on top of her head, showing a rosy and beautiful countenance, Louíse awaits Salústio, and struggles to remain balanced. She has a mixture of emotions.

Gotuza, sitting on a bench in the garden, waits; she doesn't know who will come.

The Countess has been in the north wing of the castle for some time now, helping the needy ones. The Count has left, heading for his work. The children are in the library studying, and Madelaine gives the servants orders about the house.

Life in the garden is cyclical: the perennial growth of the stems, the multiplicity and renewal of leaves, the blossoming of flowers, the colorful butterflies, the buzzing of bees in the incessant nectar, the presence of tiny insects under the precious rays of the sun that made life better, in a praise to the Creator...

Gotuza observes a whimsical nest, in which the mother nourishes the chicks in their beaks; they are fragile, greedy, and bulky. She smiles delighted.

She looks into the distance, as far as the eye can see. It's so good to live with this family... They treat her with such affection. She had forgotten the amenities of life... She had been so beaten, so despised...! After all, she was never the same...! Sometimes, she doubts she's still alive... dear Dr. Sergei smiles happily to see her better. With all the help she has received from everyone, she can calm down, take her medicine and trust in the future!

Madelaine told her that someone was coming to seeing her... Who will it be?

Breathing deeply, she remembers the cave, her sick son, how he died... He almost lost her mind and life... Still doesn't remember her past... In her mind things are mixed up... Her dreams are very confusing; in them, people she does not know appear, acting in strange ways. Sometimes she falls into a convulsive cry made of pain, of loss... For whom? For what? In these moments, Madelaine and her family console her and comfort her, affectionately... They give her tranquilizers. May God keep them safe!

With their help, she rises every day, hopeful and full of faith! If the philanthropic group of the Parish House had not found them, she would have died already, just like her beloved and missed son.

She is anxious, her heart beats strongly in expectation of something different... What will come?

She softly says a prayer of gratitude to the heavens.

Singing in chorus with her prayer, the birds sing; she smiles, moved and grateful to God.

She hears footsteps. She notices dear Salústio approaching, carrying a girl in his arms. Careful and gentle, he settles her on one of the benches. He bows his head slightly in her direction, greeting her. Then he walks away.

The girl settles down and arranges her clothes. She looks around. It looks like waiting for someone or something.

Finally, she comes across her (Gotuza is very beautiful, snowy hair, a nice pink face with classic lines. Hands in lap, right and dignified posture), who is intrigued and observes her in silence.

Sharpening her eyes, incredulous, heart wanting to jump out of her chest, barely believing Louíse whispers:

- God of mercy! Am I dreaming? My mother!

Gotuza continues looking at her thoughtfully. In her eyes, the curiosity of the moment and the perplexity of the situation.

That girl looks familiar to her! She finds her nice. Who is she? Where do she knows her from? That's why Madelaine told her it would be a memory test! Surely, 'she had seen her; maybe in the Parish House, right there in the castle... She makes an enormous effort to remember...

Suddenly, with her heart pounding, in an extreme tenderness, she recognizes her! In an almost inaudible voice, she exclaims:

- My child! Louíse! - with faltering steps she approaches, while Louíse opens her arms in the urgency of the amorous embrace so long postponed.

Hugging her, emotional and confused, Gotuza asks:

- Louíse, my daughter, where were you? André is dead!

- Poor, dear brother! God rest his soul, my mother! Nevertheless, God has preserved us for this blessed reunion!

- Beloved daughter, how I miss you! How much anguish I experienced, without knowing about you! Oh God! Why do we suffer so much?...

- Don't be tormented, Mother! These are unfathomable mysteries!

Stroking her hair, Gotuza asks:

- Why did Salústio take you in his arms? Are you sick, by any chance? Can you not walk?

- I will explain later, mama. This handicap has prevented me from to act more freely, as well as keeping me hostage to our executioner for years...

- My dear, is Lucien with you? Why didn't you bring him with you?

I miss him so much.

- Calm down, mother! We've had enough excitement for one day. You must take care of yourself. I promise you that later we'll talk about Lucien!

Seeing them well, Salústio, who was watching them from a distance, moves away.

He comes across Madelaine. Bright eyes and a broad smile on her lips, she declares:

- I feel happy, Salústio! I'll talk to them later. Now, they need to be alone; there is so much to say! God bless them!

***

AT THE PORTAL DA LUZ, François and the Turkish woman have their first meal of the day. Then François, restless and dazzled, runs free all over the entire property, breathing heavily, happy as a bird that has escaped from his cage.

***

MADELAINE SEARCHES FOR Louíse:

- Finally, duties done, I can be with you and welcome you with dignity, Louíse!

- Madelaine, the happiness you have given us is priceless! May you and your family be blessed a thousand times!

Taking a seat next to Gotuza, Madelaine receives a loud kiss of recognition.

The afternoon is gone and Louíse must return.

She says goodbye to her mother and promises to come back to see her. One more time, Salústio leads her, carrying her with unparalleled discretion and nobility.

Everyone can see how happy they are when they are together.

Once they arrived, Francois ran to meet her:

- Louíse, how are you?

- I am very well! And you, my dear?

- Ah, I can't believe I'm here, away from that fortress!

I'm happy, happy, happy! – he shouts, raising his arms towards the heavens.

- I can see it in the brightness of your eyes and the wonderful colors of your face, dear boy!

Jumpy, he follows her, pacing to wait for her. Then, suddenly stops; on the wall of the corridor, a portrait catches his attention:

- My friend André! How handsome and elegant he was!

- Yes, Francois! Your friend was very elegant! How do you feel about him now?

- I feel pity for his sufferings and his death; as well as friendship and longing, too! Poor fellow! Fortunately, he repented his mistakes; if not out of remorse, as he himself said, for fear of what he would find on the other side, carrying so much guilt! He helped me escape! I owe him my freedom!

- Good for him, Francois! May God reward him! As for you, my little one, we must plan your future. I will speak with Father Estanislau about your education.

✱ ✱ ✱

HENRY IS STILL in the hospital. Sir. Jaime and Madelaine decide to go visit him.

Pale, like the color of the sheets, in rest and with his eyes closed, he enjoys missing Madelaine. He desires to be discharged so he can go look for her.

He closes his eyes and remembers her, every aspect of her face; her features, her softness and energy, her beautiful black hair, her light feet, her crystalline and sonorous voice, her beautiful small and smiling mouth. She is his muse, his ideal of womanhood, his love...!

He hears a sound of footsteps and is surprised by their presence.

He can't disguise his emotion.

- Good news, Henry! The doctor told us that you will soon be going home and there you will complete your recovery.

- Yes, that's true. I've missed you, Madelaine!

Deliberately ignoring what she heard, she wants to know:

- How do you feel?

- Weak and dizzy; but the wound is healing well.

- That's good! Soon, you'll be feeling better! And what about the painful experience you lived?

- I feel confused. I am torn between rebellion at Eugene's extreme act and the unfortunate realization of my guilt!

- Eugene is impulsive! You defied fate, Henry!

- This is how I have lived, Madelaine! – Ashamed, he closes his eyes, interiorizing himself. Madelaine now knows her spiritual miseries... His performance as a good man has fallen apart...

What a disaster...!

Respecting his silence, guessing his sad and painful thoughts, she is momentarily silent.

Minutes later, breaking the silence, she informs him:

- Henry, someone has come with me and wants to see you.

Astonished, he asks:

- Eugene has come with you?

- No, but someone else is here.

In view of the things that have involved us all, I have become friends with both father and daughter!

Intending to get up to complain, Henry moves, but collapses back onto the bed.

Showing much annoyance, he concludes, perplexed:

- Madelaine, you brought Eugene's father here?!!!!

- Yes, Henry! I brought him!

- How could you, Madelaine? Is this something to be done? Not even asked my permission!

- You wouldn't, my friend! While you heal your body, you must begin the healing of your soul!

Disgusted, he stubbornly shuts up. Had it been someone else and not Madelaine! He would never allow himself to be told what to do! What a horrible imposition! He 'doesn't want to see his old boss.

She looks at Madelaine and realizes her disappointment. With her eyes lowered, she waits for him to speak up. He will never disregard her! Take a deep breath and agrees, in a kind voice, in which he tries to imprint a relaxed tone:

- Okay, Madelaine, let's go! After all, it's not the end of the world!

What can I do, right? You've decided for me! I know that your intention is good! Let's do it! Where is he?

- Thank you, Henry. He's at the hospital reception. I'll get him. – as she walks away, he asks:

- Madelaine, forgive my bad mood. Will you come back to say goodbye?

- Yes, don't worry.

- Thank you.

She goes off to find Sir. Jaime. He is absorbed, looking out through the window.

- Sir. Jaime, he's waiting for you.

- Daughter, I fear this confrontation. The memories run over and over inside within me, revolving like red-hot ancient iron wounds...! What will I feel when I see him?

- God will guide you! I wish you strength and peace!

- Yes, whatever God wants! This is the moment! – Thus saying, he goes towards the infirmary where Henry is. He enters without delay and recognizes him. He approaches with slow steps. It seems like he would be carrying the world on his back...

Henry pales mortally when he sees him.

The two look at each other, in silent. These are difficult moments for both.

The executioner and his victim face each other...

Bravely, Sir. Jaime takes the initiative:

- How are you, Henry?

- I'm recovering, thank you.

- What Eugene did to you was unforgivable! I thank you for the honorable way you defended her.

- I don't deserve your gratitude! You know the reasons. In the other hand, I probably would have done worse! This meeting is pretty weird!

- It is true! Between us there are misunderstandings and painful memories. But, Henry, right now I am overcoming a great challenge! It seems to me that a great weight has been lifted from my soul.

In that unhappy moment when you revealed yourself without disguise, stealing from me all that I have accomplished in so many years of struggle, if I could, I would have destroyed you! Blessed attack that prostrated me to the ground, taking away my condition to act criminally! The time that I lived sick, ignoring everything around me, was worth so that I did not seek revenge! After all that suffering, I had plenty of time to think, Henry...!

Today, after such a serious experience, I have learned much more about what we are and what we think we possess.

We often live deluded as to the goals of life in its legitimate values! What fate lends us in unexpected circumstances can change course and hands!

At this moment, before you, this truth is undeniable!

Over the years, through your various experiences, you will also learn!

It was good that I came! I owe it to this angel, who luckily is your friend and has helped us in this situation!

Be at peace; I am at peace! My heart is light!

It was not easy to come here! I fought a lot against my scruples! One day, think about this and everything you have get by betraying me...!

Now, Henry, this is no longer important. I still believe in the humans and in its possibility of transformation for better. If you need me, come to me. I won't turn you away, believe me!

- I believe in what you say, I've had plenty of time to get to know you well.

But I warn you: don't harbor any illusions about me. I cannot ask for your forgiveness, nor do I accept the peace you offer me, for now. Perhaps one day, who knows?

I thank you for your good intentions. If you can, forgive me for disappoint you again! - Henry is being sincere.

- Time makes everything right, Henry! I wish you long life to learn!

- I accept the admonition and agree with the assertion, but I would never have sought you out.

- I know that Henry. I have also had enough time to get to know you well!

Henry feels deeply ashamed. He wants that man, who carries in his eyes and in his thoughts the real assessment of his character and his faults, to go away once and for all.

- In the name of the peace that pervades me, Henry, I bid you farewell, wishing you a speedy recovery!

- Good-bye!

Sir. Jaime leaves quickly without looking back.

Henry closes his eyes. Odd and mixed feelings confuse him... Life charges him to get it right and offers him resources... silence weighs on the environment.

He hears well-known footsteps.

- Henry, as I promised, I came to say goodbye. Thank you for listening to Sir. Jaime. I'll be back to see you soon.

- I don't deserve your gratitude, Madelaine. But I'll try to redeem myself, I promise!

- I trust you, my dear friend! The best version of you will win. Farewell!

- Farewell, Madelaine! – when she has already distanced herself, he complements. – My most beloved angel...

* * *

APPARENTLY FORGOTTEN BY US, Prince Aleksei, answering to the call of his uncle, Baron Otto Svirilás, of Westfalia, who is ill, travels to see him. Aleksei is his uccessor after Willfrida, his daughter, who is now fifteen years old. She is tall, robust, blond, with big blue eyes, with a passionate and compulsive temperament.

She has dresses herself exquisitely to receive her royal cousin and the lord of her dreams.

She put on her hair lots of perfumed oils and braided them around her ears in golden spirals.

On her neck, she put on a necklace of rubies as red as blood, and in her ears, earrings of the same material under the braids.

Very fine laces finish the décolleté of the luxurious dark blue dress made of shiny velvet.

With a small waist that highlights her full hips hangs a tiny purse woven in gold threads.

The sleeves, fluffy at the shoulders, taper along the arms, ends in points on the back of her hands, highlighting valuable rings that sparkle when you look at them.

Soft leather shoes complete her toilette, as rich as it is seductive.

Willfrida took a long bath with aromatic herbs, in which her servant Erica poured a white, viscous liquid to soften her skin.

In front of the great mirror, Willfrida is proud of her own image.

She seems to await her destiny, as if in an enchantment. She bites her lips and exclaims:

- I will conquer you, Aleksei! We will be happy in this world or we will go to hell together! Let there be no woman in your life! With the sword of our ancestors, I will cut you in half before I give up on your love!

Her faithful maid asks her, docile and serene:

- What is the matter with my lady? Why are you so restless?

- As you know, "my prince" is arriving today!

- The handsome Aleksei, with eyes the color of the starless night; elegant as a god and brave as no one else?

- Yes, you describe him perfectly! You love him, don't you Erica?

- It's true, ma'am; I feel a great affection for him!

- Erica, I want him desperately!

In my nightmares, imagine, he rejects me for another woman! It's a "different time" from this one! I am not blonde; my hair is black and my eyes are the color of ebony. He, as always, as handsome as Apollo! His features are the same: virile and classic!

The other woman, my rival, is blond and beautiful as an angel!

Turning his back on me, he leaves with her!

I despair, I beg him not to go! But he laughs and disregard my love.

Mad, I took from the waistband of a soldier his shining sword and with it, I strike him a sharp blow in the back.

He falls agonizing, in shock... In his eyes, a sinister gleam of hatred condemns me...

The other woman looks at me with reproach and pity...

I hug him, cover him with mad kisses, while he breathes out in my arms... While the other woman, slowly moves away until she disappears into a distant mist...!

I wake up bathed in sweat, crying! How is it possible that these nightmares keep repeating, Erica!

- How horrible, Frida! Placate them, pray and forget!

- I know I'll love Aleksei to death, Erica! These nightmares show what I'm capable of if he rejects me!

- Oh, Frida dear, why talk about death?

- Death, life, love, it's all part of our destinies, Erica! Isn't my father dying? For me, feelings are like storms loaded with lightning that illuminate our misfortune!

- It must be the Baron's illness that makes you talk like this. I'll get your tranquilizer.

- No! I want to stay lucid! Do I look attractive?

- Dazzling!

- Will he love me?

- He'll have to be blind to resist!

- I hope you're right. Has been years since we hadn't seen each other! Aleksei is strange and pragmatic! He almost isolates himself. He creates barriers between us! I must win him over!

- Madame will succeed!

Restless, with fire in her eyes, she waits for him.

A few hours later, she hears the sound of footsteps mixing with whispers. She feels like fainting because of her emotions. Behold, he is coming!

Three men enter the hall. Two of them, are his direct superintendents. A little behind, brilliantly dressed in his uniform, the haughty and royal cousin.

One of the superintendents announces:

- His highness, Prince Aleksei Nikolai Ivanovich!

In an elegant bow, Willfrida salutes him:

- Welcome, your highness!

- Thank you. How are you, cousin?

- Very well! Did you have a good voyage?

- Not really! Highway robbers slowed us down, they kill two of our best men! I am pretty tired! Nevertheless, thank you for the warm welcome!

- If can do something to maintain the joy of your heart and the well-being of your body, count on me, without reservations!

- You are always so spontaneous, Frida!

- You know me, my cousin, I am very honest! I hope that, despite this sad circumstance, you will stay with us for a long time!

- I doubt it! I have unpostponable business and appointments in Paris. I must stay here just the time long enough to treat deal with our issues.

- I'm sorry! Anyway, let's see!

- How is my uncle?

- He's slowly saying goodbye to us, Aleksei.

- And the doctors, dear cousin, what do they say?

- We hired the best, but they don't give us any hope! We also consulted several therapists, who at start promised wonders.

Then, they concluded that the treatments did not achieve their expectations. Poor Dad!

- Can I see him?

- Certainly! Frederich, accompany his highness to the Baron's chambers! I'll be right there.

Climbing several stairs, Aleksei and Frederich reach a gloomy floor, with gothic architecture. A few minutes more and they reach a large chamber lined with rich carpets, heavy black furniture with dark green velvet curtains.

On a platform, on a wide and soft bed, under a rich canopy covered with the same velvet fringed with gold threads; dressed in a white dressing gown, cap on his head, pale like death, Baron Otto Svirilás breathes with extreme difficulty.

He puts his blue eyes on the wide door through which the wo men had just entered and says:

- Welcome, Aleksei! – between violent spasm of coughing extends his seraphic hand.

- Thank you, dear uncle! How are you?

- Not well, as you can see.

- You'll get better!

- I have no illusions, my dear Aleksei! That's why I sent for you.

Frederich, leave us alone.

- Certainly, Baron. Excuse me, your highness! – bowing respectfully, he leaves.

- Now, sit down close, Aleksei.

Eyes closed, recovering from the effort, he shuts up. His pallor is impressive.

Aleksei had never received any affection from this relative; while what his uncle sees in his nephew, with extreme pride, is the male child he never had.

Frida was born in the maturity of his life; she is the fruit of his third marriage.

He made of Aleksei his idol without him ever being interested in it and raised Frida with the same adoration, in her daughter's ravished heart, an echo for his exaggerated affection grows, his nephew – son of his dear sister, now living in Russia, where Aleksei was born.

Aleksei does not disdain the goods he will receive upon his uncle's death.

While the Baron is recovering, he, mingling thoughts, remembers Madelaine.

- Aleksei! – exclaims the Baron, I love you very much!

- My dear uncle, you have never made any secret of this affection, and I, for my part, am very honored, I am very happy, dank!

- On the verge of the grave, I must be rational and objective. I don't know how much time I have left... Hoping to be understood by you, I will open my heart; a heart that will soon be silent.

I can't tell how much I did right or how much I did wrong in the life that is now extinguished! However, what I did is done and is the reflection of my imperfect and ambitious soul.

I have almost always sought the pleasures of the flesh misleading and fleeting sensations, but which delight us!

Despite the realization of my mistakes, if I could continue living, I would not change my behavior. Painful recognition of a still incipient evolution!

Vanity, ambition, and pride have always been part of me! Everyone who knows me knows this!

- You will never hear any reproaches from me, not even veiled ones! Don't worry! This is also my behavior. You, my uncle knows! I intend to continue in the same way, as long as I have life and blood running through my veins! We were cut from the same cloth, my uncle!

- That's why I admire you; for your courage, intrepidity and ambition!

I don't know what I will find on the "other side". I confess my fear about a reality that I don't know.

What awaits me? My race carries the certainty that it must die fighting to enter the grace of the gods! Experience has taught me long ago, that the gods withdrew to the Empyrean, leaving us only with our miseries!

And God? How can I be worth of him, if I have never lived according to his laws? In these philosophical lessons, Aleksei, what is my real purpose?

- I cannot understand you, my dear uncle.

- You can't? Now, that it is so obvious!

What other purpose or thought could I have that were not focused to my beloved daughter? Especially in these major moments of my life!

- How and why could such creepy issues as these would be related to my beautiful young cousin?

- Do you admire her beauty, Aleksei?

- What man would be so blind as not to admire her?

- Right now, it is your opinion what really interests me!

The Prince begins to be annoyed by his uncle's detour speech. He can feel something different in him, something that will certainly not be good for his interests. In a remarkable effort, he continues going alone with the same issue:

- As you know, Frida was raised and led by me to have the same principles. I have encouraged her, openly, pride and vanity, ambition and thirst for power! I taught Frida to take what she wants, anything she desires! To dominate before being dominated; to be victorious against anyone, in any way, in any circumstance, at any time or place!

- Nothing more natural for someone who lives like us!

- Therefore, Aleksei, I cherish a great dream for her future.

- Yes, and what is it? – he asks, knowing in advance what the answer will be.

- To see her married. I will die soon and I don't want to see her alone!

- And does she want the same? And if so, does she already have a suitor?

- Aleksei, my dear nephew! – he says in a tone of reproach and sorrow. – Why do you pretend to ignore my daughter's feelings for you?...!When I say that I wish to see her married, I mean that I wish to see her married to you! Don't play tricks on me, please!

The Prince turns pale, upset by his uncle's confession. He feels trapped. He deliberately keeps silent.

His uncle continues:

- I understand your hostility, but have in mind that I will insist, because this is my will, Aleksei. A man on the verge of the grave is allowed anything.

Frida is beautiful, strong, rich and in passionate! She will be a worthy wife. There will be no other like her!

- That is "your" opinion! Are you forgetting that I may have other plans, uncle? Do you intend, by any chance, to decide my fate? – Aleksei's voice a adopt a certain rudeness.

- No, this is not my intention. Calm down and listen to me; I ask you in the name of my great affection for you.

What justifies my audacity is the certainty that you will not find more suitable wife for you. Frida has a feeling for you that borders on insanity, an open adoration. You will never see love like hers, Aleksei!

- This mad love, my uncle, suffocates, exasperates and destroys! – despite what he says, Aleksei recognizes that he also loves just like her.

After a few moments, in which his uncle tries to recover, he pleads:

- I intend to marry for love with someone I choose!

I desire a woman who will conquer me, and my dark soul!

- Well, well! You are no exception to the rule, Aleksei! The darker we are, the more we desire the light! How ironic, isn't it?

- Yes, indeed! I want for myself a beautiful, radiant and perfect woman!

- I conclude, in the face of such enthusiasm, that such a woman is already part of your life! Are you in love, Aleksei? Are you engaging to someone? - asks the Baron, gaining ground in his quest.

But he doesn't get an answer. Aleksei closes up like an oyster.

- And what about being unwanted? - he continues. - Choosing someone so different, you run the risk of rejection. Have you thought about this?

Unable to control himself any longer, Aleksei answers, choleric:

- I possess talents that my uncle doesn't know! I will be loved in one way or another! In this game, I will call the shot! And in this fight, I'll be the winner, don't you doubt about me! Using all the resources, I will succeed, as is my way!

Frida will be happy with anyone else. She is beautiful, intelligent and rich enough to attract excellent parties!

- Yes, now I am convinced, you have already made your choice; that is why you reject my daughter. But, Aleksei, we don't want another suitor. You are forgetting a very important detail:

Willfrida loves you!

- And because of this you intend to decide my fate?

- Far from it, dear Aleksei! But... don't forget the interests we have in common! With this marriage, my estate will not be divided! And I, seeing you together, happy or not, even dead, will smile with pleasure!

Aleksei concludes that the discussion is useless and it is better to tire him. On the other hand, he does not want to lose the assets that will be in his uncle's inheritance.

- My uncle, save your energy! You mustn't go on talking this way!

- I will rest, if you promise me that you will think about what I just told you.

- I promise to think about it, of course. You, my uncle, deserve it. I'm not ungrateful.

Baron Otto Svirilás realizes that his nephew intends to tire him and to gain time to avoid a decisive answer. Demonstrating how well he knows him; he exclaims with no strength:

- Aleksei, do not disregard me, even being who you are, you know the heraldry and fortune that you will enjoy with this marriage! We do not despise these things, and we are too close to lie to each other! Think of the great financial power you will be attaching to what you already possess!

- I will, dear uncle, I promise. Now rest, I beg you.

- Call my chambermaid, please... The pains are back. I need the narcotics! Hurry...! – he twists in the sheets, while his crisp hands wrinkle the precious fabrics, showing unbearable suffering. Aleksei laments.

The servant, a short distance away, crouching, awaits the call: he quickly obeys and goes in search of the calming balsam.

Coming across his cousin in the corridor, Aleksei asks:

- Willfrida, what sickness lies on my uncle?

- We don't know, Aleksei! The doctors say that a great evil is hurting him from the inside. Sometimes, I wish him dead to be free of the pain, and other times, I wish to see him cured, and I even believe it, deluding myself out of desperation...

- He will be cured, Frida!

She stammers weakly:

- I don't believe that Aleksei. Every moment of his life seems to be his last...

- I'm so sorry...

- I'll go see him, he's not well. Your servant has gone to prepare the medicine for the horrible pains in which he is struggling, becoming more intensely... I'll stay by his side; I hope that once he's been medicated and the pains have calmed down, he can once again fall asleep...

The orders regarding his belongings here have already been given.

Any servant that shows disregard, will be severely punished! Make yourself at home!

He follows a stiff-faced servant who precedes him to his royal chambers, which occupy three floors. The servants that come with him, will be on the lower floor. Special and luxurious service honors: from undressing to hygiene and even dressing. For his meals, with extreme servility, they offer him dishes, exquisitely prepared according to the best taste of Germania at the time.

After a strenuous day, Aleksei sleeps very well, recovering.

Awakening, he brings up the conversation with his uncle:

"What does he think? That I will submit to his whims?

Poor uncle! If you knew Madelaine, you would understand why I would never be interested in Frida!

What a bother! I must hurry! I must see Madelaine again! I miss her so much!

It would be rude for me to marry this fiery cousin! What right had him to get her hopes up in his daughter's heart? Since when does he decide my future? Surely, you don't know me as well as you imagine!"

Well dressed and fed, he slowly makes his way to his uncle's chambers. After a few minutes that seem hours to him, he reaches the hall that precedes the room. He takes a deep breath and announces himself.

He enters and listens:

- Good eyes behold you, my nephew!

- Thank you. Are you feeling better?

- Only more comforted by the drugs, which effects are getting shorter and shorter. Soon they won't help me anymore... I shudder at the thought!

- Then don't think, uncle.

- So? Have you thought, as you promised me?

- No matter how hard I tried, I couldn't come up with an answer! You must admit, dear uncle, that my future has already being decided! I was taken by surprise and I need more time! I attend to you, free as a bird, and I am offered a cage!

- But... a golden cage! With Frida's dowry added to yours, you will be invincible, Aleksei!

He listens and agrees. It is on his unbridled ambition that his uncle bets on.

- Nevertheless, I've come to ask you for more time. As I have already told you, it is my life that it is on the line!

- You will have all the time in the world, Aleksei, but I...

- I promise to do my best to give you an answer soon. Now, rest assured, my uncle, and so saying, he ends the conversation.

With wide, strong steps, thoughtful and annoyed, he walks away. His powerful mind will get him out of this predicament. But, in the meantime, he buys himself time.

*** * * ***

AFTER ANOTHER day of fun and games, Francois is getting ready for bed.

He opens his little bag and takes out a sheet of thick, yellowish paper with Bible passages in large, legible letters. He kneels beside the bed, reads it reverently, and then folds it carefully.

Some objects remain on the table. A wooden square with a religious image is standing next to the bundle.

After the prayers, he feels thirsty and goes in search of water. He returns and lies down, tired. In a few minutes he is asleep.

As usual, the Turkish woman arrives, arranges the covers, kisses him and leaves the chamber on tiptoe.

In the corridor, she comes across to Louíse, in her difficulty walking, heading that way.

She helps her as she listens:

- Is François already asleep?

- Like an angel, *Mademoiselle*!

- His arrival has filled this house with light! Ah, Betbara, he does me good, fills me with hope!

- *Mademoiselle*, this child is peace, love, light, help... Were it not for him, my life would have died out long ago for lack of stimulation! – sitting her down on a chair in the bedroom, the Turkish woman asks:

- Shall I wait, *Mademoiselle*?

- No, thank you. I'll be here for a while, don't worry. Good night!

- Good night, *Mademoiselle*!

Admiring François' serene countenance, Louíse wonders:

"Where will this little soul be while the body rests?..."

Under the flickering light of the lamplight, she sees the little bag and the objects it contains. She smiles understandingly and thinks:

"This is her little treasure! When Corine tried to take it from him, judging it worthless, it reacted with energy, surprising her...!"

She approaches it with difficulty, intending to put it away.

As she comes closer to the small wooden frame, her heart races and the past comes returns... He also analyzes the other objects. She touches them... She recognizes them.

"God! – she thinks with emotion, "Am I dreaming? That's why my heart warned me!

Reason ignored it, but my feelings denounced the ties of blood! My Lucien! It's you! It could only be! What strange paths life has taken to bring us together!

André took you, André bring you back to me! May God bless him, forgiving him for his misdeeds! Victim and executioner, friends and reconciled, without knowing it! Glory to God! Praise be!"

With trembling hands, she unfolds the paper and in tears reads:

"Job remembers his first feeling of happiness.

1. Job continued in his speech and said:

2. Ah, I wish I were as I was in the months gone by, as in the days when God kept me!"

Job, 29:1,2

She hears footsteps; it is Corine who is looking for her:

- *Mademoiselle*, I went to take your tea and could not find you! I imagine that you were here. Would you like help to go to your room?

- Yes, I would, Corine. Thank you.

- Now, are these the "goods" of our boy? They seemed to me like useless things, garbage! At least he allowed me to wash the cloth!

- Those things, Corine, are all that he possesses, or... possessed! For me, these are important points of reference!

- In relation to what, or to whom, *Mademoiselle*?

- You will know later. Please wait!

- Yes, *Mademoiselle*!

- God be praised! – exclaims Louíse, looking at François, after kissing him affectionately.

- Ad aeternum! – replies Corine, circumspectly.

Back in her chambers, Louise realizes that Corine has something to say:

- What do you want, Corine? I can see your intentions!

- Yes, *Mademoiselle* is right. I want to ask you for information about one of your friends. But perhaps you won't allow me...

- That depends, Corine. If you tell me which friend you are talking about...

- That handsome military man who comes to visit you from time to time.

- General Antoine Belfort? What do you want to know?

- What he's like, what he does, where he lives; things like that!

- He is a high-ranking military man, fearsome and powerful. He is part of the ruling power. He is a bachelor, rude and authoritarian. What else do you want to know?

- If it is not insolence... if there is any engage between you two.

- May the heavens deliver me from such a fate!

- And may they honor me!

- What did you say, Corine?

- Nothing important, Madeimoselle! I've heard what I wanted. I don't want to exhaust you; I'm going to go now.

- And dream about the "handsome" General?

Corine defends herself:

- Do I not have the right, *Mademoiselle*?

- You do, Corine. However, knowing you are so passionate about life, I wish you would not chase after nightmares.

- Rest, *Mademoiselle*. I am prudent, I can defend myself!

- There are no defenses against him, Corine. He is already older than you; if he perceives your interest, he will exploit the fact. He will not respect you!

- What if he is the hope for the future I have been pursuing for so long?

- Don't you dream of marrying for love?

- No, *Mademoiselle*! Marriage, for me, will be the solution to my problems. I want to elevate myself socially! I find you beautiful and elegant! Who knows, maybe some fortuitous circumstance will bring him closer to me?

Silently, Louíse feels sorry for her, while she sinks pleasantly in the soft sheets, dreaming of the worthy Salustius and of the unexpected happiness of having her beloved brother Lucien under the same roof. She says a prayer of deep gratitude to heaven and sleeps in peace.

※ ※ ※

IN THE PARISH HOUSE, Madelaine is scanning Salústio's feelings:

- Dear friend, am I mistaken, or do you feel for Louíse a special affection?

- We all have special affection for her.

- Don't use nicety with me, Salústio! You are clear as glass! What are you afraid of?

- That she won't even notice me! I am socially inferior to her!

- Louíse is not prejudiced!

- But the world is, Madelaine! On the other hand, my libertarian ideals prevent me from dreaming! My life belongs to France!

- Salústio, to overcome evil, we will always have to kill or be killed?! Why hasn't this "perverted and adulterous humanity", as Jesus well defined it, learned to love yet?

In these fights, my friend, what happens is the relay of tyranny! It only exchanges hands! How many are willing to fight for an ideal, are surprised further on, imposing on the vanquished. The same scourges they suffered?

I, particularly, live in a painful dichotomy; between the unmistakable realization of the urgency of a patriotic stance, in the face of all sorts of abuses that oppress our people, and the rightful fear of the excesses that could result from an armed struggle!

One, would only wish, Salústio, for moral power over all the others, the legitimate defenders of the rights of men! Generally, what we see are those who are greedy for power, masquerading as liberators, stirring up the masses, making them blind and violent!

I fear for you and for so many others who, sincere, defy so openly and recklessly, the despots! Most of them, my dear friend, end their days misunderstood, anonymous, and sometimes sacrificed by the ignominy of those whose only goal is to rise above the common people, writing their stories with tears and blood – of others!

Fortunately, I have one certainty: that one day everything will be rescued and the truth will be known. Lights forged in the codes of the great law will bathe the consciences and feelings transforming evil into good and selfishness into brotherhood!

But, while we await this time, Salústio, true history is adding martyrs! May God reward them!

The more I analyze the steps that this humanity has taken, the more I admire my father's profession, wishing him success and divine protection, when, through his powerful intelligence and his competent word, based on honesty and deep love for justice, defends the innocent and points out the guilty! – Madelaine shows the passion for what she says in the color of her cheeks and in her vehement.

Serene and reverent, looking at her after drinking in her wise reflections, he argues, questioningly:

– Sweet friend! Tell me: How many have access to this kind of resource?

– To tell you the truth, not many, compared to the great unprotected majority...

- So, Madelaine? We must put a stop to these monstrosities, legalized by the absolutist power that sucks the energies of this unfortunate people!

We will fight with whatever we have in our hands and with whatever is within our reach: guns, sticks, stones, or empty-handed!

Stimulated by pain and despair! In a mixture of justice and injustice! In a terrifying picture of fright, fear, anxiety and courage; terrible and at the same time glorious! I feel my blood boil in my veins and my head spin, just thinking in get free France! And it will be, no matter what it takes! I will give myself completely, without any kind of hesitation whatsoever! This is my destiny!

Moved, Madelaine listens to him, excited, ardent, determined.

He seems to have forgotten her presence. Distant gaze, shining eyes, enthusiastic gestures, defending his ideal with all his strength.

- May Jeanne d'Arc support the arms of those who face such a difficult undertaking! God keep you safe and reward you, dear Salústio! - she wishes him.

Asserting his patriotic ardor, already calm but energetic, he replies:

- I, Madelaine, am only a drop of water in this ocean of despair, patriotism, and intentions! What matters is that the homeland becomes free, just and fraternal!

- And what about Louíse, Salústio?

- I will be his friend. As you can see, I don't have time for love!

- I disagree with you! Listen to me; your burning heart needs love!

The time you and Louíse can enjoy will be worth it! In this world, along with so many difficulties, "every day has enough evil", as Jesus told us. What matters is the quality of life, not how long it lasts!

Anyone can die unexpectedly, regardless of age, occupation, situation or ideals, my dear friend!

To be happy, is to value every instant of our fragile and short existence!

- Madelaine, don't get my hopes up!

- Well, feed them and be happy, Salústio!

- Thank you, my friend and sister! I promise to think about it.

Now, shall we get to work?

- Of course! Duty calls!

While working in the wards, Madelaine sees a young man approaching:

- Are you *Mademoiselle* Madelaine?

- Yes.

- I bring you a note from *Mademoiselle* Louíse.

She thanks him and reads:

"*Dearest!*

I greet you in the name of God, our father!

I hope that he will find you well and happy; likewise, to dear father Estanislau and Salústio.

I pray to heaven that your loved ones will make a speedy physical and spiritual recovery. God bless them!

Nostalgic, I want to request another visit to see my beloved mother.

I know the setbacks that come with these visits, but I have surprising news! I am still surprised by the recent discovery!

We will share this happiness that now bathes my heart with heavenly celestial feelings!

I love you and look forward to a reply.

The ever-grateful friend,

Louíse of Villefort"

Madelaine smiles, trying to guess what Louíse is referring to with such enthusiasm.

While the messenger waits, she writes:

"*Dear Louíse,*

I am already anticipating the news! Whatever it is, if it makes you happy, we congratulate you right away.

Thank you for the courtesy!

We will plan a schedule and the best way to serve you. We will let you know!

I hug you affectionately.

Your devoted friend,

Madelaine D'Or Alvarado"

Receiving a coin, the boy offers to get back to the Portal da Luz with the answer.

Louíse is looking for François.

He is in the orchard, his favorite place. The regained freedom has incomparable value. François recovers, minute by minute, the years lived in shadow and solitude.

Corine goes to call him:

- François, *Mademoiselle* wants to see you!

- Coming, Corine! - quickly, he picks a beautiful flower and hurries towards the house.

Receiving the flower, Louíse kisses him with emotion.

Curious, he sits down and waits. He is strong, ruddy, with luminous skin, shiny hair.

- Did you sleep well, Louíse? - she asks him with a beautiful smile.

- Very well, François! As never before! What I want to know is the origin of those objects you have.

- Ah, I forgot to put them away yesterday! I'm sorry!

- I'm not blaming you, my little one! Make yourself at home in your chambers!

- Do you want to know where they came from? I'm not sure... Let's see... A red macaw feather and the ribbon with the buttons have always been with me. The little square I use to pray too.

- And the paper with the passage of Holy scripture?

- About Job? He suffered a lot, didn't he?

- Yes, François.

- His sufferings compared to mine were much greater!

Rachid, the Turkish woman's husband, copied it for me. He told me:

"François, keep this. The paper is strong and will last for years. Read it when you are sad and think on what is written." He did this to consoled me, one night when I was crushed by the beatings, I had received from Mr. Joubert for trying to escape once again...

Rachid was good to me until he died! The Turkish woman cried a lot when he was gone. She loved him so much, poor thing! Then, the two of us were left alone.

- May God reward him, François, wherever he is!

Do you want to know the origin of the other objects?

- Do you know?

- Yes, I know. How nice of you to have kept them! The buttons and the pink ribbon were part of your outfit, on the horrible night that decided our lives.

- My outfits... that horrible night... I don't quite understand what you are saying, Louíse...

- You will, François. Listen to what I have to tell you with patience. Then you will understand:

One nice evening, we were all returning from a pleasant visit to our dear friend Marta, considered by us as a relative. The same one who gave her the red macaw feather when she noticed your great interest. You were fascinated by it, which was resting next to Marta's inkwell.

Arriving home, happy and noisy, we were surprised by the strange men who emerged from the shadows of our garden leaping upon us.

Heavily armed, they violently subdued us. We were separated: you and I; mama and André, our older brother, the legitimate Baron André of Villefort.

Imprisoned in our own home, we did not know about each other. Strange men watched over our survival.

One day, I was summoned to the presence of an elegant, gray-haired, stiff and cruel man, who claimed to be the new Baron of Villefort!

- It was my friend... Sir. André? So, it's true? - the boy begins to cry.

- You already knew everything, Francois?

- Yes, Louíse! Sir. André told me! I doubted because he was seriously ill!

Then, at the hour of his death, the General assaulted him, while declaring that he was my tormentor! That I owed him my misfortune! He, poor man, told me that if he could, he would go back!

Regretting his actions, he asked my forgiveness and died in my arms! -

Francois cries convulsively. The recent memories still hurt him a lot. He hasn't even had time to understand them yet. Now, with what Louíse tells him, things make sense.

- "Did you forgive him, Francois?

- Yes, Louíse! I told him about Jesus and kissed him on the forehead. He, grateful, looked at me and died in peace... I hugged him tightly and cried a lot. He was my friend!

Louíse, unable to speak, draws him in and hugs him tightly, crying.

- Lucien! My darling! Listen, there's more:

The philanthropic group from the Church Our Lady of Mont'Serrat found our brother André dying in a cave, among rats and filth, and at his side, suffering and self-sacrificing, our beloved mother!

After his death, Madelaine took her under her care.

- Madelaine! Sir. André talked about her! He confessed his love for her!

He feared she would marry another while he was away!

- It's true. André loved Madelaine and pursued her, relentlessly.

This small painting of the mother of Jesus, Lucien, was made at his request, by our Arab servant, Mohamed. He was talented, a craftsman, and loved you very much.

- My name is Lucien?

- Yes, Lucien Brumel of Villefort! Soon we will visit mom. What she imagined has become true; that you were with me!

- Louíse, we are siblings and I have a real mother?!

- Yes, Lucien, we do!

- This is so good! All in once, God gave me back everything! Our mother will be angry, if I continue to love the Turkish woman as my adopting mother?

- No, my love! She too, like me, will love your good Turkish woman! She protected and loved you like a real mother! Now she is part of our family!

In a few days, we will find them, all gathered in the Alvarado's castle, to share our recent joys. Gotuza won't believe it.

Soraya and Fabian hug the boy, who unfolds to tell them his adventures, leaving them stunned, especially Fabian, for whom Lucien or François, whatever his name, is now his latest hero.

Close to Salústio, noticing his shyness and reserve, Louíse, courageous and spontaneous, decides to win him over:

- Dear Salústio, you look admirable! What elegance!

Disconcerted, he replies:

- Thank you! Even though I know that your eyes must be used to much more refined elegance!

- Nevertheless, my friend, I have never surprised anyone with such taste! Your image certainly reflects your soul!

- *Mademoiselle* Louíse, you flatter me! I don't have the graces of the great halls!

- None of those noblemen, Salústio, in spite of their luxury and display, could transmit the same as you! - Intimately, she concludes, resolutely: "I have suffered enough, my dear Salústio, to lose you now! If from now on, I have the right to be happy, may it be at your side!

She openly ignores the social distances and prejudices of the world.

Salústio realizes that Madelaine is right; he can dream and be happy! Louíse is there to prove it, opening her heart, exposing herself to attract him. She doesn't hide her interest for him. And in her beautiful blue eyes... Oh, God! There are promises of happiness! ...- wrapped in this expectation, he shows her a look that also tells her everything... his soul releases of any obstacle and surrenders to the sweetest captivity the world has ever seen...

In silence, attracted, the two remain like this, as if time had stopped. Dreaming, hearts out of sync, they are awakened from their ecstasy by Fabian, who comes running to the rescue to help a baby bird that fell from the tree.

Salústio asks permission and goes with the boy, promising himself that he will resume the conversation with Louíse. But the hours go by and he fails to do it. There is so much to say, to celebrate, to smile. The confraternization is complete and absolute.

Hours later, they enter the Portal da Luz. Lifting her in his vigorous arms, he feels his heart beating strongly. He settles her gently, on a comfortable armchair, he listens:

- Thank you, "dear"... Salústio!

- I am honored to be able to help you! By the way, I ask your permission to come to see you more often.

- Come whenever you want. I look forward to seeing you!

- Thank you! Farewell, Louíse!

- Farewell, Salústio!

✱ ✱ ✱

HENRY, AT THE HOSPITAL, bored, can no longer stand the lack of activity. Only Madelaine's visits take him out of his apathy. She makes herself present:

- Hello, Henry! How are you?

- As you can see, impatient! Finally, I will be discharged in the next few days!

- The doctors are cautious, Henry. You almost die! You must heal yourself completely to avoid relapses!

- Yes, I know. But to stay here, inert, for someone like me, is a torment! And speaking of torment, my dear Madelaine, while my body is recovering, I struggle with almost insurmountable conflicts. The worst of them is the unhappy conclusion that you have discovered my horrible soul! What can I do to solve this situation? Advise me, I beg you!

- Stop that, don't torment yourself, Henry! God finds unusual resources to help us in our spiritual miseries! At the end, the light that is in us will shine! We are or have been wrong about this or that; each in its own time. In our search to survive, we exercise our old selfishness! But the future is glorious!

- For the sake of this future, can I still count on your mercy?

Will you continue to be at least my friend? Or am I asking for too much? - Henry's eyes fill with tears. Now that he's practically in good health, Madelaine will certainly stay away from him...

Which given the circumstances, will be very understandable.

- Calm you heart, Henry! You deserve me so much! You deserve my gratitude, consideration and respect; you earned little by little in a fraternal relationship!

- You are being very indulgent, trying to rescue my self-esteem.

Thank you!

- In this world, Henry, most people struggle between good and evil! As for you, be happy! Your soul is already moving towards a remarkable transformation. You decided that by your own, when you looked after the miserable of all sorts!

- Make no mistake, Madelaine! I did it for you, not for them! Enough of lies! I need from now on, to see myself as I really am!

- No matter the reason, Henry! Nothing takes away the merits of your good acts. Those who were benefited, praise your generous hands and bless you daily! The unfortunate ones are the beloved of the Masters of masters, and you have done much for them!

How many mothers, when they feed their children; how many ill people, when they receive hospital treatment; how many old people, comforted in their last days of life; hungry or wounded, rescued from the gutters, how many of them address to the heavens hymns of gratitude in praise of those who dedicate their live to unconditional charity! And among all those who work in this sacred place, Henry, you are one of them, determined and generous, despite what you say!

He, in adoration, listens to her wise concepts. At the end, he says reverently:

- Your soul fascinates me, Madelaine! It has overcome so many obstacles!

- And many others await me, Henry! *"To whom much is given, much will be asked"* and I have received a lot from the Creator!

Your friendship is a valuable pledge to my heart. God keep you safe and support you in this task, which is the hardest: the inner battle, rejecting the darkness and seeking the light until full integration! Count on me always, my dear friend, my brother!

Eyes watery with tears, he thanks her:

- Only the heavens can tell what I feel at this instant, Madelaine! Little by little, you take me out of the mud and show me the sun! Spiritual misery is more painful than the material! I am your disciple and unconditional admirer. If I cannot conquer your woman's love, I realize that I am dearly to your heart.

Thank you!

- You have entered a path with no turning back! It keeps progressing!

It is not for everyone, just for the one who are willing to persevere! Well, farewell! I hope to see you soon in your home!

- Farewell! I pray to Mr. Kronos to fasten the wings of Mercury, in order to shorten the time, I spend away from you!

IN WESTPHALIA, ALEKSEI breathe a sigh of relief when, broken with grief pain, Frida told him of her father's death.

He had died in his sleep, under the effect of medication.

After the funeral service and the reading of the will, he, finally free (and richer), will return to Paris.

Shadowy and suspicious, Frida knows that her father had not had time to sacrament his last will.

Aleksei demonstrates openly that he is not interested in her.

He must have another woman...

A large number of people attend the splendid funeral:

On top of a marble platform that stands on its high and golden legs; in the coffin, surrounded by lighted candles and herb-scented, the Baron's body seems asleep.

His servants, friends and diners, as well as the local nobility are present, silent and reverent.

The heavy silence is cut by Frida's sobs. Aleksei, upset and insensitive, longs for the ceremony to end. Frida's glances bother him.

He is leaving Germania and his cousin as soon as possible. As if guessing his intentions, Frida approaches him and whispers:

- Cousin, do you not wish to revere him? The Germanic nobility, gathered here, waits for your reverence, the only relative and direct heir after me!

Surprisingly angered by the admonition, he accompanies her, haughtily, faking the requisite sadness. He picks up a small amount of herbs, pours them over the tripod on the embers, and approaches the coffin. There, arrogantly, he receives the condolences, while, bored, remains beside his cousin.

The carriages, coated in black and gold, await the time of the hour of the funeral. The day has dawned hazy. The wind blows as if weeping. A cold rain begins to fall.

The nobles wear black, loose, heavy, and very luxurious clothes. The final minutes are already approaching...

Frida faints and is sustained in her cousin's vigorous arms.

Leaving her in Erica's care, he follows the ceremonial closing of the coffin, with the honors due to his uncle and accompanies his entourage to the cemetery, where, in a luxurious mausoleum, the Baron ends his earthly life.

Bored and unimpressed, he returns to the castle and there, he is informed by the good Erica that Frida sleeps under the effect sedatives.

The next day, he surprises her packing her suitcases and luggage. Intrigued, he asks:

- Are you going on a trip, cousin?

- Yes! I am leaving Westphalia, definitely! Nothing more keeps me here!

- Alone with Erica? And still in mourning?

- Mourning, Aleksei, will not prevent me from achieving my goals! As for going alone with Erica, we're not really going alone!

He feels a chill down his spine. He can reach in her a higher intention, which he must be involved, or... be the main target!

To confirm what he already guessed, he asks restlessly:

- Who will you go with? Can you tell me?

- Well, don't you understand yet, my dear cousin? We will go with you!

Rising hastily from his seat, he bursts out:

- What?! Have you gone mad, Frida? I don't remember inviting you!

- I don't care if I don't have your invitation, Aleksei, because I know my father's posthumous wishes! And you will know about it too, when you open his will!

Terrified, he concludes that father and daughter have always acted the same and that somehow Frida is obeying the Baron's last will.

He shudders, indignant, and wrings his hands. While in his mind he mentally spews curses and blasphemies. He must wait for the reading of the will.

What is at stake is very important... He cannot make his statement before... Meanwhile, he decides to bear with Frida, courteously. He doesn't know what's coming next...

SIR JAIME AND HIS DAUGHTER, already into the fraternal coexistence with the Alvarado, await Eugene's definitive absolution. Her, smiling and relaxed, shows through the beautiful colors that illuminate her face that she is completely recovered from everything she has lived through. She has become closer to Madelaine, with whom she has pleasant and deep conversations, admiring the good sense and wisdom of her new friend.

Father and daughter already know the group from the Parish House, as well as Gotuza, Louíse, Lucien and Betbara.

The Count and Sir. Jaime share the same ideals of life, exchanging impressions in enthusiastic tertulias.

The children have become attached to Eugene and her care. Despite everything, Eugene misses Marianne and the twins.

Salústio and Louíse finally understand each other. Sincere and courageous, he confessed the risks he takes for his patriotic ideals. Proud of him and fully happy, Louíse accepted his marriage proposal and, between preparations and expectations, they watched time go by, anticipating the fortune to share their lives.

The wedding ceremony was very well attended and magical. Father Estanislau officiated it. The church, beautifully illuminated, was in harmony with the happiness of the two. Around them, those who love and admire them, wishing them the continuity of their love, amid much health, peace, and prosperity. If it depends on these loving hearts, they will be happy forever!

Eugene's situation officially solved, completely freed of guilt, father and daughter decide to travel. Suitcases ready, say goodbye, with anticipated longing, to those who have conquered them for good:

- Madelaine, says Mr. Jaime, I will never be able to express my gratitude! May God bless you! I leave here our address in Reims, at the Estancia Santa Sofia. I will be expecting you there in the future.

You will also have the chance to meet Natacha and her parents, the Korsanikov, who I already told you about.

- Dear friend, she answered, we are the ones who are grateful for the unique opportunity to meet you and to enjoy your kind company! Give a hug to Natacha for me and tell her how much I wish to meet her! I have a great desire to meet her at my wedding!

- We will be here on the due date! I congratulate in advance for this "event chosen by the gods"! Too bad he is traveling. I wish I could have met him.

- Thank you! I will tell him that. God be with you all!

Weeping, Eugene bids farewell to the children, who are also crying. In another room, the Count and Sir. Jaime pledge to keep their friendship. Bettine, moved, has her eyes filled with tears. She hugs them tightly, hoping to see them again in the future.

Hearts full of love and gratitude, father and daughter return to their lives. Eugene seems to be dreaming: free and happy, next to his beloved father, with a new opportunity!

CORINE APPROACHES Louíse and asks her:

- *Mademoiselle*, when will you reside in the new house, on the outskirts of Paris?

- I don't know yet, Corine. I must first settle the various pending matters of my new situation; not only as a married woman, but also try to redeem our former status, mine and my family's, the real owners of everything that the false André has taken from us, as you already know.

- *Mademoiselle*, I was almost frightened to death when I discovered the truth!

I understood so many things! Your tears and your answers, almost reticent!

- Yes, Corine, it was all abominable! Today, I am happy with Salústio, thanks to God! We will settle a little far from the center of Paris, so that I can benefit from nature and various treatments, in the hope of regaining the movement of my legs. Salústio says that this is his great and blessed desire to see me walk normally, again.!

Corine returns to her duties, while Louíse concludes that her coming to the Portal da Luz was providential. She recalls how she was solicitous, defending her; her good will in bringing Madelaine, and finally, how she had discovered Mateus's intentions to steal...

At this moment, on her mind, she sees Corine making use of her usual cleverness, in that occasion:

Seeking her, hurried and restless, she informed:

- *Mademoiselle* I must speak to you about Mateus! As you know, I am very observant and lately I have seen him in the stores, making big purchases! To my question, he answered that an uncle of his, from Ravenna, in Italy, left him an inheritance. But how did he receive it if he didn't even leave here?

- Perhaps it was brought to him, Corine.

- That did not happen, *Mademoiselle*. We haven't even had postal delivery in the last few months! And there's more, listen: I see him coming out of your brother's chambers, repeatedly, carrying poorly disguised things. Silent, with his fist closed, he threatened me, the other day, when he saw my reproachful gaze.

- Yes, you must be right. I have kept myself distracted and delaying, indefinitely, certain issues that required my attention. Mateus's behavior is one of them. Now I must take an attitude that corresponds to his excesses. Thank you, Corine, I appreciate your fidelity and vigilance!

- No need to thank me, *Mademoiselle*, but you must call the police. You can ask for help from your good friend, General Antoine Belfort.

- I don't want him here, Corine!

- All right, *Mademoiselle*, replies Corine, with no intention to obey, as is her nature. Corine only does what she wants, no matter what.

The gate bell rings, and she goes to see who it is. Louíse waits, and when she returns, informs her, smiling:

- *Mademoiselle*, guess "who" is here! - At a negative sign from Louíse, she declares, in a theatrical gesture, opening her arms, eyes shining:

- The General!

- Oh, no! Corine, tell him I'm indisposed today; I can't see him!

Cheerful, she returns to the salon and, between smiles and intentional glances, accompanying him, as she reached the garden, far from everyone's eyes, she warns:

- General, I have an important report to make!

- Well, do it! - he orders, interested.

Smiling, she replies in a soft voice:

- Not here! *Mademoiselle* must not know!

- Then come to me! Take this card. I will be at this address all day. I'll wait for you! - this he says, measuring her from head to toe, appraising her. He noticed her interest.

- I'll go without delay, today! - Corine confirms.

Continuing his analysis, he admires Corine's beautiful eyes.

Perplexed, as he scrutinizes her features, he thinks:

"By all the devils! How could I have missed it before? This young woman is the living image of Jeannette!" - While he thinks on his great discovery, she bids him farewell:

- Until then, General!

Accepting her game, seductively, he tells her persuasively:

- Don't be long! I'll be waiting anxiously for you!

Flattered, she goes along with him to the big gate, feeling the burning of his eyes.

He rides his fiery horse, forcing it to take the desired direction, while staring at Corine, who slowly enters the house. He is determined to win this new conquest.

He wanted to see Louíse again and tell her off for her marriage. He had been rejected for someone without position and power. He wanted to take revenge, condemn her. But, in a few moments, his thoughts and interests suddenly changed direction:

"What a beautiful filly! - he thought. - And how she looks like my Jeannette!' Ah, this looks promising!"

Passing indifferently between the vehicles and the pedestrians, the General continues with his thoughts:

My blood boils in my veins and my heart has gone crazy! It's like seen Jeannette back, alive and rejuvenated! This beautiful girl seems to want me with the same fire! Well! The die has been cast! I'll take everything I can from this opportunity that fate is generously offering me!

While he, amid these thoughts, speeds his horse away, Corine, with an enigmatic smile thinks:

"Ah, my handsome General!" I have so many plans! Perhaps you are one of them! Without even knowing it, you could be my trampoline to get out of this world!

While she dreams of her future, Mateus thinks of his, feverishly organizing himself to run away, taking everything he can carry. He has already hired a carriage to wait for him at the back, late at night. He fears Corine's cunning; he must hurry.

Around him, in his chambers, many packages and suitcases.

From his boss's rich cellar, he has stolen the best wine, the one he chooses for his most important visits. He drinks it non-stop, (he has already dispensed with the glass, and drinks the whole tasty liquid). Many empty bottles are piled up in a corner.

Drunk, he staggers among the volumes, falling here and there, getting up with difficulty. He latches on to everything and everyone, in a late and untimely complaint about his "miserable life", in a pasty, repetitive voice.

Corine approaches his chambers, puts her ear in the door and concludes that he is completely drunk. Silent, she looks for the duplicated key and locks the room from the outside. He doesn't even notice; falling and getting up, he continues with his noisily and recklessly activities. Returning to listen to him at regular intervals, she hears a loud snoring. He has fallen asleep overcome by alcohol. It is the moment of the flagrant, she thinks. He will sleep for a long time and Louíse is sleeping too; she won't notice her leaving.

She quickly goes to the address on the card. Makes an announcement and waits.

A few minutes pass and she is led to the General.

Surrounded by papers, he exclaims, happily:

- Well, how beautiful and elegant you are! Have a seat!

- Thank you!

- What kind of accusation do you want to present, and against whom?

- Against the servant Mateus, who is stealing from his boss! At this moment, he sleeps drunk in his room. I locked him out without him noticing!

- What a beautiful and competent servant Louíse possesses! Does she already know?

- Yes, and she intends to denounce him. But, she wasn't feeling okay today, she can do nothing. Contrary to her orders, I came on my own to put a stop to this situation before he runs away!

- So, let's catch him red-handed!

- Bravo, General! Let me just get there first.

Mademoiselle must not know that I was here.

- Of course! But tell me, what is your name?

- Corine, Sir!

- Beautiful like the mistress! Don't disappear! I want to see you again under more favorable circumstances!

- When you wish, General! - she answers smiling, as she gets up and slowly, flirty, leaves, feeling his gaze on her body. Then she hears his thunderous voice commanding:

- Jacques, organize a search and seizure party! We'll bring another rat here! Right now!

- Yes, Sir! - replies his subordinate, standing in line before leaving.

A few hours later, the General arrives at the Portal da Luz, accompanied by a properly armed detachment, to Louíse's astonishment:

- What do you want, General, with all this array?

- Make no mistake, I'm not here to visit you, *Mademoiselle*! I'm on duty!

I have received a complaint!

- Against whom?

- Against your servant Mateus!

- Yes? And who reported him?

- This information I will keep to myself. *Mademoiselle* has always ignored my influences!

Without paying him any attention, Louíse concludes that Corine has disobeyed her orders.

"Well, – she thinks –, so be it! This will solve everything."".

- Make yourself comfortable, Sir, and do your duty!

In a few moments, the General has access to Mateus's room.

Everything there condemns him. He is carried like hunted prey, without realizing what is happening to him. When he awakes from the drunkenness, he is already in jail, defenseless and poor as ever.

- Don't ruin the catch! We will come to find out more, later! - warns the General. And so, it was done…".

Louíse thanks the heavens for Corine's providential defiance and her arrival at the Portal da Luz.

* * *

AT ESTANCIA SANTA SOFIA, Sir. Jaime and Eugene benefit from nature, while they can. He, going back to his professional activities with Mr. Korsanikov, has incrised his love for the family and the place, assisted by Natacha and Eugene.

A little later, Mr. Korsanikov became seriously ill and Eugene received a letter from Marianne informing her that Sister Rosália was ill too. Father and daughter go to visit her. The two avoid talking about Henry.

In the reception of the school, Sister Inocência arrives to accompany them to Sister Rosália's chambers. The mother superior tells them that she wants to see them later.

They enter and find Sister Rosália breathing badly and looking extremely pale, with the eyes closed.

The visitors gently touch her hands and whispers gently:

- Sister, look who is here!

Opening her eyes, she smiles:

- My dears, how much we miss you!

- Us too, dear sister! - replied Sir. Jaime, moved by emotion.

- What's wrong with you, my dear mother? - Eugene asks, affectionately, disguising the urge to cry.

- My child, nothing too serious! My heart is tired!

- And the doctors, what do they say? - she goes on, sitting down next to her dear sister.

- They prescribe medicines and rest. And you, daughter, how are you? There has been so long! Did you find Henry after all?

- No, sister, I quit! - she lies. - I'm with my father at the ranch!

- Praise God! My dear friend is calmer now, is he? - she asks Sir. Jaime.

- No doubt about it! God has heard our prayers, dear sister! At last, Eugene has matured spiritually!

- I never doubted that it would be like this! And Natacha, how is she?

- She is well and wishes you a speedy recovery! Couldn't come with us because her father is very ill.

- I will pray for him! Are you still studying the things of the heavens and Earth?

- Yes, and we are intensifying our care for the unfortunate people who live around the ranch! We have developed a great work.

In this matter, we have a competent ally, a well known being to you, Sister!

- The daughter of my heart? Thank God! - Breathing hard, she shows fatigue. The two say goodbye and go to the Mother Superior's office.

After the usual greetings, the topic of conversation is Sister Rosalia's health. They fear the worst.

Mother Eulalia praises Eugene. She admires her courage in facing problems, working hard, in a permanent effort to survive.

Looking meaningfully at his father, Eugene accepts the praise, wondering what she would think if she knew about her attempted murder. Reaching out to her, he smiles at her, lovingly reassuring her.

The two stay at Marianne's house. There is a complete feeling of happiness for the reunion. The twins can hardly believe it; they throw themselves on Eugene arms, as always, in the rejoicing of the moment.

Every day, father and daughter visit Sister Rosália, often accompanied by Marianne.

Saddened, they lose hope of seeing her better.

On a bright sunny day, with birds singing, blue sky filled with white clouds, they are urgently called away.

Sister Rosália is getting worse.

Arriving, they approach to see her; with hearts tighten. She opens her eyes, looks at them tenderly, and declares:

- My dears! My heart is going to rest at last! But my love for you will never be extinguished, because it is eternal! I say goodbye to you today, to see you again one day with God! Give a kiss dear Natacha for me!

Just as those who have already leave us are watching over us, I promise you equal protection!

She stops talking and takes a deep breath, trying to gather strength to continue. Suddenly, she tries to stand up, eyes wide open. Sir. Jaime, delicate, comes over and lifts her slightly.

Accepting his help graciously, she exclaims, showing surprise:

- Oh! May the eternal father be praised on his throne, surrounded by cherubim and seraphim! To confirm my assertion, "they" are here! After so many years, I see them again! Some relatives...

"Our sisters" who over the years have gone... The dear sister Berta, among them, mother, happy and healthy...! They smile at me saying they've come to take me! Reverend Mother, they greet you respectful and moved, wishing you the blessings of heaven in this blessed labor!

- Thank you! - cries the Mother Superior.

- Ah, if only you could see what I see! Such light! So much beauty!

There is a rainbow here in the room, Mother Eulalia! I hear sounds, beautiful and impossible to translate... Now go, and take with you my eternal love! I need to prepare myself for the holy communion! I want to receive it lucid! Farewell, my beloved friends... - she looks at everyone for last time, deeply loving.

The parish priest arrives for his sacred service.

Sir. Jaime kisses her hands reverently, unable to speak, and Eugene kisses her on the cheek, wetting her tears with infinite tenderness. In a loving effort, looking at Eugene, she tells her:

- Daughter, when the wind blows, a bird sings, a rose opens or a star shine in the sky, I'll be watching over you! Be happy, Eugene! Love your father! Good-bye! I'll bring your mother news about you!

Closing her eyes, she shuts up. The Reverend, putting on his stole and speaking to his assistant, begins the ritual. One can hear the difficult breathing of Sister Rosália. Gradually she calms down and lets out a long sigh ...

The cage was opened and the bird, free, flew towards infinity, in search of God!

* * *

VISITING LOUÍSE, father Estanislau shows interest and curiosity about Francois.

The boy asks him to take him to church. He wishes to get to know the parish. When he does, he admires everything, asking a thousand questions that the priest answers with pleasure.

Father Estanislau asks him about his experiences in prison.

Concentrated, he narrates everything, leaving the priest astonished and moved. For hours, he listens to him, deeply interested, and rightly concludes that the child knows God's creatures and has already lived experiences that most people can't even imagine. His expressions are honest, concise, calm. He talks about the "fortress" with such detail that the priest feels like he is there.

At times, he felt like crying, such was his emotion. Hugging him, at the end of the narrative, he exclaims:

- You are a good boy, François! God keep you safe, my son! And bless your Turkish woman!

- Amen, Father! May I come here again?

- Certainly, Francois! Whenever you wish!

- Thank you, father.

Just like that, Lucien, or Francois, little by little, lives more in the parish than at home. Gotuza took back her legitimate name, Caterine Brumel of Villefort, and currently lives with Louíse, Salústio, Betbara and Lucien.

The kid, curious, asks Madelaine:

- Madelaine, if I want, can I become a priest?

- Of course, Francois! Or should I call you Lucien?

- As you wish, Madelaine! I like both names!

- Me too, my dear!

- But I must consult mama and Louíse, right? And dear Turkish woman too, in case I decide to become a priest!

- Yes, you must ask their consent. But if you really want it, you will get it, even if the whole world is against you!

"You were already born committed to goodness and love, dear boy!" - she thinks and says:

- If you need me to convince them, I am at your disposal!

- Thank you, Madelaine! Now I understand why Sir. André loved you so much!

- God bless you, Lucien!

- Amen!

* * *

IN HIS WILL, Baron Otto Svirilás of Westphalia conferred to his nephew, Prince Aleksei Nikolai Ivanovich, the guardianship of Willfrida Svirilás; depending of this clause his part of the inheritance.

At hearing this, Aleksei bit his lips to keep from screaming with hatred. She knew about it! They had plotted together! No matter what, Aleksei will not give up the slice of cake his uncle left him. He'll put up with Frida, but she'll soon discover how dangerous it is to push him. He will give her what she really deserves when it is the right time. His contempt for her has grown a lot. They get ready and, in a few days, they travel.

Arriving in Paris, he gives her a place in his castle, but in a distant chamber, to get rid of her uncomfortable presence. Silent, she seems to submit to her cousin's orders.

Erica joins her.

Aleksei is absent from the castle every day. He updates papers, business, and cleverly make use of his newly acquired inheritance.

He wishes to see Madelaine again and to make her marriage proposal official.

After a few days, with this intention, he goes to the Alvarado castle.

There, he announces himself and enters, haughty and arrogant, as always. Very polite, he greets:

- How are you, dear Count?

- Very well, your highness! Please, sit down!

Taking a sit, he informs:

- I was in Westphalia for some time, at the call of Baron Otto Svirilás, my uncle. Seriously ill, he wanted to see me to say goodbye. One night he died while sleeping, under the effect of medication.

After the funeral and the opening of his will, I returned to Paris.

- I am very sorry about your uncle's death, your highness!

- Now, as is my nature, I will get straight to the point, which brings me here and which is already well known to you!

The Count shudders and prepares himself for what is coming.

- I want to marry your daughter Madelaine as soon as possible!

The Count decides to make use of the sincerity that distinguished him:

- Your highness, with all the respect you deserve, I must repeat to you; my daughter is already engaged! And this time, the fact is public and notorious!

Rising abruptly, he bursts out in anger:

- Are you defying me, dear Count? And who dares to consider my rival?

At the Count's silence, he insists:

- The name, Count! The name of the candidate for Madelaine's hand!

- She is engaged to the worthy Marquess Charles D'Alençon!

- Engaged to that stupid Marquess?

How could you accept this engagement, ignoring my formal request, prior to any other? Have you gone mad? Have your philosophical thoughts in the forum thrown you off balance? Have you got confused with the things you defend? It is difficult to me to pretend not see your rebelliousness, whether in court or in your private life!

You shamelessly take the side of the king's enemies! I can only leave you to the mercy of the fate you share so well with the scum!

Have you forgotten that I am a legitimate representative of the ruling power? Your statement borders on audacity! And now, where is your famous oratory?

The Count, astonished, confirms his suspicions that his family is harshly censured by the nobility.

With courage and dignity, he answers with another question:

- Is your Highness a christian?

- What? Do you, by any chance, think I'm a heretic? Don't you know that I follow the

precepts and rituals of the Russian orthodox church?

- I mean, your Highness, inside your heart!

- The heart, dear Count, is forbidden ground!

- My question has a purpose, your Highness; that of knowing whether you intend ignore my daughter's feelings!

- Why, what a stupid question! Since when do we, men, depend on the opinion of women? If such freedom is granted to them, in a short time we will have an undermined and weakened society! In this specific matter, we already know that we will never understand each other! I warn you; I will spare no effort in this intention of mine and nor will I stop myself! With your consent or not, and above all circumstances, Madelaine will be my wife!

- Faced with such an imposition, your Highness, I must tell you that my daughter is free to decide her own life! She is used to it! As for the threats, I fear nothing, for I live with an open heart! I only fear God's judgment! His power, widely known, is also subject to the major law!

I will die, if necessary, grateful to heaven for the opportunity to sign with my blood the things I stand up for, I have no intention of imposing myself on Madelaine's life!

- What about your family's blood? Do you answer for all of them too? - Aleksei inquires, with a thin, musty smile.

- We are all children of God and we must act according to his laws, first of all, your Highness!

Aleksei gets up and walks around the room. The Count is an enemy of respect; his moral power is unquestionable... Standing to him, he exclaims, in a lower tone, amazed at his courage:

- As far as the disparity of our concepts is concerned, I admire your intrepidity, recognizing in you a rival equal to my privilege! But, Count, I don't like to lose!

In fairness, I recognize that Madelaine is a worthy heiress to you! Although, I would like to shake your hand, praising your honor and courage, instead, I warn you that I will not hesitate to impose my will! I will be ruthless! Nothing will stop me! So, think it over!

We will talk about it later! For today, we understand each other, or... we misunderstand each other, as you wish! Farewell!

Heeling, Aleksei shakes hands with the Count who matches his greet; he leans slightly and leaves.

The Count collapses onto the armchair. He knows the danger he is in; not only him, but his whole family.

Back in his castle, Aleksei comes across his cousin:

- Dear cousin, she exclaims, lamenting, we hardly see each other!

- I'm not in the mood for conversation, Frida! You have chosen a very bad time to approach me! Now, please, leave me alone! Respect my privacy!

Upset, she leaves the corridors in the direction of her chambers. Disgusted, she talks to herself as she walks:

- What kind of snake has bitten you, dear cousin? You can fight all you want, but you won't get rid of me! Don't even dream about it! Hum... I need to know about your life...!

She walks by Erica's chamber, who is carefully arranging her beautiful fawn hair. She is very beautiful and good. Frida likes her.

Erica tries, selflessly, to lead her to good path, but Frida has an unstable temper.

Frida is disoriented. Her mad love turns to hatred for Aleksei.

He is very devious; he systematically and obviously avoids her very… She will have to find other alternatives to approach him… and win him over. That's what she has come for.

Erica, as always, consoles her mistress and gives her the usual tranquilizers.

* * *

MADELEINE WAKES UP WITH THE SINGING of the birds. She opens the window and excited, heavily breath the morning air. She thinks about Charles.

She misses him. Wishes the wedding happens soon. They will be happy! They love each other too much!

Her parents request her presence in the library. She hurries up and, in a few minutes, she goes to where they are. She notices the Count's pallor and the undeniable sadness on his mother's face.

- Here I am! Has something bad happened?

- Yes, very serious, daughter, confirms the Count.

Bettine gets up, hugs her, affectionately, and asks:

- Listen, dear daughter, to what your father will say, and above all, have great faith in God!

Sitting up, frightened, Madelaine replies:

- Yes, mom. It is impossible to ignore how distressed you are! I don't know what it is yet, but we will trust in God, as we always do, whatever happens!

Worried and sleepless, her father says everything: the Prince's marriage proposal and his threats.

Madelaine listened in silence, feeling the seriousness of the moment.

Her happiness is beginning to seem distant, impossible... She pleads to God for help. In her mind, the beloved image of Charles appears... His only love; the one who keeps waiting for her... Owner of her dearest hopes of happiness; as a woman, and human being! Her handsome and noble Charles, sensitive, loving, worthy...

Will she have to give him up? Will she survive after having known and loved him?

She stays in silent. What could she say? There are no words that can express her intimate conflicts. At this moment, only faith can sustain her, besides the great love of her...

The Count understands his daughter, even if she does not say what she is feeling, and courageously defines herself:

- Darling daughter, I told the Prince that the decision will always be yours! God will be at the helm of our destinies! He sees all and provides all! We would never ask you to give up on your happiness!

Think about it and let us know about your decision. We will be by your side, no matter what. We will take the risks, together!

- Thank you, father. May our creator bless us and defend all of us! I'm going to the church right now to consult with Father Estanislau. At other times, faced with the arbitrariness of the prince, I had already had this intention without, however, doing so. Right now, I can no longer put it off. He will help me to think and to find a way out, I hope...

Rest assured, everything will be all right! - and, softly, to herself, she adds: In one way or another...!

Caring and loving, her father could hear and understand what she was saying, what is worrying her. He knows about her courage and principles. He feels sad, but try to hide it from Bettine.

The two notice Madelaine's concern not to increase their natural apprehensions. Together, they go to the chapel to pray.

Leaving their horses in front of the Church Our Lady of Mont'Serrat, Nestor helps Madelaine to get off the horse. Thanking him for the assistance, she goes to the church, which at that hour is full of faithful attending the service celebrated by Father Estanislau.

She kneels and prays fervently. Then, from the side, close to the altars faithfully illuminated by candles, in which the saints represented there seem to sympathize with her pain, reaches the sacristy and waits for the dear priest to finish the ritual.

Arriving, still in his vestments, he asks:

- What happened, daughter? I can see your physical and spiritual discouragement!

- I need help, Father. Also, advice! It seems to me that the world has fallen on me! - Madelaine gets it off her chest.

- Calm down! Wait for me for a while, please. Minutes later, sitting side by side, he listens carefully.

At the end of her narrative, she cries. Moved, he hugs her and waits for her to regain her composure. Her weeping must not be interrupted, Madelaine needs it; it is the most urgent and wise help from nature.

Seeing her wipe away her tears, a little calmer, he declares, sincere:

- Daughter, regrettably, we both know that the fate of your family is in your hands!

- Yes, Father! That's what the Prince wants! But, what about Charles?

He will destroy him... What can I do?...

Opening his arms, discouraged, as he raises his eyes to the image of Jesus, begging him for help, the good priest answers:

- May God sustain and inspire you, daughter! Your decision will be very difficult and, at the same time, very simple... It is your future that will not be easy, whatever your final answer may be...!

- Father Estanislau, an idea comes to me: What if I speak to the Prince? I could explain so many circumstances that he doesn't know about! Who knows, right? Perhaps he will change his mind and release me from this expectation so cruel to me, who loves another man and not him!

- I know his power of persuasion, Madelaine... Nevertheless, only if were you less beautiful and less virtuous, you would have any hope of persuading him to withdraw his request...

- It's decided, Father! I have no other choice! Right now, it's the only idea that I have!

- Will you go alone, my child?

- No, Nestor will come with me. I don't want my parents to know! If I solve the situation, I'll tell them myself!

- You're afraid about the Prince's behavior, Madelaine?

- No! He won't act without thinking! He's too intelligent for that, and he knows me too well! He respects me, despite his authoritarianism! I feel, Father, that this regal gentleman really loves me! I regret it, because I will never love him!

- Then, good luck to you, my child! I will stay here, standing by, and praying, with all the faith in my heart!

- Thank you, Father! Only God can help us!

Madelaine arranges with Nestor and the next day, while her parents think she is heading for the Parish House, she goes in search of the Prince.

Seeing the jagged towers of the gloomy castle, she shudders.

Noticed of her arrival, the Prince, stunned, prepares to welcome her. Proud with his own elegance, he strides downstairs with his heart beating fast.

Gracefully, Madelaine bows to him:

- Your Highness...

- Sweet Madelaine! My castle lights up with your presence! - he exclaims, kissing her hands.

By the girl's harsh look, he concludes that she has come to ask him to retire his marriage proposal.

They both sit down.

Confirming his suspicion, taking a deep breath and searching for the right words, she speaks up, delicately:

- Your Highness, forgive me for coming unannounced! To save you time, knowing your many duties, I'll get straight to the point that brought me here. I was very honored by your marriage proposal! But, already engaging to someone else, I earnestly ask you to withdraw it, accepting in exchange my pledge of eternal gratitude!

Laughing, benevolently, charmed by her presence, he replies:

- Beautiful and dear Madelaine, I can hardly believe it! It gives me immense pleasure to have you under my roof; a roof that also will be yours! I thank you for your sincerity. I reverently admire your intelligence and courage. I will be equally straight and honest with you; I have decided to marry you, and I'll accomplish my intention, no matter what! I never give up for what I consider important to me. I made your father the formal request, and I don't accept negative answers. Under these circumstances, I must protect you and guide you. You know our costumes, old and legitimate!

- You cannot decide for me! I am not yet your fiancée! - she declares, showing her indignation.

- Well! That it's only a matter of time, my dear! Which I will make it as short as possible!

Cheeks flushed, exalted, she exclaims, angry:

- Your Highness forgets two things. First: I am not your wife! Second: I am not a child who must be told what to do!

I have a mind of my own! I know the costumes of which you speak, and I despise them! My father, liberal and evolved, respects my decisions, leaving me free to choose my own path!

Aleksei smiles, complacent, fascinated by her courage and beauty, but overcoming his adoration, he replies angrily:

- That's another one of your many mistakes! When you ignore the traditions and the prevailing laws, your father despises our majesty the king!

- We live honorably, surviving at our own expenses, without weighing down the country! And we go beyond, helping many through our efforts! We are benefactors, as you know.

- Have you forgotten that I am one of them, or can you only see me as a tyrant?

- I didn't say that, your Highness!

- In a hidden way, you did!

- Your Highness is putting words in my mouth!

- Be careful, Madelaine! I'm not a liberal like your father, the Count, who, by the way, takes the risk of defying me! - threats arise - I tried to warn him about the allegiance he owes to the power! If were up to me, he would have been in jail long ago, Madelaine! You don't know my tolerance or you pretend to ignore it! You don't know it, but I am assigned to keep a close eye on the Alvarado's in their "eccentric" way of living! I use indulgence because I long to marry you! However, my dear, let me tell you something:

I know the Countess Bettine's tasks with the so-called wretched. I also know of the steps taken by the "good samaritans" of Father Estanislau's church, of which you are part and all of you break the laws, rescuing and protecting those whom the King condemns and treats harshly to the scorn of society!

I also know about Salústio, the fanatical libertarian; about Dr. Sergei, and Nestor who accompanied you here; and so many other things that you can't even imagine, my dear!

Don't underestimate my intelligence! Do you believe that I, in the position I have, would go along with traitors? If I want, I can put an end to this arbitrariness, in a snap of my fingers!

As if she had been stung by a thousand bees, she gets up suddenly:

- Traitors, us?...! From which side do you see the things that happen? Our life is clear and pure as a fountain of pure water! Our intention is always to help those who are in need!

- Criminals, not needy people! Enemies of the system!

As I have already said, I have turned a blind eye only because of you!

However, I will go beyond everything and everyone to get what I want!

- Even above me, your Highness?

- Yes, Madelaine! I know no limits! I never had one in my whole life!

- And yet you expect me to love you?

- Yes! Because I know the powers I hold to conquer you! I will make you so happy, Madelaine, that the stars themselves will envy you!

- Ignoring my will and my feelings?

- A woman's will and feelings belong to her husband!

- You don't really know me, your Highness! I may die before I submit to anyone!

- I know, Madelaine! I know your courage and your virtues and I count on them! Altruism and self-sacrifice are part of you!

You will think in the happiness of your family before your own! Right? See? I know you better than you think!

And not only yours will be in danger. There is a whole philanthropic work. The infirmaries also host so many unfortunate people...!

Have I forgotten someone or something? The fact that I have not mentioned other actions of all those who challenge the King's power does not mean that I don't know about them!

Do you understand, in fact, against whom you will be fighting?

It will be an impossible fight for anyone, especially for a fragile beautiful woman!

Collapsing, devastated, on the rich armchair, surprised, she asks; heart in her mouth, tears in her eyes:

- God! How can you do this?

He bursts into loud laughter:

- Surprised, Madelaine? There is so much more! Do you realize now how much I've been protecting them?

Silent, she doesn't answer. She's terrified. She understands that with him there is nothing she can say to change his mind; his laws are brute force, arbitrary power, slander, violence... It's his world...

- So? I need to know what do you think! - he insists, already impatient.

- I think that if God did not allow it, you could do nothing, despite all that I have just heard!

- So he is my friend! - he comments, mocking about it, ironic.

- He is everyone's friend, because he grants us what we really need. In this existence, as fragile as it is brief, we are all living according to his laws! By placing us where we are, he has allowed us the challenges to prove us make better persons! I am leaving, Prince Aleksei! Excuse me! - making the usual bow, she turns her back on him to leave, when she hears:

- I will not wait long, my dear! I want to get married and start a family by your side, my sweet Madelaine!

"-Miserable Madelaine", you should say! - she exclaims almost in a whisper, which makes him regret the situation and wish to clasp her in his arms, proving his love to her; giving her the world as a gift!

In an attempt to follow her courteously, he moves forward, but she hastens to avoid him, and calmly overcomes the distance that separates her from the carriage, and goes in, disappointed, almost in tears.

Immobile, aware of how much he has assaulted and threatened her, he watches the carriage drive away, disappearing around the bend in the road.

Exhausted from the emotions experienced before, he thinks:

"This will change Madelaine! I will win you back and we will be happy!

But do not expect from me a peaceful affection, for what I have to offer you is a mad, crazy love, that will take me to the last consequences! This is the only way I know to show you how much I love you."

He ignores that, from the shadows, Frida, disgusted, listened to the interview, shuddering with hatred and revolt at each of her cousin's words. Deplores that beautiful, unhappy woman. Disguising herself, she approaches him and asks:

- My cousin, who went out just now? I saw a beautiful woman boarding a carriage!

Snapped out of his thoughts, without looking at Frida, he answers categorically:

- Who was here was *Mademoiselle* Madelaine D'Or Alvarado, my fiancée!

Pretending kindness, she complains:

- Why, Aleksei, you didn't even introduce us!

- I had no time for formalities! We are planning our wedding!

- Oh really? And when will it be?

- Very soon, cousin! - Answering her questions, he turns his back on her and leaves.

Back in her chambers, she blurts out, angrily, breaking everything, she can, while Erica rushes in:

- Miss, how long will you torture yourself? Let's go back to Westphalia! Aleksei will not allow himself to be conquered; that is clear! Why to suffer about this? I fear for your health!

Controlling herself, she wipes away her tears, arranges herself better, while answering:

- The path I have chosen has no turning back, Erica!

Go get that crippled servant who sleeps in the stables! Bring him to me! I'll be waiting! - Leaving, she sneaks into a dark alcove, and waits. Seeing them, she makes a sign for him to come closer and orders Erica to leave.

Surprised and frightened, he waits, respectful.

Suddenly she accuses him:

- You hate your master!

- No, madam, I don't hate him at all! May God deliver me from such a disgrace! I live in a bad mood because of my leg that hurts a lot! - he replies, showing his right thigh.

- Calm down, man! I'm not blaming you! I don't care who you hate! But I ask you, and I hope to hear a sincere answer. Do you want to get a benefit from this hatred?

Stunned, he doesn't know what to do. She insists:

- There's no point in denying it anymore! I have caught you several times blaspheming against the Prince when you are alone! I know you would kill him if you could!

- No, madam, no! I do not swear against him, but against my luck!

- Stop defending yourself, man! I need your services!

Listen, you'll have to be extremely discreet. What do you say?

- What do you want from me?

- For now, to know if you're willing to obey me without no questions. After that, you will never have to work again! So?

- Never again? Oh, yes! To get rid of the unhappy life I have, I'll do anything! Command and I'll obey!

- Then wait! I'll send for you when I need you. We will always meet here! Be alert!

He leaves with a limp, and she carefully returns to her chambers. A terrible idea begins to take shape in her head.

Jealous torments her and drives her mad.

She finds Erica focus in tidying and cleaning. She, clever, discover in the girl's sparkling blue eyes her darker plans. In silence, she prays to the heavens for help. She fears for Frida and... for Aleksei...

* * *

IN THE CHURCH, FATHER Estanislau unfolds his rosary, pleading for help and assistance for the Alvarado's, especially for Madelaine, without knowing that he and the parish house are part of the same dangerous context. The prince holds them in his devil-minded regard.

Arriving back from a trip, Charles goes to the castle to see his fiancée again.

Bettine receives him warmly and warns him that the Count needs to speak to him alone.

Doing what he considers his duty, Count Luiz Santiago informs him about the recent events.

- Count! - Charles exclaims, in shock, after hearing him out. – He seemed to have forgotten us!

- He was in Westphalia, at an uncle's funeral, and stayed there for a while because of the will. When he arrived here, he imposed himself, as I have already told you.

- He will have to face me! I will not be ignored! I will defend my right to love Madelaine, with my life, if necessary!

- Beware, my son! It's public and notorious that he makes use of his power in a cruel way! The Prince is an active participant in this world of injustice in which we are currently immersed. Don't expose yourself, I beg you! At least don't be reckless, giving him exactly what he wants, there is no doubt, that this is exactly what he expects and will know how to use it.

- Dear Count, I am dazed! I wish I could be calm, but my blood boils in my veins! I must think; be at peace! When Madelaine comes, please tell her I must speak to her!

I'll be back tomorrow! See you soon!

- See you soon, Charles! And don't forget, we don't always understand God's purposes; however, we must submit to his wise and perfect will!

Without answering, Charles leaves, completely shocked. A great rebellion settles in his heart. An image of the Prince and his usual arrogance comes to his mind and upsets him. He goes home, without knowing what to do. He needs to speak to his beloved bride. He imagines how much she must be suffering.

The next day, while waiting for her fiancé, Madelaine talks to Louíse:

- When are you moving out, Louíse?

- In a week!

- How are Gotuza and Lucien?

- Mamma is slowly recovering. Lucien goes with Salústio every day; he lives more in the Parish House than in our home. If it were not for you and the philanthropic group from the Church Our Lady of Mont'Serrat, mother and I would probably never have met again. I would have gone on through life, ignoring her location and lamenting about her fate. God bless you... Her, on that memorable day when she recognized me, wanted to know why we had to suffered so much. I didn't know how to answer, but I have thought on my family, Madelaine: Lucien, so little, separated from us, taken away from us and thrown into a horrible prison, living among convicts, helping them as best he could, as a fragile child and also a prisoner. Ignoring his origin and his past, he learned to love exactly our executioner!

André, our dear and missed brother, violently taken from his family and his life to suffer inconceivable hardships in prison, without having done anything against anyone! After years of suffering, he is thrown on a garbage heap!

Me, captured with my family on that tragic night, hostage of the false André, persecuted, hurt and unhappy! Him, to terrify me more, claimed to have my dear Lucien in his possession! Those were years of much pain, insecurity and fear! Unable to move about normally, because of the violence and cruelty of the fake Baron, I thought my life would drag on like this until my death! Despite my faith, I suffered too much! God! If a bomb had exploded in my house that terrible day, perhaps it would not have caused so much damage!

- But Louíse, by the grace of God, with the exception of André, you survived and found each other again. If not all of you could be alive, most of your family is together now.

- It is true, my friend. I am very grateful for this.

What about mom? Noble by birth, accustomed to luxury and wealth, she ends up wandering the streets, forgetting who she is and where she came from... Wounded in the head by André's accomplices, she was sick and feverish for a long time, saving herself by a true miracle. She went on to live among beggars and wretched people of all sorts. She told me that, amid shivers of horror and bitter tears, when she glimpsed some recent or older facts in her memories.

During her tormented dreams, she saw faces that seemed familiar to her and on these occasions, she would awake crying loudly in pain...

Unbelievable to us that people exposed to all dangers, to constant hunger and bad weather, manage to survive!

- These are traumatizing experiences. Because of this, many adopt unbalanced behaviors, sometimes dishonest, sometimes cruel. They lose their sense of the legitimate values of life and, consequently, dignity. Those who preserve themselves from evil are rare. For this purpose, one would hope that their soul is purified. But, in our world, our imperfections prevail. Finding these environments and determining causes, they show themselves miserably. Those who have never experienced it, condemn them, insensitive and unaware, demanding from them what they themselves cannot offer for lack of merit. How can we know what we really are when we have never been challenged?...

In this world of ours, in general, what speaks louder is power and money! When, my dear friend, will humans love and respect his fellows?... - Now, it is Madelaine who is on the verge of tears.

- Forgive me, Madelaine, I am talking about things you already live with the unfortunate ones, every day... I know how much this good heart suffers for them all...

- It is not problem at all, Louíse. Not speaking, not seeing, not taking action and protective measures do not prevent evil and injustice from spreading like a deadly epidemic! Our people suffer a lot!

- In this reflection of mine, I am analyzing the facts that have reached in a fatality, to mine, but I know that many others pass or have passed through these trembling corridors. A sad fate!

- I disagree with you, Louíse. These "sad signs" point to a long old commitment with the sufferings to which they all deserved. If God is good, just and perfect, he does not commit injustice; think about this. This lack of analysis and legitimate faith has thrown many people into total disbelief and despair that leads them to all sorts of vices, to various deviations, to suicide, madness and death. The robust faith, the one that sustains us, brings us the absolute certainty that God is our father, our creator, who loves us and provides for us all. The rest depends on our negligence, needs of understanding, or debts.

Your family, for example, brings a dark characteristic, linked to prison, misery and banishment!

- You are right! It is like a stigma!

Have we made others suffer the same pains that we have experienced?

- Probably!

- And when did we do it?

- In other existences, in lives badly lived, without love and responsibility; when *"we will heap fiery coals upon their heads."* as Jesus told us.

- So, do you believe that we can live more than one life?

- If this were not true, how can we explain the "apparent" injustices of the world?

- You are right. You talk about reincarnation, don't you?

- Yes, a deep subject, worthy of study and careful analysis.

We must think with reason and faith, drawing our own conclusions; and these, without human prejudices, will lead us closer to God, reverent before his justice.

- You remind me of an ancient Indian work; the Bhagavad-Gita, in which Krishna shows the warrior Arjuna the urgent need to fight, without weakening, his "relatives".

Referring, of course, to the warrior's own imperfections.

He then teaches him about the new bodies that Arjuna would receive as many times as he needed during his spiritual evolutionary pilgrimage.

In fact, this is more in accordance with God's perfect justice. The human, in general, even the so-called enlightened ones invented a divine justice based on their own imperfections!

- Many missionaries of God came to bring him the will and to explain justice to him; almost all of them were sacrificed. But, in his infinite mercy, he goes on believing in our redemption and send us his representatives. And among these, the greatest, the incomparable model, our loving master Jesus! And what did the Earth do to him, Louíse?

- Sacrificed him too! This humanity has accumulated it a lot of guilt, doesn't it Madelaine?

- Yes, this is the reason for so much suffering. We reap what we sow! True justice is done, one way or another, today or tomorrow; as long as it lasts! We are millenary travelers in constant learning. And in these wanderings, Louíse, how many times we find ourselves again in life(s) experiences?

Diving into the memories of my heart, I only found the first time when I saw Charles. In that magic moment, was I guided by my intuition or did I remember that he was my only love? This leads me to conclude that we have lived many other times together; each time loving each other better and in a higher way. Ah, Louíse! The past, the present and the future! In them we are eternal!

Unfortunately, my dear friend, not everyone is open to understand these truths! Tell me, how was it that Gotuza met up with André, his son?

- In a great effort, mama told me that, one very cold and dark day, two men threw a body from a cart onto a nearby pile of garbage. She and her group, all miserable and sad approached curiously. It could be someone they knew. One of them, more eager, turned him over to get a better look.

Touching him, she realized that he was still breathing. Sad and in common agreement, they dragged him into the nearby cave where they were sheltering and took turns tending to his wounds. They could do almost nothing, but they could not leave him out in the streets. The poor wretch seemed to be in agony.

- According to her, misery, exclusion and total destitution have two strong and determining extremes of the various: one of them imposes itself through selfishness strongly installed in a person, through desperation and the need for survival; the other unites and strengthens, giving shape into selfless behavior, illuminating the heart with a greater love, different, that absorbs everything and redeems.

Imagine what conclusions mom has drawn from her experience! However, she knows, and so do we, that if the world were more fraternal, no one would live through this torture!

"The patient – she recounted between tears –, in a dark corner, wrapped in rags, survived, despite everything. He received from us a portion of what he could get for food and water. The food was offered to him in small quantities; he had problems swallowing.

Miraculously, he improved day by day.

A few days later, we decided to take him outside; to get some light. The cave was dark and the place where he was staying was even darker.

Carried, almost dragged, extremely weak and broken of a shocking thinness, he moaned with every new effort.

On this day, I came closer and observed his features. He seemed very familiar to me and his presence moved me too much.

Leaning back against the wall, he mumbled a few words, trying to talk... My heart soared! I recognized in that prematurely aged man, my André...! My beloved son!

So long gone from me! I held him in my arms, in tears, and tried to be recognized by him. At first it was impossible for him to remember, but as time went by, he understood me and wept, grateful to heaven for our reunion, even in those circumstances...

I improvised a bed for him and took care of him, until the group from the parish house found us and helped him in his last moments...

You already know this, Louíse..."

- How I wish I could have found my beloved brother again, Madelaine! - Louíse becomes very sad.

- Before Madelaine replies, Charles arrives and, greeting him, she says goodbye. She ignores the Prince's marriage proposal.

Taking his bride in his arms, he kisses her, rapturously. Squeezing her powerfully against his heart, he fears he will lose her.

Returning his caresses with equal intensity, she holds back to not cry.

- How I miss you, Madelaine!

- I miss you too, my Charles!

Taking a deep breath, looking sad, he declares:

- Madelaine, I already know everything. I'll do whatever it takes to free you from this hateful, imposing, unfair commitment!

- Charles, I'm afraid for you! I'm afraid for all of us! He threatens us, without disguises! And we can expect everything from him!

- And what will we do, my love? - he stares at his beloved face, fearful. He knows her courage and self-denial well enough.

- I don't know yet, but if everyone's safety and peace depend on me, I will give up everything, even my dreams! – she concludes, regretfully but rationally.

- But those are our dreams, Madelaine! And you will kill me! I will not survive without you!

- Charles, have mercy! It's as hard for me as it is for you!

Don't dismiss my pain, for God's sake!

- My life, forgive my despair, but I can painfully see that you have already made up your mind!

- You are wrong, Charles! I will wait in God until the last moment for a remedy! I don't know yet what I will do; I only know what my reaction will be, in the face of the worst! After all, even without intending to, I am the cause of this disaster!

- The Prince! Him, alone, is the cause of all that we are living, Madelaine!

- So be it! And you, Charles, are his first target! I must defend you with my love, as well as my own!

- And let me live, knowing you are married to him?! I'd rather die, Madelaine!

Covering his mouth with her delicate hands, she pleads:

- By God, don't say that! Live for everything you love in life, and for all that it offers to you! Live, my beloved, for your family, for your music, for us!

- For me, Madelaine, everything depends on the affection I carry in my heart for you! Without you, nothing else will hold me to this life, it will become impossible!

Together, they cry.

The Count, knowing what is there, approaches, but when he sees the scene, leaves without being noticed. His heart aches. He will give his life so Madelaine can be happy.

Charles leaves, goes to the Prince's castle and requests an audience. He is received by the servant, who tells him to wait in the luxurious office.

Without holding back, he walks in, restless.

After a long time that seemed interminable, the Prince introduces himself, intemperately:

- Here I am. Be brief! I have business that awaits me! I see no reason to waste my time with you!

Controlling himself, Charles replies:

- I also have important appointments, but the matter that brings me here is of interest to both of us!

- Really? I don't see how or why! It's hard for me to imagine that we have something in common!

- Your Highness, do not disdain my presence or what moves me! As gentlemen that we are, we must show respect for each other!

- The Marquess tires me with these rules of etiquette! Tell me why you have come!

- Well then! Your Highness has recklessly ignored my engagement to *Mademoiselle* Madelaine D'Or Alvarado!

Irritated, Aleksei threatens:

- Put yourself in the place you must be, Marquess, and watch how you speak to me! I don't recognize your so-called engagement to Madelaine because she was already promised to me before the pantomime set up by the Count and you! Where are the official proclamations to the King? Have you forgotten to whom you are speaking?

- My place is at my fiancée's side, defending her! I am engaged to Madelaine and I do not depend, for that, on the recognition of anyone, not even your Highness!

We love each other and you can't stop us! The proclamations will come out within the time limit set by the laws, since we are on our way to the marriage!

- We shall see about that, Marquess! You may be surprised, at the contradiction of everything you are saying now!

I was the first to court her and ask her to marry me! When you appeared, our engagement was already on the way to being made official! It was the Count who delayed us, by taking time to give us his consent, on which I do not really depend.

Beware, you are treading on dangerous ground! In the Alvarado castle, my will is already well known to all. And you, in what world do you live, ignoring the orders of your most powerful representatives?

- Do you intend to fulfill yourself by threatening and imposing yourself on Madelaine's will? Do you forget that she loves me?

- That is false! It is not what I see!

- Oh, yes, I forgot! The constituted power and its representatives make use of a different optic from other creatures, even if it is distorted! - Charles uses a lot of irony, irritating the Prince even more.

Approaching Charles dangerously, his finger cocked, he threatens in a grim voice:

- Watch out! I can throw you into a prison from which you will never get out! Your words may be your shroud! And in any case, Marquess, I shall become the husband of the lovely Madelaine!

This is fate, be content! It is useless to fight against it!

- I know that you can destroy me with the snap of your fingers! We all know about your power and tyranny! However, I warn you, I will shed every last drop of my blood to defend her! I love her and I know I am loved! Your Highness may have all the kingdoms in the world, but you will never rule that heart because it belongs to me!

- Once again you are wrong! She will learn to love me, with the pass of the time!

Intelligent as she is, she will soon understand what is the best for her and her family!

Me, for my part, will conquer her tirelessly. I'll tell you something else, I will do it with such commitment that you or anyone else could ever imagine!

I love Madelaine with such adoration that I doubt anyone could love her more, not even you! I am investing in my happiness! You promise to shed your blood! I promise to preserve mine to live and be happy! I do not believe that your naivety and impudence are such that you cannot conclude who will be victorious in this contest, Marquess!

As you see, you are wasting your time and mine in a useless conversation!

- You have strange ideas about love, your Highness. Not for a moment, I want you to know, you manage to impress me. I am sure of Madelaine's love. I feel secure and confident. I have no fear of her sincerity towards me. And, as my fiancé, I beg you to stay away from her! If you love her, even in your own way, allow her to fulfill her dreams as a woman in love!

- How dare you to give me orders? Your audacity borders on temerity! Have you forgotten the crime of "lese-majesty"?

Thank me for my patience and go away, once and for all! I don't know how I could listen to you for so long! I declare this interview, which should never have started, over! Get out of here, Marquess, and forget about Madelaine; it will be better for all!

That saying, the Prince left the office hastily, leaving Charles astonished. He will take with him the certainty of the uselessness of his attempt. It is impossible to seek understanding in the Highness Prince Aleksei.

Leaving the place, Charles goes to the Church Our Lady of Mont'Serrat, to speak to Father Estanislau. He needs comfort, rebalancing and, why not say it? Consolation as well! He is heartbroken... The latest events warn him that, for him, happiness will be an impossible dream... Unless new facts come...

Who knows? In this fragile hope, he makes his way to the church.

* * *

AT THE INN, Mr. Korsanikov shows no improvement, despite different treatments.

- Sir. Jaime, I don't know what would be of me without your help! - says Natacha.

- We are overwhelmed and, moreover, annoyed by the diatribes of your cousins. What can we do to change the situation?

- Fire them and hire new employees. In our philanthropic wanderings we have seen people who need to work. To start, we could use three of them. But we will only fire Rupert and Nikolai when we have the others here with us. Then we will be a majority! We already know how they are going to react!

- In fact, it would be more prudent to do so...

Natacha's mother arrives, very distressed:

- Please come quickly! Kostia is ill!

The two of them hurried off, and Natacha asked her father:

- Did you take your medicine, papa?

- Yes, child, he answered with difficulty.

- I'll go and get the doctor!

- Thank you, Sir. Jaime, she says, as she lovingly covers her husband, kissing his thinning hair, the color of the Russian steppes.

The doctor arrived, examined him and prepared them for the inevitable. That same afternoon, Marcel arrived, and was informed of the painful situation.

After a night of agony, Mr. Korsanikov gives his soul to God.

After the funeral, in her black clothes, Natacha was at her mother's bedside, who was sleeping only thanks to tranquillizers. Sir. Jaime asks:

- How is she, Natacha?

- A little better!

- And you?

- Trying to find peace again, but right now is lost! I will miss him so much! - she bursts into tears.

Stroking her blond hair, Sir. Jaime asked:

- Couldn't Marcel stay a little longer by your side?

- No, he had urgent commitments. He'll be back at the end of the week. - she explains, while crying desperately.

- Cry, Natacha, let it out, it will be good for you! Remember the happiest moments, lived next to your father! I pray to heavens that he is well and happy with God!

- Hope he is! Mother is so devastated...

- She will recover, my child.

- I don't know, my friend. I have bad omens...

- Because of your depressive state, daughter.

- It could be...

- I hope you and Marcel get married soon! You need to be happy, Natacha!

As he says this, he notices that the girl is transformed, changes her posture and, as other occasions, begins to speak:

- There will be no wedding!

- No? Why? - he asks, hoping for an enlightening answer.

- There won't be time for that! And besides, she doesn't intend to, to get married! Intuitively, she senses that her life will be short! Her enemies will destroy them!

- Her and her fiancé?!

- No, to her and to him who, in his present existence, is also carrying the need to pay off old debts.

- Dear God! Could my brother in Jesus be more precise? With greater references, I might be able to think in something or protect those who will be included in this painful prediction!

- Forgive me, but this is not my decision to make. It would be of no use to you, believe me. Whatever must be, will be, regardless of any circumstances. The divine law is mercifully fulfilling itself in its creatures, always aiming at their spiritual evolution.

I can, however, help you in your own discovery; remember the conversation we had before, when I told you about your daughter actions, you will find there the references you are asking for.

Stay by the side of this dear soul! May God strengthen and bless you! Do all the good you can, while you can! You will always have the support from the King of heaven, he will never fail you. God is, above all, love!

I bid you farewell, wishing you courage and much peace! - Thus, the "voice" says goodbye, raising his right hand in a gesture of blessing.

Silence reigns in the room again and little by little Natacha regains recovered. Looking at her good friend, she asked:

- What did I say this time, Sir. Jaime?

- Nothing important, daughter. Rest a little; you need it. - While she rests beside her mother, he leaves, thinking:

"Dear daughter, spirit loved and found again! I think we will share the same fate... May God sustain and strengthen us...! Who will destroy us and... when?...!"

A few days later, Nikolai and Rupert are fired. Amid threats, they pack their bags and disappear into the world.

Sacha received the news of the father's death. Deeply saddened, he regrets not having said goodbye to him. He prepares his luggage and travel to France with his family. He stops doing business in Russia. Now he needs to be with Natacha, at the head of the Estancia Santa Sofia.

- Sir. Jaime, I await my brother with anxiety! I haven't met little Kostia yet! I will prepare chambers for them on the first floor. There the sun illuminates all the rooms. The kitchen and the garden are near, and a child needs a healthy environment.

- Very well thought out, child! The arrival of this little kid will bring happiness to everyone, especially to your mother's heart and yours!

- It's true!

* * *

CAUTIOUS, MADELAINE AND HER PARENTS advised Charles to decrease his visits to Madelaine. They see each other, of course, during the tasks of love with the unfortunate in the wards. In this way, they find some time for themselves. However, they spend a few days without seeing each other. Today, Madelaine made an appointment to meet him at the Parish house, in one of its rooms, and is waiting for him there.

He arrives handsome and elegant, but physically haggard, leaving Madelaine pities him:

- My love, are you ill?

Kissing her ardently, he replied:

- In a way, yes. I suffer the torments of the Amenti because my feet and hands are tied!

- I'm so sorry, Charles!

- If you like, we can run away! Perhaps this is the only way, Madelaine! Unless...

- Unless...

- Unless marriage to the Prince is not so terrible to you!

- Charles! - she replies, upset.

- According to all that we have experienced, I must consider everything, Madelaine. If that is so, I will turn away from you, leaving the way clear for him! After all, the Prince really loves you, according to his own words, and he will also bring advantages into your life, hard for any other suitor to overcome.

In the gloomy despair that overwhelms me I can tell you, without fear of being mistaken, that no one will love you as I do! At this crucial moment, anticipating the terrible probability of losing you, I feel myself disgracefully on the verge of madness!

I have to say it again, Madelaine, I will not live without you!

Deeply distressed by his words, she exclaims, deathly pale:

- You are delirious, Charles, everything you say is because of the despair you are feeling! I won't even take these absurd ideas seriously! You know about my great love! I don't deserve a single doubt about this feeling that bathes my heart and brings me the joy of loving and being loved!

Taking her in his arms, regretting his words, he asked:

- Forgive me, my love! I am dying of jealousy, I am going mad! - and, in a whisper, he asks:

- What shall we do?...

Seeking strength in God, she replied:

- First of all, stop looking for me! The Prince can appear at the most unexpected moments.

You are in danger of death and this exasperate me! He promised to visit the Parish house. Perhaps he already knows that we are seeing each other here. This, perhaps, is his way to show that he is informed. Coming from him, everything threatens us. That's why I asked you to come, to warn you. Forgive me, my love, but we must wait for better days! Our greatest hope is in God!

- To stay away from you, Madelaine?... I can't! I do not fear the Prince! On the contrary, I feel the urge to face him! I'm as much a man as he is!

- My love! The Prince does not face his opponents on the same field; he annihilates them at a distance, by unknown hands, in the shadows and in silence! I know you know about this, Charles! Do you consider yourself immortal or indifferent to his savagery? How many of our friends have perished in a mysterious way for defied tyrants in defense of their most just rights?...! When will pain and despair overtake us, my love? When?... Sometimes it seems to me that we are delaying this fatal moment! I am, like you, desperate, don't doubt it!

- And then what should we do? Or rather, what do you intend to do?

- I'm not sure yet, but I beg you to distance yourself from me and never forget for an instant how much I love you! You are and will always be my only love! - Madelaine, trembling, cries, disconsolate.

- I knew it! I know you well enough to anticipate your attitudes! My God! This sounds like a goodbye, Madelaine! You're sealing my end! Who needs the Prince's violence?

I will die, to his delight, in one way or another!

- No, Charles, don't say that! Think, as I do; help me! We both know how many lives will depend on what I do!

Oh, God, how I wish it were not true! The weight exceeds my strength! In this terrible impasse, only you can sustain me! - Madelaine looks through the window and her beautiful eyes seem to see far beyond...

- Madelaine, I am surprised at your intention of give up at our love! Think of me! - Charles kisses her tears away and clasps her to his heart in despair.

- That is exactly what I am doing! Don't you realize that you're the most affected?

- If you have the difficult task of deciding what to do about so many things, I demand that you give me the power to decide about my life, because without you it won't be worth living! How will I survive to such a great loss, Madelaine? Do you have the answer?

- I am drawing strength from true love that liberates rather than imprison us, my dear!

- This is not enough for me! Do not underestimate me! I do not possess such a high understanding! - How much pain in the intonation of his voice -.

I would rather die than see you in the arms of another man! If I survive, I shall be a ghost instead of a man!

- Charles, don't say that!

- Madelaine, my love for you can be my heaven or my hell! Without you, nothing matters to me!

Desperate, he kisses her ardently over and over again, between oaths of love:

- I love you, Madelaine! Never forget it! I will love you for the eternity! This feeling, which at this moment makes me suffer so much, is the greatest pledge of my life! After you, Madelaine, nothing nor anyone else can gladden my heart as a man in love, in this despair into which I am being thrown, without defenses!

But I will not impose any longer! Do as you wish and I will respect your decision, whatever it may be, even if it is amidst unspeakable pain, unhappy and disillusioned with everything!

Wherever I am, in whatever time and place, because the soul is eternal, I will be with you in my thoughts! Always remember: you are everything to me! Madelaine, my only and great love! -

clasping her tightly, trembling and desperate, he kisses her, countless times, on her lips, on her face, in her hair... Then he plunges his gaze into hers, long and hard. He feels that he will never see her again. He wants to keep in his mind and in his heart her beautiful face...Finally, in a superhuman effort, he picks up his feathered hat, cloak and sword, and leaves, disappearing into the streets, without looking back. He did not notice two pairs of sinister eyes that had been following him for days...

Father Estanislau found her in tears. He supports her, silent. There is nothing to say. He knows what happened.

She returns home, devastated. A few moments later, the Prince appears, elegant and haughty:

- Father, where is my bride?

- Who is your Highness's bride?

- Do not underestimate my intelligence, Father, and do not disdain my power! Where is she?

- If you tell me of whom you speak.

- As if you didn't know! I'll show you how tolerant I can be, I'll refresh your memory: Where is Madelaine?

- Oh, yes, Madelaine! After her usual prayers, she returned to the castle!

- That's better. I want to talk to you!

Surprised, the Priest made himself available and invited him:

- Please sit down, your Highness! What do you want?

- As is my nature, I'll go straight to the point: You must relieve my fiancée from the tiresome work of the infirmary.

It is not right for a princess to do servile tasks, those are only for servants and people from the lower class.

Astonished, Father Etanislau asked:

- Did you talk with Madelaine about this?

Bursting into loud laughter, he asks another question:

- Did you? Do you also share the ideas to grant women certain rights? Watch out! You may face insurmountable difficulties! The Roman church must submit to the power of our King and to our traditions!

- The church submits only to God, your Highness!

- I see on the spot that you are a bad influence for my fiancée! From this day forward, I forbid her to come here except at the usual times of worship and prayer! - silently, he gets up, annoyed. With a slight inclination of his head, he said goodbye, leaving the good priest in shock.

Arriving home, Madelaine sees her father getting ready to go to the courthouse. Looking at her countenance, he asked her:

- Dear daughter, don't let yourself be overwhelmed! Use your freedom according to your will! Your mother and I will die before we see you unhappy!

He hugs her tightly. Leaning her head on her father's heart, she exclaims despondently:

- Dear father, there is no point in fighting back! I know very well how many lives are at stake! What will become of all of you? Of Father Estanislau, of our sick ones, dear Dr. Sergei, Nestor and so many others? Poor dears, Soraya and Fabian! Just to imagine, I think I'm going mad! The Prince, papa, must be painfully demanding something from me I owe him... If at birth I brought this, God will sustain me...!

- What do you say, child? Does the Highness the Prince threaten everyone else? – the Count shows his great surprise at Madelaine's words.

He thought that only his house was under the Prince's vigilance.

- Yes, my father. Forgive me for keeping this from you. Almost all those we know and love are included in his threats.

- Dear God! And I thought that I could, with my love and my courage as a man and a father, defend you, by giving you the rightful freedom to make up your own mind!

This regal gentleman knows how to create fatal traps! I can now, daughter of my heart, understand the great weight that you carry and the enormous responsibility that has fallen on you! Despite all this, I reaffirm that you can count on me for whatever you need and under any circumstances. I love you, dear daughter, and God will help us, trust me!

- I know, my father... Were it not for the faith that bathes my heart...

Bettine arrived and, seeing her saddened, wanted to know:

- How about Charles, my child?

- He has already understood, Mama, what the outcome of this drama will be!

- Daughter, I offer myself entirely in exchange for your happiness! Your father and I are ready for any sacrifice!

- My dears! Would I wish such a thing? God keep you safe! – They share a tender hug and remain so, supporting each other.

* * *

SALÚSTIO AND LOUÍSE are very happy. She is improving by leaps and bounds walking better, they can see the result of the treatments she is undergoing.

On moving into the new house, Corine proudly declared her new situation:

"- *Mademoiselle* Louíse, here I end my life as a servant! A bride of the handsome and prosperous General Antoine Belfort must assume new tasks!

- Are you engaged, Corine?

- Oh, yes, we are! He's in a hurry to get married. He was always a bachelor until I came into his life.

Imagine, *Mademoiselle*, that he is amazed at the physical resemblance between me and his late Jeannette!

Shaking her head to show concern, Louíse exclaims:

- That's it! When I was trying to remember where I knew you from, it was that very resemblance that struck me! You look like my friend Jeannette, reborn!

- That's what he says and he loves me so much! He can't wait for the wedding date, which by the way we have already booked! I hope to see you and *Mademoiselle* Madelaine, as well as Soraya and Fabian, at the ceremony and the party which will be magnificent!

- We'll come to the church wedding, Corine! We want to see you happy! That general of yours, at last, seems to have a heart in his chest!

- I know, *Mademoiselle*!"

In these reflections, Louíse did not realize that her husband was approaching. Kissing her, he brings her out of her thoughts:

- Louíse, Madelaine is devastated! - he informs her, sitting down beside her. - She fears for Charles' life! The Prince may want to "drive him away" for good! The two met at the Parish House and practically said goodbye! It's a shame to see how bad our dear friend is!

- Poor dears! What a problem! How would we feel if it were us, Salústio?

- The same as they are feeling. Ah, if I could help my dear Madelaine... I am capable of anything for her, but in these circumstances, I can do nothing! She seems determined to sacrifice herself.

God forbid that she should marry the Prince!

- I was jealous of you with Madelaine. But, seeing her love for Charles and her disinterested affection, I reassured myself.

- To be honest, for a time I was in love with her, Louíse. This I cannot deny. But then I learned to love her as dear sister.

- If she had loved you too, it would be you today, and not Charles, who is being persecuted!

Have you ever thought of this?

- No, Louíse. Poor friends!

- Poor friends, Salústio...

Salústio wraps his arms around Louíse, clasping her to his chest, with emotion. He is afraid of leaving her in a sudden way; he lives in constant insecurity... His life is full of dangers...

She, for her part, is aware of the risks he runs. When he lingers, her heart races with fear. He often cries in secret...

Together, they exchange caresses when they hear the chuckle of Fabian, who arrives with Soraya. They are there, with Lucien, spending a few days in the new house.

Disconcerted, they move away, listening to the petitions of the restless Fabian who pleads for some help from Salústio for anything. Hugging the boy, he leaves under the reverent gaze of Louíse, who remains talking affectionately with Soraya.

*** * ***

SACHA, OLGA AND little Kostia arrive. Hugging, the two siblings mourn the loss of their father.

The little one, with his blond hair and eyes color of the sky, immediately wins over everyone, especially his aunt who lovingly covers him with affection, guessing his desires to satisfy them.

The united family, together with Sir. Jaime's competent work, courageously and determinedly carries on the business of the ranch.

Olga is strong, healthy and friendly.

The harmony that is taking place foreshadows better times. Marcel is with the bride's relatives and suggests that they set a wedding date. He loves Natacha devotedly. He feels the urgency to have her by his side, but strangely she refuses. He concludes that she is still grieving over the recent death of her father, and Sir. Jaime remembers the prophetic warning.

Her mother tries to convince her, but it's useless. Natacha's behavior is inexplicable.

* * *

HENRY JHON, ALREADY RECOVERED and tired of waiting for Madelaine's visit, as soon as he can, goes to the Alvarado castle, only to be surprised by the sadness that seems to be in every corner, despite the efforts of the hosts to disguise it. In a few moments he understands everything. The authoritarian and unpleasant presence of the Prince leaves him in shock.

Showing, without hesitation, how much his presence displeases him, his Highness informs him of his intentions to marry Madelaine and, in a defiant posture, expects him to leave.

Madelaine, depressed, looks like a marble statue. She treated him well, but with reservations, under the Prince's hard and incensed gaze, seeming to show her would-be fiancé that he has nothing to fear from him, protecting him.

Bidding her a polite farewell, Henry left, depressed and saddened by Madelaine's remarkable disenchantment.

Salústio had also experienced the Prince's bad temper.

Visiting the castle and coming across him, he bowed slightly, and as he was leaving, heard:

- Mr. Saul Venturi, avoid coming here too often! We can live without your unpleasant presence!

- Do you speak for the owners of the house, your Highness?

- I speak for everyone! And there's more: beware of your patriotic impulses! Your aversion to the powers may be fatal to you!

Salústio felt his blood freeze in his veins.

Then, more emphatically, he threatened:

- You are being observed! If you don't take care of yourself, you will end your days on the gallows or in the infected cellars of the prisons! Surely your wife expects to live for many years by your side, doesn't she?

Salústio tries not to react, not even verbally. The allusion to his private life made him shudder with anger and concern. Clenching his fists, he keeps silent; bowing, reverent, he leaves. He will avoid mentioning these threats to his good friend and her parents. Her torments are already too many...

Disgusted, Frida watches her cousin leave and suffers his ostentatious contempt.

As he told her, he is getting ready for his wedding with Madelaine, which is happening soon.

Today she decided to approach him, before setting in motion the plans she has been plotting:

- Aleksei, I need to talk to you! Can you give me a little of your attention?

- What do you want, Frida? Well, be quick and to the point!

- Why so angry, my cousin? When will you trust in me?

- I never trust anyone, Frida!

- I want to be your friend, cousin! And, consequently, become friend with your fiancée.

- I will try, Frida, as far as I can, to fulfill your request. Now leave me, please, I have a lot to do!

Leaving the room, she thinks angrily:

"One way or another, Aleksei, I will have you! I swear it! My father, from wherever he is, will support my intentions! He will give strength to my arms and energy to my mind!"

Contrary to Aleksei's wishes, Madelaine goes to see Father Estanislau. She needs comfort. Between one issue and another, she decides to tell him something very important:

- Father Estanislau, yesterday I had a beautiful dream! I would like to tell you all about it!

- Of course, my child! I would be delighted to hear it!

- As I fell asleep, I "came out of myself" and flew towards Charles's residence like a swift bird.

He, awake, was weeping, extremely depressed and unhappy. I could read his thoughts and feel his emotions. Leaning over I cover him with great love. Blue lights poured from my heart on his chest. He nodded off, fell asleep, and "came out" of his body, rejoicing to see me.

We get together in a glorious embrace, forming a single being.

We glided along, always climbing, and reached a city of beautiful and apparently solid buildings. In the air, an untranslatable music. Enlighten beings passed by us, greeting us with loving looks.

Some wore Greek-style tunics and bare feet.

They were carefully carrying strange objects, unknown to us. I don't know how, but we learned that they were advanced instruments of medicine, astronomy, engineering, etc.

Another group of beings carried, cautiously, in transparent boxes, of different colors and sizes, living and perfect copies of our various organs, made of plastic material never seen by us before.

We saw many other things, difficult to describe for lack of analogy.

A name vibrated in the air. I remember it very well: Galeno!

Together, we walked along a path that was already known. We reached a beautiful building with a white front, exquisite gardens, wide doors and lots of light inside. In fact, we were already expected. People whom we do not know in this life, familiar to us, welcomed us there with unusual joy. A great happiness infected us all. We exchanged fraternal hugs, involved each other in great nostalgia...

After a time that I cannot determine, we left the place and crossed a luminous portal, capable of balancing our pains and frustrations. Integrated with cosmic love, we experienced the pains and joys of humanity as if we were a single being!

A glorious personality, who for us represented brotherly love, enlightened us powerfully! I felt like a star, united to my beloved Charles, and he smiled happily at me.

A radiant and extremely friendly spirit joins us, affectionate. Instructing the other luminous beings around us, he declared:

- The man will return first. She, like John, the most beloved disciple, will live much longer. It must be in that way...

I awoke, still hearing that soft, harmonious voice.

Father, if life robs me the chance to be happy with Charles, here on earth; "there", where we were, we will fulfill our dreams of happiness!

I understand now, my spiritual father, that my Charles will leave me soon! May God bless us and give us strength! Despite all the spiritual resources that reach me, my good friend, I sometimes feel so weak! - she cries freely, unable to contain herself.

- Madelaine, while the body is weakened by the struggles, the spirit is strengthened and rises to seek consolation and peace! Both of you have been spiritually restored by the grace of God.

You both bear urgent witness to renunciation and understanding.

- Father, the time granted to me by the Prince has already run out.

I must accept his proposal of marriage. I do not want to be responsible for anyone's unhappiness.

- Alea jacta est, as my dear father says! May God be glorified in us, his creatures!

- Ad aeternum, daughter!

Wiping away her tears, and tenderly and sweetly hugging the priest, her friend of all hours, she said goodbye and returned to the castle.

A few moments after her arrival, Aleksei and Frida appeared. The Prince introduced her:

- Count Luiz Santiago de Alvarado, I present to you my cousin, Baroness Willfrida Svirilás of Westphalia, daughter of my recently deceased uncle, Baron Otto Svirilás!

- Delighted - replied the Count, kissing her hand, while Countess Bettine approaches and hugs him.

Aleksei disappeared. He goes in search of Madelaine.

When he sees her, she turns pale, which makes him ask, happily:

- You are frightened by my presence! Well, well! The mirrors tell me I'm not that ugly!

She smiles slightly, without any enthusiasm.

Kissing her hands, he whispers:

- Smile, my dear! I will make you happy! I promise you solemnly!

And indeed, he loves her.

- Madelaine - he insisted - I look forward to your answer. What is it going to be?

Do you want to be my wife, my most radiant star, my fortune? Will you marry me?

- Yes, your Highness... - she replied, head bowed, voice fading.

She seemed to be signing her own death warrant...

Despite her sadness and obvious reluctance to answer, he bursts out with joy:

- Bravo! We will set the date for two weeks from now! What do you say? - he asks, like a bouncy, relaxed boy.

- That's fine with me! - she continues, without any interest.

Her words were articulated with extreme difficulty, as if they were out from a different mouth.

Bettine and Frida, followed by the Count, arrived.

Over the shoulder of the Prince, who bends down to kiss her hands, Madelaine is met by a pair of eyes as sparkling as steel.

- Your Highness - Madelaine asked him politely - who is the girl?

He answered begrudgingly:

- She is my cousin Willfrida Svirilás, from Germania, more specifically from Westphalia!

- Pleasure, Willfrida! - Madelaine exclaims.

In order to hasten the various arrangements for the longed-for marriage, Aleksei decides to leave, taking Frida with him. She, disgusted, decides, as a last resort, to declare her love, thus playing the last card.

The next day, we see her choosing the best outfit and the most exquisite props. Around her, clothes of all colors and varied shoes; jewelry boxes, open, as if they were in an exhibition. In front of the richest case, in which pieces of rare value are, she begins a strange monologue:

- How can anyone live without these? They give me strength, security, a sense of power! Many of these jewels have belonged to the victors of all peoples! How many stories have they witnessed? How many bodies have they adorned? How much greed have they been targets? How many have killed or died for them? Hard to know! It is almost impossible to discover their origins!

They're mine now! I love them! I could do anything to keep them...!

- Frida fills her hands with the pieces; she drops them on the rich bedspread, to pick them up again. She strokes her face with them and delighted in the sensation of the touch. She turns them over in his hands and is enraptured by the glow that emanates from them. She remains like this for long time, strangely fascinated.

Quietly, Erica wonders what dark stories might be behind those precious things...

- Erica, help me with this zipper!

Finally ready; satisfied with the image reflected in the mirror, she goes out determined to talk to her cousin.

Confused and astonished, he welcomes her:

- Are you going to a party, cousin?

- No! I've done my best to please you!

- To please me? I don't understand! Can you be clearer?

- All right, I'll be honest and clear, as you like, my dear cousin!

I want to speak to you with an open heart about my feelings! - she declares, heavily flushed.

- Your feelings? Are you in love with someone?

- Come on, Aleksei, don't pretend to ignore my great love for you!

- Have you gone mad, Frida? How dare you? To declare yourself like that, without the slightest modesty? Aware of my love for Madelaine and of my forthcoming marriage?! Leave me alone! Stop this!

- What do I care about modesty, Alekei, if this love burns me like a live coal and embers and torments me like the inferno of Dante?...! You're the one who is crazy! Can't you see that I'm the one that can make you happy and love you as you deserve? Are you blind? Don't you realize that we are the same? Made of the same cloth?

- And this is a positive thing to you? You have no idea how much you fool yourself! Madelaine is everything I desire and we are not equal!

- You will be mine, Aleksei, anyway! No other woman will steal you from me! - Out of control, she advances to hug him and is violently pushed away:

- Stop it, Frida! Don't lower yourself like that! I'll never love anyone like you! Madelaine is all I aspire to have!

- Without you, Aleksei, I would rather die! - she declares exaltedly.

- Then die and leave me alone! - Aleksei feels the urge to hit her, to throw her out. But he controlled himself. He crosses his arms and challenges her, his gaze hard and threatening.

Silently, she approaches again. She walks around he, like a feline before attacking, eyes shining. Staring at him, she asks, ironically, strange, in a sibilant voice:

- What do you expect from the beautiful Madelaine? That she loves you? Don't make me laugh! Her romance with the Marquess is widely known! Do you want to be loved out of obedience? That's not how it works, Aleksei! You may dominate her body, but you will never possess her soul, which will still belong to the Marquess! "Your Highness" will be scorned by all the nobility of France, Russia and Germania!

Choleric, Aleksei raised his right hand and struck her full in the face. A slap knocks her off balance, causing her to stagger.

Without a groan, she brings her hand to her face, feel the affected area and continues, out of control:

- Everything I told you is true; you know it! That's why you rebel and hit me! I humiliate myself, I offer you love, and you despise me? Me? Who would die in the name of this love, without flinching?! You will regret it bitterly! You will pay me dearly! I swear it! In the name of my father and all our ancestors! - this, she says, fist raised, looking upwards in an imprecation to the heavens.

- If you continue acting like this, taking away my freedom and imposing yourself, shamelessly, I will destroy you, Frida! And in such a way that not even your father or "our" ancestors, who must be in hell, will be able to put you back together. Get out! - as his scream echoes, he sees Erica emerge in distress and support Frida with solicitude.

She looks at Aleksei in silent reproach.

In front of her, mysteriously, Aleksei loses his aggression.

He admires her, deeply and spontaneously. He feels for this woman, almost unknown, a great respect.

Changing his voice, he suggested:

- Take her away, Erica, please! Frida has the gift of exasperating me!

And make sure she understands how wrong she is!

Hugging Frida, she invites her:

- Come, daughter, calm down! - She drags her out of the Prince's office.

He sits down with a bang. He saw the gleam of hatred in his cousin's eyes before she left. He regrets having to tolerate her and decides that somehow, he will get rid of her.

In her chambers, Frida breaks everything she can reach. She screams, reacts to the enormous frustration. She cries in despair and listens, once again from Erica:

- Frida, are we going back to Westphalia?

- No! What for? The war has only just begun! We'll see who will be the winner!

- Frida, against the Prince there is nothing you can do!

- Do you forget my privileged intelligence? He won't lose by waiting! He'll get his comeuppance and more!

Erica has seen her like this countless times and the result is always deplorable. She is not threatening in vain. She will go through everything and everyone to get what she wants, one way or another. Beseeching the heavens for help, she provides the tranquilizers for Frida.

The next day, thinking better, Frida understands that she was precipitated. She decides to change her tactics. If she continues with this, he will send her back to Germania, even if it's tied to the mast of a ship. Then it will be impossible to carry out her plans.

After breakfast, appearing calm and repentant, she will talk to Aleksei again:

- Good morning, my cousin! Will you listen to me, please?

- If you want to continue what you started yesterday, no! Greek tragedies only in the theater, with good actors and in good company!

- Take a rest! Today I come to apologize to you! My behavior yesterday was deplorable! How could I? I must, once and for all understand that you are getting married! I shall learn to conform. I'm thinking of getting married too! That's it, I'll forget about you!

- This is the ideal solution! Beautiful and rich, you won't be short of suitors!

Choose one of them and be happy!

- Thank you for your understanding, Aleksei! Be at peace!

Relieved, he took up the papers that had occupied him before, which were spread out neatly on his ebony desk. His quartermaster arrives and he dispatches orders.

His thoughts flew to Madelaine. His chest almost burst with happiness. However, Frida's words have confirmed, the Marquess' words about Madelaine's love for him.

He must think about it...

Madelaine has lost the joy of living. Her parents will find her, often weeping at the foot of the image of Our Lady of Mont'Serrat in the castle chapel.

And... the days go by, quickly, shortening the time before the marriage...

* * *

AT THE INN, MRS. KORSANIKOV fell ill. Still recovering by the recent grief at the loss of her husband, she has acquired pneumonia, which, threatens to take her away from her children and grandchild. The doctors are worried: she will soon follow her husband.

Suffering, Natacha bravely continues to run the business, now without the host couple. Sir. Jaime, in his duties, spares no effort to keep a firm grip on the financial affairs of the resort.

A week later, Mrs. Korsanikov says goodbye, leaving the world; Natacha, whom she had already been recommended to marry Marcel, Sacha and his family. Another burial and more tears of grief and anticipatory longing.

- God, I think my heart is going to explode! It's too much pain! - Natacha exclaims, weeping.

- Daughter, have strength! They must be together, and they will continue to watch over you and the resort! - advises Sir. Jaime. - As you can see, we have done everything we can, Natacha! The spiritual help you have received will certainly help you in your time of troubles. The soul newly arrived in the afterlife feels dizzy and confused, needing to use other resources; those that were forgotten during earthly life, but which are attributes of the spirit!

They, while they lived, practiced honesty, striving for survival, love for their family and friends, and for those who knew them! Your dear parents deserve peace with God. They will be fine, Natacha! You can rest your heart!

In silent, he recalled what Natacha had said to him a few days ago:

"Sir. Jaime, when I go to the woods to refresh myself and blend into nature, I sometimes feel watched, in danger!

A chill runs down my spine and I return home."

At the time, he advised her not to go too far from the resort.

There had been a lot of activity there in recent days. Employees, guests and locals have been out in solidarity and attended the funeral, reverent.

Rupert and Nikolai, who lived nearby, watched the funeral services of their aunt from a distance; while Sir. Jaime and Natacha think they are far away.

* * *

AT THE CASTLE, MADELAINE is visited by father Estanislau:

- So good to see you, Father! I was missing you!

- Me too, my child!

- How is everyone at the Parish house?

- Missing you, of course!

- I feel the same... You have no idea! However, my friend, that's how it should be, at least for now. How is our dear Salústio?

- He is fine! He hasn't been coming here because he's afraid to face the Prince and create more trouble for you. From Italian roots, our friend is hot-blooded!

- Dear Salústio! God keep him safe!

- And you, Madelaine, how are you? I notice you are very sad!

- I suffer a lot, Father. Nor could it be otherwise... I submit, but in the name of something much greater: the safety and survival of many!

With every passing minute, I move further away from my happiness... the one that is just in front of me, like a scaffold, the life I hate beckons me, sinister!

- I am so sorry, Madelaine!

- I've been thinking a lot, Father, about the situation that I'm experiencing, and I wonder: how many other women are feeling the same way right now? It is easy to answer: many! I can only imagine what your priestly ears hear in the confessional about this!

- You are right, child! I am worried!

- As long as the man is selfish and prevents a woman from deciding her own life, he is throwing her into despair, death and betrayal, Father!

- Daughter of my soul! The mistakes of men will never justify how they degrade women!

- I know, father. However, *"the spirit is willing, but the flesh is weak"*! I have no intention of betraying the Prince's trust, but countless times, my being longs for Charles!

They can subdue the matter, but the soul will always fly where it wants! The heart is sacred ground! Man can impose himself, but they will never prevent the feminine soul from dreaming, freeing itself through thoughts and will, making these dreams come true, not often, these dreams that leave the subjective field for full realization!

In our works of charity and love, Father, how many of these women do we listen to, compassionately, in order to enlighten them afterwards, to show them the right path? Why condemn instead of understanding and uplifting them? Those who fall should be helped to get up instead of being singled out and stigmatized! Our society is hypocritical!

Only God knows the moments of despair and pain experienced in silence! Yes, Father, dear friend! I, Madelaine, am just a drop of water in this immense ocean of pain and disenchantment!

- You are right, Madelaine. Let us forgive the mistakes of others, helping to the dignity of those who fall, and let us pray for all: victims and executioners! One day, man will learn to love without selfishness!

- Certainly! Without forgetting that many women, too, selfish and imposing, turn the lives of their partners, into a living hell!

Men and women act without thinking in the field of love, in general. But almost always it is the man who imposes himself, the old, and unjust laws.

Sooner or later, however, this situation will change.

No one can stop the wheels of progress.

The current position of women in society is depressing and disrespectful. And let us not forget, Father, the dramatic situation that they face in other parts of the world! Mary, mother of Jesus, will pity those who carry the sublime task of co-creators with the Father, because they are givers of life!

Well, dear friend, shall we go to the dining room? Ignácia must have cooked a tasty snack for you!

- Come on, hurry up! I appreciate Ignácia's delicacies like no one else!

* * *

HOLDING THE PACE FLAG, Frida pretends to be interested in her cousin's marriage, sympathizing with him.

Meanwhile, she calls Lugano:

- Today I'm going to check your promise! I want to know if you know someone who is expert in potions; do you know what I mean? Remedies for curing diseases, poisons... something like that!

- Oh, yes! I know a wizard who makes these things. He lives in a cave far away from here! Would you dare go to such a strange place? People say that in that place the wind howls and laughs horribly, scaring those who come near!

- Take me to him, Lugano! And don't worry about me!

- If that's what you want... I'll stay away, if the madam allows me?

I'm very afraid!

- Stay where you want! Let's go!

So, it was arranged. Shivering with dread at the appearance of the place and of the wizard, she acquires what she desires.

On her return, she pays the servant generously and shuts him up.

Despite her apparent calm, her inner self is in chaos.

Erica, careful, faithfully watches over her health and safety. The good woman keeps her soul in suspense. She knows Frida well enough to believe she is content.

With a strange gleam in her eyes, Frida warns excitedly:

- Erica, I want a glorious toilette to attend the wedding ceremony of my beloved cousin! The most exquisite from Paris!

I want a magical, unique, eternal dress! - she laughs, leaving Erica badly impressed:

- Madam, why so desperate?

-What despair? You are talking nonsense, Erica? I'm happy! Go do your duties and leave me alone!

Keeping quiet, Erica does as her madam said. But, deep in her soul, can presage terrible things.

* * *

IN A WHOLE SERIES OF DIFFERENT FEELINGS for each attendant, the wedding day arrives.

The castle, bustling, welcomes friends and relatives.

Disguising what is in their hearts, the hosts welcome everyone with dignity.

The religious wedding will take place in the castle chapel, officiated by Father Estanislau.

It is difficult to describe the pomp with which the Prince's castle awaits for his future mistress. He himself seems to be going mad with happiness. While organizing the wedding, he torments the servants with unreasonable demands.

He has already dispatched the most urgent matters from his office and, among them, an order that has made his gaze more sinister. He carries on his lips a thin smile of mockery, before the world that lives at his feet. He sometimes hates the power in which he is invested. He is aware of the power he has to satisfy his own desires.

He spent most of the hours before the realization of his most cherished dream in a feverish agitation.

He couldn't sleep at night, because he had nightmares. He has premonitions that try to repel. Any loud noise startles him. It seems to him that strange shadows, wrapped in evil omen, are moving around him. Sometimes he feels accompanied, with no one around. And to make it stranger, his uncle Otto is present in his thoughts all the time, bothering him. He seems to see him with empty eye sockets, thin hands, in patent despair...

"Well, this is all just a figment of my imagination that is anxious for my marriage! My conscience is playing tricks on me because I know that uncle Otto great desired was to see me married to Frida! That's it!

I shall think only of Madelaine and forget about these horrible thoughts! We will be very happy! She will be mine! In a few hours, I shall be the happiest man on this planet!"

Frida gets ready, luxuriously, for the event, dressing up, as never before. With persistence, she won her cousin's trust in a few days. He thought she was resigned to the inevitable. And the hours goes by...

Sir. Jaime and Eugene were present and placed themselves at the disposal of Madelaine and her family. Natacha sent a beautiful gift. It was impossible to her leave the resort at the moment.

Henry declined the invitation and sent a beautiful gift for the bride and groom.

Louíse, Caterine, Salústio and Lucien are trying to help Countess Bettine with the various arrangements for the ceremony. Betbara remained at home, in charge of everything, in Louíse's absence.

In her chambers, assisted by her mother and Ignácia, as well as by numerous maids, Madelaine dressed for the ceremony.

Silent, her eyes red from crying, she submits, indifferent.

A great sadness hung in the air.

The dress, embroidered with gold and pearls, weighs on her like the fate she is about to assume. The equally precious ornaments adorn her unique beauty.

Sitting on a bench, the volume of the dress spreads out on the shiny floor. It is the picture of disillusion. Bettine tries to cheer her up, without success. As she kissed her, trying to cheer her up, she cried once again in her arms. Bettine's heart squeezed.

Uncle Richard's rapid footsteps were heard as he entered his niece's room, saying loudly:

- Madelaine, brightest star in my sky! What has happened in this house while I was traveling? It seems to me to have taken ages out there! What happened with your engagement to my friend Charles? By any chance, did he prove to be unworthy of you?

- No, my dear uncle! Listen...

He won't listen:

- I've hardly come from the East and heard the blasphemy that you're going to marry the Prince?! I'm shocked!

- Dear uncle, this is not the right time to ask for explanations, I just want you to know that I know what I'm doing!

- I doubt it! If you knew, you wouldn't marry this despicable man!

And why these red eyes from crying? Not even makeup can't disguise them, Madelaine!

- Every bride cries, uncle.

- Of happiness, I think. Not you! What have you done with that worthy heart that loves you madly?

- He will be happy with another, uncle Richard.

- Never! I know him well, Madelaine! That heart belongs to you. He only loves once! Now I understand what I've heard from common friends: he travels endlessly, no longer plays and does not sing! Can you imagine that? I really like that boy and what you are doing to him is incomprehensible! Unless... Yes! You must be forced to do it! And your father? What is he doing about it? I'll talk to him.

- Uncle Richard, what have you heard about Charles? - Madelaine asks, deeply mortified.

- He is a shadow of the man he was! Thin and haggard, he no longer smiles.

He stayed little time in Paris, being constantly away on long journeys related with his art.

Noticing that Madelaine was beginning to cry, he was surprised:

- God, you still love him! I can see it in your eyes which never lied to me! What could be behind all this? Calm down, Madelaine, and forgive me for the outbursts! As if I didn't know the risks one takes in defying "your fiancé"! I will speak to my brother.

Why did I stay so long in the East? It seems that the world turned upside down! - He kissed Madelaine and hurried downstairs to the halls in search of Count Louis.

That's Richard; a spontaneous, outgoing, loving man.

***

IF THE KING COULD SEE THE PRINCE'S BEAUTY and elegance, he would surely envy him. Tall, slender, of flawless lines, refined, the rich attire fits him like a glove.

Frida, on the other hand, is elegant and very beautiful; but she carries a strange gleam in her eyes. She looks for Aleksei and, seeing him in his ceremonial clothes, she is breathless. Her passion knows no bounds. She shows a wide smile and compliments him:

- Aleksei, you look stunning!

- Thank you, my cousin. But what do you want? It's not polite to disturb me in these solemn and serious moments!

- Rest assured, I'm not going to trouble you. Today is the day of your happiness, and I want more than anyone to contribute to it.

- Then please be brief!

- I will! Today you get married and then I return to Westphalia!

- Have you decided that? I'm glad to hear it! Once there, try to follow my example and get married too!

- I intend to. Now I want something from you! It's my farewell! After your wedding, it's likely we'll never see each other again, cousin! Therefore, fulfill my wish, which may be the last!

- What wish is that? - His voice was filled with impatience.

- Toast with me for this special day!

Surprised at the simplicity of the request, and concluding that to do her will is the best way to get rid of his uncomfortable presence, he replies:

- Well, Frida, certainly! I'll call my private servant right now and he will bring us the best wine!

- No, cousin! We will toast with a special Bavarian wine, which is a nectar of the gods, worthy of you! I have saved it for an occasion like this!

- All right, Frida, but let's hurry! They are waiting for me at the castle of the Alvarados and I don't want to be late!

- They will wait for you as long as you wish, my regal and beautiful cousin! Shall we go then? I have everything ready in my chambers!

- You are amazing, Frida!

- Is this a compliment or a reproach?

- It depends on the circumstance, dearest cousin. Right now, it's a compliment!

As they walk, she continues, deliberated:

- Aleksei, my luggage has already been checked and Erica is already traveling to Westphalia, to accommodate everything the way I'm used to!

- But... Frida! She and I didn't even say goodbye!

- Whenever you want, you can come and visit us, with the beautiful Madelaine!

Aleksei concluded that Frida had definitely given up on him.

In a few minutes they arrive.

He is surprised by the beauty of the surroundings, the aesthetics and the luxury.

Everything seems ready for a party: flowers, chandeliers lighting, impeccable decoration.

If he were more attentive, he would notice slight facial tremors in Frida. Considering her eccentric, he disguises his bad mood, showing a false relaxation.

On the sideboard, a gold tray holds two cups of the same metal, carved with precious stones. Next to it, the bottle of wine seems to await them.

She pours the liquid into the cups in a strange ritual. Concerned and restless, he awaits what is to come. To clear his head, he compliments her:

- Frida, you look very beautiful!

- Thank you, Aleksei! Here's to your happiness! - She exclaims, in exaggerated joy.

Perhaps you've finally convinced yourself that I'll never love you? Finally! - he thinks. He breathes, relieved, and receiving his cup from her hands, he drinks the contents, without even tasting them, such was his haste to get rid of the embarrassment.

She, with a strange smile on her lips, cup in hand, waits for him to finish drinking the last drop.

Putting the cup down on the tray, Aleksei feels strangely tired. He thinks he has demanded too much of himself in arrangements for the wedding.

His head is spinning now. He has trouble for standing up.

His body feels like it's being stung by fiery sparks. An atrocious suffering begins to overtake him. A sudden thought comes to his mind:

Frida has poisoned him!

Too late! He can't defend himself... He advances towards her, but his body is heavy, he moves slowly. Gathering all the strength he has left, he cries out in a raspy, yawning voice:

- Damned! You poisoned me! I'll kill you! - he struggles to change his steps, but his legs do not obey him. Eyes unreasonably open, reflecting a frightful hatred, he bends his knees and with a deafening thud, collapses on the carpet, at Frida's feet, in spasmodic convulsions, agonizing.

She laughs, diabolical, and screams at him, tragic:

- You have despised my love, Aleksei! You shouldn't have done that! I warned you! You will be mine in death! Today, here, we will be together my cousin! Like that, we will cross the boundaries of this life and, united, we shall reach that in which my beloved and longed-for father preceded us!

Frida's voice explodes in Aleksei's ears, torturing him without him being able to fight back. The sounds he tries to articulate die in his throat, guttural. His body becomes numb.

In a mental effort, he directs his last thoughts to the only person he loves: "Madelaine! My crazy and dear love! My sweet Madelaine! Farewell! I love you and I will carry this love with me wherever I go! My last request is that you do not forget me!

Madelaine..."

She still sees Frida raising her own cup, speaking in exasperation:

- Can you still hear me, Aleksei? Look! I'm going to drink the same poison to join you! Do you know anyone who would love you so much? I doubt it! And you rejected me! Me, who loves madly! - raising the cup she offers:

- To you, my beautiful Prince! – And, so saying, she drinks the whole contents. Opening her hand, she drops it and rushes to Aleksei.

Throwing herself upon him, she hugs him, kisses him, maddened. Now he cannot drive her away...

She begins to feel the effects of the poison. Her vision is blurred, her limbs numb, her head spinning, she distinguishes shadows moving next to the two of them. Among them, she recognizes his father's countenance, tormented, surrounded by disgusting and irreverent creatures. Frightened, she is sorry. He is unhappy, that is obvious. Suddenly, she concludes that those diabolical beings are waiting for her and Aleksei. In a split second, she wants to turn back, but it's too late. All is done. Her unhappy love destroyed them... With her eyes squinting, she feels helpless in the face of the abyss that opens at their feet, dug by her own madness...

She went through the same convulsions of agony. A few minutes later, she calms down.

Baroness Willfrida Svirilás of Germania and her cousin, the Russian Prince Aleksei Nikolai Ivanovich, have tragically left the world and all it has to offer...

Lugano is the only one who can calculate the risks the castle faces.

For him, however, it matters little what happens to the tyrant who exploits and torments him.

The beautiful German has paid handsomely for his work and her complicity. In a few hours he will leave that place forever. He acts normally so as not to arouse suspicion.

* * *

IN THE ALVARADO'S CASTLE, on the wedding day, the sun has risen bright, the birds have been singing since early morning, the river sounds loud, the children running around happily, and everything seems to foreshadow a happy day. However, contrary to this enchanting scenery, hearts are deeply sad.

In the early hours of this decisive and deeply difficult day, the Condes went to the chapel to pray. The day was dawning, demanding of them an unshakeable faith. As if by a fatality, they are convinced that the only way is to wait...

Together with Madelaine, they ratified the immense love they felt for her and their pride in having her as their daughter.

Hugging, equally moved, Madelaine declared, lovingly:

- I love you devotedly and I want you to know that if only you alone were in danger, I would have the same attitude towards the Prince's imposition! I know that you would do the same for me or for my siblings! May the love that characterizes our family strengthen and sustain us in this difficult trial! Rest assured; I'll be okay! Rationally, I will overcome this situation that seems to be irreversible!

Together, between kisses and tears, it's like they were saying goodbye to each other...

Now, the hours pass slowly, demanding from everyone a lot of calm and apparent casualness, in the reception of those who arrive happily to the party without imagining the drama they are going through.

- You look magnificent, Madelaine! - exclaims Sir. Jaime.

- Thank you, my friend!

- Is there anything we can do to cheer you up?

- No, thank you.

- Madelaine, have faith, God will help you, one way or another! - says Eugene, hugging her tightly and kissing her on both cheeks.

- I will go down, Eugene, and see in what I can help more urgently with the Count - says Sir. Jaime.

He is walking to the door when he suddenly feels dizzy.

He stops and waits to understand what is happening. A little time ago the mediumistic phenomena have been surprising him.

He concludes that he must return and take care of what is now being announced.

Calmly, he asks Eugene:

- Daughter, start praying, because I can feel something urgent in the air and perhaps, I am the instrument of some warning, if God allow me. I will concentrate. Help me, as you know how, will you?

- Yes, papa.

- Madelaine, please clear the rooms. Only we should stay and participate in what is to come. I feel heavy vibrations, something terrible is happening and it concerns about the life of this castle.

Yes, sir!

In a few moments, he is answered.

A few minutes pass and Sir. Jaime seems to snore slightly.

Focus, Madelaine waits, praying. Hands in her lap, she sighs and trusts in God above all. You know that friend well, his dignity, his spiritual and philanthropic works, his admirable wisdom and his great heart. There is a silence that helps to achieve a favorable meditation.

He moves on the seat of the comfortable armchair, raises his right hand and exclaims with elegance and delicacy: - Peace be with you!

I am present because of the divine mercy that allows us to have this loving exchange and in the urgent need to help this courageous and submissive group to the father, which is now going through solemn moments of evaluation and some atonement!

Contributing to the execution of God's will, we reaffirm our eternal love for those who live here and work in favor of the legitimate love! The group is tuned with the good and the progress, directly responsible for their own evolution, are part of an endless chain, in a universal family of which we are part, grateful and reverent!

For this purpose, we help each other, evolving more every day!

Prepare your hearts and strengthen yourselves in faith, because the time is bad for all, without distinction!

Right now, "the fire has been lit" and will burn until the end. Within the principle: 'To each one according to his works', the one who today would fulfill the greatest dream of his life, in an idealization for his heart, has already entered the world of the so-called dead, in a tragic and unpredictable way!

Practicing obnoxious acts, one of them a few hours before died, he opened a dark space for hatred and revenge, in the very consummation of his fate; dying as he lived – surrounded by evil!

In a total unbalance, another being, equally violent, precipitated in middle of the events in a mad passion! I warn you that frightening things are about to begin.

- Could you tell us who this is, in the name of God? – asks Eugene, in haste.

- The one you are waiting for the ceremony that will not take place, and his relative, an unfortunate young woman who, through a crime, has attracted misfortunes that will hurt many, while others will be taken to the real world!

- My God! - exclaims Madelaine, understanding everything. She has long realized Frida's unbridled love for Prince Aleksei. - They are... dead?!

- Yes! Now listen carefully, for many lives will depend on the actions that must be taken! This, the one, who allows me to speak now, is arranging, with the help of the spiritual world, the way to protect and guide you from now on! While I am using his body, he is aware of all that I have just told you, and he is also listening to the advice of the spirit world.

Be strong and see in the events that will follow the consent of him, the one who grants us what we need for a constant evolution, respecting our free will, when we have already conquered it! The carnal suit will only serve us as an immortal essence that allows us to explore ancient and sacred paths!

We will inspire those who must take the right decisions, corresponding to the difficult situation that will arise in a few hours! - Turning to Madelaine, the entity affectionately advises:

- Daughter, beloved spirit of so many who fight for the transformation of this planet, your heart will be hurt more than the others. Be strong! We will be vigilant to spare you within the possibilities of the current situation. God our father blesses you and embrace you in gentle vibrations. We will continue for years to come always relying on your loving heart!

Trust, we will be at the rescue! Peace and strength!"

Gradually, Sir. Jaime awakes to describe what he "saw" during his spiritual disconnection:

- Without knowing the castle of Prince Aleksei, my soul went there, with God's permission.

- Arriving there, I was presented with a terrible scene! Him and a beautiful blonde, dressed luxuriously woman, are dead, together, lying on the floor, in which two cups still spill the remnants of a lethal poison. I could also see that the scene is still ignored by the other residents of the castle.

Luminous entities have warned me of the need to act quickly to avoid greater tragedies! Listen to what we will do:

Madelaine, pretend to have a sudden illness and untie yourself. Put on something more practical and wait. There is an urgent need for us all to get out of here!

I will speak to his parents and Dr. Sergei who must confirm his condition through a supposed diagnosis. Together we need to quickly put together a strategy.

– Sir. Jaime, I am stunned! How to understand all this? What reference points do we have to act without danger? What about what inevitably happen to me in this tragic situation? God help us! – Madelaine despairs.

– Calm down, Madelaine, so you can help in a positive way.

We are all confused and unsure. Save the questions for a more appropriate time, please! – Sir. Jaime pleads, taking her frozen hands.

Feeling her head spinning, she seeks the bed and lies down. She curls up, like a fetus in her mother's womb, and cries. She is in an extreme situation.

Eugene calls the maids and asks them to assist her in changing outfits.

Sir Jaime, without arousing suspicion, requests an interview with the Counts and explains to them:

– Forgive me for what I am about to tell you, but the prince is not coming!

– How did you know? – asks the Count, surprised.

– A few moments ago, I was talking to Madelaine and I was seized by strange sensations that always precede psychic phenomena, to which I am duly accustomed, as are Natacha and Eugene. In this way, I learned everything. Time is short, and we must get out of here. The prince and his cousin are dead. The fact is still ignored in the castle. Please believe and be wise and save yourself and your family!

Running his hands through his thick brown hair, the Count shows surprise and insecurity. If the prince arrives and doesn't find them, he will surely pursue them ferociously, judging them to be traitors.

Deeply distressed, in tears, Bettine identifies in that situation the answer from heaven. Confident, she asks her husband:

– Dear, let us listen to the voice of God! I feel we must listen to Sir. Jaime, please!

– Let's be quick, Count! – the good friend insists – We have in the salons several compatriots of the prince and his cousin! When the news explodes, tempers will be inflamed!

– Honey, the first suspects will be us! Our aversion to this marriage is widely known!

– You are right! I will follow this advice, although I have no major points of reference! But, despite and above all, may faith in God guide our steps! Time is short! We will quickly put together a silent and effective escape plan! I will remain in the castle, standing by!

– My dear friend, you will die if he does!

– It doesn't matter! If its God wills, let his will be done!

It seems to me that I have been living in expectation of this terrible moment! And I will not run away from it!

Bettine readily recalls the offering of both, for the happiness of their daughter.

– I will stay with you!

– No, Bettine, you mustn't!

– Give up, Luiz, your fate is my fate!

Embracing her, moved, he falls silent. His heart beats wildly. On him will depend, probably, many things decisive for everyone.

Once the strategy is set up, with care and discretion, those who will be involved are warned and moved around, each within his or her qualifications.

In a few moments, they are in two carriages: Madelaine asleep (Dr. Sergei has administered a narcotic to her), Ignácia, Sir.

Jaime, Eugene and Father Estanislau; the frightened children, Salústio, Dr. Sergei and two trusted servants.

Bettine kissed, at length, her beloved daughter, stroking her hair. The Count, kissing her, sweetly, whispered:

– Goodbye, beloved daughter of my soul! God will allow us a future reunion! I love you, God keep you safe and make you happy! – driving away, they will also reassure the children, promising to follow them in the other vehicle.

They lovingly kiss their children and, tears streaming down their faces, explain to them that Madelaine has fallen ill and needs to be taken to the hospital. Faced with Soraya and Fabian's question as to whether they should all go; they justify it by saying that Madelaine will be happy to see them all there when she wakes up.

Distressed, Bettine narrows them against her heart, only to let them go. Perhaps she will never see them again...

Before leaving, Sir. Jaime hugs the Count tightly and tells him, with tears rolling down his noble face:

– May God keep you safe and bless you! You can count on my eternal affection and my perennial admiration!

Returning the embrace, Count Luiz finds himself unable to express himself. He is stunned, as he has never felt before.

And in a desperate and silent action, the two carriages drove off, quickly disappearing down the road.

Caterine, Louíse and Lucien had returned home much earlier.

Caterine had felt ill, and her children had accompanied her back home. For her, emotions are still dangerous. They ignore the latest events.

*　*　*

IN ALEKSEI'S CASTLE, his delay begins to worry many who have arrived for the wedding. They are mostly relatives and friends, diners, and fellow politicians in the ruling power.

Unnerved, those present begin to form small, discreet groups to search. They inspect the various departments of the castle, while a closer and more eager uncle comments:

– I am very unhappy about this link, this alliance with the Alvarados! We are extremely different in the ideals of life, in religion and in customs! They live in defiance of the powers and the traditions! They ignore the king's orders, making their own lives an accumulation of nonsense!

They welcome under their castle roof the outcasts of the world, for the purpose of helping them grow socially! As if birth alone did not determine our place in society! Ingenuous, they put a price on their own heads. If it were up to me, they would have already been punished, to serve as an example!

My dear nephew, Prince Aleksei turns a deaf ear to reason. His love for that girl blinds him! And, by the way, he has good taste! She is a beautiful girl! It would make any man's head spin!

In these moments that precede this undesirable liaison, I wish that surprising events would change the course of events, freeing you from joining this family! But if this is so, without my being able to prevent the consummation of Aleksei's madness, I will be at the ready against the Alvarado, and at the first occasion I will fall upon them without mercy! They don't waste for waiting!

His peers applaud his concepts and are already enraged, stroking the weapons they carry with sinister eyes.

– Let them dare to challenge us! Perhaps the task of disciplining them is ours! What do you say?

– We are in complete agreement! Count with us! – they shout.

Thoroughly checked all the spaces in the castle, someone remembers Willfrida's rooms. The group increases with each step. They walk hurriedly and noisily.

When they reach the rooms, they retreat stupefied. Approaching, they try to lift them both, but their bodies are already stiff, dead.

The castle is in an uproar. Everyone speaks at once and no one understands each other. Servants scream and run without direction. They don't know what's coming.

The uncle who undertook and headed the search, after partly recovering from the shock and sadness that invades him, asks in a loud voice:

– Who can be blamed for this double crime?

–The Alvarado! – those around him answer in unison.

– Yes! Only them! And, what is our duty?

– Avenge our beloved prince and his beautiful cousin!

– So, let's go, before that scum gets away! We must do justice!

– To them! To them! – they all exclaim.

They then mount fast horses and get lost in the dust on the road leading to the Castle of the Meccans...

SOON AFTER THE CARRIAGES LEFT that took most of the family and friends away, the counts informed the guests that Madelaine had been hospitalized. With humble apologies, they postponed the espousals to a later date to be arranged in advance.

Very upset, putting themselves at the family's disposal and seeing their favors declined, they left for their homes, understanding that the parents want to go to the hospital to provide the necessary care for their daughter. Some commented that, in fact, Madelaine did not look well. Wishing her health and a speedy recovery, they left, leaving only a few servants and the couple in the castle. The Prince's relatives, who had gone there in advance of the royal retinue, went to his castle in search of their royal relative, whom they imagine to be well informed and therefore absent until that moment.

Careful, Bettine dispatches the servants to certain places on supposed assignments and prepares herself and her husband to expect what seems inevitable to them. As long as they are there, their family will be far enough away to get out of harm's way.

Time drains away in a terrifying way.

Together, they go to the chapel, which is beautifully lit and waiting for a ceremony that will not take place? There, despite the circumstances, the atmosphere is peaceful.

As Knights of the Apocalypse, the prince's relatives and friends gallop creepily to the shouts of "revenge!" in the direction of the castle. A cloud of dust rises and the sounds of the animals' hooves haunt by the deafening clatter, added to the clatter of their weapons.

After a difficult time of, snuggling and loving, sensing that their final moments are coming, Luiz Santiago and Bettine hear a cry, foreshadowing their end. They hug each other, tightly, while hearing imprecations...

The castle is being beaten, inch by inch, under threats:

– Where are the criminals? Death to them! What hole did they hide in? Search everywhere! Don't forget any of them!

The voices are huge, terrifying. They both fixate on the image of Our Lady of Mont'Serrat, imploring strength and protection. They have already entrusted their souls. They probably won't have time to explain themselves, and it is also useless if they manage to do so. They have already been judged and condemned. They will no doubt be executed by those who set themselves up as their judges and executioners.

In a few minutes, Aleksei's rebellious uncle comes across the embracing couple. He shouts, stentorian:

– Here they are! The criminals are hiding in the chapel, as if that would do them any good! We've come to do justice! – he advances toward the count and throws the accusation in his face:

– Lord Count Luiz Santiago de Alvarado, I accuse you of having murdered his Highness Prince Aleksei Nikolai Ivanovich and the Germanic Baroness Willfrida Svirilás!

– What do I hear? – replies the Count. – If we didn't even knew about it!

– So, Count, vile murderer, where are the guests and the bride?!

– We have not yet had time to announce to you that she, exhausted by preparations for the wedding, suddenly fell ill and was hospitalized! We were waiting for his Highness so that we could set another date for the engagement! The dismayed guests left.

The accusation you make is unfair and very serious, for someone who lives according to the laws of men and above all, submissive to the powerful will of God!

– Enough talk, Count! Your oratory skills are widely known! You don't fool us! You will pay with your life for your crime! You killed, we don't know by what criminal hands, since you are close to the rabble, easy to hire to execute his deeds, leaving you with the appearance of being innocent. You must live like this, in this abominable exchange; you give them your bread, and in exchange they do you such favors, don't they?

– A thousand times no, gentlemen! I realize that you are unaware of my true conduct! I would never do anything that would weigh on my conscience! I have a sacred commitment to myself and to God! I demand that you withdraw this unjust accusation!

– Why, he demands it! Behold, how bold he is!

– As an honorable man, I have rights before the world, which I respect and dignify with my work!

– I imagine you are thinking of defending yourself before the law with the resources so well manipulated by you and your peers, aren't you? Know that you won't have time! I am in this instance your judge and the avenger of my dear nephew! My verdict is guilty! My sentence is death! Stand back, all of you! The honor of this execution, I require only for myself!

– I warn you, you all are confused! We have done nothing, and we fear nothing because our conscience is clear!

– What are your last words, Count?

– I reaffirm to you, in the name of God, that I am innocent! I beg you, please, spare my wife! This is a gentleman's business! I will be at your disposal, taking all the risks, but let her go!

Bettine, looking at him reproachfully, clings to him, rejecting his proposal. He knows that this man enjoys the power to torment them and then kill them without the slightest pity. Ignoring his request, the "avenging uncle" cries out in a rage:

– You have destroyed the finest flower of Russian nobility and a bright hope of haughty Germania! We will proudly wash this unforgivable outrage with blood! Die!

Thus saying, he advances, sword in hand, and, in one brutal blow, pierces Count Luiz's chest. Eyes squinting, he falls, looking at his beloved wife, saying goodbye...

Horrified, she rushes over her husband's body, when she feels her blond hair being violently pulled. She stares, perplexed, at the one who savagely assaults her and slips one last glance at the image of the Virgin.

She feels a stabbing pain in his chest, brings his hand to it, and notices the blood gushing out. Her eyesight dims and she falls, overwhelmed.

Around them, the group lingers for a few minutes. Then they leave, leaving their blood-soaked bodies behind.

– Burn everything! Let nothing remain of this abject race! – explodes the assassin, to top it all off, in snarls of diabolical victory:

– Your Highness, Prince Aleksei Nikolai Ivanovich and Baroness Willfrida Svirilás, you are avenged! – and, like a madman, reinforcing the previous order, shouts at the top of his lungs:

Let everything turn to ashes! Come on, set it on fire! I want to see the fire engulfing everything!

Lugano, in the Prince's castle, at the first movement of the finding of Aleksei and Frida's bodies he dodged, hiding. In a few hours, he gathered his meager belongings in a cart and fled.

On the way, he saw rolls of black smoke, denoting a huge fire. He concludes that the Alvarado castle is burning. Rushing the horses, he gets lost in the world, leaving everything behind. He takes with him great resources to radically change his life. Anywhere, completely unknown, he will live well and be respected (count on it...).

The fateful group, after the destruction, among curses and blasphemies, returns to bury, with due honor, their dead.

In the chapel, Bettine and Luiz Santiago awaken, in spirit, and rise. Reverently, they look at their bloody spoils on the ground staining that place of peace and love. Tied together, they make a supplication to the heavens; in one thought and in one heart:

"Father of infinite mercy, protect and sustain those who remain and who cannot yet understand your holy laws! They will think us unhappy because we were murdered! However, Lord, within their lovely souls, may they hear our voices saying to them: Beloved! Sustain yourselves in faith and submission to the Father! Here today, we fulfill our destinies, repaying old debts, paying off old debts, conscious and grateful for the opportunity that has been great, enlightening us forever! Aware of what we should do, we follow the path we have been following since we took shelter in these blessed bodies that allowed us to live with everyone as a constant learning process in the exercise of good! We are all brothers because we are children of the same Father! We say goodbye now, to meet again later, happy and rewarded! Stay with God, beloved! We wish you peace!"

At the Parish House, Father Estanislau stayed, while the others went on their way to Estancia Santa Sofia.

Salústio accompanied them most of the way, until he felt them safe. Then, contrary to all expectations, he provides a fast horse, rides it, and gallops off in the direction of the Alvarado castle. He will desperately try to help Madelaine's parents.

At breakneck speed, his body shakes, strong and virile. Untiring, he shortens distances along paths he knows very well.

Both he and his mount are sweaty and tired from the effort, but neither slows down the pace of the race for a single moment. As he goes through wooded areas, the branches hurt his face, and Salústio doesn't even notice. In his heart, he senses the worst.

As he approaches, he notices a black, compact smoke rising towards infinity... He stops, violently. He has understood everything!

From his lovable chest, he emits a groan that sounds more like the roar of a wounded animal...

He speeds his mount up again, and when he arrives, he finds the flames devouring everything. As if intoxicated with pain and despair, he attacks them in a desperate search...

Impossible to continue, it would be suicide... He is already scorched. He feels the pain of the burns. A terrible certainty settles in his mind: Count Louis and Countess Bettine must be dead by now! ... The fire must be the criminal coup de grâce of those who tried and succeeded in destroying everything!

He returns outside, stepping away, unsteadily; he falls to the ground, deeply disappointed. Twice the fire robs him of his loved ones! ... He moans and cries inconsolably, while babbling, in despair:

– Forgive me, Madelaine! I failed! Dear sister, I couldn't save your parents! What will become of you?! I feel like the last of the mortals!

Exhausted by his emotions, he rises slowly, looks around and searches for his horse. A short distance away he waits, showing extreme fatigue.

He rides again and, very slowly, as if sleepwalking, he returns, devastated. Clothes in tatters, bent over the animal's neck, he feels dizzy and sick...

In this state, he arrives at the church to throw himself into the priest's arms, sobbing convulsively. The good priest understands everything... Nobody asked him nothing, there is no need. Consoling him, he prays to heaven for those dear friends who have returned to God...

Finally, under control, Salústio asks, while wiping away tears:

– Forgive me, Father! I feel like dying! During life, I lose those whom I love!

– So, it is for all of us, Salústio! Especially in these days! Let us love the ones remaining to us!

– I will do that, Father; however, I feel my blood boiling in my veins, confirming more and more the need to put an end to these misdeeds! How do we allow monstrous things like this to keep happening? Are we blind who refuse to see? ... God, enlighten our minds and strengthen our arms; to change this unfortunate context! In any way! With the sacrifice of our lives, if need be!

– Salústio, my son! Pain makes you blaspheme! Measure your words! And take care, we don't want to lose you too!

– My life doesn't count, Father! What matters is our homeland!

Salústio's eyes sparkle and he hears nothing more. Asking the priest's permission, he goes to try to pull himself together. Through the corridors, he continues in the same diapason, talking to himself:

– Idolized France! To your freedom! – raising a closed fist, shouts, strongly, through the corridors: Long live France!

Father Estanislau hears his exclamation and suffers. He fears for him, for his safety and for his admirable and useful life... He sits in one of the pews of the church and releases the floodgates of his soul crying freely...

※ ※ ※

IGNÁCIA, LOOKING AFTER SORAYA AND FABIAN, is bitter and insecure. She doesn't know what to say to the children when they ask you when they will go home. She understands that, like her, everyone who has arrived there is still unaware of the events unfolding in the Alvarado castle.

At this point, he comments to Dr. Sergei:

–Doctor, I feel remorse for not having stayed with my dear Counts! However, I obeyed their orders to stay along the boys, hoping that soon after they would come to meet us... The heart tells me that this will not be possible...

–Dear Ignácia, we think as you do, but we must remain strong so that the children do not notice anything.

–Soraya has already asked me very objective questions, doctor, and often cries, hugging Fabian who, in turn, is no longer interested in playing, despite the news and the extreme patience and care of Natacha, who tries admirably to distract them!

–Let's wait, my good Ignatia! There's nothing we can do, for now!

Several times, Soraya and Fabian went to Madelaine and lovingly stood by her side waiting for her to finally awaken to help them in their afflictions. They cuddled her and made some noise in the hope that they could wake her up. Finally exhausted, at nightfall, they fell asleep lulled by the incomparable care of Ignácia.

The singing of birds woke Madelaine. The sun illuminates everything through the curtains. She looks around curiously, not understanding where she is.

She tries to get up and can't. She is dizzy.

Suddenly he remembers the day before. Her heart beats anguished. She feels the urge to cry. What happened after she took the tranquilizer?

The door opens softly and Eugene enters. Anxiously, she inquires:

–Eugene, for God's sake enlighten me: what happened and where am I?

–We are in Reims, at the Estancia Santa Sofia, about which we told you in due time, remember?

—Yes! Yet I know it is far from my home! What am I doing here and where are my family?

– Your siblings are here with us.

– What about my parents?

– We haven't heard from them yet, Madelaine...

– Did they by any chance stay there?

– Yes! We came straight here and they didn't want to come!

– And why was I brought here?

– To protect you!

Madelaine squeezes her head with both hands and explodes:

– By what right? I must go back there! – In an attempt to get up again, she collapses again, she collapses on her bed and wants to know:

– What's wrong? Why am I dizzy?

– Because you have been given sedatives and are still under their effects.

Sir. Jaime and Dr. Sergei arrive. She asks them in distress:

– Why have you brought me here against my will? Are you ignoring my freedom of choice?

– Madelaine, calm down, you are still weak and under the effect of the medication. There's no point in struggling. If we acted this way, it was in compliance with your father's will, who, knowing your intrepidity and fearing for your life, used this resource to neutralize you, explains Dr. Sergei.

– And what happened next? How are they? For God's sake, enlighten me!

– Calm down, daughter, please - asks Sir. Jaime. – We know as much as you do! We are still waiting for the news that our dear Salústio will bring.

Madelaine cries. She closes her eyes, showing that she doesn't want to talk anymore. Tears stream down her pale face.

Respecting his wishes, everyone leaves, silent.

Natacha arrives and asks the doctor's permission to stay with Madelaine. With his consent, she disposes herself to sit by the bedside without being noticed, when, opening her eyes, Madelaine comes across her and asks:

– Are you Natacha?

– Yes, Madelaine. I am at your disposal for whatever you need!

– How are you, Natacha?

– Well, within the realm of possibility. We are all afflicted for you.

Trusting in the father, we have prayed a lot, Madelaine!

– I thank you and apologize for the inconveniences!

– Rest assured; despite the circumstances, it is our pleasure to host you!

– Do you know where my brothers are right now?

– Yes, I will get them for you. Ignatia takes care of them and your morning toilettes. I'll be right back!

– Natacha, thank you so much for everything...

– You're welcome, Madelaine!

Eugene enters slowly and asks:

– Are you feeling a little better, Madelaine?

– I strive, Eugene, to be worthy of the divine help, which I have never needed it more than now! – She starts to cry again.

Sympathetic, Eugene approaches her and, stroking her hair, exclaims, affectionately:

– Whatever happens, we will stand by you. God will give you strength! I know I don't need to tell you things like this!

– I really need them right now, thank you...

Meanwhile, Sir. Jaime tries to clear his thoughts and anxiety a bit by to Dr. Sergei:

– Dear Doctor, while we await the unfolding of events, wishing from the bottom of our hearts that everything turns out well despite our just fears, I would like to talk to you about the various therapies that I am currently studying and practicing in depth. They complement the formal medical care, benefiting, above all, the soul. For me, your opinion is very important to me, as a doctor that I admire and as a friend.

– I am unaware of such therapies! I have heard of some of them, but I have never been aware of them and I doubt their efficacy!

– I, in my turn, have had countless occasions to prove their great effects, and I can tell you my great satisfaction in seeing to see them result in health, well-being and harmony!

– I translate these effects as mental conditioning because they come from suggestion, of which the human being is so susceptible!

– As a disciple of Hippocrates, you only believe in what you can see and touch, am I right?

– Partly because, when making a diagnosis, I cannot always actually see or feel what would be of vital importance to me! Often, I can only assume and prescribe, according to the symptoms of this or that disease.

– Indeed, Doctor! Not everything can be seen and touched. Often, as you say, you have to make do with suppositions! Especially in today's branch of medicine, still very far from what it should be.

However, the seriously ill cannot wait. We must, then, help him with adequate therapies; these, in the future, will be accepted through scientific proof!

Treatments that in the past were considered absurd, and today are accepted by medical science, are no exception. Little by little, it is proving and approving differentiated and increasingly evolved treatments. The barriers are being broken down by those who dare to go beyond, based on true love and enlightened reason, to give humanity new resources for healing and balm in pain, especially in incurable diseases.

- I fully agree with your competent defense, my friend, but I am still left unable to judge what I don't know due to lack of appreciation and conclusion, as one would expect!

-So, let me proceed with what you called "competent defense". We can also recall the treatments that the medical profession inherited from ancient civilizations:

Infusions, bloodletting, the application of suction cups, therapeutic baths, poultices, hot or cold compresses, change of climate in favorable seasons, the terrible trepanations, and a countless number of measures carried out to improve and often cure the patient. Many of these practices cannot be proven scientifically with the resources that the various appropriate instruments offer, and not even by the brilliant brains of those who labor selflessly in the area of medical research.

However, they are practiced and have become established, day in and day out, because of the effects they offer, major or minor; no matter when, amid these attempts, some deeply painful, the patient perishes.

We are absolutely not disparaging these practices, all of which are based on laudable intentions that, in turn, result in admirable experiences. I myself am grateful for the treatments to which I was recently submitted and which allowed me to survive, rescuing me from a limiting situation: physically and spiritually!

- Did you say physical and spiritual? Can you explain that?

- Yes, I can! Please follow my logic:

If man is not made only of matter; if his psyche, that is, his intelligence that includes spaces still unknown to us in its variations and potentialities, makes him profoundly different and at the same time so similar to everyone else, weighs so deeply in his life, how and why treat him only in his physical, forgetting the real 'driver' of everything, which is without a doubt his eternal soul?!

– It starts from a premise that I am not familiar with and that has never interested me!

– And how can you, my dear doctor, being worthy and good as you are, ignore the things of the soul?

– I live according to my conscience; doing my duty and listening to what my heart asks of me. That's all.

– When you say "my conscience and my heart," you speak in a subjective and not materialistic, as you pretend.

– I agree. However, I don't need established creeds to be "good and worthy" as you said; I thank you for the compliments.

– They are honest, dear friend!

Continuing: I agree, completely!

When we help a sick person, we do it in the name of the Supreme Intelligence that leads us; whatever name you have, dear doctor: God? Allah? Who cares? In our imperfection that limits us too much, we are unable to define this great creative and sustaining force of all that exists! However, we can boost it for our own benefit and that of others who are our closest people!

– You have a way of speaking that reaches us in a rational and practical way, Sir. Jaime. Where did you acquire such convincing knowledge? I can listen to you with respect, admiration, and pleasure! Usually, I get tired and bored with these matters; but you, good Father Estanislau, dear friend Salústio and our dear Madelaine touch this already weary and unbelieving heart of mine sensitively... Tell me, where did you learn such profound things?

– In life itself and in current and ancient literature. To this knowledge acquired through much effort we add the practices of good. We help many unfortunate people who ask us for our disinterested help in serious and solemn moments of their existences! Mostly, dear doctor, people disillusioned with any and all official treatment, or, unable to access it for various circumstances; possible to imagine.

- Despite all that you tell me and your competent dissertations, I become more and more disillusioned with respect to faith, when I see our beloved Madelaine, good to the very top of her luminous soul, suffer what she suffers, dear friend! How can we understand?... Not forgetting our dear Counts, who by now have probably been sacrificed in the name of the wickedness that seems to rule this world! Meanwhile, the wicked and profligate nobility enjoys every possible and imaginable benefit! Where, the proclaimed divine providence is? -the lovable doctor is saddened. His eyes become clouded with tears.

Controlling himself according to the same feelings, Sir. Jaime continues the conversation:

- Well done, Dr. Sergei! I will answer you, in principle, with another question: What do you think about the physical anomalies that surprise you every day in the exercise of your profession?

- It's easy to answer that: I find plausible explanations in the malformation of the fetus, in heredity, in the problems of a complicated pregnancy, in the consequences of an extremely difficult birth; finally, in the circumstances that present themselves, inducing me to diagnoses for each particular case.

-And in these issues don't you question divine providence? I know I am asking you a question without the necessary reference points to expect a satisfactory answer. So, I explain myself, stating that I don't believe in it as being biased and arbitrary in the distribution of the different luck.

- It is implied that the dear friend is talking about justice, isn't it?

- Yes, of a perfect justice, because God is perfect!

- And how does this justice take place? I conclude from your remarks that you strongly believe in it!

- Indeed, I do! With the truth of my soul! It happens through palingenesis!

-Do you mean the philosophy of chained rebirths?

- Yes! After studying it, how can anyone doubt that these anomalies actually have a higher purpose, within the laws of cause and effect?

-Can you quote examples, illustrating your assertion?

- Yes, I can! In the innumerable examples that the Earth offers us, when we see perfect children and imperfect children, physically or mentally, for no apparent reason. The misfortunes that strike many people, as if by fatality; the determination, from birth, of wealth and misery; fortune and misfortune; beauty and ugliness; common sense and foolishness; diseases, for the time being incurable, causing those who suffer from them to perish, often, among cruel sufferings; the different social contexts that crucify us, each new day, without our having competent defenses! In other words, everything that cannot be explained through the usual ways, and that defy faith and understanding, are laws, dear doctor, installed in the being who owes and pays his debts, in the realization of "To each one according to his works...", as Jesus Christ taught us!

In the courageous testimonials of people who were born carrying within them the memories of other experiences lived in other countries, other races... Many declare where, how and with whom they lived then, and not infrequently give their addresses, names and details that are verified.

Others express themselves in languages other than their own, often, as in the "Pentecost" phenomenon narrated by the Holy Bible, without ever having learned such languages.

Many people behave correctly or mistakenly, indicating to us different maturations in relation to moral life.

And going further, dear friend: what "original sin" does the Roman Church talks about, which claims to lead Christians all over the world?

If our soul is created according to your philosophy at the time of birth, how can we have sins to purge? When they tell us about original sin, it makes us understand that we already carry old faults!

Within Eastern cultures, reincarnation is an assumed fact, without any further questioning. There they live according to it, some, forgetting the needs of the body as the precious garment of this "pilgrim of all times," gives up material progress as far as the things of the world are concerned. We are not of the world, but we are in it! We need balance, not fanaticism.

– Sir. Jaime, I confess that your lessons stun me, in a way, but at the same time, they make me very curious. As a doctor, I keep up to date with science on a daily basis. I have little time left for other things, especially for philosophies that never interested me. As for religious creeds, I have never been fascinated by their arbitrariness and, because of their pressing need to impose one over the other in a dispute, sometimes shameful, sometimes criminal...!

I believe that God, if He exists, has become a name that is exploited by humanity, which despite invoking Him, does nothing to deserve the mercy it begs of him!

I have come to the conclusion that such a force, unique and powerful, whatever it is called, should be better and greater than the image formed by the very men who claim to follow it!

In these conjectures, I decided a long time ago to do my part, in this immense context of suffering, in order to calm my conscience; dedicating love to my fellow man, without expecting anything. Those who know me already know my disbelief.

The fraternal and philanthropic group at the Parish House has tried very hard to make me finally capitulate to their religious theories. However, Sir. Jaime, if I confess that I am already somewhat shaken, it is not because of the usual polemics, but because of the innumerable examples that these same friends give me of constant abnegation. Maybe, their "God" will end up being mine too, by force of good coexistence!

Now I hear lucid and verifiable arguments from you, leading me to think more about it! I assume that when someone like me refuses to believe, it is because he has not received convincing explanations like these from anyone! After all, we are the intelligent part of this planet!

–Bravo, Dr. Sergei! Thank God for having met you and for sharing your friendship! We will have other chances for conversations like these! Now, excuse me, I must go to the reception! Then, I'm going to see Madelaine! She worries me. It seems to me that she is at the limit of her strength!

–One more thing, Sir. Jaime, what about our friend? Relying to the laws of cause and effect, just like her family?

–So it is, doctor. Not just them, but all of us! Although, regarding our dearest Madelaine, I guess she's passing bright passage among us, like a star shining in the suffering night of this debt-ridden planet! But I must also add for the sake of clarity of all that I have told you, "Sowing is free, but the harvest is obligatory!"

–What's done here, you pay for it here?

–More or less! On other occasions we will talk more, if it interests you! See you!

– Certainly! Now, I'm going to Madelaine to give her another dose of medicine. I want her to continue to rest for a few more days! days! Goodbye, Sir. Jaime!

– Goodbye, Doctor!

In the meantime, Soraya and Fabian have finally been able to speak to Madelaine and ask her for an explanation of what they are experiencing:

– Madelaine, Soraya asks, "if you are better now, shall we go home?

– Later, my dear, we still have some matters to resolve. How are you?

Fabian climbs into bed, kisses Madelaine, squeezing her neck tightly, and cries softly.

–Why are you crying, my love?

– I don't know, Madelaine. I'm sad and I miss mom and dad! I want to see them!

– We all do, Fabian, but we need to wait a little longer, yes?

–No, I don't want to wait any longer, Madelaine! Let's go home, now!

– Have I ever, my darling, denied you that which I could do for you?

– No!

– So, trust in me, will you? - She starts to cry.

Soraya hugs her, certain that Madelaine cannot attend to them, for some major reason.

–Madelaine, we will wait! I'll convince Fabian, you bet! Are you feeling better already?

– Better, Soraya, but still not very well.

– Daughter, how are you? - asks Ignácia from behind the children, as she leans over to kiss her forehead.

–Slowly getting better Ignatia, although...

– What were you going to say, child? She asks in a rush.

–Later Ignácia. Take good care of our dear ones, mom is counting on it!

–I know, Madelaine. Don't worry about them.

– Pray, Ignácia, with all the faith of your good heart! For all of us!

Ignácia understands Madelaine's message and shakes her hands in loving understanding.

–All right! Everybody out! I want to examine my sick one! Let only Natacha stay! Please!

Following the doctor's orders, everyone leaves, except for Natacha who arrived with him.

RUPERT AND NIKOLAI, nearby, watch the happenings at the resort from afar. They accompanied, unseen, the two burials, and watched Sir. Jaime and Natacha's steps. They saw their cousins and baby Kostia arrive.

* * *

THE NEXT DAY, WHILE DOING his duties, Sir Jaime hears voices at the reception and comes across Salústio. Hugging him, he hears that he needs to talk to him and Dr. Sergei. Attended, extremely weak, showing wounds on his arms and hands, remarkable pallor, he declares with difficulty:

– Dear friends, I bring terrible news! Prepare yourselves to hear it, and may God help us to overcome so many misfortunes! – Salústio takes a deep breath and continues, controlling himself with remarkable effort – Our dear Counts are no longer part of this world; they have given their luminous souls to God! The castle was destroyed by a terrible fire... They either perished in the flames, or were killed before the blaze... I tried to save them, but failed.

I even burned myself, as you can see. Deeply saddened, I returned to the church to tell Father Estanislau, venting their my despair at the irreparable loss of our beloved friends. The next day, not yet recovered from the first blow, we learned that the Marquess Charles D'Alençon, former fiancé of our beloved Madelaine and dear friend of us all, had been found dead in one of the streets of Paris, with a dagger in his back! So, Madelaine has not only lost her parents and the castle, of which only blackened walls now remain as shadows, but also the only man she ever loved in her life...!

Silent under the impact of the painful revelations, they hear a muffled scream, followed by a deafening thud. They get up and find Madelaine lying unconscious outside by the half-open door. She had heard Salústio's voice and, getting up, went out to look for him, listening, appalled, to his statements. She is rescued and returned to bed. Under the care of Dr. Sergei, she comes to her senses. When he comes across Salústio, she asks in tears:

–Salústio, by God, is what I heard true?

–Yes, Madelaine, unfortunately! It took a lot of courage to bring you this news! Forgive me, for being the herald of your unhappiness, dear friend!

She doesn't answer, covers her face with her hands and bursts into convulsive weeping.

Ignácia, who has come to see Salústio, asks nothing, understands everything.

She hugs Madelaine and cries too.

The children, who have followed behind Ignatia, realize that something very bad is happening and begin to cry. Soraya rightly concludes that her parents are dead. Disconsolate, she sits down and lets her tears flow freely. Natacha hugs her, silent.

Fabian climbs into Madelaine's bedside and bursts into uncontrollable despair:

– Madelaine! What happened? Why are you crying? Where are mom and dad? Answer!

– My dear, mom and dad have gone with God!

– You mean they died, Madelaine?! No! I don't believe it! I won't let God take them! I won't! – He whimpers violently, causing Salústio to carry him and lead him outside in an attempt to calm him down.

Dr. Sergei prepares tranquilizers for everyone and distributes them efficiently. Natacha and Eugene diligently assist.

Everyone stands in solidarity with the family, supporting them in every way possible and imaginable...

✱ ✱ ✱

FATHER ESTANISLAU INFORMS Henry where Madelaine and their family are.

He tells him that the counts had been murdered and incinerated in the castle itself and that the Marquis Charles D'Alençon had been found dead. "I wonder how Madelaine is?...! And the children?..." – he thinks, deeply saddened.

Henry senses in these linked events a fatal and painful predestination... The Prince died, but he still prevented Madelaine from being happy! She never hid her veneration for her fiancé. She will never love another, she confessed, several times.

Address in hand, he leaves for Estancia Santa Sofia.

When he arrives, he runs into Sir. Jaime and Eugene.

Disconcerted, he concludes that the occasion is ripe to reconcile with both of them. Affable, he approaches them:

–Sir. Jaime, how are you?

–Very well, thank you. And you? – He answers, pleasantly surprised by the hand Henry extends to him.

–I'm recovering. And you, Eugene, how are you doing?

Pale, she shyly and confusedly answered:

–I am fine. Except for the sadness that overwhelms our friend Madelaine...

–That's why I'm here. Poor Madelaine, what a fatality!

–You are right.

As they talk, Eugene analyzes Henry's features and discovers something different, for the better. She feels happy at this.

Learning that Madelaine is sleeping under the influence of sedatives, he asks Eugene to accompany him on a tour of the surroundings.

Side by side, they talk and exchange apologies. Eugene discovers that all he wants most is to be by her side, like right now.

He, gazing at her from top to bottom, declares:

–Eugene, you have matured into a fine young lady! And now, I am being sincere!

–Because the other times it was falsehood, wasn't it, Henry?

–Forgive me, at that time I won your friendship out of interest. If you could forget these unpleasant facts, I would be very grateful!

–Forgotten are you! That's it! And have you forgiven me for making an attempt on your life?

–Well… That is not very easy, you must agree!

Deeply disconcerted, she comments:

–How would I feel if someone tried to kill me? You have the right to deny me your forgiveness! Although you were the one most guilty of my crazy gesture!

–I'm just kidding you, Eugene! I have today a new proposal of life! It is I who must make myself forgive! In this regard I have plans that will reconcile us. Wait for it!

–I look forward to it!

Returning, Henry decides to speak to Sir. Jaime. He will not delay any longer.

–Sir. Jaime, please, I wish to speak to you!

–No, you don't. I am at your service! Speak up!

—Dear Sir. Jaime, the social skills that I exercise so well, at this moment, are of no use to me! I feel intimidated by what I intend to say to you!

— I never knew you were shy, Henry!

— And, in fact, I never was. However, with the changes that I impress on my character today, trying to change myself for the better, treading falteringly on new and somewhat unknown ground...

—What do you really want, my dear man, with this lecture? Stay calm! Speak without fear!

—I intend not only to ask your forgiveness, but also to tell you that I will retract my statement in front of you and Eugene. I don't know how yet, but I will figure out the best way to do it!

—I forgave you long ago, Henry. As for the coins, they only escape us when they don't really belong to us! If they were ours, really, Henry, even your privileged intelligence couldn't take us! Everything is in its place. I have already rebalanced myself through my work and thank God I have adjusted to the new reality!

—Nevertheless, I want to refund you! Only then will I be at peace with my conscience!

—Your transformation is remarkable, Henry, and was predicted by the late sister Rosalia!

—And how was that? She, more than anyone else, could penetrate my soul!

—She warned us that you would surprise us, and that is what is happening right now!

—Interesting! I owe this inner reformation of mine to Madelaine. She, with her sincere friendship, her respect for my person, in a dignified and honest posture, tolerated me without ever condemning me, even though she recognized my spiritual miseries.

With her example and your loving advice, she were able to reach this heart that has lived so long hardened and ignorant of the true laws that govern us above all!

- Lovely, suffering friend of us all! - laments Sir. Jaime.

- Yes, poor Madelaine... But, continuing with my attempt to explain myself, I owe the fraternal and charitable group of the Parish House enormous gratitude as well. In the good coexistence, I mirrored their good souls and their incomparable examples; gradually becoming ashamed of the performance I had created to approach and conquer Madelaine... They, together with the Lord, are "my Damascus Road" as our dear Father Estanislau preached last Sunday.

–Henry, why do you say this? I could do nothing for you, despite my good intentions!

–You are wrong, dear benefactor! By taking me off the streets, courageously and confidently, to offer me a better life and prepare me for the future, you have sown in my heart the good seeds that are sure to sprout and bear mighty fruit now!

Moved to tears, the two hug each other.

Eugene, who watches them anxiously from afar, rejoices happily. This reconciliation meets their new expectations...

When Henry is gone and Madelaine awakens, Eugene communicates:

- I have some news for you: Henry came here and couldn't see you because you were asleep. Best wishes for her health and peace!

He will return soon to see you.

- Did you talk, Eugene?

- Yes, and we did it like old friends. With my father things were stronger because they embraced each other fraternally. I watched from afar and conclude that they understood each other.

–Am I mistaken, or is there a new gleam in her eye?

–How perceptive you are, Madelaine! Indeed, I am taked by new yearnings, or not so new, who knows?

–Are you discovering yourself, Eugene? I dare say that between you there has always been something greater; something that only now, through maturation, you are both beginning to understand.

–Goodness! You have summed it up so well! At least for my part I have found that no man has ever interested me because of his existence! After all, he crossed my path without even asking my permission!

–Which despite everything, you would never deny him, right?

–Right!

–And on Henry's part?

–I notice his interest. His seductive eyes look at me differently now. I feel that we have a chance!

Be happy, Eugene! Don't let the opportunity go by...

Taking a short, introspective hiatus, Madelaine declares, moved:

Yesterday I dreamed about my parents, Eugene. They were hugging and happy! They wrapped me, loving, asking me for calm and faith. They were beautiful! They were like a unique being! Mom used to say:

"We are grateful to God! We have come to the end of this journey by doing his good will! We love you and we will always be protecting you! Be happy and endure adversity with courage and spiritual strength! There is still much to do, Madelaine! Take care of your brothers and sisters and continue in the blessed task of helping the unfortunate, who are the beloved of Jesus Christ, our Lord!"

Then my father hugged me tightly and told me with a radiant smile:

"I love you, stay in peace! From where we are we will protect everyone and each one in particular! Thank you, beloved spirit of my soul, who has allowed me to live by your side valuable experiences in a highly beneficial exchange! The love that surrounds our family group is eternal! We will be recognized by how much we love each other! Our united souls will overcome the differences in planes! God protect you, daughter. Be strong!" Then we embraced and were also a single being! In ecstatic with happiness, but with my heart overwhelmed with goodbyes, I woke up in tears and soon fell asleep again...

Weeping, Madelaine thanks her friend for her affectionate embrace and gets it off her chest:

–I feel physically exhausted, Eugene; I'm not well...

–And I let you talk so much! Oh, if my father could see! I'm sure he would scold me. Sorry!

–Don't worry, it was nice talking to you. – She closes her eyes and internalizes herself again. Two thick tears roll down her beautiful face, falling onto the pillows. A few minutes later, she is asleep. Eugene comes downstairs and runs into Natacha. She wants to tell Madelaine that her brothers will come to see her in a few minutes.

※ ※ ※

LATELY, HENRY REMEMBERS his mother insistently. He would like to know her fate, if she is alive... Finally, he wants to hold her close in his arms, ask her for forgiveness and his blessing...

When he sees Madelaine again, he intends to tell her about this new yearning. He fully trusts her good sense. She misses her friend as she starts to see her at last. Eugene's image towers over her, dominating, changing the direction of her feelings.

At the inn, a week goes by and Madelaine's health worries Dr. Sergei. She seems unresponsive to the most varied treatments. Slowly, she seems to want to say goodbye to the world. She is visibly losing weight, rarely smiles, spends most of the time with her eyes closed, and only her brothers and sisters are able to pull her out of her apparent immobility. Everyone tries in vain to help her. With a weak smile of gratitude on her lips, she shows her gratitude, yet continues in her sadness.

–Daughter, come back to life! Your brothers need you! – says Sir. Jaime.

–I know, thank you for the efforts you make to help me. I have no intention of contradicting you. However, I lack the strength to react, believe me! I feel like someone who is slowly going away, dear friend, in a strange lethargy...

–I will speak to Dr. Sergei, Madelaine. Be strong and have faith, my dear!

– God will help us, I trust in him!

– But, daughter, do your part, will you?

Silently she starts to cry.

Finding the doctor, Sir. Jaime tells her:

– Dear doctor, Madelaine seems to get worse every day!

– I am seriously considering, Sir. Jaime, taking her to a hospital or even to the wards in the Parish House. His body is increasingly weakened.

–When do you plan to do this, doctor? I have something in mind...

–As soon as possible! In truth, I'm afraid the journey will be too tiring... I know what you're thinking; you think you can help Madelaine with your knowledge, don't you?

–Bravo, doctor! It seems that little by little we speak the same language!

–Could you tell me how you intend to proceed in this case?

–First of all, to request your permission!

–Despite our understanding about it, I have no points of reference, Sir. Jaime, to judge the exercise of these practices! Tell me:

Are they contrary to my prescriptions? Will they cause her any harm or painful impression?

–Not at all! Your remedies will be respected and will continue to accomplish their goals. Therapy is quiet, subtle, and gentle. It is carried out with great respect and discipline. It will act from the inside out, in Madelaine's soul, rescuing her vital forces.

–If so, you can try. However, I want to be there! In the face of any risk or harm to my patient, I will prevent you from continuing. This is my condition.

–I thank you, doctor, for your permission and for your presence, which will do us great honor! I will hasten to make the necessary arrangements in view of the urgency that presents itself! I warn you: all those who attend must follow a certain diet, in which abstinence from alcohol is included, so as not to interfere negatively with the expected results!

–I got your message, rest assured, I will leave my usual vodka aside. I have every interest in seeing her well! – He answers with a certain embarrassment, clearing his throat to disguise it.

–Thank you. Tomorrow, before nightfall, we will meet in Madelaine's house, except for the children and those who are not in tune with our goals. First, I will consult Madelaine. She is free to choose whether she wants to benefit from the spiritualist practices or not. Goodbye, doctor!

Thus saying, he goes to her and explains to her the great possibility of helping her through mediumistic and spiritualized work.

Grateful and hopeful, she accepts.

On the appointed day and time, the children stay with Olga and Kostia, while Ignácia offers to attend the session.

In the room are Sir. Jaime, Mr. Sergei, Natacha, Eugene, Ignácia and two other mediums with whom Sir. Jaime is used to working in the vicinity on behalf of the unfortunate and sick.

Lying comfortably on the bed covered with white sheets, dressed in light clothes (as are all the others), introspective and serene, Madelaine waits, in silence.

Eugene holds the Bible in his hands, open at the New Testament.

In large jars, medicinal herbs flood the room with a harsh, healthy fragrance.

Thick curtains seal out the light from outside, covering the windows. In the environment, a night lamp illuminates faintly.

Minutes before, Sir. Jaime locked the door with recommendations not to be interrupted after the session starts.

On chairs arranged around the bed and some distance away are Eugene, Natacha, Ignácia, Dr. Sergei and the other two mediums.

On a round table covered with a white lace tablecloth, a vase of flowers decorates the room. And on another table, in the corner, a jar filled with drinking water covered with a starched towel.

In the distance, Soraya's violin is heard.

The sounds pleasantly reach Madelaine's ears. She believes that Lucien would like to be there, among them, at this divine banquet... it reminds her of her priestly vocation... She interiorizes herself, deeply... She sees on her mental canvas the image of Nossa Senhora da Mont'Serrat, in the chapel of his beloved castle... She thinks of her beloved parents, of Charles, her great and only love, and cries, in a moving silence...

In a few minutes, her light snoring can be hear; she is deeply asleep.

When it is necessary to speak, they do so quietly, respecting the necessary introspection of each one in particular.

Rising from his chair, Sir. Jaime, in a dignified posture, with an audible, contrite voice, recites Psalm 91. As the last words come to a close, the bells of the nearby church are heard pealing, sorrowfully.

He asks Natacha to make a prayer to the heavens for Madelaine, and she stands up, respectfully and internally, eyes closed exclaims:

−Praise God!

May he keep us obedient to his unchanging and righteous laws so that we may be worthy of his mercy!

Father, have mercy on us, former convicts in this valley of tears of tears! Suffering the injunctions of our misunderstandings, sir, we rehearse the first steps towards true love!

Give us strength to follow the examples of our master Jesus!

May your mercy be upon us who are still dying in this life, and upon those who, having departed, have already given an account of their existences! Give them peace and the balm of oblivion! May they live in our nostalgia and in our prayers!

Our greatest purpose today, Lord, is to pray for our dear Madelaine, your dedicated worker, who in these moments of great pain has momentarily lost her physical strength and the courage to go on living!

Allow, Jesus, that in a fraternal embrace, gathering our greater and better energies, we may help her in Your name! May from our hearts, added to the hearts of our beloved spiritual protectors, lights pour down upon Madelaine's body and soul, invigorating her!

May she be enveloped in Your incomparable and sublime blessings!

Lord, extend these blessings also over Soraya and Fabian; over Sacha, Olga and little Kostia!

Hear our petitions, but above all, may God's will be done, today, now, and forever!

In a harmonious whisper, she fell silent, deeply moved.

Juliette, one of the mediums, describes what she sees:

−Luminous Entities appear among us, carrying in their hands devices unknown to us, and transparent vials in a shining crystal box. Now they posture themselves around those who are here and await our proceedings. One of them, Sir. Jaime, says with an affectionate accent in his voice, "Get started! We will give you the backing you need!"

–Reverently, we thank these presences, in an honest proposal to follow the examples of the master Jesus, for a lovable work of solidarity and love! Let us now read, Eugene, the Gospel, previously chosen!

–Yes, my father! It is the gospel of Mark, chapter 4, verses 1 to 9, and is entitled "The Parable of the Sower".

Taking advantage of the reading, Sir. Jaime, together with those who already have the habit of evangelical explanations, discourse about it with wise and clear words.

–Natacha, Juliette and Eugene, do the work of laying on of hands! – they obey and at some distance raise their arms and spread their hands in Madelaine's direction, concentrated. One on each side and another at the foot of the bed.

Sir. Jaime goes to the bed and, raising his hands, starts, starting from Madelaine's head, without touching her, respecting the distance of a few centimeters, longitudinal movements, as to free her from something that is supposedly glued to her body, releasing even her feet to return to the same movements three times.

After that was done, he take a deep breath, raise his hands again, and impose them more slowly, following the same direction as before and the same procedures, but this time, he loosens his hands in a light manner, also moving his fingers, as if he were "raining" invisible energies on Madelaine's body.

Juliette continues:

–Over our heads a faint silvery-blue rain falls. Those who have come here with the instruments and the vials approach us and light up reflectors of colored lights; these, bathing Madelaine, are absorbed into her body. One of them gently pours on her lips the subtle liquids from a few different bottles, interspersing them...

God, what a wonderful thing! I can see his various organs absorbing the luminous medicines, reflecting the same colors, vivid some and faint others!

Now, as in a microscopic constellation, their organs are moving in different directions, under the impact of the medications and the gestures that these entities give them, in intense directions and speeds!

They smile and advise me:

"Go on narrating what we are doing! In the future, these treatments will be known and practiced wisely in transforming diseased energies into positive, healthy energies, through the cosmic ether that surrounds us and that is one of the forms of our Creator's presence!

Understand what Jesus told us:

"Seek and you shall find; Ask and you shall obtain; Knock and it shall be opened to you!" These words make us aware of the great power of the Creator in his infinite goodness!

However, we will always need fraternal hearts in this selfless and competent donation, based on true love and legitimate faith! And, quoting once again and always, our lovable master Jesus:

"Only love covers the multitude of sins!"

Be in peace and always count on our support in this work! May our purposes always be in harmony!

Our patient deserves us, and she will be fine! In the name of life and in the name of progress, we need this beautiful Spirit very much! May God keep her safe and strengthen her!

Much peace and may the Architect of the Universe bless you all..."

Bowing, reverent, they withdraw slowly and silently.

They turn back and disappear just as they came! – Juliette cries profusely, such is her emotion, infecting everyone.

Moved to the core of his soul, Sir. Jaime says a heartfelt prayer of thanks, while Natacha and Eugene lay their hands on the jar of drinking water.

All closed, he calls the session over, advising them to leave slowly so that Madelaine stays asleep.

Eugene, who has been slowly developing "eyes to see and ears to hear," reports that Madelaine's parents were present at her side and that sister Rosália also appeared, luminous and rejuvenated.

Restless and curious, Dr. Sergei approaches Sir. Jaime:

– May I, Sir. Jaime, ask you for details of everything I have seen and heard?

– Certainly! Speak up, doctor!

–First of all, I must confess to you that I felt very well during this session that was so well programmed and conducted by you.

Now, my questions:

Why the plain clothes?

–Because they reflect the light better and also demonstrate the cleanliness of the garments. As in the beds and doctors' clothes, in hospitals.

–To continue: you asked us for discipline and did not warn the boy who, sleeping all the time was externalizing a rather unpleasant sound from his throat!

Smiling, Sir. Jaime explains:

– The function of our lovely Justino is exactly this: to donate energies, so that the spirits can work more efficiently when they need to "materialize" the medicines and surgical interventions on patients! The good results of the works in question often depend on this donation. In truth, we may say that not all who have this faculty necessarily need to snore, as you have found, but our brother is an extremely charitable and hard-working person who is devoted to the good of others; his work is respected and accepted by us with joy.

—And what about that girl's narratives? Hard to understand!

—Are you in the habit of reading the bible, dear doctor?

—To be honest, no.

—Well, I recommend it to you: in the Old Testament, Samuel I, chapter 28, "Saul consults the medium of En-Dor", and in the New Testament, Mark, chapter 9, verses 2 to 8, "The transfiguration". Read and analyze, also, the healings that Jesus did; which disciples He chose, almost always the same ones, in a need for specific characters that he knew so well.

—How about saying that Jesus was Jesus? He could do miracles!

At least this is what we hear every day!

—Doctor Sergei, the holy scriptures prove, through impressive facts, the countless possibilities for the human creature to overcome barriers, promoting incredible phenomena in this long-suffering journey in need of differentiated resources! If God's laws are perfect, the "miracle" would be the derogation of these laws.

Jesus said: "*I have not come to destroy the Law, but to fulfill it...*", referring to the higher law and not to the law of men. And he also told us: "*You are gods! Everything I do, you can do and much more!*" Despite this, some unsuspecting factions believe that he has invested this or that one, in a specific, privileged and hierarchical way, to represent him! However, experience shows us, at every angle of the path, that this is a choice and a sacred right of every child of God; all that is needed is the courage of inner transformation, based on the incomparable examples of Jesus! No one is granted the authority to "distribute the gifts of heaven" that belong only to God! An elevated, responsible, conscious soul can do a lot; regardless of any permission from this or that organized creed! Do not forget that much evil has been done in the name of the "Lamb of God"! In his name, people have been killed, burned, plundered and persecuted! It is necessary to analyze the different behaviors, independent of labels, dogmas, impositions, "pomp and circumstance"! Good and love meet where truth is lived and the courage to faithfully follow Jesus! *"By the fruit you know the tree..."*

—I admire, more and more, your wise insights! Going further, with my curiosity, I wish to know: what are the herbs, the closed windows, and the drinking water for?

—Let's go slowly: The herbs flood the environment with salutary effluvium, assisting in environmental hygiene; the windows are darkened because the imponderable materials used by the spiritual plane resent the strong light. To preserve them, the material light must be dimmed. And the drinking water has been transmuted into medicine for our Madelaine, who will take it, little by little, throughout the week, until we have another session like todays.

—Is it then a treatment with a deadline?

—More or less; these are periods of opportunity for the patient's body and soul to rebalance. For some people this time is short; but as for Madelaine, three sessions will suffice, for the credits this lovable spirit possesses.

—Now, the most important: what about medical treatment?

—It completes the spiritual and vice versa.

—So they are two therapeutic sides?

—Exactly! One acts on the body, and the other acts on the soul, as I have already told you on another occasion!

—I understand... Allow me to abuse your patience a little more...

—I am very happy, doctor, with this conversation!

—And what about the different movements she was making with her hands, what do they mean?

—In the first instance, I did a "cleaning" in Madelaine's aura. Our world is polluted in all ways. The creature resents the coarse energies, and thus becomes impregnated with a dark, viscous cloud enveloping his physical and spiritual body.

Then, assisted by Eugene, Natacha, and Juliette, I poured the healthy and healing energies that come from God and that are agglutinated in our hands, our hearts, and our thoughts, when turned to true love!

Supporting us powerfully were the entities that were described by Juliette, who can easily, like Natacha and Eugene, see the spirits!

–What does the presence of other people represent and what addition do they bring?

–The increased interest in the patient. Their affections vibrate strengthening the work. For this reason, Jesus asked family members to stay in the sick room and asked everyone else to leave. Love is a powerful lever; healing, uplifting, and enlightening!

–Sir. Jaime, without any intention to belittle anything, I compare everything I saw, to a very beautiful true fairy tale, if I may put it that way! It seems like going back to childhood to prove that the magical powers of those beings were real!

–Dear Doctor! – exclaims Sir. Jaime, laughing heartily - true life, lived in depth and plenitude, is indeed a wonderful fairy tale, where anything can happen, and our wishes can be fulfilled, provided we know the ways and techniques! Happy analogy! I congratulate you!

–And what about the healing of the patient, if it happens, going back to the subject of therapy: what actually cured her? The official treatment or the alternative, subjective one?

–This does not interest us! The task accomplished fills us with Christian joy! The happiness of seeing our patient better fills us with peace! Faith intensifies in our hearts and we submit ourselves, more and more, to Divine Providence!

There are, however, circumstances that lead us to clear conclusions: when the poor wretch has not had access to the other form of treatment!

–Indeed! I'll give you that!

–And what about our dear Madelaine? What is your medical opinion?

–That she will benefit from this love you speak of and from the refined techniques you study and exercise so well! Onward, dear Sir. Jaime. Proceed with the arrangements in this particular regard, and I in turn will continue to medicate her to the best of my knowledge! Right?

–That's right!

– See you then!

– So long, dear doctor!

Once the treatments with the fraternal group and Dr. Sergei were concluded, Madelaine was more serene and strengthened, and she emerged to the new life that awaited her, different from the one she had dreamed of.

While she is fully restored, she enjoys the lush beauty of the place, with his friends and brothers. She goes for walks in the surroundings and also has the chance to exercise his philanthropic habits there. Along with Sir. Jaime, she joins the ranks of the selfless.

Henry now frequents the estancia, adding two pleasures: seeing Madelaine again and exchanging ideas with her on various subjects, while openly winning over Eugene, who has become the main reason for his new life. There he recovers from the tiring world of finances.

At this moment, Madelaine, blushing and smiling, walks side by side with Natacha through the garden alleys.

–Dear Madelaine, what do you intend to do in the future?

–To return to Paris and my life as it was before. Naturally, on a new basis. However, the life of my brothers will follow the same directions as always, in the direction of the plans established by our dearly missed parents! They will from now on be my only concern, apart from the work in the wards of the Parish House, which I miss so much! Even though I have not realized my dream of love with my beloved Charles, my life proposal has not changed at all. Wherever he is, he will continue loving me, I know it. One day we will meet again, happy and grateful to the Father for the wonderful experience we had. Better to have conquered him and lost him than never to have loved him at all, Natacha...

–I agree with you... It makes me wonder... I wasn't born for great love, Madelaine...

–You surprise me, Natacha! And Marcel, this handsome boy who adores you, who is dear to everyone and longs to make you happy?!

–Poor Marcel! I suffer for surprising his hope and disappointment each time he insists on getting married, while I keep postponing the date, indefinitely! Someone else would have had enough!

–Why do you do that?

–I'm not sure, but it seems to me that I won't have time to get married...

–How strange, Natacha! Do you have reason to think so?

–No, and to be honest, I don't even know if I love Marcel. At first, I was dazzled by his visible qualities, by his physical beauty that fascinates any woman of good taste, but little by little I realized that he, and only he, truly loved.

–And what will you do? You must make up your mind!

–Yes, I've decided to speak frankly to him and let him be free! To be happy with someone else!

–It's pitiful! You seem made for each other!

–Everyone says so. My parents loved him, but life is full of surprises...

–And the heart, a mysterious land, Natacha!

After a few weeks, Madelaine is preparing to return.

She will be missed...

She bids farewell to everyone with deep emotion. He will miss each one and everyone too much. She kisses little Kostia and hugs his parents. Her heart goes out to Eugene and Natacha, whom she has learned to love as sisters.

–We will visit each other whenever we can! - exclaims Eugene.

–Certainly! - confirms Madelaine, while strangely moved by the feeling that she will never see Natacha again. The latter, at that moment, tearfully bids her farewell.

Sadly, she goes to the waiting car, where Sir. Jaime is waiting to say goodbye. The children cannot keep themselves away from little Kostia, who screams and wants to follow them. Soraya cries. Fabian kisses the sweet baby many times and goes in the direction of the vehicle.

Sir. James affectionately embraces Madelaine, promising her a visit soon. He wants to see his good friend Father Estanislau again. He sends him hugs and best wishes..

Once again, Madelaine's heart seizes in an anticipatory feeling of loss: she will never see him again... His face and sisterly smile are print in her mind...

For the time being, she and her brothers will stay at the house of Salústio and Louíse, on the outskirts of Paris; a large and comfortable house, where they will reorganize.

Henry looks for a small villa for them not far from Louíse.

Ignácia and Dr. Sergei have long since returned. She is visiting some relatives, then settling in with Madelaine and the children. The doctor resumed his work in the office and wards of the Parish House.

So, supported by her friends, Madelaine starts over.

She did not go to see the ruins of her beloved castle. She wants to keep it alive in her memory as in the good times. She has become more reserved and quieter, without being sad.

She received the lute from Charles' parents, in a magnificent black velvet box. Not infrequently, he hugs the rich instrument and presses it against his heart, in an attempt to feel its presence... And in those moments, she cries a lot...

In his patriotic ardor, Salústio becomes increasingly involved in the libertarian movements, struggling between these and numerous other commitments. No matter how hard he tries, he can't divide yourself well. In his prolonged absences from the Parish House, the priest thinks he is at home, next to Louíse, and otherwise, Louíse imagines him busy in his various assignments, next to the priest or in Dr. Sergei's office... Salústio is falling apart.

Corine, informed of Madelaine's return, goes to visit her:

–*Mademoiselle* Madelaine, how I miss you!

–Corine, what a surprise! How are you?

–Very well married and happy, thank God! My general adores me and covers me with luxury! *Mademoiselle*, have you recovered from the tragedy?

–With God's help, I try not to feed useless suffering. But only time will heal the wounds of the soul...

–I understand, *Mademoiselle*. I came to bring you my new address. We are now living in a bigger and more comfortable house. When you can, come visit us!

–Thank you, Corine. In order not to lose the old habit, I advise you not to get too attached to what is ephemeral.

–If I ever must give it all up, *Mademoiselle*, I will have enjoyed it enough! We are different; *Mademoiselle* likes more what speaks to her soul; I like the pleasures that life can offer me! *Mademoiselle* is spiritually strong and full of faith, full of common sense! I admire you, but I don't intend to imitate you! I am happy with Antoine and wish to remain so! When life whitens my hair, I will think of my soul, which at last is not bad, *Mademoiselle*!

–Just ambitious!

–So that's how it is, but I love people and have managed to be happy!

–I wish you luck and much joy, Corine! And don't forget God!

–I won't! Good-bye, *Mademoiselle*!

–Good-bye, Corine!

Bowing, she leaves, elegant and facetious, as usual.

Madelaine thinks, "Be happy, Corine, and may God keep you safe!"

Father Estanislau and Henry, now great friends, talk to each other:

–Father Estanislau, in my dreams, I see my mother crying; aged and unhappy... I have often reproached her, blaming her for my character vices, but today I think differently. Who am I to judge anyone, especially my own mother?

Where will she be, Father? I am so rich and she, who knows, will be in need, if she is still alive...

In this new life proposal of mine, will God allow me the grace to see her again and perhaps support her?

Father Estanislau answers:

–Life has surprised us with seemingly impossible things, don't you think? Who knows, perhaps you will make this wish come true? God is infinite mercy!

–Now, tell me: how is your relationship with Eugene going?

–Well done! In the just purpose of giving them back everything that, unfortunately, I once took from them, I am amazed at an unexpected solution, in this affective involvement! I am fascinated by Eugene's beautiful eyes, his privileged intelligence, and his filial devotion.

–I'm happy! Try to be happy! I want to officiate this wedding!

–If she wants to, and I believe she does, the dear priest will do it for sure! Well, my dear friend, I must go. I have an appointment and I have already taken up too much of your time! Keep praying for me!

–You can always count on my prayers, dear Henry! – the two embrace, fraternally.

Picking up his elegant hat and cane, in a few minutes Henry is on the streets. In every lady he thinks to find the traces of his mother.

Sometime later, at the ranch, walking side by side with Eugene, he confessed:

–Eugene, I want to get married; I want to start a family!

–Do you really want this, Henry?

–Yes, and I don't think I'm wrong when I conclude that you do, too!

–How can you know? – She, blushing, asks him, her heart pounding.

Taking her by the shoulders, looking into her eyes, seductively, he states in a caressing voice:

–Your eyes, your gestures and your words betray your feelings, to the delight of my passionate and submissive heart at your feet! I love you! Some time ago I discovered this, happy and thankful to the heavens! I know that you love me too! Will you marry me? Isn't that what you've always wanted, Eugene?

Giving up denial, snuggling into his broad chest, she lovingly confesses:

–Yes! And even when I said I hated you, my heart betrayed me by loving you!

–Wise heart! – He exclaims, kissing her, in love, amidst the exuberant vegetation and the perfumes of the flowers...

At that moment, going to the window to rest their eyes from the countless bills, Sir. Jaime surprises them. Smiling, he thinks:

"Be happy, dear daughter! I can now return to the arms of my Eugenia! Were it not for Henry, you would never be happy!

Sister Rosália, wherever you are, you will surely see your prophecy fulfilled!"

Returning to work, he hears a light knock on the door. He answers and is confronted by the two of them. Eugene kisses him and shows him a bouquet of flowers:

–Look, daddy, how beautiful! I brought them for you!

–Thank you, daughter!

–Sir. Jaime, we want to talk to you!

–So, speak up, I am all ears!

–We want to ask for your consent to get married!

–May God make you very happy because I already am! This makes me happier than you can imagine! – He hugs Henry and kisses his daughter.

–Thank you, daddy!

–I want grandchildren! Although... I won't see them...

–What did you say, dad?

–Nothing, child, I was talking to myself...

–Shall we tell Natacha? She suggests, and they both go off in search of the girl.

Henry heard and understood what Sir. Jaime said, but he kept quiet, he didn't ask questions. He must surely have his reasons for saying what he said... "Is he sick again?" - He thinks. When he sees Natacha, he momentarily forgets what happened...

Nearby, living in a crude house made of tree trunks, live Rupert and Nikolai. Their appearances are frightening: long beards, unkempt hair, sun-tanned skin, and cruel eyes. They survive by doing some small jobs for the local residents, and not infrequently attack others farther away to take what they carry, sometimes hurting them. More brutalized than ever, in a fierce coexistence, they nurture in their hearts an unjust hatred for Natacha and Sir. Jaime, blaming them for all their misfortunes.

* * *

A FEW YEARS GO BY and yet another sorrow befalls the Parish House group: Salústio sacrificed himself for the ideal.

Activist in meetings and pamphlet propaganda, he was followed, arrested and executed. How was that known?

Father Estanislau received an unusual visit from a strange character, dressed in rags, with a strange air, who loudly demanded urgent confession.

Attending him, intrigued, he notices a remarkable transformation in his gestures and speech during the aforementioned confession:

–Father, I know you and I have come to bring you tragic news! Salústio has just been murdered in a dark alley, near the Largo da Concórdia!

I was willing to defend him, but I didn't even have time. It all happened so fast! The killer who stopped him executed him right there, with a pistol shot. From a distance, I tried hard to reach them and help him, but it was impossible!

Salústio, stronger, was defending himself bravely, when the shot reached him in the middle of his chest! The flyers were scattered on the floor.

He was carrying them for the usual distribution.

When I arrived, I could only hold his head and hear his last words:

"My ideal companion, tell Louíse to forgive me for leaving her... That I will continue to love her in eternity... Tell Father Estanislau that I am dying for the beloved Homeland! Tell him to ask God to understand sacred intention of the fulfillment of my duty! May God bless you all and protect you! ... Thank you, my partner!" In a last effort, he raised his right hand with a closed fist and shouted at the top of his lungs, "Long live France!" – He choked with his blood, went into convulsions and quieted down. I seemed to see in his last expression a smile of victory, Father...

I will give you the coordinates so that you can give him a proper burial. His body is covered with cardboard and some rubble.

Indicating the location in the best way, the strange character even vaticinates before leaving:

–Goodbye, Father! Another dark alley may be waiting for me! Our fate is tragic! Long live France!

–Long live France, my son! And may God protect you!

He stands up, looks carefully around him, and adopts his former appearance. In slow, dragging steps, arm seemingly crippled, mouth crooked and gaze crazed, he walks out.

Drawing back the curtains of the confessional, the priest still sees him at an angle of the path and then loses sight of him. What is his name? He will never know! He regrets his fate...

Estanislau tries to help himself from the great pain that overwhelms him, bursting into sobs?

–My son, my dear Salústio! Why did you leave? Only God can judge him! How long will I endure such pain? – His whole body shakes with convulsive weeping. A few minutes later, he wipes away his tears and goes out to find the body of Salústio to give it a proper burial.

At the funeral, Louíse is the picture of desolation:

–My great love! I will never recover from this pain! However, I want you to know how proud I am to be the widow of a hero! May God receive and reward you!

Hugging her by the shoulders, Madelaine asks:

–Come and get some rest, Louíse!

–No, Madelaine! After these painful hours, I will never look upon this dear countenance again! I always knew it would be like this! I've been happy, Madelaine, as happy as one can be in this world! When he asked me to marry him, he was sincere, exposing to me his ideals and his intentions! I love him, even more, for who he is and what he represents! - embraced, the two weep.

Admiring that manly, noble and serene face, Madelaine whispers:

–My brother and my friend, you will be so missed... Go in peace and take our undying love with you! May the angels of God surround you with affection, for you deserve it! Until the next opportunity, Salústio! ...

–Arranging her strong hands, covering them with fragrant jasmine, Madelaine walks away, leaving Louíse in her reverent contemplation. Next to him, Lucien reads a prayer book. He prays for his good friend and brother-in-law. He accompanied Father Estanislau in the office of extreme unction post-mortem. Little by little he is exercising the functions of a future priest.

A few days after the funerals, following a strong intuition, Father Estanislau goes to the little room that Salústio occupied as a bachelor, confirming his suspicions: Salústio kept that room to partly divert the attention of his persecutors.

He sits on a stool and meditates. He hears footsteps on the stairs.

On the landing, a young woman appears who, by the way she dresses and her exaggerated painting, leaves no doubt as to her profession. Surprised by the priest's presence, she wants to know:

–Were you a friend of his?

–Who are you talking about, my child?

–Salústio! - She exclaims, lowering her voice.

–Oh, yes! He was one of my parishioners!

She no longer hears the answer. She searches through the furniture drawers for clothes and objects...

Disconsolate, she sits on the floor with the pieces in her hands as she exclaims:

–When will it be my turn?

Approaching her, the priest asks:

−Can I help you?

−Yes, father! Tell me I am right, when I leave my son, for the sake of the freedom of France! - Forgetting the previous reenactment, she bursts into sobs.

−Let it out, child, it will do you good!

Wiping her eyes on the clothes she carries, she explains:

−I am an activist, like Salústio! I left my son with my mother, to protect him from this life I lead, Father! However, I miss him and I suffer horribly!

−And what drove you to it?

−Rebellion and the desire to hasten the punishments that our executioners deserve!

−You exude good manners and finesse! Where do you come from and why did you engage in such a dangerous movement?

−I am the widow of a nobleman, plundered by power. Thrown into prisons, I never saw him again. Our property was annexed to the wealth of those who left us in misery. Outraged, I threw myself into this fight. I hope that my beloved son, who is now only four years old, will understand me when he grows up!

−I am sorry for your fate, daughter, and I pray to heaven for you!

−I'm out of here, Father. The death of Salústio can compromise me! I will find another place to live. I will pursue my ideals, and if I die before I see France free, my soul will be with those who are at the front, in the struggles to come. I believe that Salústio and many others, who have already given their lives for the Fatherland, will swell the ranks! United, living and dead, in the same intention, we will liberate our beloved France, when the decisive moment comes!

Father Estanislau asks:

−Why don't you go see your son?

–To protect him! But how many nights do I lie awake missing him!

–God will find the resources to help you! I will pray for you!

–Thank you, Father! Before I go, I must tell you that nothing existed between Salústio and me except a great friendship. We set up this farce to protect his private life. He has always been faithful to his wife. Tell her that. Any woman would like to know how much she was loved!

–She is sure of that, daughter. Salústio was an honorable and sincere man. One of the best I have ever known!

–Good-bye, Father!

–Be prudent! Farewell!

A few days after this, the priest began to notice strange presences in the church. Some officials of the regime were investigating the work of the Parish House. He kept quiet and put them at ease. In a few days, realizing that charity in that hospital was legitimate and practiced with love and honesty, they disappeared.

All this shaking and the advanced age, makes the priest sick, worrying his friends and demanding the competent care of Dr. Sergei, who also feels worn out.

* * *

FOR TOO LONG we have left our characters to their own devices. Now we return to them:

Eugene is happily married to Henry John.

Recovering the old house in which she was born in England, she went to live there after she was married. They have three children: Henry John, age eight, has his father's features, posture and gestures; Jaime Luis is six. He is pink, resembling his mother, black eyes and dreamy like those of his maternal grandfather.

And now, let us pay attention to an Argentinean voice that sings: it is Natacha Eugenia, four years old. She looks like a doll.

She enters the room, barefoot and dancing in graceful, studied twirls.

The family admires her, delighted.

Eugene tries to put on her feet, without success. She rejects the socks and shoes:

–Little one, don't be rebellious! Barefoot, you can get sick or hurt yourself!

–I don't want these ugly shoes! Daddy, buy me nicer ones! – She whines.

With infinite sweetness, Henry replies, agreeing:

–I promise to buy it, my pretty little doll!

–So you spoil our little one, Henry!

–For so little? Calm down, Eugene, our little Natacha is docile and understanding, despite her young age! What does it cost me to take care of her shoes?

–Ah, sweet little fairy, you always get what you wish for! – Eugene covers her with kisses as she laughs heartily.

Henry John moves closer to his father and inquires:

–Daddy, we are English, aren't we?

–Yes, we are! Why?

–Why does our little sister have a Russian name?

Setting aside the book he was trying to read, Henry pulls his son to himself and, while stroking his hair, clarifies:

–Natacha is the name of someone very special to me! She and her grandfather Jaime lost their lives tragically...

Eugene comes in, after leaving Natacha Eugenia with the nanny, and listens to her husband's last words. With a tight heart, she remembers how it all happened:

"Newly married to Henry, reclaiming the old house, moved her father's heart overmuch, and he began to reverse his travels: he worked at the ranch and rested in England beside them. Henry returned to him at a profit all that he had taken from him. Selling the Rue-de-la-Chapelle mansion in Paris, he preserved the works of art, returning them, likewise.

Rich again, Sir. Jaime invested even more in philanthropy.

Following the experiences of the Château des Patrons and the Parish House of the Church Our Lady of Mont'Serrat, he founded a large complex of schools and infirmaries, aimed at the destitute, under the name of the Santa Sofia Foundation.

On very solid bases, he created the institution, which will always depend on an administrative board, chosen by the community itself. In this way, when he could no longer direct it, others equally responsible would do so.

A few months after the realization of this ideal, Eugene and Henry are rushed to Reims. Sir. Jaime and Natacha were found dead nearby. Eugene almost went mad with grief. Once there, they were notified that they were returning from their usual walks, attending to the needy in the area, when they were surprised by assailants who murdered them. Sir. Jaime was the first to succumb, in defense of Natacha, who soon after was shot down…

In righteous indignation, the local population organized and went out pounding meter by meter in search of the killer or killers. Someone remembered that nearby lived two strange and shabby-looking men. They set out there, armed with sticks and stones, determined to arrest them. When they arrived, they ran into Rupert and Nikolai preparing to flee. It was enough to make them jump on them. Under pressure, they confessed their long-standing hatred of the dead and their authorship of the crime.

Sacha was astonished when at the police station he recognized the fateful cousins! Informed of a crime committed by them in Russia, she harshly accused them and denounced them to the authorities.

Rupert and Nikolai were deported to Russia, and tried and convicted there."

Eugene sobs, wistful and nonconforming. She still has the painful image of the two funerals in her retina…

Henry comes forward, hugs her affectionately and asks her:

–Forget it, Eugene! Get used to it, dear, and pray for them! They were only doing good, and they must have been rewarded by now! Have you noticed, my dear, how our youngest resembles her namesake? Would she have returned?

–How to know? My father believed this! To imagine that she is the same, delights me! And you?

–Me too! Your father, for us, will always be the greatest example of wisdom and goodness!

Snuggling closer to her husband, she agrees:

– You're right, Henry! We will strive to follow his examples! May God bless us all and grant us much peace!

They kiss passionately when they notice Jaime Luis' jealous face. Attracting him, the three of them hug each other, affectionately.

* * *

LUCIEN IS NOW father Francois.

In the exercise of his priesthood, he preaches admirable sermons from the pulpit of the Church Our Lady of Mont'Serrat, during the mass ritual, assuming his ministry with great love. Now he is the parish priest.

Father Estanislau, aged and worn out, has his chair near the altar, from where he watches, with pleasure, the work of his beloved disciple. There, he sometimes pretends to sleep, while his mind goes over the facts of his already long life. He now lives more the spiritual life than the material.

Father Francois has also taken over the work in the wards from Madelaine, who at this very moment is sitting in one of the last pews in the church, looking for a little refreshment.

She misses those who are gone infinitely... Her father, her beloved mother, Charles, Salústio, Natacha, Sir. Jaime... His beloved uncle Richard, who a few months after the tragedy that engulfed the Alvarado castle died sadly; he had lost his former joy. He was visibly wasting away... On the fateful day, after an understanding with his brother about the impossibility of reacting against the prince, he had gone out to have some fun with one of his girlfriends... Having faced an unforeseen event on the way, and taking longer than expected, when he arrived, everything was consummated...

On her mental canvas, Madelaine reviews everyone and each one in particular. With tears in her eyes, she remembers the routine in the castle: waking up in the morning full of promises; her mother's efforts in conducting everything, closely accompanied by her: the help to the unfortunate; the festive Sundays... She remembers Charles arriving smiling, with the lute on his back, in love... She can almost hear his voice, singing, invading her whole... Her siblings, happy and dynamic, following the bustle of all the activities...

Remember her father defending the innocent...

The long-suffering Pierre was finally acquitted, after his strenuous efforts. After all, that family was reunited again. Some time later, Pierre found an occupation and with dignity began to support his family... Bettine helped them for months on end... Oh, so many memories! Too many for one life!

Today, Soraya is engaged to an officer-at-arms who looks remarkably like her late father. Could this resemblance have influenced her choice?

Fabian is a handsome military man, requested by women. Vain in his uniform, dates them all, but commits to none. He loves Madelaine and lives for her. He guesses her smallest desires in order to satisfy them.

Louíse has become a beautiful matron; she looks like her mother in every way. Almost fully recovered, she is a bit of a mother to Soraya and Fabian, supporting Madelaine.

At prearranged times, she works in the Parish House, helping the disadvantaged. There, she feels closer to Salústio.

Sometimes she can see him walking between the beds with his bright eyes, wide smile, in bright white robes... He smiles at her, approving her charitable actions. In these moments, she thinks she is dreaming with her eyes open...

✲ ✲ ✲

LEAVING THE WORK OF THE PARISH FOR A WHILE, father Francois goes to the fortress from which he escaped so many years ago. He will request from the authorities the approval to exercise his priesthood there, periodically.

In the vehicle, he recalls the day of his escape, together with the Turkish woman. She surrendered her soul to God in his arms of her adopted son. A short time later, as if they had arranged it, Caterine, his dear mother, left too... Insistent tears fall down his young, perfect face. Splitting the jagged towers, his heart beats frighteningly. He feels the urge to go back, to forget... How many painful pictures are in her retina! He reviews, point by point, the events with the false Andre; the one who took away his freedom, only to give it back to him later... At that time, He could never suppose that this suffering and misguided man was using a name that by right belonged to him, just like the title of Baron...

The vehicle stops in front of the big gate. He gets down and announces itself as God's minister in the exercise of his duties.

Led to the head jailer, he identifies himself, asking for Joubert and Gothardo.

- Reverend, they are still here. One of them, blind, is very old and lapsed. They live in the back of the prison, in a little house attached to the fortress. The other supports him, with admirable zeal! Come, I will show you the way!

Walking again through those dark corridors, Francois feels himself weakening. He remembers every meter of that ground and the steps he took countless times, in a painful coexistence, with those who died there in life, among blasphemies and despairs!

Passing by the old workshop where the Turkish woman's husband worked, he seems to see him leaning over the workbench, as in the old days. He sends him thoughts of gratitude and affection and continues in the direction of the rustic dwelling.

He entered the large courtyard that rewarded him with sun and rain, where he could breathe better and talk to the stars (remembering gives us back the past, as if by magic!)

Father Francois looks down at the black sheath and the shiny shoes, groping to make sure that time really has passed...

They stop in front of the door so familiar to him and the attendant informs them:

– They are there, Reverend. Make yourself at home!

Taking the knocker, he knocks lightly, with trembling hands. He hears slow, dragging footsteps that he recognizes at once.

– Who is it? asks a pasty, raspy voice.

– I am the pastor of the Church Our Lady of Mont'Serrat!

– I'll be right there, Father! – creaking on the rusty hinges, the door opens, revealing the huge, aged Gothardo, with his eyes increasingly narrowed.

– Come in, Father! – he says, reverently.

In the small room, the grimy floor reminds Francois of how the Turkish woman used to keep it polished. Some old furniture is piled up, clothes are strewn on the floor, the scene is desolate...

– Sit here, Father, suggests the giant, as he hurriedly cleans a stool with his big hands.

– Thank you. Are you alone?

As if to answer him, he hears a groan in the next room, where his and the Turkish woman's bedroom used to be. A body stirs in the bed and a voice, that brings back the past, inquires:

– Gothardo, by all the devils! Tell me, who is there?

– Mr. Joubert, we have a visitor!

– Send him away! I don't want to see anyone! It's enough that you eat all my food, man!

Slowly approaching, Francois asks:

– Mister Joubert, I need to talk to you...

– Who are you, and how do you know my name? – he replies, as he struggles to sit up in bed.

– After so many years, you are still sick?

– Where do you know me from?

Taking his hand, which he spreads in the air, in the direction of her voice, Francois answers:

– Right here, Mr. Joubert; where I lived for many years in my childhood.

Pulling sharply on his hand, he exclaims in astonishment:

– You are... Francois?!

– Yes! Today, to the world, I am Baron Lucien Brumel of Villefort, and to God, I am Father Francois!

– And I, I must be dead! Francois or Lucien must be dead by now!

Did you come back to condemn me? – he cries, terrified. But if I am already dead, and I am certainly in hell, what are you doing here?

– Calm down! We are both alive and I didn't come to charge you with anything! Just rest! – watching Gothardo who is dozing, oblivious to everything, he continues. – Listen to me and try to understand me.

– You've been told I'm obsolete, haven't you? Well, that's a lie! It's the pains that hallucinate me! You must remember how much I need to drink to bear them! Now even that doesn't help me anymore!

– You should see a doctor instead of drinking, Mr. Joubert. It pains me to see you still in this state...

In short, Francois tells him how he escaped and what he experienced after that.

Understanding some passages and oblivious to others, he listens without much attention. At the end of the narrative, rolling his eyes in an attempt to see, but failing to do so, he asks:

– You are very important now, aren't you?

– No, Mr. Joubert, I am the same as before. I just became an adult and took on a new life.

– And what have you come here to do? What do you want?

– Absolutely nothing, or rather, I have come to ask your forgiveness!

Disarmed, he exclaims:

– But... I am the one who should ask for your forgiveness! What should I forgive you for?!

– For not having been able to help you as I needed to! For the trouble I created for you by disappearing... You must agree that I needed to get out of here!

– Okay, I forgive you! And can you forgive me the beatings?

– I must have deserved them, one way or another. May God have mercy on you and on Gothardo! I intend to resume my duties here, this time as a priest.

– Therefore, can you give me your blessing?

– Of course!

– Wake up Gothardo and come receive the priest's blessing!

Rising hastily, the lout stands in reverent position awaiting the aforementioned blessing.

With abundant tears washing his face, which can neither be seen by Joubert nor understood by Gothardo, Father Francois blesses them, while imploring: "Father, help them in their greatest need! Forgive them Father, and in your mercy, rescue them to repentance, leading them to the paths of goodness! I thank You for having known them in this existence! Through them, in the ensuing sufferings, I have learned much! As Your minister I must forgive them and love them!"

Lying down again, in a few minutes Joubert is asleep.

Turning to Gothard, Francois exclaims:

– My friend, I owe you the freedom and the chance to be today what I am!

Disconcerted, grimacing, he replies:

– Your friend, Father?! You must be confusing me with someone else! I am bad and ugly! Very bad and very ugly! – Thus saying, he hides his face with his huge hands.

Opening his arms, Francois asks:

– Will you give me a hug, my friend?

Awkwardly, he agrees, and in a fraternal embrace, Francois deposits a kiss on his forehead, while telling him:

– My dear big guy! I am Francois, your friend, remember?

– Francois is still a boy, Father! I have never seen him again! How much I miss my little friend!

– Now you will be able to see it many times, Gothardo! See you!

Without understanding, he reverently opens the door and follows him through the large courtyard and the corridors, as if no time had passed...

Already in the carriage that will take him back, Francois hopes that his brother André and André de Montmar have already reconciled.

Suddenly he remembers that Louíse is waiting for him at home because Ignácia is ill. Spending a few days at Louíse's house, she unexpectedly fell ill. She's already quite old, the good Ignácia... He gives the driver the address and sits back. He now reflects on his usual visions:

During the various rituals, he catches a glimpse of those who have already departed, as if they were still alive, seeking breath at the altars, and sometimes he surprises them crying freely, asking for prayers... Some he has seen when alive in the church benches, others are strangers to him...

Entering the church, he comes across others on the steps, in the courtyard, or at the door looking in. Clothes in strips, dirty, provocative, with malicious glances... Some mockingly fall to the ground laughing so hard at the arrogance of those present and their luxurious but dubious elegance. They hang from the rich carriages and point out the coats of arms and heraldry. They imitate, debauched, the sanitarians in their airs of studied piety...

When Father Francois passes through the two crowds, the living salute him reverently, and the specters walk away respectful and ashamed of their deplorable behavior.

Time and again, he watches from the altar processions of luminous beings who enter and pray to God and then go up in smoke, not before smiling at him with joy, aware that he sees them.

This close coexistence with the two planes of life makes Father Francois a different person, introverted without being sad; on the contrary, his eyes seem to live smiling.

A few months after his new acquaintance with Francois, Joubert said goodbye to the world, begging for prayers. After extreme unction, Father Francois kissed his rough hands in a gesture of humility.

Another period of time passed and the good Father Estanislau, serene, said goodbye to life, snuggled up with so many who had loved and admired him over the years.

Soraya got married and has a beautiful little daughter named Bettine. She still plays her violin and often performs the pieces she used to play with her family, only to cry of nostalgia soon after...

She never went to the castle again. She promised Madelaine that she would keep it in her memory, as it was before the tragedy that destroyed it. She is pregnant again. If it is a boy, his name will be Luiz Santiago.

Unlike Soraya, who has resigned herself to never seeing the castle again, Fabian has never given up on it. With his sister's consent, he finally goes to meet the past.

Garish, mounted on his fastest horse, he overcomes the distance that separates him from the ruins, anxious. Drawing closer, he can make out the blackened and bare walls like crystallized specters...

Making the horse neigh, he comes closer, emotional.

Leaning over the animal's neck he cries; he can't control himself. The sounds of hooves ring out loudly, making an echo in that lonely place. He remembers that other riders, in other happier times, arrived there, elegant and happy for festive Sundays... And still others, apocalyptic, passed by in a stampede, destroying the lives of their parents and all they could reach...

He stops the animal and climbs down. He ties the harness to a rough piece of wood, a piece of an old staircase that he recognizes. On this, at the last level, he was defying danger. Madelaine, in great distress, ran to get him out of there, then hugged him lovingly against her warm and soft lap...

Falling to the ground, his chest exploding with pain he exclaims in despair:

– Madelaine! Never come here, my dear! – bent over himself, he goes on weeping convulsively. With faltering steps he goes to the remains of the chapel and there he prays, fervent, amidst those vestiges of a happy time...

In this state she remains until he feels a strange numbness.

Suddenly, he seems to hear his mother's beloved voice saying to him in a deeply loving inflection:

– Fabian! Forget the past, my son! Live the present and be happy! Our love will join us forever, above the circumstances of this brief life we live there, on this suffering planet in need of much elevation to God, Our Father! Our pains were part of our purification! Kiss Madelaine and Soraya for us and be at peace, dear son!

Did he indeed hear the voice of his longing mother, or did he wish it, and from his heart those words rose to his brain? Either way, a strange peace comes over him, and so he returns, riding his horse again. He leaves behind that rubble, determined never to return there again.

Arriving, he looks for Madelaine and she wants to know:

– So, my love, was it worth it?

–Yes and no, Madelaine! On the one hand I suffered horribly, on the other I exorcised the ghosts that accompanied me in the ignorance of what reached me in a painful way, marking my heart forever! The information I received never satisfied me!

– You were so small, Fabian!

– But I remember everything, Madelaine! What I didn't see, I caught, or else I fantasized about! To this day I can feel our mother's desperate kiss, and the hug she gave me, as she put us in that carriage, never to see us again! - he bursts into sobs, as if the events had just taken place...

Madelaine hugs him and cries too. Slowly, he settles down and asks:

– Forgive me, my sister! It seems to me that now, at this very moment, I am burying my past!

– Good, Fabian. Our loving parents are always nearby protecting us. Sometimes I see them beautiful and smiling as they have always been. Don't forget the real life; here, everything is ephemeral! Our real life is eternal, without goodbyes and without separations! Forget the past, Fabian, live the present, and be happy!

– Madelaine, that's what mama told me!

– And how was that?

– Or I thought I heard her, I'm not sure... You just repeated her advice to me!

– Remember that she and I shared the task of educating you, and in this we harmonized! And so it continues to be, Fabian.

Kissing him affectionately, she bids him farewell and returns to her duties with the sick.

Some years later, Fabian falls madly in love with a beautiful girl and decides to get married. Surprisingly, he returns to the castle and restores it, point by point. The Castle of the patrons resurfaces, as if nothing had happened. Married, Fabian moves in. Everything there enchants him; every angle speaks to him of love and progress. Following his parents' example, he sets up the festive Sundays again, and after a long hiatus in time, the castle regurgitates with performers of all kinds, looking for a chance to perform.

The wards of the Parish House have been transformed into a hospital with new techniques, specializations, and many doctors and nurses.

The years go by, inexorable...

* * *

TODAY AS LIKE MANY OTHER DAYS, father Francois officiates the masses, full of love and responsibility.

He looks at his parishioners with affection, regardless of their virtues or vices. Involved in the "greater love", he has a filial feeling for them. They are children who need patience and guidance, he thinks... At the end of the ritual and the sermon, everyone leaves, forgetting in a few moments all the warnings received and the stimulus to walk on straight paths. They will learn slowly, by repeating the inappropriate behavior countless times, until, suffering, they learn definitively. May Jesus enlighten and protect them in goodness and progress! – he asks.

One mass is followed by another, and he tirelessly fulfills his obligation without faltering.

The church fills and empties, like the tides...

At the end of the last mass, he sees Madelaine arrive. Steps faltering, she sits down in one of the last benches. François is inexplicably emotional this morning.

Think of Madelaine; analyze her selfless life... Intense hours of work, in which she barely eats for lack of time... she sleeps very little, in a total dedication to the unfortunate...

In one of the ritualistic movements, he remembers her beautiful, young, elegant and full of dreams...

"You are the consecrated host in the form of a woman! You are an angel who dressed in flesh to illuminate the earth! My example of life is you, Madelaine!" – his heart cries out. He feels the urge to cry and a huge desire to go to her, to hug her, affectionately, fatherly...

Why this feeling of loss?

Normally, he doesn't disperse during his priestly duties, but today he finds it difficult to concentrate.

The mass is coming to an end. The hymns evolve through the air, echoing in the acoustics of the souls... Little by little, everyone leaves silently...

When the liturgy is over, he takes a longer look at dear Madelaine, and then he falls down, flabbergasted at the foot of the altar! A crowd of luminous beings burst into the church. They are angelic beings. Incredibly beautiful, shimmering colors of light pervade the entire environment. There is a great celebration. Of what?!

Madelaine stirs slightly; her slender body loosens on the seat and her arms hang over her knees; her head falls to the side... Her gray hair falls across her face... She seems asleep.

Asleep? No! Madelaine is leaving! – Francois suddenly concludes.

Now he sees Charles arriving, elegant, lute on his shoulder, smiling. He holds out his hands to Madelaine and she comes out of her cocoon; luminous, gorgeous!

Charles envelops her, affectionately, blending into her light; the two become a single being. It is difficult to describe so much beauty...

There are two Madelaines: one sitting, inert, and the other glowing in the arms of her love...

The counts, present, wait their turn to embrace her, which they then do. Oh, also dear Salústio is there and lovingly embraces his dear Madelaine. He looks at Francois, greeting him, smiling...

There is a divine music in the air that sounds inside the church and rises to the heavens.

Francois continues to see them arrive and parade before him, reinforcing the plethora of luminous beings who have come for Madelaine: his mother Caterine; Betbara, his dear Turkish; dear Father Estanislau smiling at him, kindly, Dr. Sergei!

Francois wipes away the tears that insist on falling to better see the scene: Madelaine looks at the body that served as her dwelling place and bows reverently before it, grateful in a salute?

Now, she looks at Francois and, with a unique smile, with shining eyes like stars, she reaches out her hand in a romantic gesture of farewell...

Without articulating words, François asks her:

"Dear angel, don't forget us! We will miss you! We love you!"

Responding to him in the same way, without speaking with her lips, but with her thoughts, she expresses herself:

"I love them too! I will never leave them alone! Say goodbye to my siblings for me! To all, my love and my blessing!

For now, goodbye, Francois...!"

She joins the others that, amalgamating, form a single light of brilliant and chromatic colors, in a vast luminous wake, like a silent comet that dizzily rises into the heavens!

The music still sounds in the air.

Sitting on the altar steps, Francois cries freely.

He gets up and walks towards that body that has already fulfilled its destiny. He hugs it tightly against his heart and cries a lot...

Getting a grip on himself, he finally calls an auxiliary. He must warn the others, set up the space for the last earthly farewells, as well as administer the last rites post-mortem...

Stroking her hair white from time and struggle, he declares, lovingly:

– One day, Madelaine, we will see each other again! Praised be you, Lord, for this servant who returns to her true home today!

While he waits, he recalls that some years ago she had the good fortune to recognize among the unfortunates of the streets of Paris a woman who, feverish and exhausted, cried out to her beloved son to ask his forgiveness before she died.

Your son's name? she had asked him, only to hear perplexed, from his parched lips, the name Henry John Stanford, from England!

Called to Paris as a matter of urgency, Henry was able to give this suffering and disoriented being his forgiveness. He granted her optimal medical treatment, which unfortunately came too late. After introducing her to Eugene and his children, he said goodbye to her, grateful to heaven for the opportunity. Between tears of gratitude, she entered the spirit world.

EPILOGUE

DIVINE JUSTICE REACHES everyone in this immeasurable universe.

Henry, responsible for financial and moral bankruptcies, some with suicide aggravations, is punished for what he has sinned.

Persevering in the transformation begun in the same existence, determined to do good, deeply changed, this time he is unjustly accused. However, he complies with the law of Talion, which is automatically executed.

A former cause of ruin of so many families, he is definitively separated from the one he loves most: his beloved son.

Stirred by reminiscences of this past that is now present, those who accuse him are merciless and vengeful.

Not understanding with his reason, Juan Gadelha (Henry) feels himself in a purifying atonement.

Supported admirably by his faith, he acquits himself of the great Law.

While awaiting execution, his heart stopped, bidding farewell to life and sparing him greater pain and humiliation.

It ascended to a better world to rest from struggles and sufferings, while it remakes itself for new endeavors on Earth, in the pursuit of an incessant evolution.

His son Charles, a ruthless spirit, will live to honor the memory of his father who was wronged by the laws of the world.

Leaving Spain, Charles will study law in England and, once he graduates, will prove his father's innocence.

In the process of multiple existences, humanity redeems itself as it climbs the steps of Jacob's Ladder and weaves its wings for the flight of liberation.

One day, we will sing Hosannas, deeply grateful for the paths we have traveled, in this chain of lives that harmonize with each other, in an endless chain of evolutionary experiences.

Jesus, ruler of our planet, said to Nicodemus:

"*Truly, truly, I say to you, no one can see the kingdom of God unless he is born again.*"

And, Allan Kardec, common sense reincarnated, revealed the maxim:

"*Be born, live, die, be reborn still, and progress always – such is the Law.*"

ROCHESTER

Rio de Janeiro, November 13, 1990

Zibia Gasparetto's Greatest success stories

With more than 20 million titles sold, the author has contributed to the strengthening of spiritualist literature in the publishing market and to the popularization of spirituality. Learn more of the author's successes.

Romances Dictated by the Spirit Lucius

The Life Force

The Truth of each one

Life knows what it does

She trusted in life

Between Love and War

Esmeralda

Thorns of Time

Eternal Bonds

Nothing is by Chance

Nobody is Nobody's

God's Advocate

Tomorrow Belongs to God

Love Won

Unexpected Encounter

On the Edge of Destiny

The Sly One

The Morro of Illusions

Where is Teresa?

Through the Doors of the Heart

When Life chooses

When the Hour Comes

When it is necessary to return

Opening for Life

Not afraid to live
Only love can do it
We Are All Innocent
Everything has its price
It was all worth it
A real love
Overcoming the past

Other success stories by André Luiz Ruiz and Lucius
The Love Never Forgets You Trilogy
The Strength of Kindness
Under the Hands of Mercy
Saying Goodbye to Earth
At the End of the Last Hour
Sculpting Your Destiny
There are Flowers on the Stones
The Crags are made of Sand

Books of Eliana Machado Coelho and Schellida

Hearts without Destiny
The Shine of Truth
The Right to be Happy
The Return
In the Silence of Passions
Strength to Begin Again
The Certainty of Victory
The Conquest of Peace
Lessons Life Offers
Stronger than Ever
No Rules for Loving
A Diary in Time
A Reason to Live

Eliana Machado Coelho and Schellida, Romances that captivate, teach, move and
can change your life!

Romances of Arandi Gomes Texeira and The Count J.W. Rochester

Lancaster County

The Power of Love

The Trial

Cleopatra's Bracelet

The Reincarnation of a Queen

You Are Gods

Enigma

Books of Marcelo Cezar and Marco Aurelio

Love is for the Strong

The Last Chance

Nothing is as it Seems

Forever With Me

Only God Knows

You Make Tomorrow

A Breath of Tenderness

Books of Vera Kryzhanovskaia and JW Rochester

The Revenge of the Jew
The Nun of the Marriages
The Sorcerer's Daughter
The Flower of the Swamp
The Divine Wrath
The Legend of the Castle of Montignoso
The Death of the Planet
The Night of Saint Bartholomew
The Revenge of the Jew
Blessed are the poor in spirit
Cobra Capella
Dolores
Trilogy of the Kingdom of Shadows
From Heaven to Earth
Episodes from the Life of Tiberius
Infernal Spell
Herculanum
On the Frontier
Naema, the Witch
In the Castle of Scotland (Trilogy 2)
New Era
The Elixir of Long Life
The Pharaoh Mernephtah
The Lawgivers
The Magicians

The Terrible Phantom
Paradise without Adam
Romance of a Queen
Czech Luminaries
Hidden Narratives
The Nun of the Marriages

Books of Elisa Masselli

There is always a reason
Nothing goes unanswered
Life is made of decisions
The Mission of each one
Something more is needed
The Past does not matter
Destiny in his hands
God was with him
When the past does not pass
Just beginning

Books of Vera Lúcia Marinzeck de Carvalhoç and Patricia

Violets in the Window
Living in the Spirit World
The Writer's House
Flight of the Seagull

Vera Lúcia Marinzeck de Carvalho and Antônio Charles

Love your Enemies
Slave Bernardino
the Rock of Lovers
Rosa, the third fatality
Captives and Freed

Books of Mónica de Castro y Leonel

In spite of everything

Love is not to be trifled with

Face to Face with the Truth

Of My Whole Being

I wish

The Price of Being Different

Twins

Giselle, The Inquisitor's Mistress

Greta

Till Life Do You Part

Impulses of the Heart

Jurema of the Jungle

The Actress

The Force of Destiny

Memories that the Wind Brings

Secrets of the Soul

Feeling in One's Own Skin

World Spiritist Institute

www.ingramcontent.com/pod-product-compliance
Lightning Source LLC
LaVergne TN
LVHW041737060526
838201LV00046B/833